THE PELICAN HISTORY OF ART

EDITED BY NIKOLAUS PEVSNER

z25

SCULPTURE IN THE NETHERLANDS,
GERMANY, FRANCE, AND SPAIN: 1400–1500

THEODOR MÜLLER

Michael Pacher: High Altar, 1471–81. Detail. *St Wolfgang*

THEODOR MÜLLER

SCULPTURE IN THE NETHERLANDS, GERMANY, FRANCE, AND SPAIN

1400 TO 1500

PENGUIN BOOKS

BALTIMORE · MARYLAND

WRITTEN FOR THE PELICAN HISTORY OF ART
TRANSLATED FROM THE GERMAN BY ELAINE AND
WILLIAM ROBSON SCOTT

★

Penguin Books Ltd, Harmondsworth, Middlesex
Penguin Books Inc., Baltimore, Maryland, U.S.A.
Penguin Books Pty Ltd, Ringwood, Victoria, Australia

★

Text printed by Richard Clay (The Chaucer Press) Ltd, Bungay, Suffolk
Plates printed by Balding & Mansell Ltd, London
Made and printed in Great Britain

★

CONTENTS

The Plates

LIST OF PLATES

ABBREVIATIONS

A.P.   Archives Photographiques, Paris
F.M.   Foto Marburg

*Where not otherwise acknowledged, copyright in photographs belongs to the museum,
gallery, or owner cited as the location*

FOREWORD

THE task of making a comprehensive survey of fifteenth-century sculpture in the Netherlands, France, Spain, the German lands, and Scandinavia is fascinating indeed. The high aesthetic values one is going to meet are indicated by the names of Claus Sluter, Nicolaus Gerhaerts, or Veit Stoss. The sculpture of Great Britain also belongs to the great unity of European sculpture north of the Alps, but it has already been treated separately by Lawrence Stone in The Pelican History of Art.

To appreciate fully the common bond between the sculptors of the fifteenth century in the countries I have mentioned, one need only compare their work with that of contemporary artists of the Early Renaissance in Italy. The very nature of the tasks which sculptors north of the Alps had to fulfil was completely different from that which faced their Italian counterparts. In his Randglossen zur Skulptur der Renaissance, Jacob Burckhardt has indicated features which were common to Italy in general but which we encounter either not at all or only on the periphery of Quattrocento sculpture in European countries other than Italy. On the contrary, this latter still belongs entirely to what Huizinga has called 'the Waning [or Autumn] of the Middle Ages'.

My task, though fascinating, was also extremely difficult, as becomes apparent as soon as one tries to deal adequately with the individual figures within so vast a domain. These are difficulties which arise from the nature of the task itself, and also from the differences between the various regions.

The prescribed limits of my survey have compelled me to concentrate upon certain nodal points, and thus it was impossible to do full justice to all the artistic monuments of all regions. Especially with regard to the vast number of such monuments preserved in Germany and Spain, my selection had to be radical. As far as Late Gothic sculpture in Hungary, Czechoslovakia, Poland, Scandinavia, and Portugal is concerned, I have tried, by choosing the most important examples, to indicate to what a large extent the art of these countries forms part of the subject we are surveying. I am fully aware that my examples fall short of giving the complete picture. In my bibliography, too, I have had to restrict myself to the most important monographs and studies, in which the reader may find further material.

Another source of misunderstanding is the fact that my survey is confined solely to sculpture. The creation of large altarpieces was one of the most characteristic achievements of Late Gothic, and moreover colouring is a salient feature of Late Gothic sculpture; thus by subdividing a historical survey into the categories of painting and sculpture, we lose sight of the fructifying energy which is generated by the intercommunication between the two arts. I should like to stress the fact that this is not a fault of arrangement of The Pelican History of Art. On the contrary, it is a complete misconception that it is only in the case of those Late Gothic masters who are known or assumed to have been both sculptors and painters that an essential community between the two arts can be recognized. However, this subdivision of the arts into various separate categories has unfortunately become an almost universal characteristic of art history. We have only to think of the complex significance of Roger van der Weyden's art and of the miraculous altarpieces of

Netherlandish Late Gothic to be clear how much our insight into the inspiration behind them would be increased, if we could but realize how closely sculpture and painting were interwoven in the opus completum. *In fact, R. Stiassny in his monograph on Michael Pacher's altarpiece at St Wolfgang called this unity of the two arts the 'master secret'. In the history of the Gothic masons' lodges of the thirteenth and fourteenth centuries it is just as impossible to separate architecture from sculpture. In the same way the intercommunication between sculpture and painting is an essential feature of the 'Waning of the Middle Ages'. Similarly, the exhibition 'European Art around 1400' held in Vienna in 1962 demonstrated vividly the incredible powers of visual imagination contained in the illuminated manuscripts carried out, usually for aristocratic patrons, in the late fourteenth century. Out of the wealth of ideas in these illustrations, certain* imagines *gained extensive currency via pattern books, just as certain drawings of the lodges from Villard de Honnecourt onwards had done. It was not a question of 'taking over' or 'translating' certain motifs, but of using a common reservoir of sources for those conceptions which took shape in the painting and sculpture of the fifteenth century.*

In the nineteenth century research into Late Gothic painting was pursued more intensively than was the case with sculpture of the same period. One result of this seems to me to be that even today in accounts of Late Gothic painting, the personalities of the individual masters – including those who have had to be designated by makeshift names – stand far more in the foreground than in the predominantly anonymous history of Late Gothic sculpture. Specific inquiries into the contribution of the painters of works of sculpture to the original appearance of Late Gothic statuary and altar carvings prove again and again how far this sculpture is still rooted in the opus completum *of the Late Middle Ages.*

Another problem was the chronological limit of my survey. From the aspect of nodal points in a history of European sculpture, the demarcation between the fourteenth and fifteenth centuries is as fruitful for the sculpture of Florence as for that of Burgundy. But this is not true if we are investigating the growth of individual phenomena. I would remind my readers for example of the work of André Beauneveu, or of the most advanced portrait-busts in the triforium of the choir of Prague Cathedral, or of the sculpture in St Stephen in Vienna, executed under Rudolf the Founder, to indicate the difficulty which confronted me in my endeavour to ensure that these incunabula *of the new style of c. 1400 should not be overlooked. It is yet more unnatural, particularly in the case of German sculpture, to draw one's chronological frontier at 1500. This makes a meaningless incision across the careers of such outstanding masters as Gregor Erhart, Veit Stoss, and Tilman Riemenschneider. But since the general arrangement of the book made such a chronological limit unavoidable, I could only strive to draw the consequences of it – and this method too possesses its own peculiar truth – and to let the similarity of contemporary phenomena emerge with the greatest possible clarity within these prescribed historical boundaries. In this way the subdivision of the individual chapters of the book stems from the framework of the whole. Against this background I have always tried to show the personalities of various artists and the peculiarities of regional development as independent curves.*

Finally one last difficulty: the different degree of preservation of the monuments in different regions and the different states of the research undertaken on them. It is not only certain epochs whose style appears obscure, but also certain regions. Research into Late Gothic sculpture has been pursued most actively in Germany, Austria, Switzerland, and Spain. In the Netherlands and France particularly religious conflicts, revolutions, and wars have wrought unbelievable havoc among the monuments themselves, in the main centres as well as in the remoter provinces. But in many districts of Germany and Austria too the iconoclasts, and later to a no lesser degree the expansion of Baroque, have brutally eradicated the wealth of Late Medieval art. Statues used for liturgical purposes have often received no better treatment. Even up to the present day restorations have created a situation which makes it scarcely possible to recognize the original appearance of a work of art. From investigations into Late Medieval sculpture extending over large areas in remote places, and from lodges concerned with the restoration of Late Gothic churches, important discoveries may be expected, and cautious efforts to rid famous original works of their disfiguring additions will bring about a radical change in our ideas.

In addition, there is the problem of the relative value of the publications on my subject and the enormous and seductive emphasis – especially at the present time and in the sculptural field – on reproduction. In France the decisive pioneer work was done by Christian archaeology, by research into archives, and through the plaster-cast collection of the Trocadéro. In the new arrangement of the plaster casts in the Palais de Chaillot, the Late Gothic examples have taken second place to the earlier sculptural works from cathedrals and monasteries. The sympathies of the authors of recent general surveys of French medieval sculpture (e.g. Marcel Aubert in 1946) have inclined in the same direction. Georg Troescher made a comprehensive survey in 1940 of the fundamental significance to European art of the early fifteenth century of that Netherlandish–French sculpture generally designated as Burgundian. I am specially indebted to Paul Vitry and Pierre Pradel for their study of the transition from Late Gothic to Renaissance in French sculpture of the late fifteenth century. Since the war, exhibitions and publications inspired by an increased interest in French regional art have brought to light important Late Gothic statues.

Wilhelm Pinder more than anyone else paved the way for our knowledge and comprehension of 'Deutsche Plastik vom ausgehenden Mittelalter bis zum Ende der Renaissance', as the title of his memorable handbook goes. He was the most eloquent interpreter of the Expressionism of Late Gothic. What he has to say on the genesis of the 'primitive' style of the fourteenth century, the spirit of the 'Fair Virgins', and the centrifugal energy of sculpture in the time of the Master E.S. is so revealing that in his work the phenomena of the developing Renaissance recede into the background. Walter Paatz in his Prolegomena *of 1956 was able to make some corrections to Pinder's ideas concerning the sources of the artists round 1400. The publication in 1962 of Dr Kutal's research has thrown new light on the great importance of Bohemian sculpture.*

I should like to mention a third such survey, the Escultura gótica *by Juan Ainaut de Lasarte and Augustin Durán Sanpere. The authors of this book have made a strict selection of the most important works in Spain and thus provide us with a balanced perspective such as is still sadly lacking in many important fields of European art, for example the Netherlandish altarpieces and their widespread export.*

My statements in the following pages are only the result of tentative investigation and, as I well know, in many respects fragmentary. The more I worked upon this book, the more I doubted whether I was the right person to undertake the survey and interpret its theme. I became increasingly convinced that the vital stimuli are to be found above all in the Netherlandish–North-French field of sculptural activity, for the interpretation of which basic investigation is still lacking, though the exhibitions in Amsterdam (1958), in Bruges and Detroit (1960), and in

FOREWORD

Vienna (1962) pointed the way. Special reference must be made to the scholarly importance of the catalogue of the Bruges and Detroit exhibition, produced as a result of collaboration between the Detroit Institute of Arts and the Centre National de Recherches Primitifs Flamands in Brussels.

By my occasional introduction of 'arti minori' in ivory, alabaster, or gold, I did not wish to imply that these small-scale works were merely an echo of monumental ideas that had been lost. On the contrary, I believe that in Late Gothic, as in every late phase of a monumental style, such apparently peripheral works exhibit a sublimation of qualities and are possessed of great influential force. It is no accident that Albrecht Dürer was the son of a goldsmith.

Finally, I must thank all those who have helped me by supplying me either with information or photographs. It is impossible to mention everyone by name. But my gratitude to the photographic section of the Kunstgeschichtliches Institut of Marburg University and to all the museums who were kind enough to put their valuable photographic material at my disposal is great, and must here be recorded.

And a last word to thank sincerely Mr and Mrs Robson Scott, the translators, who have gone to endless trouble to overcome the considerable difficulties that my text could not help placing in their way. I am very much indebted also to Mr John Woodcock, who drew the maps and thereby made it possible for readers to locate the far-scattered places where the works discussed are (or were originally) to be found.

MAPS

NOTE

These maps are intended to orientate the reader historically rather than to be a complete guide to places in which sculpture has been preserved. Hence, places which contain well-known museums or private collections but which are historically unimportant do not appear. A complete list will of course be found in the index.

A selection of places in which there is no longer any sculpture mentioned by the author is indicated, and these places are distinguished on the maps by being noted in a smaller script and having a pierced circle as marker.

Inset

Kloosterzande
Antwerp
Geel (Gheel)
Dendermonde (Termonde)
Malines (Mechelen)
Tongerlo
Hulshout
Merchtem
Diest
Hasselt
Louvain (Leuven)
Brussels
Anderlecht
Etterbeek
Maestricht
Halle (Hal)
Forest (Vorst)
Zoutleeuw (Léau)
Wisbeca
Hakendover
Braine-le-Comte ('s-Gravenbrakel)
Hollogne-sur-Geer
Liège
Soignies (Zinnik)
Nivelles

120 mls
200 kms

NETHERLANDS

Bolsward
Haarlem
Amsterdam
Deventer
Leyden
Eemnes
Utrecht
Arnhem
Delft
Oud-Zevenaar
Zaltbommel
's Hertogenbosch (Bois-le-Duc)
Venraij
Breda
Maaseyck
Bruges
Ghent (Gent)
Antwerp
Beek
Maestricht
Oudenaarde (Audenarde)
Brussels
Louvain
Ypres
Courtrai (Kortrijk)
Liège
St Omer
Tournai (Doornik)
Antoing
Basècles
Lille
Douai
Valenciennes
Le Crotoy
Noyelles-sur-Mer
Arras
Cambrai
Abbeville
Amiens
Fécamp
Colleville
Folleville
Laon
Avioth
Le Havre
Beauvais
St Martin-aux-Bois
Metz
Bec-Hellouin
Rouen
Bulles
Pierrefonds
Louviers
Écouis
Fresnoy-le-Luat
LaFerté-Milon
Ancemont
Pont-à-Mousson
Wuisse
Neuwiller-lès-Saverne
Haguenau
Bernay
Écos
Méru
Taverny
Le Mesnil-Aubry
Meaux
Épernay
Châlons-sur-Marne
Vic-sur-Seille
Saverne (Zabern)
Marienthal
Évreux
Poissy
Paris
St Denis
Nancy
Strasbourg
Le Folgoët
Vincennes
Dangolsheim
Sélestat
Hittenheim
Vitré
Marcoussis
Vert-St-Denis
Lhuitre
Kaysersberg
Chartres
Rampillon
Troyes
Bayel
Colmar
Villeneuve-l'Archevêque
Lautenbach
Isenheim
Châteaudun
Montargis
Sens
Chaource
Thann
Solesmes
Malicorne
Tonnerre
Rochefort
Vieux Thann
Jarzé
Lude
Cléry
St Benoît-sur-Loire
Asnières-en-Montagne
Flavigny-sur-Ozerain
Basel
Angers
Bueil
Vernou
Epoisses
Semur-en-Auxois
Turcey
Fontaine-lès-Dijon
Pesmes
Saumur
Tours
Limeray
Morogues
Charny
Bussy-la-Pesle
Dijon
Auxonne
Nantes
Mehun-sur-Yèvre
Châteauneuf-en-Auxois
Arcenant
Rouvres-en-Plaine
Loches
Bourges
Autun
Beaune
St Jean-de-Losne
Nevers
Laizy
Seurre
Bessey-lès-Cîteaux
Poligny
Poitiers
Bourbon l'Archambault
Ternant
Moulins
Fribourg
Azat-le-Riz
Montluçon
Souvigny
Cluny
Baume-les-Messieurs
Villebret
Varennes
Jaligny
Brou
Sion (Sitten)
Riom
Ambierle
Geneva
Limoges
Clermont-Ferrand
L'Hôpital-sous-Rochefort
Lyon
Auzon
St Didier
Vienne
Ste Fortunade
St Antoine-en-Viennois
Bordeaux
Conques
Rodez
Caderousse
Moissac
Villeneuve-lès-Avignon
Avignon
Albi
Apt
Aix-en-Provence
Toulouse
Quarante
Perpignan

FRANCE
BELGIUM
Garonne
Seine
Oise
Rhine
Rhône
Wissembourg
Luxembourg

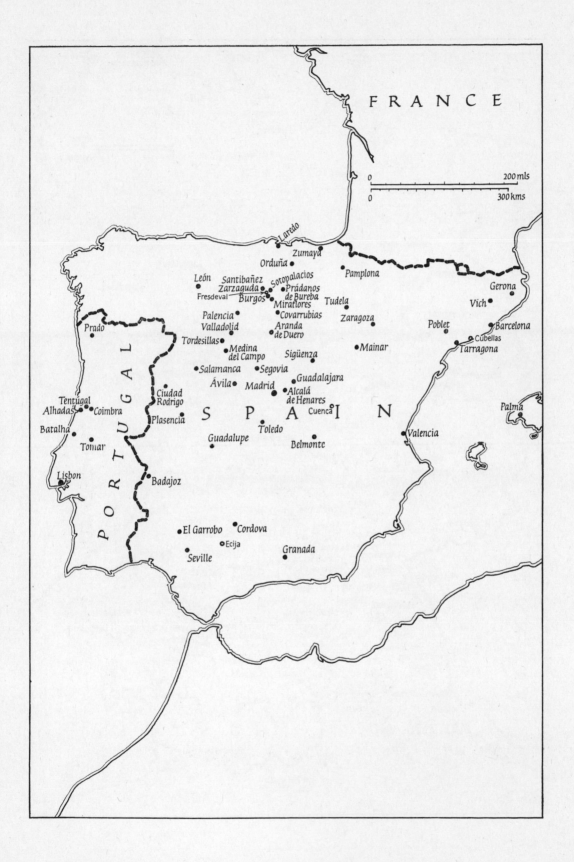

FRANCE

200 mls
300 kms

PORTUGAL

SPAIN

Laredo
Zumaya
Orduña
Pamplona
Gerona
León
Santibañez
Zarzaguda
Sotopalacios
Vich
Fresdeval
Burgos
Prádanos
de Bureba
Barcelona
Miraflores
Tudela
Palencia
Covarrubias
Zaragoza
Cubellas
Valladolid
Aranda
de Duero
Poblet
Prado
Tordesillas
Tarragona
Medina
del Campo
Mainar
Sigüenza
Salamanca
Segovia
Ávila
Madrid
Guadalajara
Ciudad
Rodrigo
Alcalá
de Henares
Palma
Tentúgal
Alhadas
Coimbra
Plasencia
Cuenca
Batalha
Guadalupe
Toledo
Valencia
Tomar
Belmonte
Lisbon
Badajoz
El Garrobo
Cordova
Ecija
Seville
Granada

Stralsund

Lübeck
Marienwohld
Hamburg
Lüneburg
Bremen

Wismar
Güstrow

0   60 mls
0   100 kms

Havelberg

Berlin

Schledehausen
Minden

Hanover

Magdeburg

NETHERLANDS

Münster
Emmerich
Cleves   Grieth
Kalkar   Xanten
Gaesdonck
Rheinberg   Wesel
Dortmund   Unna
Iserlohn

Telgte
Soest

Halberstadt

Wittenberg

Göttingen

Halle

Kassel

Düsseldorf
Zons
Heinsberg
Cologne   Altenberg
Aachen   Siegburg
Cornelimünster Bonn

Marburg

Merseburg
Naumburg
Pforta
Kapellendorf
Erfurt   Jena
Arnstadt

Meissen

G E R M A N   Y
Braunfels
Limburg   Hirzenhain
Karden   Oberwesel   Kronberg
Lorch   Hallgarten Frankfurt
Ockenheim   Mainz   Steinheim Aschaffenburg
Clausen   Lohr
Pfalzel Oppenheim Darmstadt Rimpar
Trier   Worms

Römhild

Münnerstadt

Hassfurt

Maidbronn
Würzburg

Bamberg

Zwickau

Saarbrücken
St Arnual

Eberbach
Heidelberg
Speyer
Wimpfen
Heilbronn
Maulbronn

Mergentheim
Schöntal
Öhringen
Weinsberg

Creglingen
Dettwang
Rothenburg
Schwäbisch Hall

Nuremberg
Schwabach

CZECHOSLOVAKIA

Grosskomburg
Tiefenbronn   Heutingsheim Ellwangen
Baden-Baden   Schwieberdingen
Strasbourg   Lichtental   Stuttgart   Bopfingen
Honau   Horb   Tübingen
Lautenbach
Rottweil   Heiligkreuztal Heggbach
Biengen   Altsimonswald Zwiefalten Oberstadion
Freiburg   Ochsenhausen
Staufen   Waldsee
Überlingen   Meersburg   Bellamont
Constance   Ravensburg Wurzach
(Konstanz) Weissenau
zürich   St Gallen   Weingarten

Weissenburg
Öttingen
Nördlingen
Kaisheim
Vorderried
Blaubeuren Ulm
Wiblingen   Jettingen
Fürstenfeldbruck
Mindelheim Landsberg
Buxheim
Kaufbeuren

Regensburg
Straubing

Eichstätt
Ingolstadt

Landshut
Moosburg
Freising

Passau

Heiligenstadt

Munich   Altötting
Ramersdorf Feichten
Wasserburg   Seeon
Tegernsee

Salzburg

Berchtesgaden

FRANCE

Basel
(Bâle)
Neuchâtel

SWITZERLAND
Bern

Chur

Innsbruck

A U S T R I A

Sterzing
(Vipiteno)
Marienberg
(Monte Maria)

Brixen
(Bressanone)
Bozen
(Bolzano)

Brione

Lübeck

Tujec
(Tiegenhagen)
Gdańsk
(Danzig)
Frombork
(Frauenburg)
Elbląg (Elbing)

Toruń
(Thorn)
Włocławek

Poznań (Posen)
Gniezno (Gnesen)

P O L A N D
Warsaw

Berlin

G E R M A N Y

R. S. S. U.

Meissen
Dresden
Zwickau

Radibor
Görlitz

Lubiąż (Leubus)
Wrocław (Breslau)

0   120 mls
0   200 kms

Chlum Sv. Maři
(Maria-Kulm)

Prague

Cracow

C Z E C H O S L O V A K I A

Karlštejn
(Karlstein)

Šternberk
(Sternberg)

Plzeň
(Pilsen)

Jihlava
(Iglau)

Brno
(Brünn)

Lomnička
(Kleinlomnitz)
Bardějov
(Bartfeld)
Levoča (Leutschau)

Regensburg

Třeboň (Wittingau)
Kájov
(Gojau)
Český Krumlov (Krumau)

Znojmo
(Znaim)

Trenčín

Danišovce
(Diensdorf)
Košice (Kaschau)

Passau

Vyšší Brod
(Hohenfurth)
Kefermarkt
zwettl
Hollenburg
Klosterneuburg

Hlohovec-Galgóc

Linz

Danube
Göttweig
Vienna

Bratislava
(Pozsony-Pressburg)

Laufen
Irrsdorf
Inzersdorf
Herzogenburg
Heiligenkreuz

A U S T R I A

Esztergom
(Gran)
Budapest

Salzburg
St Wolfgang
Frauenstein
Mariazell
Wiener
Neustadt

Innsbruck
Gries
St Sigmund
(S. Sigismondo)
Pfalzen (Falzes)
Hallstatt
Aussee
Admont
Grosslobming
Graz

H U N G A R Y

R O M A N I A

Altenmarkt
Tamsweg
St Lambrecht

Sighișoara

Sterling
(Vipiteno)
Brixen
(Bressanone)
Bruneck (Brunico)
St Lorenzen (S. Lorenzo in Pusteria)
Maria Saal

Bozen
(Bolzano)
Klagenfurt
Viktring
Ptuj
(Pettau)

Manapfarr
Murai

Venzone
Ptujska Gora

Sibiu
(Hermannstadt)

I T A L Y

Montemerlo
Venice
Trieste

Y U G O S L A V I A

Brașov
(Kronstadt)

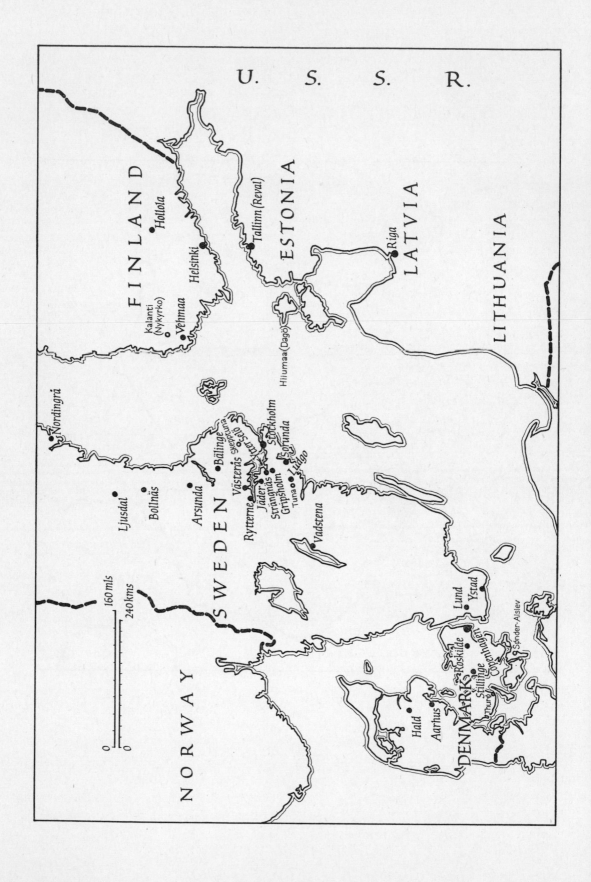

U. S. S. R.

FINLAND

Hollola

Helsinki

Kalanti (Nykyrko) Vehmaa

Tallinn (Reval)

ESTONIA

LATVIA

Riga

LITHUANIA

Hiiumaa (Dagö)

Nordingrå

Bälinge

Stockholm

Västerås Skeppruna

Sörunda

Lilla Sejö

Ljusdal Bollnäs

Arsunda

 Rytterne Jäder

Strängnäs

Gripsholm

Tuna

Lidgo

Vadstena

NORWAY

SWEDEN

160 mls

240 kms

Lund

Ystad

Sönder-Alslev

Roskilde

Stillinge

Copenhagen

Hald Aarhus

DENMARK

Thurø

CHAPTER I

INTRODUCTION

PERHAPS it is a good sign that art historians have become embarrassed by the very ambiguity of the stylistic terms that they themselves have devised; indeed they avoid putting to the test the validity of their boundaries between styles and themes. From the title of this book, which embraces the sculpture of the fifteenth century in the Netherlands, Germany, France, and Spain, it will be quite clear that what we are concerned with is the Late Gothic style: but if in the following pages I use the term 'Late Gothic', it must be explained that by restricting the theme to the fifteenth century certain aspects of this subject may well be lost.

The main examples of Late Gothic sculpture are to be found in the sculpture of portals, on altarpieces in cathedrals, and also in the *imagines* of tombs; and with all these, both with regard to their genesis and their appearance – in the sense of the medieval *ordo* – the stylistic influence of the building as a whole played the decisive role. Every altar shrine, every tombstone, every figure on portal or pier was a constituent part, a microcosm within the transcendent macrocosmic whole.

This monumental religious art – and we shall have little to say of secular art – died beneath the hammer blows of the Reformation. Indeed, one might well consider whether 'Late Gothic' does not really continue up to this religious crisis. The iconoclasts destroyed many of the most important works of ecclesiastical art; members of the traditional crafts of carvers, painters, and painters of carved figures became unemployed. Actually, especially in the Netherlands and Germany, the careers and activities of the great masters at the end of the Late Gothic period continued into the second and third decades of the sixteenth century. It is nevertheless clear that the turn of the century cuts like a knife through a series of organic growths.

However, it was not at a moment of inner exhaustion that Late Gothic art came to grips with the canons of the Italian Renaissance: it was the Dürer of the Apocalypse who called for these new ideals. The 'Sturm und Drang' experienced by Lucas Cranach in Austria in 1502 is the most striking proof that this problematic first decade of the sixteenth century brought with it the decisive turning point for Northern art. From now on new criteria prevail to so large an extent that the *liberalitas* of an *arte moderna* makes a complete break with Late Gothic traditions. This decade stands like a watershed between the two epochs.

From 1400 on Italian sculpture had achieved a new autonomy of style, deriving from its inner affinity with the Ancients – this is to be seen most clearly in the work of Ghiberti and Donatello – while the Late Gothic sculpture of Northern Europe is marked by the very absence of this autonomy. In Late Gothic sculpture stone carving went hand in hand with architecture, wood carving with painting, whether through the colouring of the woodwork surface or through the combination of the carved

I

altarpiece with wings which were painted. The masters often presided over workshops where both carving and painting were carried on. Often, too, the same man combined both talents. This is certainly true in the case of Michael Pacher, for example. When Pacher was in North Italy, his style of painting was decisively influenced by the work of Mantegna. But in his sculpture we seek in vain for any echoes of the Italian sculpture of the Early Renaissance – so different in this sphere were the attitudes of north and south. It is interesting to observe in this phase of Late Gothic painting and sculpture such fundamental differences of reaction to the Italian Early Renaissance. We may assume that even the earliest works of Italian sculptors in Northern Europe – e.g. those of Francesco Laurana and Guido Mazzoni in France or of Adriano Fiorentino at the Dresden court of Frederick the Wise – also seemed new and strange. From 1506 on Michelangelo's Madonna was to be seen in the Church of Notre Dame in Bruges in all the lucent white of Carrara marble, and in 1521 Dürer in his diary did not fail to make a note of his encounter with this work of art.

In France the sculpture of the feudal civilization of the late fourteenth century had already produced astonishingly assured monumental representations of the human figure. Unfortunately it is almost impossible to gain any idea of the true significance of this sculptural art, since vast quantities of its most outstanding monuments were destroyed in the Revolution. But perhaps Holbein's drawings of c. 1524–5 of the marble statues by Jean de Cambrai of Duke Jean de Berry and his wife Jeanne de Boulogne in the Sainte-Chapelle in Bourges (Basel, Kupferstichkabinett)[1] will serve to show the affinity between this French monumental sculpture of the years round 1400 and the spirit of the Early Renaissance at the beginning of the sixteenth century. In reality, in the development of French sculpture in the fifteenth century we can see very clearly a certain adherence to formal conventions in both choice of subject and composition, so that there the harmonious and lyrical style of the early years of the century continued longer than in Netherlandish and German sculpture, where divergent, opposing tendencies followed hard on one another.

With the end of the House of Valois (Charles VIII died in 1498), the Late Gothic style ceases in the sculpture of France. Charles's successor, Louis XII of the House of Orleans, conquered Milan in 1500. The earliest indigenous works of Renaissance sculpture are in France Michel Colombe's tomb of François II of Brittany and Marguerite de Foix (1502–7) in the cathedral at Nantes, and in Germany the sculpture of the Fugger Chapel in the church of St Anna in Augsburg (1509). Typical of both is the extent to which the artist's vision was determined by the ambitions of the patron, and also the extent to which preliminary sketches by painters provided the sculptor with an impetus for stylistic innovation.

Let us now return to the earlier limit set to this volume – the art of the years round 1400. Is this demarcation an artificial one? Sculpture of the late fourteenth century was still dominated by the co-operation of architect and sculptor in the masons' lodge. What developments in this tradition are to be seen at the turn of the century?

I think it will be found easier to answer this question if we first of all direct our attention to the state of German monumental sculpture at the end of the fourteenth century.

The most important factor in this field was the far-reaching influence of the Parler family; in particular, the contacts which radiated from Prague had a beneficial and rejuvenating effect on the traditions of the masons' lodges in Austria, Franconia, Thuringia, and Silesia. But the most striking thing is the international character of these connexions; and this is to be explained not merely by contacts between the lodges and by exchanges of workers over vast distances – we find for example the work of Matthias of Arras in Prague, that of the Frenchman, Nicolas de Bonaventure, in Milan, and of German workmen and masons in Milan,[2] Bologna, Orvieto – but also by the generosity of the patrons. When we notice, therefore, the similarity between individual busts in the triforium of Prague Cathedral and contemporary statues of Parisian court art, we are reminded of the connexion between the Emperor Charles IV and the court of Charles V of France.[3]

In this sculpture from the triforium of the cathedral of Sv. Vít in Prague, which dates from 1374–85, portrait busts of the master masons, Matthias of Arras and Peter Parler, stand alongside members of the Imperial family and high ecclesiastical dignitaries;[4] and we experience the gradual emergence of the 'portrait' from the abstract architectural background, culminating in the astonishingly concise three-dimensional power of the bust of Wenzel von Radecz (Plate 45A), existing as it were in its own right. No doubt this bust was one of the latest. At the same time and in the same geographical area – Austria, if not in the political, in a more generalized sense of the word – there emerged a few outstanding examples of metal sculpture, remarkable also in their strange isolation: the bronze group of St George by the Brothers Martin and Georg von Klausenburg (1373) on the Hradschin in Prague;[5] somewhat later the gilded copper reliquary bust (allegedly of St Ladislas) from Trenčin (Trencsén, Trentschin) in the Nemzet Múzeum at Budapest;[6] and another reliquary bust, also in copper, from Southern Tyrol, in the Kunsthistorisches Museum in Vienna (Plate 46B).[7] In this series of metal statues we may trace the same stages of development as in the busts in the triforium in Prague. To me it seems symptomatic that the first signs of a new style in the years round 1400 are to be found in the maturest examples of cathedral sculpture and in the transition from bronze and copper figures to the art of the goldsmith.

Considering the impossibility of explaining the reliquary bust from the Tyrol now in the Vienna Museum in any regional terms, it might not even be out of the question that it was made in Prague, after the Emperor Charles IV had given the silver bust with the relics of St Dionysius to the church of St Ulric and St Afra at Augsburg in the year 1351. On the other hand, the reliquary bust of St Donatus of 1374 in the cathedral of Cividale shows how this process of icons achieving the preciseness of individual appearance is a change on a European level in which the leading masters of northern Italy also had their share.

On the basis of these Latest-Trecento traditions there arose – once again most recognizable in the Austrian lands – certain religious statues in a stone of a particularly fine, marble-like texture or cast in finely ground limestone. Generally they are figures of the Virgin, and they were obviously not merely part and parcel of the church architecture in the traditional way, but had their own independent significance as statues. The earliest dated example of this type (1381) is perhaps the stone figure of an upright Madonna with Child on the Altstädter Rathaus in Prague whose counterpart is to be seen in the Eligius-kapelle in St Stephen in Vienna. These are the *incunabula* of the so-called 'Fair Virgins' which we meet more and more frequently from 1390 onwards. Dated representations in illuminated manuscripts by Bohemian and Austrian masters in a corresponding style confirm this chronology.[8] We shall see that at the same time we have representations of the Pietà in specially fine stone showing this same independence of setting.

There arises therefore around 1400 in the transition from the monumental sculpture of the fourteenth century, still conditioned by its architectural setting, to the carved altar sculpture which became typical of the Late Gothic style of the fifteenth century, a type of sculpture which, though still of stone, is remarkable for the conscious selection of fine materials. The high quality of these works, existing independently of the altars themselves, is proved to us by the fact that they were later frequently venerated as 'miraculous images' (Gnadenbilder). Unfortunately, not a single one of these 'Fair Virgins' appears to have been preserved in its original setting, apart from those examples where the 'Fair Virgin' is a corporate part of the contemporary altarpiece itself. The manner of presentation is still confined within the boundaries of the block, in the style of the Trecento, but there is proof of a new ability to reveal in the round the towering stature of the figure and to carry the movement of the body over into the melodious lines of the richly flowing drapery.

In Netherlandish and French sculpture of the late fourteenth century the co-existence of traditional methods alongside radical innovation is yet more marked. If we take as an example the series of papal tombs in Avignon, it is striking how in the midst of these preponderantly impersonal effigies, which are artistically of little significance (in so far as they are recognizable at all after the defacements of the French Revolution), suddenly we meet the clear features and the deep solemnity of the chiselled head of Pope Urban V (d. 1370, Avignon, Musée Calvet; Plate 26A).[9] It is not by chance that one senses an affinity between this work and the busts of the triforium in Prague. There is the same search for a new truth, which is evidently felt to be a bitter truth.

There followed *c.* 1376–80 the statues on the 'Beau Pilier' on the north tower of the façade of Amiens Cathedral,[10] the tombs of members of the Dormans family from the Collège de Beauvais in Paris, the statues of Charles V and Jeanne de Bourbon from the porch of the chapel of the Hospice des Quinze-Vingt (Paris, Louvre),[11] the statues on the Donjon de Maubergeon (built by order of the Duc de Berry) in the château of Poitiers, and the statues, commissioned by the same patron, of Charles VI, Jeanne de Boulogne, and Queen Isabel in the Salle des Gardes of the present Palais de Justice in Poitiers. I mention these works together in order to emphasize the astonishing scope of these pioneering achievements in French sculpture in the years from 1380 to 1390, still recognizable in spite of later defacement. In the examples cited we see – as in Prague – the gradual emergence of the human form from the abstract block of stone, part of an architectural ensemble, and the realization of the individual in the *imago*. At the same time these French works are distinguished from their Austrian and Bohemian counter-parts by a more logical clarity in presentation and by a more radical emphasis on the individual features. Already something is visible of the *verismo* of portraiture which was to become – along with other traits – one of the two poles in the development of artistic activity in northern Europe during the fifteenth century.

In France there followed in the last decade of the fourteenth century those achievements which were to usher in a new vision of the function of sculpture. I refer to the sculpture of the Dutchman Claus Sluter on the portal of the Chartreuse of Champmol, near Dijon, which dates from about 1393 (Plates 2, A and B, and 3A). Any account of Late Gothic sculpture in Northern Europe in the fifteenth century must take these works as its point of departure.

There is one further factor that we must consider when distinguishing the features of fourteenth- and fifteenth-century sculpture – i.e., the different uses to which it was put. In the fourteenth century the architectural function of sculpture was decisive, even where an apparently isolated figure was involved. I would quote as an example the stone figure of the seated Virgin of 1334 which is in the apse of one of the two choir aisles of the cathedral of Sens. Even the devotional images originated as part of a comprehensive programme. The altar retables appear to have been in the beginning mostly made of stone, and the same applies to the reliefs on rood screens and choir screens. But already by the end of the fourteenth century – this is clear, in spite of all that has been destroyed – the art of wood carving was on the increase and was used more and more frequently to embellish the growing number of detached altars,[12] i.e. altars conceived as independent objects in the church. Work for the altars became one of the great tasks of the stone and wood sculptors, supplanting their traditional task of architectural sculpture. Since the painted panel assumed equal importance with the carving in these altars, there arose a new community of the arts.

Germany is rich in fourteenth-century examples of altars which combine painting and sculpture. In both the Netherlands and France for the most part fragments only have survived. All the more significant therefore are the French 'vierges ouvrantes', figures which can be opened and which thereby reveal in symbolic form the synonymous nature of body and shrine.[13] At the end of the fourteenth century we meet the first fully developed example in France of the *Gesamtkunstwerk*, the union of painting and sculpture in one and the same altar. Once again it is at Dijon where, in the museum, can be seen the two big triptychs commissioned by Philip the Bold from Jacques de Baerze for the Chartreuse of Champmol (Plates 15B and 16).

Sculptural representation in these altars of about 1400 is still definitely additive, in the manner of the fourteenth century. But, later, the fifteenth-century tendency to render everything concrete and dramatic permeated this branch of art, making it the most comprehensive and suggestive *speculum humanae salvationis*. The culmination of this we see in Veit Stoss's altarpiece in St Mary at Cracow (Plates 134–5), where the moment of transfiguration is reflected in all the figures of the altar.

There are also cultural and historical considerations of a general kind which fundamentally separate the fourteenth and fifteenth centuries, but we must always bear in mind our reservation that the end of the fourteenth century has a unique twofold significance. It was the time of the last flowering of a feudal culture – 'the Waning of the Middle Ages', as Huizinga called it; but at the same time – on the fringe as it were – in the north and not only in Italy there were portents of things to come, which point to a future beyond the Late Gothic epoch. As a striking example I would cite the imperial medals of the Duc de Berry[14] which were made in Flanders or in France, and their enigmatic connexion with the art of Antonio Pisanello.

All the more telling was the naturalism of this bourgeois Late Gothic art, which reacted against the feudal style of the years round 1400 and supplanted it. This new bourgeois element produced regional variants in expression and style in Late Gothic sculpture which by the end of the fifteenth century had become so strong that it needed the formal canons of the Renaissance to reveal once again the supranational validity of common artistic ideals.

Finally, a few words on the political order of the countries whose fifteenth-century sculpture is to form the subject of the following chapters. This political order also was under the sign of the change from the Middle Ages to the Modern Age. The Middle Ages meant the *imperium*, and especially the continuation of that Holy Roman Empire of the German Nation whose territories stretched from Holland, Brabant, Hainaut, the Free County of Burgundy, and Savoy to the diocese of Trent and the lands of the Patriarch of Aquileia. The Middle Ages, however, also meant feudalism as it appears at the end of the fourteenth and the beginning of the fifteenth century in its most blatant form in the division of France into aggressively competing dukedoms and counties. The Modern Age promised national states. The tendency towards national states debilitated increasingly the supranational ideology of the medieval *imperium*. The emperors in the fifteenth century were no more than representatives of a past reality, concerning themselves mainly with their own territorial possessions. At the time of the Emperor Maximilian this attitude, as the backward-looking ideology of his funerary monument at Innsbruck with such mythological ancestors as Arthur and Theodoric proves, had assumed an almost romantic retrospectiveness.

At the same time, however, the Modern Age is also heralded by a growing mercantilism which strengthened supranational trading companies and ports such as Bruges, Antwerp, and Venice opening themselves to the world. Indeed the most eminent early representatives of the new Modern Age are arrived middle-class men of the type of Jacques Cœur at Bourges who endeavoured, still within the waning feudalism, to create similar supranational, mercantilist constellations. In art on the other hand regional characters increased, most explicitly in the astounding *floraison* and the far-reaching expansion of the workshops of the Netherlands. This also reflects the transition from the Middle Ages to the Modern Age, in so far as the basis of all this activity was the middle classes, but the most important patrons were not only the churches and their congregations, but still the outstanding representatives of feudalism.

Yet another strange fact can only be indicated. The time of the most enchanting *incunabula* of the International Style of 1400 and of their glowing harmony is also a time of tragic political conflicts everywhere. Perhaps this drifting of art away from political circumstances, this cleavage between the world of art and the social world must also be interpreted as a sign of that emancipation of the arts which belongs to the Modern Age.

6

FRANCE AND THE NETHERLANDS AT THE TURN OF THE FOURTEENTH AND FIFTEENTH CENTURIES

THE traditions inherent in the sculpture of Western and Central Europe in the years round 1400 found their most monumental expression in the work of Claus Sluter. We can trace the origins of Sluter's work in various traditions of the fourteenth century; but the essential point is that, in him, these traditions were endowed with a completely new reality and that the individual personality now emerges of a sovereign master who exercised a decisive influence on European sculpture. Sluter's name first comes to our notice among the members of the stonecarvers' guild in Brussels round 1379. When we compare this date with the birth dates of the masters who were of the greatest influence in the Renaissance of Italian sculpture, we will see that Jacopo della Quercia was born *c.* 1374, Lorenzo Ghiberti in 1378, and Donatello *c.* 1386. If, as I hope to show, determining features in that 'discovery of the world and of man', to which Jacob Burckhardt refers when speaking of the earliest evidence of the Renaissance in Italy, are already present in Sluter's work, they will provide the strongest proof, I think, of the expressive power latent in the monumental sculpture of Northern Europe in the fourteenth century. This expressive power reached its fulfilment and culmination in Sluter's amazing *œuvre*, of which Dijon is the scene.

In 1363 John II of Valois, king of France, invested his son Philip, later called 'the Bold', with the fief of Burgundy. Through his marriage with Margaret of Flanders, Philip the Bold succeeded in uniting Flanders and Artois with Burgundy and Franche-Comté. This formed the basis (1384) for the reconstruction by Charles the Bold (1467–77) of the Middle Kingdom created by the Treaty of Verdun in 843; this Middle Kingdom ran like a corridor between 'Austrasia' (more or less identical with the later Germany) and 'Neustria' (the embryo of the later France). The short resurrection of this Middle Kingdom – immediately before their growth as national states rounded off the boundaries of Germany and France – may appear as a late product of feudal domestic policy; but it is in reality characteristic of the place of Late Gothic between the medieval and modern worlds that at such a moment, immediately preceding the emergence of national states, the common characteristics and the individual significance of the arts in the Netherlands, Lorraine, and Burgundy should once again have had such fruitful results for the whole of Europe.

When Philip the Bold took over the rule of Burgundy, Dijon, the capital, had no suitable native craftsmen to carry out the commissions of the new sovereign; he therefore looked to Paris. Thus the Carthusian monastery near Dijon was built according to the plans of Dreux de Dammartin, who had previously been in the service of King Charles V of France. In 1372 the Flemish sculptor Jean de Marville, born probably in Lorraine, became 'ymagier' to Duke Philip,[1] and soon the number of Flemish names in the records increases. It would seem in particular that the double wedding of Philip's son and daughter in Cambrai in 1385 led to the employment of craftsmen from Flanders and Brabant for the ducal commissions in Dijon. Philip's ambition to vie in splendour with the court of his brother John, Duke of Berry, in Bourges and that of his nephew King Charles VI of France in Paris seems to have grown ever more insistent. It is astonishing to note that in these other most important courts of feudal France in the late fourteenth century also, sculptors of South Netherlandish origin received out-standing commissions. Examples are Jean de Liège, André Beauneveu, and Jean de Marville.

In 1383 Philip founded the Carthusian monastery at Champmol near Dijon, and here, in 1384, Jean de Marville was commissioned to erect a tomb of marble and ala-baster for the duke. It appears from the documents that his main concern was the architectural and decorative framework of the tomb, just as it was in the case of the portal of the Chartreuse (begun in 1385/6). Jean de Marville died in 1389, and in the same year Claus Sluter, who up till then had been his second assistant, was put in charge of the workshop which he had joined in 1385.

In the list of the Brussels guild of stone carvers in which Sluter's name appears about 1379, his place of birth must be read to mean Haarlem.[2] Thus Sluter's life stretches like an arc from Holland and Brabant to Burgundy, like the Late Medieval policy of the Burgundian dukes. We would seek in vain, however, for the origins of Sluter's sculp-tural style in his native diocese of Utrecht, and for this the wholesale destruction of the Late Medieval sculpture in this district may be to blame; all the more numerous are the echoes of his work in the monumental sculpture of the Southern Netherlands of the late fourteenth century, though this too is preserved only in fragmentary form.

The nearest approach to Sluter's particular style is to be found in the eight stone figures of seated prophets, together with their carved corbels, from the tower portal of the old town hall in Brussels (now Musée Communal).[3] These figures with their voluminous drapery are astonishingly full of movement, and their faces are highly individualized. However, they probably date only from c. 1390, and can consequently not be the work of Sluter himself, who by this time had long been active in Dijon. But they do prove that Sluter's style is anchored in a workshop tradition which, as illustrated by these Brussels figures, shows an unequivocal likeness to his own work. The artistic signi-ficance of this tradition is indicated most clearly in certain pieces of architectural sculp-ture of which only fragments remain: we see it for example in the remarkable sense of volume of the beautiful corbels from the town hall in Bruges, now in the Gruuthuse Museum, which were executed in 1379 by Jean de Valenciennes and in similar corbels from the town hall at Malines (Mechelen) (1383–5), which were perhaps the work of Jan van Mansdaele in Brussels.[4]

Most impressive in their effect are the numerous stone statues in the pilgrimage church of Halle (Hal) near Brussels. The figures of the apostles[5] follow in general a traditional type, but as far as the faces are concerned they reveal new and remarkably realistic emotional qualities. The new 'picturesque' style is most clearly seen in the Fair Virgin of the south-west portal (c. 1390–1400). This figure is a late offshoot of the Netherlandish-Lorraine style, and at the same time a sister figure to Sluter's Madonna on the portal of the Chartreuse of Dijon. A similar stylistic phenomenon is offered by the stone-carved Coronation of the Virgin on the portal of St Jacques in Liège, which is of slightly later date (Plate 10).[6] Here also we find the emergence of a new and powerful three-dimensional quality, the filling-out of the drapery to give a sense of dynamic amplitude, and the individualization of both gesture and feature. The expressive and very characteristic treatment of volume in the surviving pieces gives the impression that they must reflect the existence of a monumental late-fourteenth-century sculpture in the Southern Netherlands of which the best works have perished. In any case there can be no doubt of the pre-eminence of these territories from which such known masters as Jean de Liège, André Beauneveu, and Jean de Marville were called to France to be given the most prominent commissions. It is here also that the sources of Sluter's personal style must lie.[7] Sluter moreover appointed his Dijon assistants at first mostly from Brabant.

We have ample documentary information concerning the works commissioned by Philip the Bold. This too is something new. The statues of St John the Baptist and of St Catherine in the porch of the Chartreuse date from 1391; the statue of the duchess from 1393. The portal was completed in 1397. In 1395 work began on the monumental Calvary in the cloisters, which is usually called the Moses Fountain. The crowning Crucifixus was erected in 1398/9, and in 1403 the last three figures were finished. In 1404 came the contract to complete within four years the funerary monument of the duke, who had died at Halle. Sluter himself died in the winter of 1405/6. His nephew, Claus de Werve, summoned by Sluter from Holland in 1396, was appointed his successor.

A new monumentality is already visible in the figures Sluter carved for the portal of the Chartreuse.[8] If we compare them with the more or less contemporary figures on the south-west portal of the church of St Martin at Halle, we shall notice a new attitude to space in the relationship between sculpture and architecture. The brackets for the figures in the jambs project unusually far, and thus provide the statues with an appropriate base for their astonishingly life-like corporeality. The result is an unprecedented realism of the total composition. The portrait statues of the kneeling donors are flanked by the vast figures of St John and St Catherine (Plate 2A), and by means of the overhanging canopies and the weighty corbels with imposing figures of prophets which they all have in common (Plate 3A), groups are created of an unexampled cohesion. Their fluidity of movement, moreover, leads the eye to the central figure in the *trumeau*, a veritable 'Vierge Dorée', a wonderful projection of reality into the space of the whole portal (Plate 2B). The great weight of the brackets in particular contributes to produce a truly theatrical effect. Sculpture and architecture flow into the dynamic gesture of a proscenium inviting one into the church interior.

The realism of the individual figures is also new and impressive. The characterization of the figures of the two donors and the portrait-like individualization of their features is so marked that we are reminded of contemporary accounts of the appearance of Philip the Bold and Margaret of Flanders. Equally human and at the same time

C

9

monumental are the figures of the patron saints who accompany them as if they were their paladins, though it is clear all the time that they belong to that religious *ordo* which reaches its apotheosis in the sublimity of the central Madonna.

The whole composition is thus a testimony to a new sense of realism in the portrayal of the human figure, in the sense of an ex-voto, but it is at the same time raised to a super-individual monumentality. Carvings on funerary monuments, such as are here and there found in Netherlandish sculpture in the fourteenth century, may be regarded as the source of the composition; we also meet similar compositions in the reproductions of donors in contemporary Netherlandish and French illuminated manuscripts. Special mention should be made in this context of two pages of the Très Belles Heures du Duc de Berry, which are particularly close thematically (Brussels, Bibliothèque Royale, MS. 719, fol. 10). These portray Duke John kneeling in prayer before the Virgin Mary, flanked by his patron saints, St John the Baptist and St Andrew, and were painted by Jacquemart de Hesdin about 1390–1400 in grisaille in imitation of sculpture. In a series of tapestries presented by the Duke of Berry in 1406 to the cathedral of Chartres there were King Charles V (d. 1380) and his queen and children kneeling in prayer, attended by patron saints. Sluter was the first to make of this traditional ex-voto type a realistic representation of the donors as monumental figures kneeling at the church door. (The kneeling stone figures of the Duke of Berry and his wife in the Lady Chapel at Bourges are funerary figures.)

In the prophets on the corbels of the portal at Champmol we already see the human face portrayed with that remorseless penetration which endows Sluter's later works in Dijon with their deeply moving gravity. If these figures appear three-dimensional in a way entirely new to Western sculpture, it is not the surrounding space which makes them appear so; rather the body itself seems to be endowed with an immense radiating power, and the gestures – e.g. the way in which one of the prophets holds an open book (Plate 3A) – have an expressive force which is not found again until one reaches the sculpture of Michelangelo.

The other great surviving work of Sluter's – and we have not sufficient space to deal with works whose authenticity is in doubt or which are known only from written accounts – is the Moses Fountain (Plates 1, 3B, 4, 5, and 6).[9] That this Calvary forms part of a fountain, or was made to be a Calvary because of forming part of a fountain, is connected with the conceit of the 'Puteus Aquarum Viventium'. Here also the bold combination of purpose and content opens the prospect to a new future. A hexagonal base, over 10 ft in height, rises from the centre of the fountain. Against the recessed sides of this base stand the powerful figures of Moses and five prophets on projecting corbels. Above their heads six angels with wings outspread support a platform on which was raised a Crucifixion – the Crucifixus with the Magdalen kneeling at the base and the attendant figures of the Virgin and St John.

It is not easy now to conceive the original effect of this unique work, because it has suffered cruelly at the hands of time. There remain for us today only the carved base, and in the Musée Archéologique at Dijon a fragment of the Crucifixus. Work carried out after the last war on the figures of the prophets, the angels, and on the base itself has brought to light beautiful remnants of the original colouring and gilding. According to documentary evidence this was started by a painter called Guillaume from Dijon and was finished by the ducal court painter, Jean Malouel, a native of Gelderland.[10] This addition of painting to sculpture – typical of the Late Gothic style – was an essential feature; for in this way the suggestive force of the sculpture was enhanced. Realism indeed went so far that a copper diadem for the Magdalen and a pair of spectacles for Jeremiah were commissioned from a Dijon goldsmith!

In the prophets of the Moses Fountain, something amazing makes its appearance. The abundance of draperies in Sluter's works is no longer merely decorative – as it is for example in the so-called 'soft style' (Weicher Stil) of contemporary German sculpture – but structural. The body and its drapery are both functions in the posture and movement of the figure, and they are completely independent of any limits claimed by their architectural setting. Hence the boldness of the movements that link the figures and bring them into contact with each other. What we see and feel here is not emotion, but the power of truth. Hence, too, the uncannily penetrating individualization of the faces, ranging from the meditative to the magically visionary. No less rich in contrasts is the range of expressions seen in the angels (these are probably mainly the work of Claus de Werve), and they too are boldly independent of the architectural setting. The zenith of this humanization is achieved in the Crucifixus. The features are torn with pain, and on the brow is a strangely twisted crown of thorns: an entirely new image of Christ, remote from the idealized Christs of the late Trecento. It is sad that we can only guess, thanks to related figures by inferior pupils of Sluter's school, at the great tragic gestures of the accompanying figures.

The vast stone figure of the hermit St Anthony must date from between the sculpture on the portal of the Chartreuse and the Calvary. The upper part of this figure is preserved in the Musée Archéologique at Dijon. The face wears an expression of human kindness achieved by a delicate, naturalistic treatment whose wealth of modulations is in contrast to the sharpness of line of the prophets on the Moses Fountain.

A decade divides Sluter's Calvary from the early works of Donatello, from the seated St John the Evangelist on the façade of Florence Cathedral and the statue of St Mark at Or San Michele. It is of great significance for the internationality of the style of European sculpture round 1400 that an affinity is here manifest between the sculpture of Italy and that of the countries north of the Alps, such as we do not meet again before the end of the fifteenth century. When we remember that Sluter, from a chronological point of view, or to be more exact from the point of view of generation, still belongs to the late fourteenth century, this affinity with Donatello's beginnings makes one realize to the full the revolutionary nature of his art.

When Philip the Bold died suddenly in 1404, his tomb in the Chartreuse, for which he had commissioned Sluter's predecessor, Jean de Marville, was as yet unfinished. In July 1404 Duke John concluded a new contract with Sluter for its completion. This no doubt related chiefly to the over-life-size recumbent effigy of the deceased, which was to have at its head two angels, bearing a helmet as a symbol of the duke's rank. Unfortunately, this figure has been so badly restored that one can no longer distinguish any trace of Sluter's handiwork. But we may certainly attribute to him the transformation of the traditional mourners in relief on the base of the tomb[11] into a new composition, in which a solemn funeral procession of detached figures is seen moving through open arcades, just as had in reality taken place when the duke was brought to his last resting-place in the Chartreuse. Forty mourners were carved in alabaster. The procession is headed by choirboys, a cross-bearer, a deacon, an abbot, and singers, then follow monks and the court in mourning robes. In this way the traditional motif of the mourners, customary on funerary monuments, has undergone a metamorphosis into the realistic representation of an actual event. Once again the 'portrait' was put into the foreground, not merely as an individual likeness, but as the permanent record of a situation which was meant to become part of history.

Unfortunately these 'ymages pleurants' on the tomb of Philip the Bold have suffered a sad fate. When the tomb was transferred to St Bénigne at Dijon in 1792 they were dispersed. At the reconstruction of the monument in the Museum at Dijon in 1827, those of them that could be found were crudely restored, completed, and put together in so arbitrary a fashion that the original arrangement of the funeral procession could only be re-determined by conscientious archaeological research.[12]

Philip the Bold's monument was still not finished when Sluter died in 1404/5. The task of completing it, which was only achieved in 1410, fell to his long-standing assistant, Hennequin de Prindale, and to his nephew and successor, Claus de Werve.[13] While we assume that the carving of the figure for the monument was the main personal responsibility of Sluter in the last years of his life, it would appear that the majority of the 'pleureurs' are of later date. But in any case Sluter will have devised the plan of this composition and left authoritative examples and models for his successors. What we know of Claus de Werve's work from other examples (e.g. the stone reliefs in the altar retable in the church of Bessey-lès-Cîteaux) – he carried on the workshop in Dijon and in 1419 became court sculptor to Duke Philip the Good – shows no marked artistic talent but merely the reaction of a later, more painterly style to the heritage of Sluter.

All the more forceful is the impression of creative power which we feel in these last authentic works of Sluter, namely those 'pleureurs' from the monument of Philip which we can recognize to be his own work. As an example I would like to cite the figure of the old weeping monk in the Musée de Cluny (Plate 8A),[14] which unequivocally betrays the master hand: witness the feeling of sorrow communicated by the hunched figure, the sense of movement in the surface of the flowing garments, the confluence of elemental emotions in the poignantly carved facial features, the overwhelming sense of isolation. Just as magnificent – and also certainly from Sluter's hand – is the monk in the Musée de la Ville at Dijon, whose face is completely hidden by his hood so that the whole figure becomes a symbol of mourning (Plate 8B).

We shall go into greater detail concerning the vast range of Claus Sluter's influence in Dijon, Burgundy, and beyond. His sovereign significance in Dijon will be most clearly realized if we consider the outstanding works of other masters which were produced in immediate proximity to Sluter. In this context one thinks pre-eminently of the two triptychs (now in the Dijon Museum; Plates 15B and 16) which were commissioned for the Chartreuse in Champmol by Philip the Bold in 1390 from the woodcarver Jacques de Baerze at Dendermonde (Termonde, near Bruges), after a journey through the Flemish provinces which he had inherited.[15] The altars were sent for gilding and painting to the court painter, Melchior Broederlam, at Ypres. Broederlam was responsible for the painted wings, and he set up the altars in 1399 in the Chartreuse. Jean Malouel – the court painter of Dijon – the Master of Flémalle, Jan van Eyck, and other Netherlandish painters were also responsible for altar paintings at Champmol.[16]

The additive arrangement of scenes and figures within the altar shrines of Jacques de Baerze corresponds completely with the traditions of the stone retables of the fourteenth century, many examples of which have been preserved in France. But already in the fourteenth century, in both France and the Netherlands, there existed also wooden altar shrines which presented figures and groups of figures arranged in cycles.[17] The finest surviving example of such a composition in the art of the Southern Netherlands and Northern France is the magnificent alabaster group of the Presentation in the Temple now in the Musée de Cluny (Plate 21B),[18] where the subtle arrangement of the figures and the delicacy of the treatment of the surfaces immediately herald the painterly sculpture of the years round 1400. To the close connexions of this type of sculpture with the art of Beauneveu I shall revert later.

Noteworthy in the altar shrines of Jacques de Baerze is his tendency to embellish the framework very elaborately and to load it with small figures. This tendency may be observed too in the more or less contemporary painted Grand Diptyque du Bargello. But even in those portions of the altars from Champmol where the carved sculpture approaches closely the new use of space and naturalistic vividness, the linear outlines of figures and action still predominate in the individual details. Perhaps most impressive of all is the Crucifixus,[19] now in the Art Institute of Chicago, from the Crucifixion Altar at Champmol. Comparing it with the usual idealized late-fourteenth-century figures of Christ, its almost crude *verismo* is something entirely new.

It was rivalry with the brilliant luxury of the castles of the French princes which produced the art of the Burgundian ducal court. King Charles VI of France (1380–1422) had been mentally deranged since early youth, and this fact increased the power of subsidiary rulers, in particular that of the Dukes of Berry, Bourbon, Burgundy, and Orleans and of the Count of Anjou. It also led to a decrease in the central significance of Paris and to the rise in fame of regions and towns which both earlier and later were only of secondary importance.

Bourges in particular, as the neighbouring capital of the Dukes of Berry, vied with Dijon. From 1386 at the latest André Beauneveu was the court sculptor of John of Berry. He came from Hainault, and was probably born at Valenciennes. Before being summoned to Bourges he had worked in Flanders[20] and for King Charles V of France in Paris, as the marble monuments in St Denis testify. Beauneveu was also a painter. It suffices to mention his illuminated Psalter of the Duke of Berry (Paris, Bibliothèque Nationale, MS. fr. 13091), which must date from *c.* 1385.[21]

It was the personal initiative of the duke which was responsible for the building and decorating of the impressive castles at Bourges, Poitiers, Mehun-sur-Yèvre, Riom, and other places. The architect for these works was Guy de Dammartin, the brother of the architect of the Chartreuse of Champmol. In 1392 the duke ordered the building of a Sainte Chapelle[22] for his castle at Bourges (dedicated in 1405), where his funerary monument was to be erected, an obvious parallel with Champmol. All these were undertakings of a very ambitious nature. Destruction and renovation have eradicated all the brilliance of these buildings, and only a few isolated pieces of sculpture remain to bear testimony to their original richness. I must restrict myself to the naming of the most important. First, the monumental statues on splendid figured corbels on the Tour Maubergeon at Poitiers, the work of Jehan Caillou, Henniquin de Bruges, and Jehan de Huy c. 1385. In addition we have the splendid decorated chimneypieces (1386/7) and the impressive statues of King Charles VI, Queen Isabel, and the Duchess Jeanne de Boulogne in the Salle des Pas-Perdus in the former castle of Poitiers. Further, from the Sainte Chapelle in Bourges the marble group of Notre Dame-la-Blanche now in Bourges Cathedral survives (though unfortunately only in a completely disfigured form). It is a work of André Beauneveu, as are also the three fragments of heads from statues of the Apostles (now in the Museum at Bourges; Plate 23A) and the so-called 'petits prophètes' which are from the workshop of Beauneveu.[23] When we compare these works with Sluter's, though we sense a common direction of artistic purpose, we feel that the sculpture never takes flight from the stone; it is only in the rendering of facial features that we perceive that penetrating individualization which proclaims the new human insight characteristic of the fifteenth century. Probably Beauneveu's birth date precedes Sluter's; he is in any case exclusively a representative of the late four-teenth century. The smoothness in the surface of the huge heads of the Apostles at Bourges is sufficient proof of this.

Charles VI of France had also conferred upon the Duke of Berry the sovereignty of Auvergne, and so in 1388 a Sainte Chapelle was erected at Riom (Puy-de-Dôme) on the Paris model. To the portal of Notre-Dame-du-Marthuret at Riom belonged a statue of the Virgin (recently transferred into the church; Plate 24A), and this statue, taken in conjunction with André Beauneveu's work and with the general state of sculpture in France at the end of the fourteenth century, is of outstanding importance. It is a completely homogeneous piece of stone, from which the individual parts (especially the massive seated Child, which is seen in sharp outline) emerge with a re-markable abstract objectivity. Just as striking – one might almost say mysterious – is the sense of volume in the generous, flowing drapery and the austere beauty of the facial features. I think we can trace a similarity of style between this work and the royal monuments of St Denis which came from Beauneveu's workshop and even more the two Apostles on the jambs of the middle west portal of Bourges Cathedral, and these are certainly from Beauneveu's own hand. There even seems to me to be still an echo of Beauneveu's marble statue of St Catherine in the ducal chapel of Notre-Dame at Courtrai (Kortrijk), which was made shortly after 1364. I also believe that the 'Vierge à l'Oiseau' at Riom is closely connected with André Beauneveu's work at Bourges in the years round 1390. In contast to this work, the spirit of the younger generation and the radical novelty of Claus Sluter's Dijon sculpture, which is distinguished by its spatial depth, makes itself felt. On the other hand, similarity of style between the statues of the Virgin in the chapel of the town hall of Prague (c. 1381) and in the Eligiuskapelle of St Stephen in Vienna show again the intercommunication of sculptural developments in the leading North European centres in the late fourteenth century. In this context, the marble group of the Presentation in the Temple which is now in the Cluny Museum ought again to be mentioned (Plate 21B).[18] Its relation to the group of sculpture connected with Beauneveu's style is so close that it has been considered part of an altar donated by the Duke of Berry.

Beauneveu died in 1401. His assistant and successor as sculptor to the court of Bourges was Jean de Cambrai, born at Roupy, near St Quentin. The recumbent marble effigy of the Duke of Berry (d. 1416) on the slab of his tomb (begun in 1405),[24] which was transferred from the Sainte Chapelle to the crypt of Bourges Cathedral in 1757, is Jean de Cambrai's work (Plate 22). This figure is remarkably firmly shaped; it is angular in outline and only slightly engraved on the surface, so that it does not give rise to that melodious interplay of light and shade which is so characteristic of the Burgundian works of Sluter and his school. All the more pronounced is the *verismo* in the facial features. The kneeling stone figures of the duke and his second wife, Jeanne de Boulogne (as drawn by Holbein on his journey through France in 1524/5, when they were still in their original positions on either side of the Virgin on the high altar of the Sainte Chapelle),[25] and the clearly and firmly modelled Virgin (Plate 20A)[26] which the duke gave to the church of the Célestins at Marcoussis (Seine-et-Oise), are also works of Jean de Cambrai. The substructure of the monument of the duke originally bore the figures of his mourners, but only four came from the hand of Jean de Cambrai. They are of marble and now belong to the museum at Bourges, whereas the majority of these mourning figures, now dispersed, are in alabaster. They were made after Jean de Cambrai's death in 1438 by Étienne Bobilet and Paul de Mosselman[27] at the instance of King Charles VII. In accordance with the Burgundian traditional style the mourners were originally arranged in a funeral procession passing under arcades.

Further surviving individual pieces of sculpture from Bourges dating from the opening of the fifteenth century prove most convincingly what an immense significance was accorded to sculpture at the Duke of Berry's court. First we must mention the magnificent fragment of a head from a statue of an Apostle, taken from the chapel of the château of Mehun-sur-Yèvre (1408–16) and now in the Louvre (Plate 23B).[28] This is a massive stone head with sharply chiselled surface details and alive with an incredible inner tension, which, however, does not, as in Sluter's work, turn into an expression of relaxed freedom. Can this be a last work of André Beauneveu? I do not dare to make this assumption, since the surface of even Beauneveu's later works (e.g. the Apostles' heads from the Sainte Chapelle of Bourges) is softer and more fluid in the Trecento sense, while the head in the Louvre is characterized by an almost metallic exactitude of feature and a powerful use of depth. But if this work is really by Jean de Cambrai, we may judge from its excellence what his other surviving works, especially his effigy of the duke, have lost in sharpness of surface during centuries of maltreatment.

A very fine stone relief of God the Father now in the Louvre[29] also came originally from Bourges (Plate 25A). He is in the midst of an angelic host, receiving a soul into Paradise. Here again we see a very carefully defined linear structure, an abundance of movement in the arrangement of the surface, and the whole treated with a remarkably abstract objectivity. In the museum at Bourges there is a fine stone relief of a three-quarter figure of a Man of Sorrows (Plate 25B). He is portrayed with an attendant angel and with the donor, a cleric, kneeling in worship in the foreground.[30] A kind of frame to the relief is indicated by a curtain hanging from a rod – a motif which was already used in presentations of the Nativity in the fourteenth century[31] and is of course specially appropriate in that particular context. Here, in the early fifteenth century, by its use in connexion with an 'imago pietatis', it creates an illusion of real depth anticipating the pictures with curtains usual in Holland in the seventeenth century.

Finally I would like to draw attention, on account of their common style and origin, to another group of three stone figures, which is to be found today in the out-of-the-way village church of Morogues (Cher), near Bourges. This group, together with the magnificent carved sedilia also in Morogues church, is said to have come originally from the Sainte Chapelle of Bourges. In this group, the statue standing by the (cruder) central figure of the Virgin and Child attended by St John the Baptist is said to represent Louis de Châtillon, the Duke of Berry's son-in-law (Plate 24B). It is remarkable for the suggestive quality of its simple, austere lines.[32] In all probability the works I have enumerated are by a number of different masters, presumably from the Southern Netherlands or Northern France. I cite them in order to show how complex and how fraught with significance for the future was the sculpture in an important town like Bourges at the outset of the fifteenth century. We shall have to remember this fact when we come to discuss the character of the Sluter school in Burgundy, which in comparison was much more homogeneous in character.

As examples of sculpture at the court of the Dukes of Bourbon (at Moulins) I can only refer to the marble monument of Louis II of Bourbon (d. 1410) and his wife Anne of Auvergne (d. 1412) in the Chapelle Vieille of the church of St Pierre at Souvigny (Allier). These are statues of immense sculptural tension, whose corporeality is strangely enhanced by the exceptional size of the slab; it is the work of a master similar to Jean de Cambrai. On the upper side of the canopies which surmount the tomb we find representations in relief of the Crucifixion and of the Coronation of the Virgin of striking delicacy and poignancy.

At this juncture we must mention the sculpture produced at the papal court in Avignon. Unfortunately little of this survives, and that which does is in poor condition. The most impressive pieces are the magnificent relief of a demi-figure of God in Benediction, surrounded by a halo of clouds (Plate 27B), and the fragmentary figure of a bearded Apostle, both from the Église des Célestins and now in the Musée Calvet. The first is a work of concentrated and visionary power and its surfaces are full of movement. The architect of the church was Perrin Morel of Lyon (from 1396 onwards), and we know that he was also a sculptor. Perhaps we may therefore associate his name with these impressive stone figures.[33]

Mention should also be made here of a very fine figure on the pulpit of St Pierre at Avignon. It represents a prophet reading and, with its devout seriousness of expression and the rich abundance of its drapery, reminds us of the corbel figures at the entrance to the Chartreuse of Champmol. There are also in the Musée Calvet the assembled fragments of the wall-monument of Cardinal Jean de la Grange (d. 1402) originally in St Martial (Plate 27A). The kneeling figures of King Charles VI and his brother Louis, Duke of Orleans, are attended by apostles, and the deep wall niche is filled to overflowing by these statues. In its details the style is relatively austere. The monument is in two tiers. On the lower level we see the corpse of the deceased, portrayed with the maximum realism as 'speculum vanitatis' (Plate 26B). On the upper level lies the cardinal in full regalia. The cardinal had previously been bishop of Amiens, and there in 1375 he had commissioned the statues for the 'Beau Pilier' on the north tower of the front of the cathedral, including a portrait of himself. We may assume therefore that the craftsmen summoned to Avignon for the erection of his tomb also came from the northern provinces, where similar realistic tendencies are visible at this time.[34]

A connexion with Northern France and the Southern Netherlands appears, in my opinion, already in the marble fragments of the monument of St Elzéar (Plate 20B) and Ste Dolphine de Jabran from the Franciscan church at Apt (Vaucluse), which is as early as c. 1373.[35] The soft modelling of the surfaces, especially of the kneeling and praying saint, shows brilliantly those painterly transitions between concave and convex which are characteristic of the international style of the seventies and occur for instance also in Bohemian sculpture and painting. But over and above that, the figure has a strange and moving dynamic power, struggling, as it were, to liberate itself from the stone block, but not yet free to spread into the surrounding space.

Robert of Geneva, who was in residence in Avignon from 1378 to 1393 as Pope Clement VII, appears to have been the donor of the west façade of the cathedral of St Maurice at Vienne (south of Lyon).[36] The rich sculpture on the portals dates from c. 1410–20 and shows figures of great delicacy and beauty of movement with a marked feeling for depth. Stylistically they are derived from neither Bourges nor the Dijon School, but would appear to be the work of a French school of sculptors who also had contacts with the Netherlands. Closely related to these figures is the sculpture on the soffits of the west portal of the abbey church of St Antoine-en-Viennois (Isère). These are of a slightly later date, c. 1425.

The partly enamelled silver bust containing the relics of St Valerius (Plate 13)[37] and the reliquary busts of two canonized deacons, given in 1397 to the cathedral of Zaragoza by the Anti-Pope Benedict XIII (a member of the Aragon nobility), now kept in the sacristy of La Seo, are of unique interest. These busts succeed in combining a painterly fluidity of surface with great precision of detail, and are thus one of the most impressive examples of that magic and at the same time dynamic quality which immediately precedes the sculptural hardening and pulling together of the early fifteenth century. Perhaps it is true that this style found its most articulate expression in the work of the goldsmiths. In my introduction I emphasized the fact that, apart from a few of the boldest innovators, the discovery and the comprehension of the new sculptural possibilities at the end of the fourteenth century were most fully exploited by the workers in metal. In this context the three magnificent silver busts in Zaragoza follow naturally on the examples already quoted. Doubtless all three originated in Avignon – a fact which is indicated by a certain Italian character both in the structure of the busts and in the peculiarity of their enamel. This is only to be expected at Avignon, where at the time of the popes many Italian artists were active, even if they did not in fact influence the stylistic development of French sculpture.

On account of the extensive destruction in the Île-de-France and in Northern France, it is particularly difficult to gain a clear idea of the forces which contributed at the turn of the century to the development of Late Gothic sculpture there. Even of the most important achievements – for example the Louvre and its *vis*, i.e. the newel staircase (built by Raymond du Temple in 1365, with sculpture by Jean de Saint-Romain) – we have only documentary evidence and vague indications. But in places where series of funerary monuments have been preserved – especially at St Denis, but occasionally also in remote spots, e.g. in St Laurent at Eu (Seine-Maritime), where the members of the house of Artois are buried in the crypt – we gain the impression that the style of figure sculpture remained relatively constant until the turn of the century, although it is clear in the latest works of the fourteenth century that an interest in the realistic presentation of human features had become an important factor to the sculptor.

All the more remarkable in this respect are the royal tombs at St Denis by André Beauneveu; for here we see that consideration for elegance of line yields place to a new feeling for the weight and volume of the figure. The same is true of the magnificent statues of Charles V and his wife Jeanne de Bourbon (*c.* 1390) from the portal of the chapel of the Hospice des Quinze-Vingt, now in the Louvre.[38] The fact that these statues are in the guise and to the honour of St Louis and Queen Marguerite sheds light on the spiritual climate at the end of the fourteenth century. It is a striking example of the new desire to offer oneself to the saint. In any case I think it is right and proper to emphasize how different the interest in physiognomy and volume exhibited by these statues is from the work of Jean de Liège,[39] who was a 'faiseur de tombes' in Paris, worked for Westminster Abbey too, and died in 1382.

At St Denis we see the complete turn to the new realism of the fifteenth century in the effigy of the Connétable Bertrand du Guesclin (d. 1380). This dates from 1397 and is the work of Robert Loisel (formerly an assistant of Jean de Liège) and Thomas Privé. Perhaps the effigy of Guesclin's successor, Louis de Sancerre (d. 1402), is by the same artists. Both these works testify to the urge towards a new vividness in sculpture, a new firmness of style, and a new three-dimensionality.

The most striking piece of sculpture of the years round 1400 in the Paris area is the vast relief of the Coronation of the Virgin at the château of La Ferté-Milon (Plate 12A). It is set on the outer wall high over the archway. Around the recess in the wall is a framing hollow with a wide trelliswork border of realistic leafwork, and openwork trefoils. We are thus presented with a perfect stage for the Coronation and Benediction of the Virgin, and this splendid composition is spread out horizontally with a compositional ease until then unknown. Angels as in a court ceremonial bear the train of the

Virgin, who kneels in devotion, and light and shade plays round the figures. A sharply protruding edge separates the base, and three angels are placed against it in relief, bearing the arms of the lord of the castle, Louis, Duke of Orleans. The date of the building enables us to be sure that the piece was executed between 1392 and 1407. What we have here is an example of painterly sculpture developed freely in space. Its antecedents are not any regional development within the Île-de-France, but the Netherlandish sculptors, of whose services French feudalism, as we have seen, frequently made use. A related work is the gigantic statue of the Virgin which, together with fragments of other figures, was found in a very damaged condition in the château of Pierrefonds (Oise), a château also built for Louis of Orleans. It is the work of a great master, probably likewise from the Southern Netherlands.

Our surmise that even in Paris at this time the tone was set by sculptors who had migrated there or been summoned there from the northern provinces or from the Southern Netherlands is borne out not merely by records, but also by the style of the ruined statues that are all that remain of the splendour of the former decoration of the Sainte Chapelle in the château de Vincennes. The frequently repeated coats of arms of Charles VI and the Bavarian arms of Queen Isabel prove that they date from after 1379.[40]

Among the most astonishing and impressive works of tomb sculpture of this time are the marble tablets of Pierre d'Évreux-Navarre, Count of Mortain (d. 29 July 1412) and of his wife, Catherine d'Alençon, from the Chartreuse of Paris (now in the Louvre; Plates 28 and 29).[41] On 1 October 1412 Catherine was married again to Louis of Bavaria, Queen Isabel's brother, who went to Ingolstadt in the same year and assumed power. Apparently Catherine did not follow him. In 1462 she was buried in the abbey church of Ste Geneviève in Paris. Everything would therefore appear to suggest that the marble statues now in the Louvre and originally in the Chartreuse must date from 1412/13. The carving of the features on the tombstone of Connétable Louis de Sancerre at St Denis is an immediate precursor of their magic realism; their sensibility conveys a remarkable feeling of modernity. It is not merely the sculptural substance which strikes us – as it is in Sluter's sculpture – but the differentiation in the interpretations of the human face. It is this quality which lends them, in spite of all their *verismo*, a delicate veil of mystery such as we also sense in the paintings of van Eyck. Incidentally, up to the death of Charles VI in 1422 the reins of government in Paris were in the hands of Queen Isabel. The double monument of Charles VI and Isabel (d. 1435) in St Denis, made in 1425–9 by Pierre de Thury, is a relatively conventional piece of work.

Very effective stone sculpture directed by the same principles is to be found in the now remote but formerly famous church of Notre Dame at Écouis (Eure). Here we have a group of the Annunciation, where the kneeling angel – whom we see sideways with his richly feathered wings – looks up at the figure of the Virgin, standing with folded arms in an attitude of devotion (Plate 11A). Her face, soft and full, is carved in white marble.[42] The corbel is composed of three angels reading together, one of the most charmingly lyrical inventions of the early fifteenth century. It seems but a step from this group of angels to the beautiful votive stone relief from the Abbaye du Trésor, now in the parish church of Écos (Eure; Plate 11B). This shows, as in a picture, kneeling votive figures, male and female, gathered in prayer together with St Michael and St William of Aquitaine around an 'imago pietatis', and lateral angels seizing a curtain. A regional affinity exists here with the charming stone figure of a saint in the Musée Archéologique at Le Havre, which is perhaps only slightly older.[43]

A series of over-life-size stone figures of the Apostles and the Evangelists in the church of Ste-Croix at Bernay (Eure) also has its roots in the Southern Netherlands and Flanders. Originally in the neighbouring abbey church of Bec-Hellouin, they are examples of a tensionless, decorative style and are probably earlier in date than might be assumed from records of payment made to a certain Sandrin in 1433 for painting them.[44]

In addition to monumental sculpture, much small work was made, and here French feudal civilization of the period round 1400 found its most adequate expression. Evidently Paris was the centre of production of these objects in ivory, gold, and gold enamel, but judging from the inventories of court and ecclesiastical treasuries so many of them have been destroyed in the course of time that it is difficult to form a true picture of their original variety and abundance. They occupy as prominent a place in the French sculpture of this period as do the exquisite illuminated manuscripts in contemporary French painting.

In this category, the beginning of the new century is marked by that delightful gold-enamel group in the treasury of the collegiate church of Altötting in Bavaria which has become famous under the name of the 'Goldenes Rössel (Plate 14).[45] This was the New Year's gift of Queen Isabel to Charles VI in 1404. In the next year the Goldenes Rössel, together with other works in gold-enamel and regalia, of which we have exact information, was given in pawn to Queen Isabel's brother, who played an important part at the court of the feeble-minded French king and who later became ruler in Ingolstadt under the name of Duke Louis the Bearded. He saw to it that these precious objects were taken from Paris to Bavaria.

The Goldenes Rössel group presents us with a miniature stage. The Virgin is enthroned in an arbour grown over with flowering climbers and adorned with pearls and precious stones. At her feet are white-robed children representing John the Baptist, John the Evangelist, and St Catherine, to whom the Christ Child presents a betrothal ring. In front of the Virgin's throne are the kneeling figures of King Charles VI and his Marshal, who offers the king's helmet, the symbol of his sovereignty, to the Virgin, while on a lower level a page boy holds ready the king's white horse. The group has a radiance and a lyrical beauty and moreover some charming anecdotal motifs – almost as in a genre picture – which remind us of the intimate and yet aristocratic atmosphere pervading the finest contemporary illuminated manuscripts. Although each detail is clearly stated, there is a delicate veil of idealization over the whole, an atmosphere of paradisal innocence, like that of the contemporary paintings of the *hortus conclusus*.

A survey of the few surviving works of the Parisian goldsmiths of *c.* 1400 is enough to convince us of the rich variety they must have presented. There is the mysticism of the reliquary from the Chapelle de l'Ordre du Saint-Esprit in Paris and of the thorn reliquary from the Vienna Hofburg, now in the British Museum; the dignified representation of the Trinity on the medallion of Pope Alexander VI (Washington, National Gallery of Art); the profound suffering of Christ in the reliquary of Pope Sixtus V in the cathedral treasury of Montalto (Marche); in the Christ of Pity and the Mater Dolorosa from the small reliquary altar in the Rijksmuseum at Amsterdam; and in the double-sided 'Pace di Siena' in Arezzo Cathedral. Then there is the terrifying icon of John the Baptist in the 'Platter of St John' in the treasury of Genoa Cathedral, and finally the sublime Calvary in the treasury of Esztergom (Gran; Hungary; Plate 75). These miniature works of the goldsmith's craft offer us an immense abundance of vivid inventions, which appears all the greater when we remember how little has survived from the vast number of such treasures in France, enumerated in the inventories of the time.

The courts of the French dukes vied with the royal court in Paris; for example, the most precious piece of work in the style of the Goldenes Rössel appears to have been a representation of the Trinity made at the order of the Duke of Berry.[46] Similar miniature carvings in ivory and silver[47] which have survived prove to us the broad artistic and social basis on which this art flourished and, in addition, its dependence on the traditions of the late fourteenth century.

When we place a few of the outstanding examples of this gold enamel work in chronological order, we realize the dominant place occupied by these works in the artistic output of their period, and they also enable us to test our understanding of the character and development of major sculpture at this time. Symptomatic of the epoch is that sculpture no longer remains bound by the tectonic rigidity of the Trecento, and that there is an increasing contrast between body and drapery, between core and envelope. The imagination allows itself more and more free play in the painterly treatment of the surface.

In this chapter France and the Netherlands have by necessity been treated together, because leading talents in French sculpture were of Netherlandish origin, and also because the extent of the destruction in Flanders and the Netherlands makes it easier to study the sculpture of the latter region from the masterpieces which have survived the storms of time in France. Scholars in recent years have coined the term International Gothic Style of 1400 for the phenomenon of the arts in Europe around that time. This collective term represents a partial truth, in so far as for instance the similarity of the works of Jacopo della Quercia to those by Sluter is indeed great. At the same time, however, there is no mistaking the regional character of the creative renewal in Europe, the principal origins being first the Netherlands and France, second Bohemia and Austria, and third Italy with Pisanello and the artists of Florence and Umbria. The characteristics of these groups are in my opinion so striking that it would be ill-advised to go on with the term International Style of 1400. Surely in the arts of the Trecento international communications were by no means less pronounced.

In the border districts of present-day Belgium and Northern France the continuity in the development of sculpture at the turn of the fourteenth and fifteenth centuries may still be seen in the numerous surviving reliefs on wall tablets at Tournai, Lille, Arras, etc. These tablets (many executed in Tournai marble) are however but the echo of more important works of a monumental kind which have been lost. Thus the representation of the Virgin on the monument of Simon de Leval (d. 1407) at Basècles near Tournai[48] is still reminiscent of the Coronation of the Virgin on the north portal of St Jacques at Liège, which has its connexions with the regional traditions of that district, such as are to be seen most clearly in the figure of the Virgin on the south-west portal of St Martin at Halle (Hal; Plate 9B).

The climax of the new statuesque tendencies of sculpture within the traditional architectural framework is the sculpture of the Beau Pilier or Grand Contrefort of the north-west tower of Amiens Cathedral which dates from 1376–80.[49] I have already said that one of the figures is a monument to Cardinal de la Grange, whose funerary effigy at Avignon has been discussed earlier on. The way in which the volume of these statues spreads into space is astonishing. Here, it seems, one experiences for the first time that calculated painterly use of highlights and shadows which was to give to sculpture about the year 1400 a completely new optical value. The parallel to Beauneveu and the beginnings of Sluter is consistent. The power of communication of the Amiens figures is reduced by damage and restorations. Even in their present state, however, the initial force of these pieces can be gauged. Emanating from monumental sculpture of the fourteenth century, the new possibilities of an autonomy of sculpture begin to appear which make themselves equally felt in the late sculpture of the Parlers at Prague. Furthermore, another typical sign of the new urge to individualize is apparent at Amiens: the introduction of the portrait specially successfully in the Jean Bureau de la Rivière.

Perhaps the most important document in this connexion is an alabaster group, clearly from an altarpiece, of the Presentation in the Temple[18] (Paris, Musée de Cluny; Plate 21B). It has been attributed to André Beauneveu. However that may be, the group tells of a closer and immediate contact with those traditions of sculpture in the South Netherlands and Flanders in the fourteenth century which favoured delicate and gently-reflecting materials. These districts would appear to have been especially sympathetic to the development of the tender and introspective qualities characteristic of the years round 1400.

This beautiful, image-like Presentation in the Temple also goes to show, I believe, that the sculpture of Flanders and the Netherlands at the end of the fourteenth century was the source of those altarpieces which needed to be seen at close range and which were to assume such significance in the course of the fifteenth century. Altar carvings have suffered even more destruction than stone sculpture. It is fortunate therefore that at least one example of this genre remains to prove, along with the altarpieces of Jacques de Baerze at Dijon, how tradition-bound it was, in spite of the vast new possibilities revealed in the work of Claus Sluter. The example to which I refer is the carved retable of the high altar of St Sauveur at Hakendover, near Tienen, probably a piece of Brussels work from the years 1410–20. This and similar carvings and fragments of groups in the Musée du Cinquantenaire in Brussels[50] are characterized by a vivid narrative quality and an amazing amplitude in the flow of lines (Plate 18). The details however are conventional, lacking both spatial depth and the tension of a new individualization. They can be no more than an echo of destroyed masterpieces. The carved altarpieces of this period which were taken from Brabant and Flanders to North-West Germany and Scandinavia (e.g. the Altar of the Passion in the Reinoldikirche at Dortmund; Plate 19) will be dealt with in the next chapter; for these works had a lasting effect upon the sculpture of their host countries.

But there is one example of sculpture from Flanders whose clarity and bold, impressive form command our attention. It is the carved group of Christ carrying the Cross in the Musée de Cluny,[51] which belongs to the same time and has the same premises as the alter carvings of Hakendover and the stylistically similar fragments (Plate 15A). But it is more assured in the development of the relief into a new depth and is therefore of special significance for our comprehension of the influences emanating at this time from the Netherlands. The composition is still dominated by a fluidity of line, and we have still another decade to wait for the emergence of a new solidity. Symptomatic of this is the development within the same region in the early fifteenth century from the Christ and St John the Baptist in the Musée Cinquantenaire in Brussels to the more concentrated statuesque quality of the wooden St John the Baptist in the Louvre (Plate 17A).[52]

I should like to take two works from this enigmatic field of Netherlandish sculpture at the turn of the century which, although they pose problems, nevertheless serve to show the innovatory character of this art. Firstly the silver-gilt reliefs of the legend of St Servatius from Maestricht, now in the Museum für Kunst und Gewerbe at Hamburg (Plate 12B).[53] It is assumed that these reliefs originally came from the base of a reliquary bust (later completely restored) of St Servatius in the treasury of St Servatius at Maestricht, given to it by Henry Duke of Bavaria in 1403. They bear testimony to that story-telling quality which constitutes the enchantment of Netherlandish illuminated manuscripts from the beginning of the fifteenth century. Here the shimmering gold sublimates the objectivity of treatment into the realm of lyrical symbolism. Presentation and narrative come together, and we see how the idealizing magic of the fourteenth century approaches the naïve naturalism of the fifteenth. Instead of the blue of the sky characteristic of the illuminated manuscripts we have the groups of lozenges of close crossed hatching. The compositions have so complex a painterly movement that there seems to me to be no doubt of the origins of these silver reliefs in early-fifteenth-century developments of painting, even if their association with the bust of St Servatius of 1403 is not fully established.

Perhaps there already existed in the Netherlands at this time small carvings in hard wood, such as were to become so much favoured at the turn from Late Gothic to Renaissance. A very early example of this genre – still dating from the fourteenth century – is a small relief in boxwood of St John the Baptist, in the Staatliche Museen in Berlin.[54] This shows the same melodious grace of surface and the same tension in the minutest detail as we find in the goldsmiths' art. In the same tradition of artistry is the boxwood statuette of a Fair Virgin in the Carrand Collection in the Museo Nazionale in Florence,[55] with its slender proportions and tenseness of surface in the rich folds of its drapery. It is impossible to say whether such a work came originally from the Netherlands or from the Cologne region, but in the general impression the predominating resemblance is to bronzes from the Southern Netherlands.

A further early manifestation of the spirit of the new century in Netherlandish sculpture, which must be mentioned in this connexion, seems to me to be the alabaster statue of the Virgin in the Rijksmuseum at Amsterdam (Plate 21A).[56] Here we have the same fine, dully-reflecting material in which the sculptors of the Southern Netherlands in the fourteenth century loved to work. The statue has a fine freedom of treatment, and the Virgin's expression exhibits a simple naturalism which, in spite of certain charming details, remains tentative and somehow veiled. Here again illuminated manuscripts provide us with the closest parallels. In any case I see no contact with French sculpture of this time. A more likely antecedent is the monumental style of the carvings on the south-west portal of the pilgrimage church of Halle (Hal). If this is so, then the so-called Franco-Flemish, but certainly South-Netherlandish, stone figure of a standing Virgin and Child in the Victoria and Albert Museum in London[57] presents an intermediary stage.

From documentary evidence and from the works which survive we know how much Western European sculpture owes to the rich inventiveness of the Netherlands in the years round 1400, although in the Netherlands themselves so few of these works are extant. Even a figure like the black marble effigy of a member of the Drakenborch family, transferred from the Wittevrouwen Convent to the Centraal Museum at Utrecht, is no more than an echo of the greatness of monumental sculpture in the Netherlands about 1400. All the more reason have we to try and trace what reflects that greatness. I think for instance that this is possible when we regard the North Netherlandish silver reliefs from the Maestricht reliquary bust of St Servatius and the apparently South Netherlandish alabaster figure in the Rijksmuseum at Amsterdam. The appreciation of this kind of sculpture of the turn of the century is proved by the grisaille painting of carved figures on altars which are the work of the following generation. In addition there is the fragment of a stone statue in the museum at Utrecht[58] which will be discussed later; the spatial monumentality of this statue is the most eloquent witness of the creative significance of Netherlandish sculpture at the outset of the fifteenth century, even though the statue itself is of a somewhat later date and hence only retrospective evidence.

CHAPTER 3

GERMANY IN THE EARLY YEARS OF THE
FIFTEENTH CENTURY

SCULPTURE in the Lower Rhineland and specially in Cologne was closely intertwined in its development with that of the Southern Netherlands. The ecclesiastical province of Cologne stretched far west and created a permanent tie with the Meuse districts which were so rich in artistic production in the Middle Ages. We find therefore in the sculpture of Cologne and the Lower Rhineland during the fourteenth century many features which unite it with that of Brabant, Wallonia, and Lorraine. In addition there were the connexions between the different cathedral lodges and of the much ramified families of their masters. Cologne was of paramount importance. It was here that the work of the Parler family had its origins. The sculpture on the Portal of St Peter in Cologne Cathedral[1] is their work, and in the limestone bust of a woman which bears the Parler L-square on its scutcheon (Cologne, Schnütgen Museum; found in the Margareten-kloster near the cathedral) and which is probably a work of Heinrich IV Parler,[2] we sense the same triumph at the 'discovery of man' which is evident in the most advanced busts of the choir triforium in Prague Cathedral (Plate 45A). At the same time the Annunciation on the west portal of the Cistercian church in Altenberg proves that as early as the late fourteenth century a pronounced Cologne manner of facial expression had become perceptible.

One of the main works in Cologne sculpture at the turn of the century are the figures of the prophets from the Rathaus, now in the Schnütgen Museum.[3] These figures, carved in oak and painted, with their narrow-shouldered rotundity, the diagonal flow of their draperies, and the mobility of their features bear a family likeness to the 'small prophets' of the Sainte Chapelle in Bourges; for although they are of wood, the Prophets of Cologne descend from architectural sculpture and are closest akin to the prophets from the portal of the town hall in Brussels.[4] The stone figures of the Emperor, the Electors, St Peter, and the Prophets on the Rathaus in Bremen, carved by Master Johannes in 1405–7,[5] have similar connexions.

The western origin of these works is even more clearly discernible in that greatest example of early-fifteenth-century sculpture in Cologne, the monument of Archbishop Friedrich of Saarwerden. This is in the cathedral and dates from before the Archbishop's death in 1414. The bronze lid with the effigy of the Archbishop (Plate 31) bears the signature 'Eilogius Lodgus', that is Eligius of Liège. It is a magnificent example of the style of metal sculpture which flourished in Wallonia and Brabant. The most telling testimony to the parallelism of growth of sculpture in metal in the Southern Netherlands, and monumental sculpture in stone in the style of the prophets from the portal of the Old Town Hall at Brussels, is the small gilt bronze figure of a kneeling prophet in the Louvre.[6] But – to return to the Saarwerden monument – the sandstone reliefs on the walls of the tomb-chest, though they show affinity with South Netherlandish sculpture, reveal in their clarity of form and the delicate intimacy of their facial expressions a character eminently typical of Cologne and the Lower Rhine (Plate 30A). Perhaps the earliest recognizable work by this master is the stone figure of a Virgin and Child from a town gate at Zons,[7] and this in turn is clearly related to the figures of the Virgin on the north and south-west portals of St Martin at Halle (Hal), near Brussels.

This style continues in the voluminous demi-figures of prophets and angels with musical instruments on the corbels of the choir of the Andreaskirche in Cologne (begun in 1414), the magnificent angels against the brackets of the piers in the chancel of Aachen Cathedral, and in the particularly beautiful but sadly damaged figures from the Lady Chapel of the Charterhouse of Cologne,[8] which date from *c.* 1427. Here again the Cologne character expresses itself in the gentle melodic flow of the figures, ready, as it were, to enjoy to the full all that is noble. The Virgin of the Annunciation, as she kneels before a rippling curtain, shows most clearly the new spatial quality of this sculpture. Drapery and body incorporate space within themselves and at the same time radiate an atmosphere of blissful harmony. The vigour of the forms – particularly striking is the rich feathered detail in the pinions of the angels – is of a metallic precision. There is no immediate link between this sculpture and the work of the Parlers as exemplified in the Portal of St Peter in Cologne Cathedral; the decisive influence seems rather to have come from the South Netherlandish successors of André Beauneveu. Although it is impossible to gain an adequate picture of this monumental sculptural art in Belgium today, we may surmise its excellence from the small Fair Virgin of boxwood already referred to in the preceding chapter and now in the Carrand Collection at the Museo Nazionale in Florence. The limestone figure of the Virgin from the Lady Chapel of the Charterhouse (Schnütgen Museum) is the Cologne echo of this style. A fragment of a figure of St Andrew, belonging to the same category, has an inner strength reminiscent of Sluter's works.

Similar in its effect is the limestone fragment of St Elizabeth with a donor-monk from Bremen Cathedral. The clear accentuation achieved through the distribution of light and shade in the structure of this nobly proportioned block of drapery conveys a remarkably strong impression of free existence in space. In looking at it we are reminded of the Fair Virgins of eastern and south-eastern Germany.[9] As in these, the contrasts of light and dark in the articulation of the surface of the St Elizabeth are almost exaggerated. What dominates the impression is a rich, painterly ensemble rather than that sublime objectivity as it appears in the most magnificent Netherlandish form in the works of Sluter. It is for this reason that I believe the Bremen fragment, in contrast to the works from Cologne here discussed, to be the outcome of a development whose possibilities had already appeared in the late works of the Parlers. This does not, however, imply that the St Elizabeth need be an actual import from Bohemia.

In assessing sculpture north of the Alps during the early fifteenth century we tend, I think, to make too sharp a distinction between 'eastern' and 'western' stylistic sources. A page from the so-called Codex Boccaccio of 1402 (*Livres des femmes nobles et renommées*) provides us with the western prototype of the Fair Virgins.[10] On this page we see a woman artist engaged in painting just such a statue of the Virgin. On the other hand we also learn from contemporary sources of carved figures of the Virgin which were brought from Prague as far as Strasbourg.[11] Naturally on reading such an account we think pre-eminently of the Fair and Suffering Virgins which reached such a peak of excellence in Bohemian sculpture of the late fourteenth century.

We do not lack examples to show that the theme of the 'Fair Virgin'[12] enjoyed a rich abundance of variations in the sculpture of the Lower Rhineland during the first decades of the fifteenth century. It is a proof of the translation of the Late-Trecento idea of the Virgin[13] into the sphere of human experience and charming vividness characteristic of the new century, just as happened at the same time with the painted panels. As examples I would cite the carved Madonna figures in Cologne, St Gereon; the Suermondt Museum at Aachen; Maestricht, O.L. Vrouwe Kerk (generally known as 'Ster der Zee');[14] Maestricht, St Servatius; Aachen, St Foillan (1411); Cologne, St Maria Lyskirchen; Cologne Cathedral. In these works we witness an increase in splendour and amplitude and a development of the carved Virgin into a new sculptural independence.

Owing to the quantity of what has been preserved, a survey of the most important known works and masters of the years around 1400 in North Germany reveals a remarkable variety of sources. On the one hand we have the continued existence of the lodges, where the influence of the Parlers played the main part in creating the new style of the fifteenth century; on the other we have the activities of the masters in the workshops, where altarpieces were made and where therefore painting, sculpture, and the painting of sculpture were carried on side by side. In addition to these there was the thrust and counterthrust of local traditions and foreign influences, whether from the east (Prague) or from the Lower Rhineland and the Netherlands.

Relatively early, the personality of an individual artist emerges – Master Bertram of Minden, whom the records prove to have been active in Hamburg from 1367 onwards and who died before 1415. The settlement of accounts concerning a St Christopher 'to be made and painted' in 1385 in Hamburg would seem to prove that the 'pictor Bertrammus' was also now and then a carver of statues. The carved figures in the altar-pieces extant (e.g. a calvary group and statuettes of saints with surmounting canopies from the Grabow altar of 1379 from St Peter in Hamburg and the beautiful relief of the Nativity from the Harvestehude altar, both now in the Hamburg Kunsthalle) show, it is true, the purely additive character of fourteenth-century sculptural composition, but at the same time they are permeated with a charming immediacy in their narrative style.[15]

We take a decisive step into a wonderful world of new visual perception if we move on to the reliefs for the St Barbara Altar of Master Francke from the church of Kalanti (Nykyrko), (now in the museum of Helsinki), which may possibly have been made for the Ratskapelle in Hamburg Cathedral some time between 1412 and 1415. In this altar, the carved centrepiece represents the Death of the Virgin, flanked by four reliefs of episodes from her life. We may assume that sketches for these reliefs were made by Master Francke; for the pictorial element is paramount in the presentation of the subject matter, and even in the style of the reliefs themselves. It is not known where Master Francke lived before he moved to Hamburg: on the lower Rhine or in Westphalia, or in the adjoining dukedom of Gelder. In any case in these reliefs we sense a measure of that charming inventiveness of Netherlandish and French illuminated manuscripts which exercised so decisive an influence on the formation of Master Francke's style of painting.[16]

Owing to Lübeck's significance as a trading centre, the abundance of these cross-connexions in her sculpture at the opening of the fifteenth century is particularly striking. The series of oak figures in an altarpiece of the Coronation of the Virgin from the abbey of Marienwohld near Mölln (formerly Berlin, Museum)[17] is still quite conservative in style and exhibits the traditional form of the late fourteenth century in a grave and almost austere local style. Strikingly different are the charming stone figures dating from 1399–1401 which come from the Burgkirche in Lübeck and are now in the St Annenmuseum there (Plate 30B). They are by a Westphalian master who had previously been responsible for statues on the south portal of the Wiesenkirche at Soest.[18] They are delightful by virtue of the freshness of their narrative quality and the clarity of their sculptural accentuation. In this – in contrast to Mölln – they are products of a new age. The iconographical type is Lower Rhenish. Compared with their Netherlandish sources, the Lübeck series strikes one as stiff, as though the artist had tried, in a somewhat naïve way, to do more than he could manage. True to fourteenth-century traditions, the series as a series is what matters here, not anecdotal variations. There followed in Lübeck in 1406 a series of stone figures for the Bergenfahrerkapelle in the Marienkirche (now St Annenmuseum) and in 1420 the stone figure of the Virgin (destroyed in the war) from the altarpiece given by Johann Darsow to the Marienkirche. Both these works are of an austere, monumental character. I would assume that the linear element in the treatment of the surfaces is Netherlandish, and I feel reminded, for example, of the similarity in the chiselwork here and in an almost contemporary head of St Peter in the Gemeente Museum at Arnhem.[19]

The outstanding master in Lübeck was Johannes Junge, of whose activity we have documentary evidence between 1406 and 1428. The magnificent stone figures from Niendorf in the St Annenmuseum are his work (Plate 32A), and so too are the elegant St Catherine at Tujec (Tiegenhagen; West Prussia) and the delightful little head of a Virgin from the abbey of Marienwohlde, now in the Landesmuseum of Schleswig-Holstein at Schloss Gottorf; also the alabaster carvings (completed in 1423) on the monument of Queen Margaret of Denmark (d. 1412) in the cathedral of Roskilde.[20] The alabaster Pietà by Johannes Junge for the church of Sønder-Alslev on Falster, now in the National Museum of Copenhagen, is of about the same date. It is a work of balanced harmony, and serves to show how much beauty of detail has been lost to us in the tomb of Queen Margaret through crude alterations. Clearly the Southern Netherlands are the stylistic source of these works. It is the sphere of activity we have already discussed which stretches from the Coronation of the Virgin on the portal of St Jacques at Liège to the Apostles at Bernay in Normandy.[21] The essential feature is the union of a beautiful and happy naturalism with an abstract austerity of style. This proves a forceful influence from the idealizing art of the West, whether this came through precept and training gleaned by Junge in his 'Wanderjahre' or through his acceptance of certain types of representation. In the case of Queen Margaret's tomb it may also be that the court had given the artist certain instructions, which in turn were based on an acquaintance with the courtly art of the West.

The stone figures on the rood screen in the Marienkirche in Lübeck, which date from before 1428, are remarkably delicate and harmonious in form and expression. The tendency to a gentle serenity which they reveal deserves all the more emphasis, when we remember that most of the early expressions of naturalism were characterized by a certain naïve violence, to which the term 'Soft Style' for the International Gothic of 1400, which has become current in German art history, in no wise does justice.

The expressive element – as it characterizes the German Late Gothic – is very much more strongly marked in the wooden carvings which are to be found in large numbers in Lübeck itself – beginning with the high altar of the Marienkirche of 1415–25 – and in the wide area to which its artistic products were exported. The greatest animation of expression is to be found in the magnificent statues in the church of the convent of St Brigitta at Vadstena (Östergötland), in the grand maturity of the Crucifix at the choir entrance, the bitter solemnity of the Man of Sorrows, the gentleness of the life-size figure of St Anne with the Virgin and Child (1427), and in the impressive and remarkably assured figure of St Brigitta.[22] Whether we can claim that these wooden statues are the work of Junge, who is known to have been a sculptor both in stone and wood, I should not like to say with certainty.

Of specially high quality are the carvings on the Burgomaster's Bench in the town hall at Tallinn (Reval) in Estonia. The parts dating from 1374 appear to be of Lower Saxon origin. More outstanding are the bench ends with their poignant representations of Samson and Delilah, Aristotle and Phyllis, David and Goliath, reliefs of an astonishing spatial suggestiveness. There is much to indicate that these reliefs, dating from about 1430, are the work of the Lübeck sculptor Marquard Hasse, who was active at Tallinn between 1426 and 1459. I believe that the magnificent head of St John the Baptist and the Vernicle[23] are of similar date and by the same master; for they display the same penetrating, painterly vividness and the same sense of free spatial movement. The head of St John sparkles with life and is at the same time heraldically severe in its stylization, in which respects it forms a parallel to the head of the Crucifixus at Vadstena. The next of Marquard Hasse's works is the beautiful Virgin of the Apocalypse from Uusikaupunki (Nystad), in the Helsinki Museum.

In North-West Germany in general at this time we witness a similar stratification of native traditions through alien influences with their stimulating effect on indigenous style.[24] The reliefs on the wings of the altarpiece from Coesfeld (Münster, Westphalian Landesmuseum), the high altar in the Marienkirche at Iserlohn, the high altar from the Ägidienkirche at Lübeck (the so-called 'Grönau Altar') now in the St Annenmuseum, the Crucifixion Altar from Bokel in the Niedersächsische Landesgalerie at Hanover, the high altar of the Reinoldikirche at Dortmund (of soon after 1421; Plate 19) are all products of workshops in Brabant and Flanders, though we shall seek in vain for such products in their own countries. The export of these works reached as far as Scandinavia and Finland. The manner of arrangement of the figures in the framework of the shrines is still purely additive, as it had been for example in Bertram's Grabow altarpiece (1379–83) and in the high altar in Lund Cathedral (1398). Only the centre groups in these altarpieces attain to a picture-like concentration in compositions filled with painterly movement and sculptural stresses and tensions. The high altar in the Reinoldi-kirche at Dortmund is the most effective of these altars, by reason of the fine crescendo in the central Calvary group and the metrical abstraction of the closely detailed archi-tectural surround, which contains pairs of Apostles beneath canopies, set on each side of the Crucifixion, like the 'pleureurs' on Burgundian tombs.

The sense of drama of the Dortmund altar makes one realize to the full that the sculptors of the altars made in the Southern Netherlands at the beginning of the fifteenth century possessed already that ability to express themselves with complete incidental details which became typical of the late fifteenth century in the same regions, though what was at first described as in a novel later assumed the characteristics of the anecdote. At the same time one senses that the only early altarpiece remaining in Belgium, that of Hakendover, can be no more than an echo of more important lost works.

Now we must direct our attention to the cases in which models from the Netherlands were assimilated into the regional style of North German sculpture. Among a profusion of examples still extant, the most splendid is the 'Goldene Tafel' from the high altar of the abbey church of St Michael at Lüneburg (Hanover, Niedersächsische Landes-galerie),[25] dating from c. 1410. If we compare it with its presumptive models in the style of Jacques de Baerze in Dijon, we shall see that the sculptural expression has hardened and that characteristic individual traits are more emphasized. We sense a delight in the abundant and the close which serves to indicate the Lower Saxon origin of the sculptor. Similar features are to be seen in the small carved figures (1402) of the retable in the Jakobikirche at Göttingen. The majestic altarpiece from the cathedral of Minden (Berlin (East), Staatliche Museen)[26] fits into this broadly based regional development in West-phalia and Lower Saxony and is an example of the painterly presentation of the mature style of the period round 1420.

A further series of examples begins with the stone figure of a Virgin with Child from Doesburg (Gelderland) in the Archiepiscopal Museum at Utrecht. In this series we must include the stone Virgin in the Museum in Berlin (East)[27] and the sandstone figures of the Virgin and St John the Baptist in the church of Ludgo (Södermanland, Sweden), which date from the years round 1410–20. Here, and especially in the figure of St John, we may deduce a Netherlandish type, which also finds an echo in later Burgundian replicas. Again, side by side with imported pieces, there are the indigenous ones reflect-ing important Netherlandish originals which have been lost.[28]

The second great centre in the Rhineland was Mainz, the seat of an archbishop. Near at hand is Frankfurt, the old Free City, with its trading and industrial contacts to north and to south. It is therefore not surprising to find along the Middle Rhine sculpture which has close affiliations with the contemporary style in Cologne.

Madern Gerthner[29] (1391–1430), whom records show to have been both sculptor and architect at the lodge of Frankfurt Cathedral, was a figure of outstanding power. We are not however sure that the group of works we are about to discuss is by him, though they certainly show close contact with his work. Once again we may observe a phenomenon characteristic of the years round 1400 – the emergence of an individual sculptural style out of the traditional lodge sculpture – and it is typical too that Gerthner's architectural works should show connexions with the school of the Parlers.

First of this group we must mention the monuments of Werner Weiss of Limpurg in the Karmelitenkirche[30] and of Siegfried zum Paradies in the Nikolaikirche, both in Frankfurt. These works reveal a painterly presentation new in sculptural style, though at the same time they are still rooted in the magical objectivity of the late fourteenth century. The new painterly and at the same time lyrical character reaches its full maturity and charm in the sculpture on the south portal of the Liebfrauenkirche in Frankfurt (c. 1420; Plate 35) and on the 'Memorienpforte' of the cathedral of Mainz (c. 1424–5; Plate 34A); in both these a harmonious unity of architecture and sculpture is an essential feature. The relief of the Adoration carved in soft tufa on the tympanum of the Liebfrauen portal is indeed a painting translated into sculpture.[31] The surrounding arches provide the spatial effect of a curtain. The sandstone saints of the Mainz portal have the same gentle sinuous movement. Their naïve and sweet expressions seem to belong to some fairy-tale world. Moreover, sculpturally speaking, the delicate lines of the surfaces flow with a beautiful rhythm.

The outstanding masterpiece of the Gerthner group, however, is the effigy of Archbishop Konrad von Daun in Mainz Cathedral. The figure achieves an almost abstract luminous clarity through the sculptor's use of shade and depth. The effect is enhanced by the rhythmic ripples of the melodiously modulating accompanying minor movements of the folds. The climax is reached in the expressive features of the face. Konrad von Daun died in 1434, so that if there really is a direct link between this work and Madern Gerthner, a fellow-sculptor who survived Gerthner must have been responsible for the Daun tombstone.[32] In any case, a survey of the groups shows first and foremost a regional similarity of style so that, in spite of many relationships and affinities, we are not justified in ascribing the figures of the 'Memorienpforte' in Mainz personally to the artist responsible for the Saarwerden monument in Cologne. All that is unmistakable is their typically Middle Rhine character.[33] The same applies to the charmingly delicate effigy of the eleven-year-old Anna von Dalberg (d. 1410) in the Katharinenkirche at Oppenheim.

The same regional ring can be heard still more clearly in the scattered examples of wood and terracotta sculpture which began to flourish at this time. Works of the late fourteenth century such as the wooden Virgin with Child (Schloss Braunfels, near Wetzlar) and the stone Virgin with a Rose Bush from the Carmelite monastery at Mainz (now in the museum there) show once again the uninterrupted transition from monumental architectural sculpture to detached carving. They reveal too the continuity of an organic development which, owing to the altered requirements in church fitments, had, since the turn of the century, produced outstanding figures for altarpieces, like the statue of the Virgin from Oberwesel (now in the Rhenish Landesmuseum at Bonn), and those in the parish church of Ockenheim (Rheinhessen) and the Seminarkirche at Mainz (originally in the old Liebfrauenkirche).[34] The statuette of the Virgin in the Thyssen Collection in Lugano (formerly Cologne, Seligmann Collection) and the 'Virgin in the Sun' at the Schnütgen Museum, Cologne, both dating from the end of the fourteenth century,[35] prove that carvings of a similar kind were also rooted in Cologne traditions. The Fair Virgin from Caub (in the Hessisches Landesmuseum, Kassel) is also strongly reminiscent of similar figures in Cologne.

In this context a special significance attaches to the presentation of the Pietà. Two examples carved in wood survive, and they break away completely from the 'horizontal' style of presentation prevalent in Germany in the early part of the fifteenth century, which we shall discuss later. They are the Pietà from Unna, in the Westphalian Landesmuseum in Münster (Plate 32B), and that from Oestrich (Rheingau) in the Städtische Skulpturengalerie in Frankfurt. The first of these groups is deeply moving in its fusion of the huddled figure of the Virgin and the dead Christ, lying slantwise across her. Roger van der Weyden's Lamentation of Christ on the Granada altar, dating from the thirties of the century, is similar to a certain extent, but I see no tangible connexion between the two. I would suggest that it is more likely that the sculptor of the Unna Pietà was influenced by Italian paintings of the Madonna dell'Umiltà.[36] The character of this statue in Unna is obviously early, i.e. still Trecento. The slightly later Pietà in the Frankfurt Museum breaks away completely from the homogeneous unity of the Unna group – the way should be noted in which at Unna the polygonal plinth with its concave sides is part of the same block as the figures – and replaces it with the dynamism of the early fifteenth century. Both groups are deeply spiritualized. They certainly are not by the same hand, but they are both probably of Middle Rhine origin, and they reveal the rich variety of treatment in the sculpture of religious subjects at the beginning of the new century.

Another world opens to us when we turn to the sculpture in terracotta which was highly developed on the Middle Rhine at this time. The soft material, with its opportunities for subtle modelling, lent itself most readily to the innate lyrical vision. The hand of a great master is visible in the multi-figured group of Christ in the Procession to Calvary from a votive shrine in the Martinskirche at Lorch (Berlin-Dahlem, Staatliche Museen; Plate 33A), in the group of the Pietà for the Burgkirche at Dernbach (Limburg, Diocesan Museum), and in the Tondörffer tablet of the Man of Sorrows at St Lorenz in Nuremberg.[37] These are delicately balanced compositions with a beautiful sense of atmosphere, stage-like in arrangement and yet, through the use of light and shade, preeminently painterly. Alongside the idealized presentation of the biblical figures we have the *verismo* of the portraits of the donors. In the terracotta head of Joseph of Arimathaea from a three-quarter life-size group of an Entombment (*c.* 1420, Darmstadt, Hessisches Landesmuseum; Plate 46A) this same master transcended the miniature quality of the works we have enumerated and attained to a new monumental quality in his treatment of the human figure. It is remarkable in this connexion how strong is the echo of works of Netherlandish sculpture, which the master had probably looked at two decades previously but which he has transformed into a totally original creation.[38] To the same sphere, but not the same workshop, belong the charming terracotta figures from the altarpiece in the priory church at Karden on the Moselle and those dating from about ten years later from the Marienaltar at Kronberg (Taunus). These also follow a Nether-landish type of altarpiece.

A group of individual terracotta statues, named after a figure of the Virgin in the parish church at Hallgarten (Rheingau), is also of Middle Rhine stock. The Hallgarten Virgin is a slender, upright figure, dressed in noble raiment which flows down, weight-less and without any sharpness or hardness of contour, as in earlier Gothic statues – a return to the pure accents of earlier types, but without their linear abstraction. The same may be said of the sublimity of her features. An almost identical terracotta Virgin comes from Eberbach (Rheingau) and is now in the Louvre.[39] The similarity between these works by the 'Master of Hallgarten' and the alabaster Virgin in the Rijksmuseum at Amsterdam is no accident – it proves that many Western European sculptors round 1400 turned to the grace and dignity of the early fourteenth century for their models.

The bishoprics of Aschaffenburg and Würzburg, geographically adjacent, lie within the orbit of Middle Rhine sculpture. The clarity and lyrical quality in the Annunciation relief on the north portal of the Marienkirche at Würzburg, for instance, is Middle Rhine in character (c. 1425). The figure of the Virgin on the *trumeau* of this church, which is of almost identical date and is a harmonious and self-contained piece of work, follows a type we often meet on the Middle and Upper Rhine (Plate 33B).[40] This type resembles that of the Virgin of Hallgarten, but is without its Early Gothic echoes. A striking feature of the Würzburg Virgin is its breadth of treatment, which lends it a decidedly imposing character. Otherwise among the extant works of Lower Franconian sculpture of the early fifteenth century it is the artistic significance of the memorial tablets that domi-nates the picture, e.g. those in the cloisters of the monastery of Himmelpforten; in St Burkard and the Marienkirche in Würzburg; from the Burgkapelle of Hohenburg now in the Bayerisches Nationalmuseum, Munich; in the parish church of Lohr; in the collegiate church of Aschaffenburg; and in the Katharinenkirche of Oppenheim.[41] These all exemplify the organic transition from the idealized portrayal of the human form in the eighties of the fourteenth century to the realistic presentation of the 1430s.

Among the products of Franconian sculpture a special place must be allotted to a goldsmith's work: the bust of St Alexander in the treasury of the Stiftskirche of Aschaf-fenburg.[42] This is a sublimely idealized work of magical beauty. Its calligraphic character is totally different from the more elementary nature of the sculpture of the Middle Rhine, and suggests initial stimulus from works of Netherlandish and French gold-smiths (c. 1420–30). This is corroborated by the connexion between the large and splendid, partly enamelled breast-clasp of the bust and Netherlandish and French gold-enamels.

Nuremberg was also an important centre of terracotta sculpture. An Altar of the Twelve Apostles of c. 1420, perhaps from one of the Nuremberg monasteries, provided the series of seated Apostles in the Germanisches Museum (Plate 37); in their firmness of outline and in their articulation they are derivatives of the Parler style, but the ample use of flowing drapery places them within the painterly style of the early fifteenth cen-tury. An exception to the others is the St Bartholomew.[43] The figure is differently organized and its rhetorical stance and gesture remind one of the new freedom in western monumental sculpture at the turn of the century. The demi-figure of God the Father from a Mount of Olives in the Moritzkirche [44] (destroyed in the war) proved the affinity between this terracotta sculpture and the monumental architectural sculpture carried out up till then by stonemasons. Of outstanding significance is the terracotta St John the Evangelist in the choir of St Sebald, which was donated by a member of the Tucher family. This remarkably ample figure is a late fruit of the 'Soft Style'. Compared with the tectonic tautness of the wooden Virgin from the Lobenhoferhaus in the Germanisches Museum (c. 1420), the late character of the abundant Fair Virgin with nimbus in the choir of St Sebald [45] is patent (Plate 38); its decorative richness of form and naturalism of style ally it closely to the St John of the Tucher family. It is particularly noteworthy that in Nuremberg the step forward to bronze sculpture was taken already at this time. It is known that in 1428–9 a 'bildemacher' of Nuremberg made the bronze effigies of Konrad of Weinsberg and his wife for the abbey church of Schöntal.[46] The most telling example of self-confidence in the human image is the effigy of Bishop Albert, Count of Wertheim (d. 1421), in Bamberg Cathedral, which is also a beautiful example of the expansion of volume and the new wealth of *valeurs*. Late Nuremberg pieces are the wooden altar figures of the Deocarus Altar in St Lorenz, whose date is ascertained by a dedication inscription of 1436–7.[47]

Franconian influence spreads northward deep into Central Germany, and the south–north 'corridor' of the archdiocese of Mainz extended yet further contacts made through patrons and craftsmen. It is therefore easy to understand why a Franconian and Middle Rhine character appears to be the dominating feature in the most important sculpture of Central Germany at this time, in so far as it manages to free itself from the inheritance of the lodge sculpture of the previous century, which was generally of the Parler School, radiating from Prague. A specially close affinity existed between Nuremberg and Erfurt in the Late Middle Ages.[48] At Erfurt a fine series of monuments is still extant. We can trace in them the development of a regional style which increases in firmness of presentation from the indistinctly atmospheric conceptions of the beginning of the century (Lorenzkirche, Erfurt, memorial tablet of Günther von Saalfeld, d. 1405, and his wife) to the clear, three-dimensional tangibility of the monument of the Margrave of Kirchberg (d. 1410) in the abbey of Kapellendorf, near Weimar, and of the memorial tablet of Gottschalk-Legat (d. 1422) in the Predigerkirche and of the Viceregent of Mainz, Johann von Allenblumen (d. 1429), in the cathedral of Erfurt. The effigy of Bishop von Goch (d. 1422) in Naumburg Cathedral is related in style.

Against the background of this regional sculpture it is surprising to encounter the alabaster figures of an Apostle and of St John the Baptist, together with donors and the arms of the Gerbstädt family, on their striking separate bases in the Dommuseum at Erfurt (c. 1430). We know that the material for later alabaster carvings in Thuringia and Lower Saxony was obtained from quarries on the southern edge of the Harz Mountains. Can the magnificently painterly sense of movement and the vivacity of expression in the alabaster figures in the Erfurt Dommuseum be of native growth? In any case there are no immediate parallels in Bohemia, which would be the most likely source. The nearest formal similarity is to be found in the statue of St Elizabeth from Bremen

Cathedral. Alabaster had already been used for the monuments of Bishop Johann III of Wöpelitz (d. 1401) in the cathedral of Havelberg and that of the Margrave Georg of Saxony (d. 1402) in the abbey church of Pforta near Naumburg. We may trace the ancestry of both these works immediately to Northern France and the Netherlands.

The limestone Pietàs in the Jena Museum, in Magdeburg Cathedral, and in St Elisabeth at Marburg may well have been imported from Bohemia. We may also pre-suppose Bohemian influence in the Fair Virgins in the Marienkirche at Heiligenstadt (sandstone, 1414) and in the Liebfrauenkirche at Arnstadt. In the latter, with the elegiac delicacy of her expression and the flowerlike magic of the soft, rich drapery, we have a particularly beautiful and no doubt indigenous example of this type.

At one moment only it appears as though this curtain of fairness were to be drawn aside and we were to be permitted a glance into spiritual depths: in the stone statues by Conrad von Einbeck[49] in the Moritzkirche at Halle. The Man of Sorrows (dated 1416) and the Mourning Virgin especially possess a shattering fervour of expression, such as we have not met anywhere else. Characteristically enough, Conrad von Einbeck was an architect. He was active at St Moritz in Halle from 1382. His sculpture has the constraint of the late fourteenth century, and from this comes the rigidity and the heavy mood of his style. Conrad's self-portrait bust in the same church also bears testimony to this (Plate 45B). He was a Lower Saxon by birth. A similar expressive violence already characterizes the reliefs of the Passion on the choir stalls of the cathedral of Havelberg (in Brandenburg, that is also Lower Saxony), which date from 1390–1400. Faces are here grimaces. This sculpture is certainly of Bohemian inspiration, and Conrad von Einbeck was its last, and a typically Central German, offshoot in an epoch which used a crude naturalism to lend added emphasis to the ardour of its message.

As regards the Upper Rhine and Swabia, we hear of the dedication at Strasbourg in 1404 of a 'cunningly wrought statue of the Virgin from Prague', made by the Junkern of Prague. A Junker would be a gentleman, or really a young member of the gentry. When we then learn that this statue 'was called the sad one', we have to imagine one of those Pietàs which we meet in such an astonishingly wide radius around 1400 and which are so remarkably similar to one another. At that time, therefore, the influence of Bohemian sculpture reached as far as Alsace. The inscription 'Juncker von Brag gemacht' is to be found on some drawings[50] portraying figures in the style of the sculpture of the Parlers of about 1380.

We know also that the architect Ulrich von Ensingen was summoned from Ulm to Strasbourg in 1399 to complete the upper storeys of the west façade of the cathedral. When he took over the direction of the lodge in Ulm Cathedral in 1392, Ulrich von Ensingen had entered into the inheritance of the Parlers. However original and signi-ficant his architectural achievement at Ulm Cathedral may be in comparison with what went before,[51] his monumental sculpture in those parts of the cathedral for which he was responsible is thoroughly Parleresque in style. This refers to the beautiful corbels for the figures on the piers of the nave, although they are already liberated from all austerity and heaviness and are charmingly embellished with naturalistic detail. The same may be said of the figures of the Martyred Apostles and of the Wise and Foolish Virgins in the archivolts of the main portals. In 1417 Ulrich handed over the direction of the Ulm lodge to his son-in-law, Hans Kun. From the same year onwards, according to entries in the lodge records, alongside workers drawn from Bohemia, Moravia, and Silesia there was active a certain Master Hartmann, who may be regarded as the sculptor chiefly responsible for the extensive sculptural decoration of the west portal (stone statues on the jambs, a cycle of stories on the wall above the portal; Plate 34B).[52] Though we may here too sense Bohemian influences they are outweighed by a gentleness which already shows certain qualities also to be found in contemporary Swabian altar sculpture. Once again we are confronted with the translation of an art which sprang originally from architectural sculpture and which developed through the wide ramifications of the lodges into a native style of wood carving, possessing a charm of manner familiar from the panel paintings belonging to the same altars. The altarpiece from Dornstadt near Blaubeuren, now in the Württembergisches Landesmuseum in Stuttgart, is a striking example of this common unity between carved and painted sculpture (in the style of Master Hartmann) and painting.[53]

A collaborator of Hartmann attached his mason's mark to the seated apostles in the archivolts over the double doorway in Ulm Cathedral, a mark which recurs on the base of the limestone Fair Virgin at Horb (Württemberg). This figure and the terracotta Swabian Pietà from Steinberg (Württemberg) now in the Städtische Skulpturengalerie at Frankfurt[54] are clearly connected with Austrian prototypes, which I shall discuss later. As we have seen before, in the sculpture of the early fifteenth century we constantly witness the combination of a complex character with regional particulars.

The situation at Strasbourg is impressive indeed. As regards architectural sculpture, the statue of a monk against the north-west pier of the octagon stage of the cathedral steeple shows how, about 1390, the volume of a figure is dynamically reconsidered. This transformation is carried yet further in richly undulating surfaces in a wooden St Paul from Lower Alsace, now in the Musée de l'Œuvre Notre-Dame.[55] Then Ulrich von Ensingen started on the building of the north tower of the cathedral above the flat top of the west front. The tower proper is surrounded by four stair-turrets. These end in a passage which connects them with the tower. On the parapet of this passage are stone figures[56] looking up to the top of the spire – a sculptural personification of the dynamics of the architecture, which incorporates the spectator's experience into the architecture itself in a completely novel way. Among these figures are two holy Virgins, two prophets, a bullock, a bear, the Virgin, and Ulrich von Ensingen himself, marked by a shield bearing his mason's mark. Is this a votive offering of his own person, as it were? Was Ulrich, in the tradition of the Gothic lodges, architect and sculptor at one and the same time? The fact that the mason's mark is used in the sculpture proves that these figures were carried out under his personal supervision, that is, before his death in 1419. Both in their motifs and in their form these figures are unprecedented. They are the first-fruit of a fully detached statuesque sculpture no longer projected on to a building, surrounded by light, which models by means of the contrasts of light and shade. Human body and soul have been quickened into a new artistic significance. Drapery and the play of its folds have lost their decorative function; they now serve to emphasize the physical form. This is effected most boldly perhaps in the figure of St Catherine (Plate 36). Similarities have been suggested between this figure and the style of the pier figures in the vestibule of Ulm Cathedral, and again between the latter and the reliefs on the sides of the Saarwerden tomb in Cologne Cathedral. In reality we have here a far bolder hand and a far freer imagination. Nor is there, as has been suggested, any contact with Sluter's style. What is more likely is that this unknown sculptor, whose inventive power is never again equalled in the sphere of Ulrich von Ensingen's great architectural activity, was acquainted with Netherlandish sculpture of the years round 1400 – so often, as we have seen, the mysterious source of the emancipation of North European sculpture at the beginning of the fifteenth century.

The phases of sculptural development in the neighbouring city of Basel are no less striking. The stone Retable of St Anne of Canon Johannes Camerarius (d. 1391) from the cathedral, now in the Historisches Museum; the group of statues on the Spalentor (c. 1408); and the carvings on the base of the fountain in the Fischmarkt, now also in the Historisches Museum, show, in a style that is still determined by tradition, how around 1400 a new naturalism begins to claim the ascendancy.[57]

In the surviving examples of contemporary carving on the Upper Rhine we sense a special precision and concentration. The tectonic clarity and visionary quality of these carvings prove to us that here there existed an atmosphere which – as in neighbouring Burgundy – was conducive to the development of an expressive, autonomous style of sculpture. I should like to cite as outstanding examples from the first and second decades of the fifteenth century[58] the high relief group of the Holy Family from Strasbourg (Berlin, Deutsches Museum); St John the Evangelist from Molsheim (Stuttgart, Württembergisches Landesmuseum); a Virgin from the district round Belfort (Basel, Historisches Museum); the relief of a Man of Sorrows formerly at Freiburg (Berlin, Deutsches Museum); the Virgin enthroned with Child at Hüttenheim (Alsace); the group of Christ and St John from Colmar (Strasbourg, Musée de l'Œuvre Notre Dame); St Barbara from Glotterbad (Freiburg, Augustiner-Museum); and the carvings in walnut on the sides of the choir stalls in Basel Cathedral. In all these works there prevails a striking precision of outline, which distinguishes them noticeably from other South German sculpture of this time, where sharpness of outline is made subordinate to a melodious and pleasing appearance. An interesting indication of French influence in these regions is provided by the distant echo of the style of Beauneveu perceptible in the figure of St Catherine (c. 1420) in the abbey of Magerau at Fribourg.[59]

The Upper Rhine extends as far as Constance. This city, the scene of great church councils, was the seat of the largest German bishopric in the Late Middle Ages, reaching as far as Bern, up to the gates of Basel and northwards as far as the Neckar. On the eastern side it adjoined the bishopric of Augsburg. In an attempt to define the extent of Swabian art in the Late Middle Ages we must consider in the first place the geographical area covered by the old dioceses of Constance and Augsburg. Out of the rich array of individual carvings in Upper Swabia I should like to draw attention to the carvings on the choir stalls in Überlingen Minster; the figures of the Virgin from Bronnweiler near Tübingen (now in the Württembergisches Landesmuseum, Stuttgart); the works of the so-called Master of Eriskirch near Ravensburg (the most important of these are in the Lorenzkapelle at Rottweil); and – outstanding in their expressive content – the group of mourning women from a Crucifixion scene from Mittelbiberach (Berlin (East), Museum).[60] The terracotta figure of a man bearing the Cross in Überlingen Minster is equally poignant.[61] This Upper Swabian sculpture is characterized by an abundance of feeling, ranging from gentle, lyrical contemplation to controlled but violent passion.

This regional character is no less marked in the area of Augsburg. The outstanding examples here – typically, we might say – are once again in terracotta. I refer to the figures of the Virgin in St Peter's, Augsburg; in the parish church of the former Carthusian priory of Buxheim near Memmingen and in the parish church of Vorderried near Wertingen; and the demi-figure formerly in the Deutsches Museum, Berlin (destroyed in the war)[62] which used to be (erroneously) regarded as Bohemian. In my view we are here concerned with the products of a workshop centred in Augsburg, which translated into plastic clay and spread abroad the ideal of the Fair Virgin, as we find it in the contemporary paintings from Benediktbeuern (now in the Bayerische Staatsgemälde-sammlung, Munich) and in Augsburg Cathedral.[63] Augsburg was also a decisive influence on the terracotta sculpture at Eichstätt:[64] the charming Adoration of the Virgin on the north portal of the cathedral, the monumental Virgin from Buchenhüll inside the cathedral, and the Enthroned Virgin in the abbey of St Walburg, which is already in the realistic style current round 1435–40.

It is perhaps no accident that among the remaining sculpture from German-speaking districts in the early years of the fifteenth century, Austro-Bavarian and Bohemian-Silesian pieces are the most numerous. It seems, too, as though the organic development from the late fourteenth century into the early fifteenth appeared here at its clearest. This is certainly true of Prague and Vienna.[65] In both places it is noteworthy that the traditions of the masons' lodges underwent a decisive renewal in the second half of the fourteenth century, thanks to commissions given by the court.[66] This situation is reminiscent of that of the same period in France. Thus Bohemian[67] and Austrian sculpture about 1400 forms a counterpart to Western sculpture largely under the influence of the Netherlands. However, the multiplicity of events proves that one should not define the situation in terms of a polarity. Instead variations are evident everywhere.

In the sculpture of the lodges a new type of statuary was created, statues no longer tied to architecture, but existing independently in the church interiors as 'fair' devotional images carved of specially fine and easily workable stone. It seems wrong to me to try and attribute the finest of these pieces of Austro-Bohemian and East German sculpture to one master, tentatively called the Master of the Fair Virgins. His origin has been surmised on the Lower Rhine ('perhaps round Aachen or Cologne').[68] This latter suggestion shows how impossible it is, in spite of evident regional distinctions, to differentiate between West and East during these years. Why is there that difficulty? Because this new statuary is the outcome of the Parler style, i.e. a lodge style, which extended from Cologne to Milan, Prague, Cracow; thus e.g. the limestone group of St Elizabeth from Bremen Cathedral (see Note 9 to this chapter) has been attributed to the master of the Fair Virgin of Toruń (Thorn). How could one succeed in recognizing in the whole of this activity those places where an organic tradition had grown and where reputation had become such that export is likely? And how could such export, sometimes to distant places, be distinguished from cases of mere influence and from works by itinerant artists? Italian instances show how far their radii stretched. It is the heritage of the Parlers which, on the strength of anyway more than regional lodge traditions, spread a kind of statuary liberated from architectural fetters.

The following are incunabula of this new statuary: the busts on the triforium of Prague Cathedral[69] and especially that of Wenzel von Radecz with its amazing power of expression (Plate 45A), the sculpture of the Týn Church (Plate 42A), and the two Virgins of the chapel of the Altstadt Town Hall (consecrated in 1381) and the Eligius Chapel in St Stephen in Vienna.[70] Similar to these is the substantial wooden Virgin from Sonntagsberg in Lower Austria now in the Kunsthistorisches Museum in Vienna.[71] The origin of this statue leads back to the sculpture of St Michael's church in Vienna.[72] Within architectural sculpture at St Stephen, as it can be traced without a break from the Herzogswerkstatt onwards,[73] a Salvator Mundi of stone (now in the Museum der Stadt Wien)[74] represents for the first time the full maturity of the harmonious and balanced style of about 1400.

A striking fact is how prominent within this sculpture – side by side with the Fair Virgins – are Pietàs, or, as they are called in a document at Strasbourg in 1404, 'sad images of the Virgin' (*traurig Marienbild*). The Virgin is seated and bends forward towards the body of Christ lying horizontally across her lap – an icon of a sublime harmony comparable to the Fair Virgins. It is typical how close the correspondences of these images are with the subjects and interpretation in painting of the same date; noble in their statuesque appearance and glowing in their light hues. The spread of these Pietàs, almost identical even in details, and made of cast stone or limestone, extended as far as that of the Fair Virgins, and the problem therefore arises again, where the centre was and when the type was created. Again in the way of incunabula just one example: the Pietà of St Thomas at Brno (Brünn).[75] It is highly significant that such inventions of types found an echo at once in many regions and in materials including wood and terracotta. Even Italy must be included.[76]

The artistic, material, and ideal link of the early Pietàs with the early Fair Virgins is undeniable. I doubt whether it will ever be possible to identify particular workshops for the early development of the types. What is undeniable, however, is that their sources go down into the Austro–Bohemian sculpture of the late-fourteenth-century Parler lodges. At the same time they may well presuppose initiative on the Rhine, and that joins them to the sculpture of the same period in the Netherlands and France.[77]

The renewal of vigour took place first in the sculpture of the lodges. Were the 'Junker von Prag' exponents of the Parler rule? Were they the pioneers of the new, no longer architectural, stone sculpture for interiors? Examples of the echo of this in wood are the fragment of a St John Evangelist from the rood screen of the abbey church of Třeboň (Wittingau) and the beautiful St Nicholas from the collegiate church of Vyšší Brod (Hohenfurth).[78] They are in my opinion not a continuation of local traditions in wood carving, but documents of the change which had taken place in interpretation and representation in stone sculpture. The same phenomena could be illustrated equally patently with Austrian and Silesian examples. The most famous of Fair Virgins is that of limestone in the Kunsthistorisches Museum, Vienna, which comes from Český Krumlov (Krumau) in Southern Bohemia (Plate 39).[79] It is an enchanting piece, sensitive in expression and melodious in composition. The features are of the sweetest innocence. The attitude is one of gentle movement, but richly varied by means of the *valeurs* of light and shade. Yet a basic frontality is preserved and any columnar roundness avoided. There are replicas of the Krumau Virgin e.g. at Aussee and also, in a red cast stone, in the National Gallery in Prague (from Hallstatt in Austria; recently purchased). The justification for the replicas was the perfection of the original. Where was this made? I consider a perhaps slightly later work by the same hand the cast-stone Seated Virgin in the tympanum of the main doorway of the Benedictine Abbey of Marienberg (Monte Maria) in the Vintschgau, close to the frontier between Southern Tyrol and Switzerland (Plate 40B).[80] Again the extensive spread is evident. Was the original workshop in Prague, in Southern Bohemia, or perhaps at Salzburg, see of the archbishop? It is known that cast-stone sculpture was made at Salzburg,[81] and similar sculpture in a molasses limestone from the foreland of the Alps could well be Salzburg work too. What is certain, to say the least, is that Salzburg was connected with the spread of this new type of sculpture, although the town had no important share in the development of lodge sculpture of the Parler kind at the end of the fourteenth century.

As regards dates, there are traditions connected with five pieces which point to *c.* 1400 and therefore, for the incunabula, necessitate dates before 1400. A Pietà in the church of St Elisabeth at Wrocław (Breslau) is of the type described above and which, as we have seen, is typical of the early fifteenth century; yet a date 1384 has been connected with it.[82] A Salzburg Pietà of limestone, at Admont in Styria, belonging to the same type, has been connected with a date 1394. The limestone Fair Virgin of Altenmarkt in the Pongau may be the image mentioned in 1393.[83] Two indulgences of 1400 for the chapel of St George in the castle at Krumau refer explicitly to the 'de pulchro opere imago virginis Mariae Gloriosae'.[84] We may easily conclude that this refers to the so pre-eminently aristocratic Krumau Virgin and that this image therefore was given by the Rosenberg family and stood already then in the richly endowed chapel of the castle. The fifth date is that of the alabaster Virgin in the Dominican church at Cracow. This has a St George in relief on its base, and the relief is mentioned in an indulgence of 1401.[85] The line went from the broad and voluminous pieces of the late fourteenth century to a blocky compactness characteristic of *c.* 1400 and then an ever more relaxed painterly expansiveness. The Fair Virgins of Krumau and Marienberg are perfect representations of Late Trecento conceptions rooted in an aristocratic class of patrons.

Too much survives to be referred to here. I can only mention the very best: the Pietàs from Baden near Vienna formerly in the Deutsches Museum, Berlin, from Admont in the museum at Graz, from Kreuzenstein in the Diözesanmuseum in Vienna, and the other Pietàs at Gdańsk (Danzig), Jena, Magdeburg, Marburg, and the Bayerisches Nationalmuseum in Munich (from Seeon Abbey; Plate 41), and the Fair Virgins in St Peter and the Franciscan church at Salzburg, in Altenmarkt in the Pongau (see above), and – this one seated – in a private collection in Munich (from Styria).[86] In the same context belongs, or so it seems to me, the Fair Virgin in the Szépmüveszeti Museum in Budapest which comes from an art dealer in Frankfurt (Plate 47A).[87] Its origin is alas unknown to us. The compactness of the block suggests an early date. The child, still dressed and not yet comprised in the outline of the figure, is very similar to contemporary French representations.

At the same time in the same regions translations of these still relatively monumental images of the Virgin into local wood carving are frequent, and there are even translations of the Salzburg type of Fair Virgin into goldsmith's work. One such is the gilt silver statuette in the Carrand Collection at the Bargello in Florence. The motif is almost literally that of the 'Maria Säul' of St Peter in Salzburg.[88]

A parallel are the limestone figures from Grosslobming in Styria, now in the Kunsthistorisches Museum in Vienna and a German private collection.[89] The master was probably Viennese; for several undoubtedly Viennese works exist showing the stages of transition from architectural sculpture to the new, more painterly presentation. They are the Fair Virgin from St Stephen in the Stadtmuseum, the Virgins at Heiligenkreuz and Klosterneuburg, and the grandiose Man of Sorrows of the chancel of St Stephen. A specially interesting *locus* for Styrian stone sculpture is the pilgrimage church of Ptujska Gora near Celje in Slovenia, with pieces of before 1421 on portal, high altar, and pulpit. Other Slovenian churches also are rich in local versions of the 'Soft Style'.[90]

Bohemian and Austrian sculpture extended its feelers as far as Hungary and Transylvania[91] and also Italy. Here we have not only many exported Pietàs which in their turn were locally copied, but we can even recognize individual itinerant artists.[92] Thus the (Carinthian?) master of the image of Maria Saal seems to have made also the Pietà (1424) and the Seated Virgin at Venzone in Friuli. His may also be the beautiful stone Annunciation and a stone Bishop in the choir of St Mark's in Venice, whereas the limestone Fair Virgin from a convent in Venice, now in the Düsseldorf Kunstmuseum, must be Salzburg export;[93] she is a sister of the Virgin of the Franziskanerkirche at Salzburg.

To return now to Bohemia,[94] I want to mention from the early fifteenth century the Fair Virgins of Třeboň (Wittingau), Chlum Sv. Maři (Maria Kulm), Šternberk (Sternberg),[95] the parish church at Plzeň (Pilsen), the lovely seated wooden figure in the Týn Church in Prague, and the St Catherine in the church of St James at Jihlava (Iglau). The same union of majesty and lyrical grace as in the Fair Virgins appears in the still perfectly coloured wooden St Catherine in the chapel of Karlštejn (Karlstein) Castle. Full maturity of the late 'Soft Style' is represented by the Crucifixus below the choir gallery of Prague Cathedral. Already on the way to *verismo* on the other hand are the magnificent wooden Men of Sorrows in the Altstadt Town Hall and the Historical Museum (from the saloon in the Neustadt Town Hall) as well as the imposing yet tender group of the Crucifixion in the Týn Church (Plate 42A).[96]

Ties between the kingdom of Bohemia and the territories of the Margrave of Moravia and the Duke of Silesia were close about 1400. Again only the most valuable pieces can be mentioned: a Pietà (of 1384?, see above) and the enchanting Fair Virgin (Plate 40A), both from St Elizabeth at Wrocław (Breslau),[97] a St Catherine also in the museum of the same town (perhaps from the abbey of Lubiąż or Leubus), and the 'Sancta Maria Gravida' in the museum of Görlitz. Perhaps all these are the work of one man. Links with architectural sculpture are proved by the stylistic similarity to the boss of St Hedwig in Holy Cross at Wrocław. A variant of the Pietà of St Elizabeth is in the Sand Church. The most beautiful stone Pietà of the mature 'Soft Style' from Silesia is in the Chapel of St Barbara at Cracow (Plate 44A).[98] The origin of this Silesian style in the traditions of Bohemia comes out clearly in the limestone Man of Sorrows of the Goldsmiths' Altar from the church of the Magdalen, now in the museum at Wrocław.

The nearest neighbours of this Bohemian and Silesian sculpture are in the former territory of the Prussian Order, and especially at Toruń (Thorn) and Gdańsk (Danzig).[99] Above all others in quality is the limestone Fair Virgin once in St John at Toruń with the amazingly monumental demi-figure of Moses against the bracket growing out of the leaping flames of the burning bush (Plates 47B, 48, and 49), and the delightful stone statuette of the 'Sancta Maria Gravida' in Toruń Museum,[100] the latter on an uncommonly high plinth with the bust of a man (donor or carver?). Both pieces are by the same hand. The carving is clearly organized and sparing. The absolute compactness of the outlines points to a date before 1400. Almost identical with the Fair Virgin of Toruń is that in the Rheinisches Landesmuseum at Bonn (Thewalt Collection), the provenance of which is unfortunately unknown.[101] Once again the question arises whether in this wide spread relations of masons' families are reflected. The placing of the bust of Moses below the Toruń Virgin and the bust below the Toruń Gravida is a usual trait in the architectural sculpture of the Parlers, though at the same time the inexorable expression of the Moses is reminiscent of Sluter. The parallelism of development went far indeed. Only in the early fifteenth century does it become possible to recognize regional peculiarities and to ask such questions as Burgundy or Bohemia, Silesia or Austria?

With the pieces at Toruń the cast-stone Fair Virgin in the Reinhold Chapel (Plate 43B) and the Pietà in St Mary at Gdańsk (Danzig) are connected, though they are clearly by a different hand. A particularly impressive Pietà, similar to that in St Elizabeth at Wrocław, is in the Hermitage in Leningrad[102] and comes probably from one of the Baltic states. At Toruń this group is continued in an important piece which must be slightly later: the Ascension of St Mary Magdalen in St John, a combination of cast stone and limestone parts, lyrical and painterly. The later date, say the 1430s, is suggested by the noticeable sharpening of the surface.

Only now that we have concluded this survey of a style reaching from the Baltic to Venice can we turn to some local workshops in the Austro-Bavarian, the Sileso-Bohemian, and the Polish and Baltic area. Again no more is possible than some brief paradigmatic observations and notes. A general symptom is the favouring of relatively soft stones which allowed gentle transitions from rising to falling. A specially suitable stone in Austria was the limestone from Plan. Where no such stone was quarried, cast stone or terracotta was used.

In Bavaria, Regensburg was the centre. The architectural sculpture of the cathedral between 1375 and 1400 is immediately connected with the Parler lodge at Prague.

Spread over the west façade is a life of the Virgin in many tenderly and chastely treated figures. They date from about 1400–10. The triangular porch with its multitude of sculpture in the mature and rich style of the early fifteenth century is the result of a new plan.[103] The same workshop must have been responsible for the grand St Peter of limestone inside the cathedral and the sharply modelled figure of a man, probably the sculptor or mason himself, on a bracket (Plate 50). His features are passionate and restless.

Characteristic of the new desire for space in sculpture is the stone retable of 1424 in the chancel of St Martin at Landshut. It backs on to the tabernacle containing the Holy Sacrament, and the scenes in the shrine of the retable are still distant progeny of the Parler sculpture of Prague. This applies also to the beautifully linear, yet solidly rounded limestone groups of the life of the Virgin, St Martin, and the Passion of Christ in their monumental framework. A sandstone Visitation in the Germanisches Museum at Nuremberg which comes from Passau Cathedral has an intimacy closely related to the Landshut retable. Once again it must be stressed that this new type of statuesque sculpture is still rooted in the traditions of the lodges. Thus the Landshut retable is no doubt due to the lodge of the master mason of the church,[104] that 'hans steinmezz', i.e. Hans of Burghausen, who died in 1432 and whose monument on the external wall of the church shows a demi-figure of the Man of Sorrows, carried by the bust of the master himself (Plate 53B), a bust of a sharpness of carving and an intensity of physiognomical characterization entirely new in its exploration of the individual. Retable as well as monument may be the work of a certain Hans Stethaimer of Landshut, who, we know, was stone mason as well as painter.

It is impossible to separate the funerary sculpture of Bavaria during these years from that of Austria. The favourite material in both countries was the red marble of Salzburg, and Salzburg was indeed the place where this art flourished most profusely. However, the marble was also exported in blocks, so that the use of Salzburg marble does not necessarily mean that a monument was made by a Salzburg workshop. But wherever works were done and whether they were done at the request of ecclesiastical or secular patrons, the dependence of style and type on the tremendous figures on the tomb-chests of the chancel chapels of Prague Cathedral by Peter Parler and on Parler's St Wenceslas of 1373 is undeniable.[105]

The beginning is an extensive group of monumental Salzburg tomb-slabs. The first of them is that for Count Palatine Aribo at Seeon (Upper Bavaria), made by Hans Haider, c. 1390–1400. The climax is the memorial to St Vitalis in St Peter at Salzburg, a piece of great harmonious beauty. The end is the impressive monument at Mindelheim (Allgäu) to Ulrich, duke of Teck, and his second wife (c. 1429), and the red marble monument in the Bayerisches Nationalmuseum at Munich (from Ursberg) to Wilhelm I of Thannhausen.[106]

Outside this group, the work of one characteristic personality is the tomb-chest to Duke Albrecht II, the Younger, in the Carmelite Church at Straubing. The duke died in 1397. The effigy, by the closed eyes characterized as dead, is played over by rich, tender, and decidedly painterly line-work, a gossamer-fine veil of beauty as it were. The monument at Mindelheim turned the same motif into realism. If one can take the

Straubing monument as the perfect testimony of the noble, idealized manner of representation of the first decade of the fifteenth century, the question must at once be asked, whether the same master can have carved the red marble monument of Ulrich Kastenmayr, burgomaster of Straubing (Plate 53A). This dates from before 1431 and is in the church of St Jakob. The surface of both monuments has the same gossamer precision. But the Kastenmayr monument has a wholly new character of painterly reality and spatial reality, though it is still an ideally enhanced reality. If the hand is indeed the same in both monuments, then contacts with the art of the Netherlands must be presumed for such a metamorphosis. After all, Straubing belonged to the Dutch line of the Wittelsbach dynasty.

The most splendid example of the continued effects of Salzburg on adjoining Upper Bavaria is the tremendous Virgin at Feichten.[107] This is of cast stone; carved in wood on the other hand are many contemporary pieces, specially worthwhile the works of the so-called Master of Seeon, resident probably in or near Salzburg.[108] His Virgin Enthroned in the Bayerisches Nationalmuseum in Munich shows the complementary function of three-dimensional form and painted surface which is typical of the altars of these early years (Plate 51). Among the prototypes, foremost is the Visitation on the doors of Irrsdorf church, dated 1406,[109] among parallels foremost are the Fair Virgins of Inzersdorf and Hollenburg and of the Palace Chapel in Vienna.

Completely preserved altarpieces with carved principal figures and painted wings – and this equivalence of sculpture and painting is essential for the 'opus completum' of c. 1400 which is the replacement of the equivalence of building and architectural sculpture – are at St Sigmund (S. Sigismondo) in the Pustertal (c. 1425–30)[110] and in Vienna Cathedral (originally from the Cistercian abbey of Viktring near Klagenfurt).[111] The altarpieces are of types already in existence in the fourteenth century: at St Sigmund a row of three figures, in Vienna two tiers with a row of three figures below, a Coronation of the Virgin above. Nothing in these altarpieces gives as yet an indication of what glorious stage-sets the shrines of the second half of the century were going to be. The altar-sculpture of Viktring (with additions of 1447) is similar to the slightly later Virgin of Maria Saal.

A Styrian master, Hans von Judenburg, has, thanks to research of the last few years, become an individually recognizable personality. In 1421 a contract was made with him for the high altar of Bozen (Bolzano) parish church.[112] In 1471 Michael Pacher was told that he should make the Coronation of the Virgin for his altar at Gries near Bozen 'to the same measurements as the altarpiece at Bozen' – a rare sidelight on the still conventional conditions under which wood carving was commissioned in the Late Gothic era.[113] It is specially noteworthy that the prescribed pattern here was a full fifty years old. Important parts of the altar of 1421 are in all probability the Coronation of the Virgin in the Germanisches Museum at Nuremberg (Plate 52), two statues in the Schnütgen Museum at Cologne, and the reliefs of the wings. The style is characterized by a great clarity of form and sculptural precision combined with charm, naïvety, and even a certain sentimentality. If Hans von Judenburg is also the master of the Crucifix in S. Giorgio Maggiore in Venice,[114] he would be in the same receptive relation to North

Italian types of sculpture as Aegidius of Wiener Neustadt, who is documented at Padua between 1422 and 1438 and in 1425 made the stone figure of St Michael at Montemerlo near Padua.[115]

The Hungary of that time has many, if dispersed, examples of altar carving of the early fifteenth century. Workshops were active among the Germans of the Zips (now Czechoslovakia) and Transylvania (now Rumania). The initiative came from Bohemia, Silesia, and Austria. The type of altarpiece with a main figure in the centre and left and right two lower niches for other figures is derived from the retables of the late fourteenth century. Figures of c. 1420–30 particularly worth mentioning are the Virgin in the Budapest Museum from Topperz, the Magdalen of Danišovce (Diensdorf), and the statuary of the Altar of the Virgin at Lomnička (Kleinlomnitz). Of great pre-eminence, also for its masons' lodge, was Košice (Kaschau). Here, in the wonderful hall church of St Elizabeth, a monumental wooden Crucifixion of c. 1430 is preserved.[116] The character, by and large, is Sileso-Bohemian. Wood carving at Cracow is most impressively represented by the Fair Virgins of Kruzlow (near Grybow) and of St Nicholas, Cracow, now in the Museum Narodowe (Plate 44B).[117]

Perhaps the most copious surviving material of wooden sculpture is that of Silesia.[118] The quantity of pieces allows one to see the transition from the late fourteenth to the early fifteenth century with exceptional clarity. The most impressive work is the painfully agitated Crucifix from the church of Corpus Christi at Wrocław (Breslau), still entirely that expressive type of Christ crucified which belongs to the Late Trecento and is most movingly represented by the Crucifix of the cathedral on the Wawel at Cracow, traditionally connected with the name of Queen Hedwig of Poland, who died in 1399.[119] Of about 1400 are the sandstone statues of the Virgin of the Rose-Bush and the Man of Sorrows in St Dorothy at Wrocław. The bulk of early-fifteenth-century Silesian sculpture cannot be separated from that of Bohemia. Some examples are the Virgin of the Museum in Berlin (East),[120] the Virgin and the St John Evangelist at Radibor in Saxony, the apostles of the Goldsmiths' Altar in the church of the Magdalen at Wrocław, and a Virgin in the museum at Görlitz (from St Peter's). Most characteristic of the local version of this style at Wrocław and its significance is the monumental rood in the church of Corpus Christi. This must belong to c. 1420. The calmer beauty of the Crucifixion in the Dumlose Chapel in St Elizabeth must be about ten years later (Plate 42B). Supple lines of rich drapery flow round sturdy figures. The details of the body of Christ – just as in the case of the Crucifixion in the Týn Church in Prague (Plate 42A), to which reference has already been made – are astonishingly naturalistic, though at the same time austere and noble.

The most charming piece of sculpture from Wrocław on the other hand is the delightful silver-gilt reliquary bust of St Dorothea[121] in the Muzeum Narodowe in Warsaw (Plate 43A). This comes from the Chapel of the City Council and is of c. 1410–20. The small, girlish head on steeply sloping shoulders is infinitely gentle, yet grave, and the metal precision enhances these values. Here the humanization of the icon is completely achieved. But memories of the blissful expression of the Fair Virgins have still not disappeared.

To round off this survey, a conspectus of sculpture in wood in the former lands of the Prussian Order must be added. Here it is the 'shrine-Virgins'[122] that attest the surviving traditions of the Trecento. Fine examples are in the church of the Virgin at Elbląg (Elbing), the Kunstindustrimuseum in Copenhagen, and the Germanisches Museum in Nuremberg. The initiative once again came from the style of the Fair Virgins. A masterpiece is the more-than-life-size Crucifixion given to St Nicholas at Elbląg by the man who was rector from 1400 to 1414. The figures are tall, erect, extremely intense in facial expression, and in the draperies never merely decorative. The same master[123] may have carved the Death of the Virgin in St Mary at Gdańsk (Danzig). Even more moving is the monumental rood in St Nicholas at Tallinn (Reval) of c. 1430.[124] Close similarities to Silesian sculpture have led to the suggestion that the master came from there, but it is quite conceivable that the creative forces in the Baltic States were strong enough on their own to produce such pieces.

Baltic art, as we see it here, remained permanently in touch with the Hanseatic cities. The Virgin on an altar in the Nikolaikirche at Stralsund, given by the Junge family (a Lübeck family) about 1425,[125] is literally the same as the Fair Virgin of Toruń. But the Stralsund Virgin is of walnut, and therefore probably imported from the Netherlands – and this shows once more, and in a new light, the problem of West and East during the years with which we are concerned. On the other hand the bronze font of Lübeck Cathedral, cast at Hamburg in 1455, shows how long in local workshops inventions of the supple style of the early fifteenth century remained paradigmatic. The same phenomenon is demonstrated time and again by the general character of sculpture in Scandinavian and Baltic churches. Just one instance from many is the broadly composed, amazingly monumental wooden St John Evangelist at Hollola in Finland,[126] although it shows already some signs of that freezing-up which belongs to the years after 1430.

46

CHAPTER 4

FRANCE, THE NETHERLANDS, AND SPAIN TO THE MIDDLE OF THE FIFTEENTH CENTURY

THE memorials to Pierre d'Évreux-Navarre and his wife Catherine d'Alençon of 1412/13 (Plates 28 and 29)[1] mark the splendid opening of the fifteenth century in the monumental tradition of funerary sculpture in Paris. In view of their realism, one should not be tempted merely to admire the perfection of their 'portraiture'. On the contrary, despite this seeming realism, the effigies are still ideal images of the feudal lord and his widow. The individual features are sublimated into a higher reality. To the same type belong the tomb (1427–38) of Philippe de Morvillier, President of the Parliament of Paris (d. 1438), from St Martin-des-Champs in Paris (Plate 54); the tomb of Anne of Burgundy, Duchess of Bedford (d. 1432), from the convent of the Célestins, also in Paris (both are now in the Louvre);[2] and the tomb of Guillaume du Chastel (d. 1441) at St Denis. The tomb of Anne of Burgundy is – this can be proved – the work of a Flemish sculptor called Guillaume Vluten (d. 1450); it is extremely naturalistic in the rendering of costume and detail, but lacks a deeper power of portraiture. On the basis of the general situation which we have already discussed, it may be assumed that for the carving of such important funerary sculpture in Paris talent was drawn from the Southern Netherlands.

However, though this funerary sculpture is so intensely concerned with the individual human appearance, it would be wrong to regard the tendency to realism as the decisive factor of the style. More essential are the growing independence of sculpture from its architectural background, the increasing significance of the subject portrayed, and the strengthening of the expansion into space of the sculptural form. Fine examples of this are the simple stone reliefs on the tomb of Marguerite de Bretagne (d. 1420), the betrothed of Guy de Laval, from the collegiate church of La Madeleine, now in the museum of the château of Vitré (Brittany). In these reliefs, and especially in the one portraying Christ's apparition to the Magdalen, a sculptural image of peculiar quality emerges from the latent sense of movement and space.

When reviewing the achievements of German sculpture around 1400, we saw that the figure of the Virgin in particular gave rise to the development of autonomous types of sculptural representation, and we were surprised to observe how complex and rapid was this development, which was based clearly on a generally accepted climate of religious feeling. In order to indicate the western parallels of this development, I have already cited pages from the *Livre de Prières* of Philip the Bold in the Bibliothèque Royale in Brussels[3] and from the Cyrena manuscript in the Codex Boccaccio (*Livre des femmes nobles et renommées*, 1402, in the Bibliothèque Nationale, Paris).

In fact Fair Virgins are to be found in Northern France which are similar in origin and bear a family resemblance to those we have met in the Rhineland. The stone figure of the Virgin from the north portal of the church of Le Mesnil-Aubry (Seine-et-Oise),[3] column-like and self-contained, and impressive in its corporeality, belongs to the end of the fourteenth century (Plate 60B). This is followed by the development to a new stress on representational frontality in the marble figure of the Virgin by Jean de Cambrai at Marcoussis[3] (given by the Duke of Berry to the Célestins in 1408; Plate 20A). The more supple and lyrical type characteristic of the early fifteenth century is to be found in examples like the Virgins at Auzon (Haute-Loire),[3] at Bonneville-sur-Scie,[3] in the Gallery of Vassar College, Poughkeepsie, U.S.A. (Plate 61B),[4] and in the museum of Chartres. In this connexion we are reminded once again of the alabaster Virgin in the Rijksmuseum in Amsterdam (Plate 21A), whose provenance is so hard to determine (Netherlandish?).[5]

The famous Virgin in the Sainte-Chapelle of the castle of Châteaudun (Eure-et-Loire)[3] also belongs to this type and probably dates from the middle of the first half of the fifteenth century (Plate 60A). In any case the rhythmic delicacy and nobility of this statue are essentially different from other works of sculpture in the chapel, which was built between 1451 and 1468 and which we have yet to discuss. This figure of the Virgin is preceded by Notre-Dame des Fers on the rood screen of the church of Taverny[6] (Seine-et-Oise).

The regional character of the sculpture of Lorraine is recognizable in two Fair Virgins in the Louvre[7] from the early years of the fifteenth century. In their breadth of treatment they are akin to contemporary Rhenish Virgins. The increasing painterly enrichment of the middle of the first half of the fifteenth century is particularly clear in the Entombment group at Pont-à-Mousson and in the stone figures of St Mary Magdalen, which probably derive from and are almost identical with the Entombment groups from the church of Ancemont (Meuse), now in the Louvre, and in the museum of the Église des Cordeliers in Nancy.[8] With these the stone figure of an angel from the Strasbourg Cathedral lodge[9] should be compared. It is not Burgundian influence, it seems to me, which is revealed by these statues, but the independent significance of Lorraine sculpture and its mediating role between the sculpture of Central France and the Rhineland. Other examples of this are the monumental group of Christ carrying the Cross (in the Louvre) which came originally from the neighbourhood of Nancy and the stone figure of St Paul in the museum of Metz.[10]

Burgundian sculpture was remarkably prolific and influential in the generation following Sluter. We know from records how numerous were the craftsmen summoned from the Southern Netherlands to work for the dukes of Burgundy. Even though in many cases they may have exploited the heritage of Sluter, this does not suffice to explain the astonishing power of Burgundian sculpture at the beginning of the fifteenth century. It is evident that in many places, native sources which had lain dormant in the stultifying local developments of the late fourteenth century now sprang into new life.

The large number of surviving examples makes it possible to gain insight into the genesis of this influential school. Particular types of representation were repeated often with only slight modifications – whether in the leading workshop at the ducal court in Dijon or in other workshops. Hence it is difficult to distinguish 'originals', which after all themselves derive from certain conventions – sometimes even of painting – from 'replicas'. Such links can be traced most easily when the originals enjoyed a high reputation,[11] e.g. Sluter's Calvary in the Chartreuse of Champmol. In the course of the generations, however, it happened that the creative forces in the ducal workshop, when Claus de Werve stepped into Sluter's shoes, dried up, whereas in other workshops the boldness of Sluter's inventions acted as a stimulating force. Thus we shall have to draw attention particularly to those sculptural achievements which enrich our understanding of Sluter's works, even though they may date from after his death.

We have for instance a report of 1390 about a Pietà of Sluter's, intended for the chapter house of the Chartreuse of Dijon, an apparent replica of which from the early fifteenth century is to be found in the Städtische Skulpturengalerie, Frankfurt (Plate 57B).[12] This is a work of so autonomous and so assured a character that the contemporary German Pietàs appear old-fashioned in comparison. How small a step it is – both in form and spirit – from this creation of Sluter's to the Pietà of Germain Pilon in the Louvre, a hundred and fifty years later! At the same time such a comparison shows how rapidly and how radically Sluter's successors adapted themselves to French ideas and expression. Thus in the Burgundian sculpture of the fifteenth century there are many portrayals of the Mourning of Christ which are still rooted in Netherlandish prototypes, but which had long become an essential ingredient of the iconography of French Late Gothic. The same applies to other motifs.

In the same way Sluter's type of the Virgin is given a new dignity. I choose this word deliberately, because in the works of Sluter's successors the frontal aspect of the statue receives an ever more dignified emphasis, whereas the quality of depth which had such significance in Sluter's statues is neglected. The same tendency is to be observed in the arrangement of the figures. Frequently it is a question of figures standing against a wall, as for example in the reredos of 1448 in the church of Rouvres-en-Plaine (near Dijon), which may be ascribed to Juan de la Huerta and which is crowned by a figure of the Virgin (Plate 7)[13] flanked by the two St Johns. The altar is probably the replica of a no longer surviving altar in the ducal chapel of the Chartreuse of Dijon, and consequently a good example of the varying repetition of conventional motifs characteristic of Burgundian sculpture at this time. A similar figure to that of the Virgin of Rouvres is in the hospital at St-Jean-de-Losne (Côte d'Or), and a descendant of the John the Evangelist in this group is in the Städtische Skulpturengalerie at Frankfurt. The Baptist at Rouvres belongs to a type which is also represented by the slightly older one in the Warburg Collection, New York, and by the definitely later statue in the church of Châteauneuf-en-Auxois, which can be dated to the years 1457–60.[14]

The number of surviving examples is as difficult to survey and classify as in the case of the Fair Virgins in Germany.[15] Another parallel to the latter is to be found in the charm and gentleness of the facial expressions and in the delicate treatment of the surface of these Burgundian works, which are carved in a soft limestone. It is typical of the age that they tend to lack individual character.

An outstanding example is the stone figure of St John the Baptist from Autun Cathedral in the Musée Rolin[16] which is still relatively austere and therefore early in date.

Another noteworthy work is a Virgin from a house in the rue Porte aux Lions at Dijon, now in the Louvre[17] (c. 1410–20; Plate 9A), magnificent in the economy of its outline. The influence exercised by this figure is testified by statues in the Kunstmuseum at Basel and in the Musée de Cluny, and by one with a particularly charming expression in the Städtische Skulpturengalerie at Frankfurt. Somewhat later this restrained type of figure began to be transformed into a more 'Flamboyant' version. To take only outstanding examples from the large number extant, I would cite the Virgin from Plombières-lès-Dijon now in the Louvre,[18] that from the doorway of the Château St Apollinaire near Dijon, now in the Musée de Cluny,[19] and above all, on account of its majestic size and radiant painterly amplitude, the Virgin in Notre-Dame at Auxonne (Plate 57A).

There are but few places in Burgundy today where these sculptural achievements may still be seen *in situ*. Generally these are works which owe their origin to feudal overlords and ecclesiastics. One such place is Poligny (Jura). In the neighbourhood of this little town there were at one time quarries which *inter alia* supplied alabaster to the workshops of Dijon. At Poligny itself there were, I believe, sculptural workshops, whose products we may still see today in the church of St Hippolyte (founded in 1415; choir consecrated in 1422). Here is for example an over-life-size Crucifixion carved in oak, admirably clarified and sharply accentuated in form, as if the 'soft style' had been subjected to a new process of abstraction.[20] All the more remarkable is the broad and weighty impasto of the monumental stone figures in the same church: the noble donor Jean Chousat (d. 1433), some Apostles, and, a climax of painterly magic, the figure of the Virgin, almost rhetorical in its emotional intensity, but unfortunately completely distorted by over-painting. Related to the magnificent gesture of this Virgin are the stone figures of St Paul (Harkness Fund 1922) and of St John the Baptist (Pulitzer Bequest 1934), both now in the Metropolitan Museum in New York, and both originally from Poligny (Plate 56, A and B).[21] No less 'emancipated' is the Baptist from the church of Mouthier-le-Vieillard. In this statue a human dignity and formal harmony have been attained which are closely related to Sluter, although it is a question of works which probably date from as late as 1420–30. One of the most impressive examples of the growing objectivity visible in French sculpture in the second quarter of the fifteenth century is the almost life-size figure of a kneeling donor from the Église des Jacobins at Poligny, now in the Louvre.[22]

South of Poligny lies the former abbey of Baume-les-Messieurs. In its church may also be gained a good idea of the former wealth of sculpture from Burgundy's golden age.[23] Here the Abbé Amé de Chalon did a great deal towards renewing the decoration. In his funerary chapel stands his tomb (d. 1431), and that of Alix de Vilars. Among the numerous individual statues special attention may be drawn to the St Michael, the impressive composition of which suggests that it has been influenced by a lost work of Sluter's. We know that a St Michael was made in Sluter's workshop for the Chartreuse in 1395/6. The St John the Evangelist, with the harmonious vertical flow of its straight breadths of drapery, perhaps belonged originally to a series of the Apostles. The most impressive of these statues is that of St Mary Magdalen, clothed in a rich robe whose folds express the lyrical melody of the 'Burgundian style' in its purest harmony. In the somewhat later marble figure of a Virgin and Child in the church of Pesmes (Haute-Saône), the three-dimensional quality is already translated into an almost linear frontal emphasis.

Perhaps the particularly beautiful stone figure of St Mary Magdalen in the Musée Rolin at Autun,[24] with its rich and melodiously flowing drapery, is also an echo of a work of Sluter's. But when dealing with such widely scattered individual works – I would quote as an additional example the fine figure of St Barbara in the church of Turcey (Côte d'Or) – one must always reckon with the parallel influence of immediate contacts with the Southern Netherlands and Flanders.

Such influences are mirrored in the scattered examples of walnut carving, some of which are still lavishly coloured and gilded, all of them more or less the same size (about 2 ft high) and formerly component parts of altar shrines. We are still not sure where these carvings were made. Certainly one should not necessarily assume them to be Burgundian, as was formerly done, however close they approximate to the style of Sluter and his followers. An indication of origin is given by the narrow wooden figure of St John the Baptist in the Louvre, which is not in my view of French but of South Netherlandish provenance and whose characteristic base with indications of soil and plants proves it to date from the early fifteenth century.[25] I regard these walnut statuettes[26] as dating from the second quarter of the fifteenth century in France and as coming mainly from altar shrines which were supplied by North French and Flemish workshops. An early example of French wood carving is the fine oak reliefs in the choir stalls of the abbey church of St-Benoît-sur-Loire (1417).

Toulouse was the centre of important sculptural workshops,[27] whose influence incidentally played a significant part in the development of Spanish sculpture. Unfortunately only a few outstanding products of these workshops remain. The stone figure of St Michael from a destroyed church in the suburbs of Toulouse, now in the Musée des Augustins, is clearly a derivative of the Burgundian School (Plate 58B). The archangel is a knightly, boyish figure, clad in a cloak, whose wide, swinging folds reveal its contact with the Burgundian style at the beginning of the century. The monster which rears up at his feet is a magnificent invention, exhibiting a realism which at the same time has a certain fairy-tale quality about it. I believe that this figure belongs to the post-Sluter generation and dates from about 1430–40. To the creator of this figure we also owe the splendid statue of 'Nostre-Dame de Grasse' in the Musée des Augustins in Toulouse, which probably came from the pilgrimage church of the Dominicans, Notre-Dame de Grâce, at Bruguières near Toulouse (Plate 58A). This work still has the charmingly child-like and radiant expression of the style of the early fifteenth century, a comely amplitude in the wide folds of drapery, and a delicacy of surface treatment such as we do not meet again, it seems to me, in the local sculpture of Toulouse in the second half of the fifteenth century. In any case it is most probable that the origin of these two works[28] is to be found in the Burgundian tradition.

The monument in marble and alabaster which King Charles III (the Noble) of Navarre (1388–1426) caused to be erected for himself and his wife Leonora in his chapel in Pamplona Cathedral (1416–20) by the sculptor Janin Lomme from Tournai is also mainly of French origin.[29] The type is as usual: the effigies of the two deceased lie on the slab, with the figures of the mourners in Burgundian style in niches along the sides of the tomb-chest. Lomme is known to have been resident at Dijon between 1405 and 1410, and so it is understandable that the style of the mourning figures should be reminiscent partly of Burgundian and partly of Flemish prototypes. A similar confluence is also to be sensed in the formal character – somewhat different from that of Lomme's works – of the figures on the recessed wall-tombs of Prince Lionel of Navarre (d. 1413) and his wife in the cloisters of Pamplona Cathedral and of Bishop Sancho Sánchez de Oteiza (d. 1425) in the cathedral itself. The same is true of the tomb of Mosén Francés de Villaespesa, chancellor of Navarre (d. 1421), in Tudela Cathedral. Sculptors of the most varied origins occur in contemporary records of payment. It is important to emphasize how markedly the Burgundian style is already disintegrating under the impact of a new linearism. Even the dress, and above all the portrait features, have a sharpness such as we have not met before. This character appears in the most important tombs of this period in Spain and Portugal and must be considered a feature of Iberian sculpture, even where the work was done by foreign artists.

The sepulchral sculpture of Castile is also subject to Burgundian influence. Specially notable are the effigies on the tombs of Archbishop Pedro de Luna (d. 1414) and of Cabarello Don Juan de Luna, Conde de Santistebán, in Toledo Cathedral. Most impressive of all is the powerful alabaster tomb with the effigies of Gómez Manrique and his wife Doña Sancha de Rejas from the monastery of Fresdeval, which they founded, now in the Museum of Burgos, which dates from about 1430 (Plate 55). Despite the monumental austerity of these figures, a degree of naturalism has been achieved such as we do not find in contemporary French sculpture, even though the latter is the origin of this style. Similar in kind, though more elaborately decorated, is the double tomb in marble (c. 1433) of the Portuguese King John I and his wife Queen Philippa of Lancaster in the Founders' Chapel of the abbey of Batalha.

French and Netherlandish influences are also to be observed in Castilian altar sculpture; indeed in many cases altarpieces were actually imported from these countries. It is in fact not easy to decide between these two possibilities, in view of the later painting-over of the wood carvings in strong colours. An example of this is the shrine set up in the style of the Netherlandish 'group altar' in the Founders' Chapel in the Convento de S. Clara at Tordesillas near Valladolid. Reliefs of the Passion are arranged in two tiers under high Flamboyant canopies. The pictorial style of representation is reminiscent of the altar fragments at Hakendover. Composition and content, however, are much more strongly expressive in character. On the other hand the large oak figure of the Virgin from Majorga (Province of León) of the early fifteenth century (Louvre) is French in type.

Individual religious figures from the early fifteenth century in Portugal[30] also show a preponderantly Netherlandish and French character; for example the figures of St Peter and St Paul[31] in the Ernesto de Vilhena Collection in Lisbon, a stone figure of the Virgin in the Museu de Machado de Castro at Coimbra, and similar statues at Alhadas and in the private collection in Lisbon just mentioned.

The most astonishing example of this foreign character is the Fair Virgin of about 1420 at Prado near Braga (Plate 61A), which is a sister figure to the French figures of the Virgin at Taverny and Vassar College, providing us with an additional and – on account of the quality – weighty argument for the Franco-Netherlandish origin of the so-called Fair Virgins. Alongside the Madonna at Prado one should place the unusually large Virgin in the church of Tentúgal.

The foremost example of Aragonese sculpture is the recessed wall-monument of Bishop Alonso Carrillo de Albornoz (d. 1439) in the cathedral of Sigüenza (Plate 64A). At the back stand figures of St John the Baptist and St John the Evangelist, immediate derivatives of the post-Sluter style in Dijon. At the same time, on account of the relative certainty of their dating, the two figures are instructive for the chronological sequence of Burgundian stone sculpture of this period. In front of the tombs there are three reliefs of outstanding quality, which, according to an inscription, date from 1426. These three reliefs flow one into another like a painting. The figures stand out almost in the round, thus achieving a remarkable 'frontal' vividness. Their origin one must seek again in the contemporary Netherlands, but on account of the lack of sculptural examples there it is the illuminated manuscripts with their increasing sense of space which provide us with the closest parallel.

Hand in hand with this tendency goes a new capacity to present facial features in a way that is both suggestive and abstract, the most remarkable examples of which are the tombs of Caballero Gómez Carillo and his wife Maria of Castile (d. 1441 and 1448) in the Capilla Mayor of Sigüenza Cathedral. This sculptural style reaches a high degree of perfection in the marble effigy of Doña Aldonza de Mendoza (d. 1435) from San Bartolomé at Lupiana (Guadalajara), now in the Museo Arqueológico in Madrid (Plate 63); for here the fine smooth features are permeated with an astonishing assurance, as though contacts with the Early Renaissance in Florence and Siena had been established.

In Catalonia the leading sculptor round 1400 was Pedro Sanglada. In 1394, after he had been in Flanders, he began to carve the choir stalls of Barcelona Cathedral. They are filled – like illuminated manuscripts translated into the medium of sculpture – with a new feeling for the charm of anecdote and narrative. The tombs carved by Sanglada for Barcelona (1406) and Gerona Cathedrals are more conventional. On the sides of the marble tomb-chest of Bishop Escales in the Capilla de la Santísima, erected by Antonio Canet in Barcelona Cathedral, we encounter again mourners in the Burgundian style, whose violence of expression once more appears as a characteristic feature of Spanish sculpture. In the exhibition 'European Art around 1400' held in Vienna in 1962, Catalonian wooden sculpture was represented by a St Peter from a retable from the church of Cubellas now in the Museum Marés at Barcelona.[32] This work is impressive by virtue of its monumental proportions, and it is as austere and assured in form as a piece of stone sculpture. The close affinity between this work and the particular spiritual essence of contemporary panel-painting in Catalonia is evident. At the same time it is clearly allied to the South Netherlandish type of monumental sculpture of the late fourteenth century, an echo of which we have already discerned in the Apostles in Ste Croix at Bernay.

The most important Catalonian sculptor of the first half of the fifteenth century was however Pedro Johan, probably identical with Pedro de Vallfogona. He was the master of the beautiful tondo with the figure of St George on horseback (1418) on the balustrade of the façade of the Palacio de la Diputación (Generalidad de Cataluña) in Barcelona. Between 1425 and 1436 he was commissioned by the archbishop of Tarragona to carve the alabaster reliefs of the high altar in the cathedral there (Plate 62). In the sculptural precision and in the painterly richness of these reliefs we sense once again, it seems to me, a contact with Italian art of the early fifteenth century, just as we do in many important works of contemporary Catalonian panel painting. The same is true of the decorative stone work by Pere Oller on the high altar of the cathedral of Vich (1420). In the alabaster reliefs in Tarragona, too, the painterly element comes to the fore – a characteristic tendency of the time. The result was a truly enchanting grace of style. In 1441 Pedro Johan was further commissioned by the archbishop of Tarragona to erect the high altar of the Seo at Zaragoza.[33] However, only the base reliefs and the donors' coats of arms are by his hand. After his death (c. 1445) the work was carried on by others, and we shall deal later with its completion by Hans von Schwäbisch Gmünd.

The statues at the entrance to the cloisters in Barcelona Cathedral have a special character. Here again French influences seem to predominate, as a comparison between the St Eulalia and the Fair Virgin of Vassar College will most clearly show. The same applies to the wooden Fair Virgin from S. Pedro at Tarrasa, in the Museo Nacional, Barcelona.

Between 1418 and 1424 Giuliano Fiorentino[34] was responsible for twelve marble reliefs on the rood screen in the old choir of the cathedral of Valencia. These compositions show a typically Tuscan mastery in the treatment of the new relationship of body and space.

At this time a sculptor came from Spain to France who was destined to continue the tradition of monumental funerary sculpture in Dijon.[35] This was Juan de la Huerta of Daroca (Aragón). In 1439 at Chalon-sur-Saône Count Louis de Chalon-Arnay commissioned him to erect three tombs with the usual mourning figures for the family chapel at Mont-Ste-Marie (Doubs). Probably it was the impression made on Philip the Good by these tombs (destroyed in the French Revolution) which caused him, after the death of his *tailleur d'images*, Claus de Werve, in 1439, to entrust Juan de la Huerta with the long-planned completion of the tomb of his father, Jean Sans Peur (d. 1419), and his mother, Margaret of Bavaria (d. 1423), in the choir of the Chartreuse of Champmol. The monument was to be in alabaster and of the same size as that of Philip the Bold and to resemble it also in other respects. The contract envisaged a period of four years as the time for completion. The Spaniard, however, with a certain cunning, was able to get the contract justifying his stay at Dijon repeatedly prolonged, and work on the monument progressed but slowly. In 1456 completion appeared to be at hand, for paint and gilt were being bought for the final colouring. But then the sculptor disappeared, and Antoine Le Moiturier from Avignon (at Dijon for the first time in 1462) had to complete the tomb (1466–70). The two main effigies are his work. Apart from this, it is scarcely possible to establish which of the varying hands was responsible for the different parts. The monument suffered serious damage during the French Revolution – as did also that of Philip the Bold – and was over-restored when it was set up again in the museum of Dijon. In the tomb of Philip the Bold the influence of Sluter is clear, although there is a simplification of the details, e.g. in the copying of certain mourners, a broader frontality, and a reduced three-dimensionality. The personal style of Juan de la Huerta is seen most clearly in the compressed shape of the four angels with helmet and scutcheon kneeling at the head of the effigies. Records prove these angels to have been completed in 1451.

In the contract drawn up at Lyon on 24 June 1448 between Charles I of Bourbon (d. 1456) and the sculptor Jacques Morel of Montpellier (son of Perrin Morel of Lyon, mentioned earlier), the monument of Philip the Bold in Dijon was again expressly cited as a model; this time it was for the alabaster tomb for the Neuve Chapelle of the abbey of St Pierre at Souvigny (Allier) for the duke and his wife Agnes, daughter of Jean Sans Peur (Plate 64B). As we know from records, Morel had been active in the previous decades at Lyon, Toulouse, Avignon, Rodez, and Montpellier. His gold reliquary bust of John the Baptist[36] in the abbey church of Quarante (Hérault) still survives.

The tomb at Souvigny appears to have been completed in the scheduled time of five years. Apart from a few fragments, the magnificent effigies still survive; they are badly damaged, but not ruined by restoration – like the effigies at Dijon – so that we may still sense their original character. The figure of the duke is distinguished by the generous amplitude of his cloak with its ermine collar. The features of his face, surrounded with luxuriant curling hair, are strikingly chiselled and reflect a noble character. The figure of the duchess bears testimony to a new kind of realism, which does not however in any way reduce her dignity. Antoine Le Moiturier, active at Avignon, a nephew of Jacques Morel,[37] collaborated in this tomb. Duchess Agnes recommended him to her brother Philip the Good in 1462.

Another work probably by Jacques Morel is the alabaster tomb at Loches (Indre-et-Loire) of Agnes Sorel (d. 1450),[38] mistress of King Charles VII, who was long resident in the château of Mehun-sur-Yèvre. This tomb was re-assembled and completed after having been badly damaged in the French Revolution, so that the impression we now have is not quite authentic. But a certain terseness and austerity of form is very typical of the increasing tendency towards a new objectivity in sculpture in the middle of the century. Of all the sculptors in the succession of Sluter, Jacques Morel had the strongest personality and a keen sense of clarity and vigour. He is representative of a French, non-Netherlandish, school of sculpture in the valley of the Rhône (Avignon–Lyon). Remarkably close to his work is the Nostre-Dame-de-Grasse of Toulouse. Unfortunately further works of Jacques Morel, e.g. the tomb of King René and his wife Isabelle of Lorraine, undertaken in collaboration with the architect Jean Poncelet in 1453, as well as the Holy Cross Altar in the cathedral of Angers were completely destroyed in the French Revolution. Morel died at Angers in 1459.

The completion of the double tomb of Jean Sans Peur and his wife by Antoine Le Moiturier in 1469/70 marks the end of monumental funerary sculpture at Dijon. With the death of Charles the Bold in the Battle of Nancy (1477), the splendour of Burgundy came to an end.

On the other hand, the number of individual statues still surviving from the years 1430–60 is large, and the fact that they are to be found in remote churches spread over a wide area reveals to the full the fertility of Burgundian sculptural art in the middle of the fifteenth century. We can mention only a few particularly important examples. First, the group of three figures (already referred to) in the altar donated to the church of Rouvres-en-Plaine near Dijon by Philip Mâchefoing, treasurer of the Burgundian ducal family, which is probably a work of Juan de la Huerta (Plate 7).[13] The mourning figure of an abbess, now in the Louvre,[39] came originally from the abbey of Mont-Ste-Marie (Doubs); and since Juan de la Huerta was responsible, during the years 1437 to 1447, for the tombs of the family of Count Louis de Chalon in this church, it can be assumed that in the enclosed, block-like nature of this statue and in the linear articulation of its surfaces we may discern the style of the Spanish master. Whether or not this work was carried out by him personally is a question not so easily answered. The alabaster figure of a Virgin in the ante-choir of the church at Laizy (not far from Chalon, south of Autun) has a similar character, with a perhaps even more pronounced personal stamp. I think that in these works we can see the master adapting himself in his individual way to the sculptural tradition of Dijon.

The stone statue of St Jean de Reôme, originally in the palace chapel of Rochefort (Côte d'Or), now in the church of Asnières-en-Montagne, is a wonderful piece of great charm, great sensitiveness, and deep religious feeling (Plate 59c). The breadth and the gently moulded surfaces of this figure are very different from the narrow verticality and more linear austerity of the stone statue of St Bernard in the church of Fontaine-lès-Dijon, birthplace of the saint (Plate 59A).[40] Is this statue perhaps the work of Antoine Le Moiturier, who was resident at Dijon until 1494? In any case the distinguishing features of these two statues are typical of the stylistic divergence between the old and new generations in Burgundian sculpture in the middle of the century. We must add at this point the monumental stone group of St Martin on horseback with the beggar at his side in the church of Arcenant (Côte d'Or). This is a composition in which horizontal and vertical lines are sharply differentiated and which from its setting in the tympanum acquires a remarkably powerful effect.[41]

A work which is characteristic of the new tendency and in which the artist liberates himself increasingly from traditional types and forms, seeking his own individual and strongly realistic style, is the Vierge au Poupon in the Musée Rolin, which comes from the chapel of the Hôtel Rolin at Autun (Plate 59B).[42] Here the effect of beauty is achieved through the sculptural terseness of the towering figure and through the radiant clarity of its intimate expression. The St Jerome in the Musée des Arts Décoratifs in Paris is perhaps by the same hand, and similar in style is the Virgin in the Louvre, who, with her left leg slightly forward, holds the sprawling Child on her lap.[43] The painterly spread and abundance which were characteristic of the sculpture of the early part of the fifteenth century appear in works like these to have yielded to an abstract objectivity, without in any way reducing the charm of human portrayal.

The almost life-size stone Entombment in a chapel of the former hospital at Tonnerre (Yonne) dates from between 1451 and 1454 and was given by a rich citizen, Lancelot de Buonfosse (Plates 66 and 67, A and B). The masters of this work were Jean Michel and Georges de la Sonnette,[44] about whom we have no further information. The idea of the composition derives from the close connexion between the visual arts of the Late Middle Ages and the mystery plays. So we see theatrically effective elements translated into monumental sculpture: the framing is provided by the massive figures of Nicodemus and Joseph of Arimathaea (Plate 67B), figures filled with solemnity and seriousness; the frontal plane is emphasized by the tomb on which the body is being laid and behind this – rendered with all the spatial illusion of stage depth – are the demi-figures of the Virgin, supported by St John, and the three Holy Women (Plate 67A). Earlier examples of such three-dimensional Entombments in France can be traced back as far as 1408, when we hear of one set up by Jean de Prindal at Dijon; but this no longer survives. Jean de Prindal came from Brussels, and thus once more a connexion between a French type of representation and the Netherlands is set up.

Alongside the Entombment in Tonnerre we must mention the impressive stone Virgin from Poligny (Jura), now in the Metropolitan Museum in New York,[45] which is equally monumental in structure, amply flowing in the drapery, and endowed with great clarity in its thematic richness (Plate 65). The Virgin holds the Child seated on her lap; the Child turns over the pages of a book and, at the same time looks up to his mother. The group has been entitled 'l'éducation de l'Enfant', and this translation of the anecdotal into the monumental is typical of the mid-century. The New York figure is of unique importance, since its surface still shows a considerable amount of colour. We should imagine the almost contemporary Entombment from Tonnerre in the same vivid colours. As far as their formal character is concerned, both works show the predominant influence of Sluter. At any rate it is Sluter who heralds most clearly the feeling for volume in sculptural form and for rich physiognomical detail which we see in them, although at Dijon at this time, as the Entombment of 1459 in the Hôpital du Saint-Esprit there shows, there was no talent to emulate Sluter's.

To this, other sources must be added: a group of later sculpture which is best represented by the weighty monument of the bearded Jean II de Vienne, Seigneur of Pagny (d. 1436), in the castle chapel of Pagny (Côte d'Or).[46] This tomb was set up on the instructions of his niece, who was the wife of Jean de Longwy. At Tonnerre too – for example in the beautiful female head with a large, ponderous, turban-like hood – we are reminded of impressions made by the younger generation of Netherlandish artists, though it is not possible to quote precise individual details. In any case it is the epic, as opposed to the lyrical, intensity of the visual representations which is characteristic of mid-century sculpture. The large numbers of imitations to which the Entombment at Tonnerre gave rise in its own generation proves its outstanding significance.

Here a reminder might be appropriate of the impressive stone statue of St Valerie in the Louvre, because in this figure too the combination of pillar-like sculptural austerity with a delicate calligraphic wealth of detail suggests, in my opinion, that this figure also dates from the middle of the century. The draperies are treated in remarkably wide, flat areas, with the folds drawn as sharp linear notches. The provenance of the figure is not known, but on the basis of its life-history and the regional veneration of St Valerie in the district, the Louvre catalogue ascribes it to the area around Limoges. An exhibition of sculpture from the Late Middle Ages at Limoges[47] has indeed since shown that the peculiar abstract beauty of this figure is linked to the charming, austere stone sculpture of the Limoges and Bourbonnais districts in the second half of the century. It is important to emphasize this, since such regional continuity of style in France is clearly recognizable only in relatively few places on account of the destruction of such vast numbers of monuments.

The sculpture of the Hôtel de Jacques Cœur at Bourges reveals a completely different aspect. Jacques Cœur, raised to the nobility on account of his incredible success as financier to the king, was the richest man in France,[48] and he resolved that the house he built for himself at Bourges should be an expression of his personality. In 1450, the year when it was taken into use, it was not yet finished, and it was still not completed when Jacques Cœur was arrested in 1451. Then the work was brought to a premature end. The sculpture is not of outstanding quality, and restoration has robbed it of much of its authenticity. Nevertheless it is deserving of special mention because – probably on account of the directions given by the extremely self-willed owner – it shows to what bold flights of imagination sculpture at this time could soar. The carvings provide us with an insight into a new world of illustrated associations, such as is afforded us in no other building, and which comes nearest to the bold glosses in the borders of contemporary manuscripts. What we find is a frank fondness for the anecdotal exploitation of emblems, allegories, myths, and genre motifs such as we have up till now met in sculpture only in a clandestine form, as for example in the carvings on choir stalls. The illusion of the reliefs is heightened by the fact that the representations cut through their architectural framework. Traditional aesthetic frontiers are ruthlessly violated; for example in two sham windows on the façade there are busts of a man and a woman looking out on to the street (Plate 100), and behind a balustrade there is the sham relief of a watchman with halberd (surviving only in completely restored form). In one of the rooms, over a fireplace, is another sham window with couples seated at it, and above a fireplace are little recesses with couples in them. We do not know where Jacques Cœur found his architects and sculptors, but probably there were Netherlandish influences at work.

In Paris at this time the Flemish sculptor Guillaume Vluten (d. 1450) was active. He erected *c.* 1442 the monument of Anne of Burgundy, Duchess of Bedford[2] (d. 1432), for the church of the Couvent des Célestins. The effigies of Jehanne de Savernes, wife of Count Charles d'Artois (d. 1448), in St Laurent at Eu (Seine Maritime)[49] and of Jeanne de Montejeau (d. 1456) in the church of Bueil (Indre-et-Loire) are similar in style. Head and hands of the latter figure are in marble, while the body is in sandstone. Beauty in this statue is deeply felt and very personal. Probably it is also the work of a South Netherlandish sculptor, foreshadowing the noble monumentality of the bronze figure on the tomb of Isabella of Bourbon in Notre-Dame at Antwerp (see p. 92).

In the history of French sculpture in the first half of the fifteenth century we frequently come upon names of important artists who are connected with towns in Artois and Hainault, in Flanders and Brabant. It is therefore all the more galling to find in these very districts only a few works surviving to prove the significance of the influences emanating from them. In the sphere of tomb reliefs in Tournai marble,[50] which we have already discussed, one observes during the fourteenth and fifteenth centuries a continuity in the organic development of a style such as is perhaps visible nowhere else in the sculptural monuments of this period, although in general it is a question of works of only second-rate quality.

By the end of the fourteenth century already these tomb-reliefs showed suggestions of a new three-dimensionality, as is proved by the monument of Jehan de Pluvinage (d. 1376) from St Nicaise in Arras, now in the museum there. In the fifteenth century the line of development led very rapidly from the stress on beauty in the tombstones of the Colart de Seclin (c. 1401) and Cottrel (c. 1400) families in Tournai Cathedral and of Simon de Leval (d. 1407) in the church of Basècles to the austerely linear stylization of the tomb of Béatrice de Beausart, wife of Jacques de Melun (d. 1409), and her son Guillaume (d. 1407) in the church of Antoing.

This development had important contemporary parallels in the carving of monumental and votive tablets, where the figures were either cut in stone or engraved on metal. I cite as an example the line of development which leads from the relief projection of the figures on the tomb of Robert li Rois (d. 1421) from Arras Cathedral (now in the Museum) to the three-dimensional stage translated into relief on the monument of Friar Jehan Fiefvés (d. 1425) from the Couvent des Recollets at Tournai, now in the Musée du Cinquantenaire in Brussels (Plate 68), and to the spacious treatment of the figures on the tomb-relief of Jehan du Bos (d. 1438) and his wife Catherine Bernard (d. 1463) from the Franciscan church and now in Tournai Cathedral. The finest example of this graphic quality combined with intenser emotional significance – no doubt from the second decade of the century – is the tablet with the image of the Man of Sorrows in the church at Écos (Eure) which has already been mentioned (Plate 11B). One especially typical feature here is the way the figures emerge from the relief projection and jut out beyond the deep mouldings of the frame. Just as suggestive is the delicate sculptural feeling and the spatial development in the movement of the figures in the votive tablet of Ditmar de Brême, doctor at the ducal court and canon of Anderlecht (d. 1439; Plate 70) in Brabant. We may assume that Ditmar erected this memorial himself, and that it was therefore made before 1439 – an astonishing date for the richly flowing linework, which is usually to be found in sculpture only towards the mid-century.[51] An equally surprising early example of this fine, clean, graphic quality after which the new and essentially draughtsman-like style was striving is the votive relief for Canon Maistre Miquel (d. 1436 or 1437) in St-Omer Cathedral. This work is in the black stone which is characteristic of funerary sculpture in Tournai, and it has been partly painted and gilded (and unfortunately crudely restored) in a way that enhances the radiance of the whole. A charming Virgin is enthroned under a canopy, flanked on one side by a bishop and on the other by the Archangel Michael, at whose feet the donor kneels in prayer. This relief has a charm and a brilliant sharpness of line such as we meet generally only in small-scale sculpture.

The style in these reliefs has much in common with contemporary monuments at St Bavo in Ghent[52] (Margarete von Gistel, d. 1431), and at Kloosterzande (Jan von Gistel, d. 1433), but these are in such poor condition that we can no longer form an idea of the individual masters concerned.

The ultimate conclusion in both form and content has been drawn in the skeleton lying on a straw mat on the black marble tombstone (dating from 1446) of Guille Lefrachois, dit Potier, doctor of medicine and canon of Béthune, now in the museum of Arras. For here the skeleton is no longer – as in 1402 at Avignon (Plate 26B) – merely an 'imago vanitatis', but an almost completely three-dimensional figure, expressing movements that give a remarkable impression of the struggle between life and death.[53]

From all these works we may glean a hint of the significance which the sculpture of this area – nowadays a frontier district between Belgium and Northern France – possessed for the decisive turn in the development of sculpture in the second quarter of the fifteenth century – only a hint, in so far as in some of the examples we are surprised by the bold 'modernity' of their content and in others by the relatively early date of their composition. But in general we have the feeling that these funerary reliefs are only the echo of more important works of sculpture no longer extant in Artois, Flanders, and Brabant. Or else works of a highly monumental character survive, but they are so terribly damaged that we can only just sense the original delicacy of surface. The tomb-relief of Jean du Sart (d. 1456) and his wife Marguerite de Gerles (d. 1453), originally in St Nicholas at Tournai and now in the Musée Lapidaire at Ghent and dating from c. 1466, is a complete translation into stone of the kind of composition in space typical of Roger van der Weyden.[54]

The entire range of the new possibilities of spatial representation is revealed in the life-size stone Annunciation in Ste Marie-Madeleine at Tournai (Plate 69, A and B). The group stands on corbels with strikingly carved angels bearing coats of arms, but unfortunately the authenticity of the effect has been sadly impaired by repeated restoration. Judging by the coats of arms, there is no doubt that we may assign to this group the bill for carrying out the will of Jean de Bus, paid in 1428 by his widow Agnes Piétarde to Jehan Delemer, 'tailleur et ouvrier d'ymaiges', and to 'Maistre Robiert Campin pour sa desserte d'avoir peint de plusieurs couleurs les dites ymages et capitaux'. This will explain the fact that the boldly linear stylization which succeeds the three-dimensionally rounded style of the early fifteenth century is seen here at Tournai already in 1428 in all its bold spaciousness and new dynamic independence of figures. This could be realized through the close cooperation of the sculptor with the painter, Robert Campin (the so-called Master of Flémalle), who, like Roger van der Weyden, was one of the first to achieve a new feeling for space in contemporary painting. This example of impressive spatial quality in the Annunciation group at Tournai is a proof that the decisive step into a new world, leaving the gigantic sculpture of Sluter behind, has been achieved through a union of painting and sculpture.[55] The stylistic parallels with the painting of Robert Campin or Roger van der Weyden are obvious, and this not only with those grisaille paintings which, out of reaction against the naïve naturalism of the years round 1400, strove after a new abstraction and monumentalization.

The paintings of Roger van der Weyden spring equally readily to mind when we look at the impressive, harmonious, and serene composition of the stone-carved Holy Sepulchre in the church of St Vincent at Soignies (Zinnik; Plate 72A).[56] In the austere, deep lines of the stone surfaces the abstract features characteristic of Roger's art are unmistakably present. But the group is not – and this must be expressly emphasized – a painting translated into sculpture; on the contrary, in both feeling and form there is such an immediacy that – even if it dates only from towards the mid-century, i.e. the generation succeeding Roger van der Weyden's – we may incline to the belief that the origin of the stage-like composition of Roger's paintings may partly lie in sculptural traditions. We have here then a situation in which painting and sculpture were mutually fructifying, a typical Late Gothic phenomenon.

The great tradition of South Netherlandish funerary sculpture in bronze, which we have already discussed in relation to the lid of the monument of Archbishop Friedrich von Saarwerden in Cologne Cathedral, cast in Liège before 1414 (Plates 30A and 31), was also continued in the second quarter of the century. Jehan Delemer, mentioned in 1428 as 'tailleur' of the Annunciation in Ste Marie-Madeleine in Tournai, is probably synonymous with Janne de le Mer, the 'beeldsnijder' who, together with the brass-founder Jacoppe van Gerines and Roger van der Weyden as 'polychromeur', was responsible for the bronze tomb of Joan of Brabant (d. 1406) and William I of Brabant (d. 1410) in the Carmelite church in Brussels.[57] This work was commissioned in 1458/9 by Philip the Good. Was Roger van der Weyden also the designer? Jacques de Gérines was active as a brassfounder in Brussels and died in 1463/4. At the instance of Philip the Good he cast in 1454/5 the tombs of Count Lodewijk van Mâle (d. 1384), his wife Margaretha of Brabant (d. 1368), and his daughter Margaretha of Flanders (d. 1405) for St Pierre in Lille. Both these tombs have been destroyed, but we know from engravings what they looked like, and they are clearly reminiscent of the type of the Burgundian ducal tombs in Dijon. On the side walls of the tomb-chests, set in deep arcades, were the figures of mourners, presented no longer as a court retinue, but as members of a participating family. We have here therefore, as it were, a genealogical participation extended to embrace 'perpetual adoration' such as the Emperor Maximilian later sought to achieve on a monumental scale in his tomb at Innsbruck. The effigies and the bronze statuettes were so well-known on account of the personalities they represented that they were repeatedly reproduced in drawings and engravings.

The monument of Isabella of Bourbon (d. 1465), provided for the abbey of St Michael in Antwerp by Mary of Burgundy in 1476, follows the same pattern. The recumbent bronze effigy from this tomb, now in Antwerp Cathedral (Plate 106), is an excellent example of the way in which a new beauty radiates through the realism of Late Gothic art. The bronze figures of the mourners on the sides of the tomb-chest seem to have been modified versions of the family figures on the monuments in Lille and Brussels; more difficult of explanation is the fact that the figures were reproduced in mirror-image and were given other names. It is probable that ten bronze portrait statuettes representing Philip the Good of Burgundy and other members of his family, which are now in the Rijksmuseum at Amsterdam, and which were in the town hall in 1691, belonged originally to this tomb (Plate 107, A–C).[58] Judging by these and by drawings made from them (e.g. by Dürer, Rubens, and Rembrandt) and from graphic reproductions, we may deduce the stylistic character of the lost bronze figures of the tombs in Lille and Brussels. From the statuettes in Amsterdam we get the impression of a remarkable discrepancy between the striking immediacy of their invention and a certain inconsistency and flatness in their execution. This is most easily explained if we assume that the statuettes in Amsterdam are bronze replicas, dating from 1476, done from slightly earlier originals, and that they followed the motifs of these so faithfully that the style of the preceding generation may be recognized in the very details. This reduplication is characteristic not merely of the continuity of the genealogical set-up of the ducal tombs, but also of the influence of earlier models in the brassfounders' workshops. When considering bronze figures of the Virgin on chandeliers and of evangelists on fonts in the fifteenth century, we always have to reckon with the possibility that the model comes from a supply handed down in the workshop, just as it may be proved that Peter Vischer's bronze-foundry in Nuremberg used earlier models.

The names of Robert Campin at Tournai and of Roger van der Weyden in Brussels introduce a style which brought a complete innovation in sculptural methods of representation: the strange, dynamic style of the second half of the century. We meet a new magical naturalism, which is receptive to data in nature and anxious to recapture dramatic movement, without however yet rejecting the concepts of the traditional 'icon'. The finest example of this is the wooden 'Vera Icon' in the Diocesan Museum at Arras,[59] an Ecce Homo full of truth, but nevertheless still belonging to the realm of idealized representation.

Among examples of Netherlandish monumental sculpture, so sadly reduced in number, we meet one work which, although only a fragment, possesses such spatial weight and such brilliant articulation of composition that memories of the powerful structure of Sluter's figures are evoked. This is the lower half of a richly draped female figure which was found on the balustrade of the former church of Holy Saviour at Utrecht and is now in the Centraal Museum there (no. 6363). The rise and fall of the surface causes a ceaseless interplay of light and shade; the sharpness of the ridges of the drapery suggests that the figure dates from c. 1430. The large recessed wall-monument erected before his death in 1443 by Engelbrecht of Nassau for himself, his wife Johanna of Polanen, and his son Jan I in the Groote Kerk at Breda (North Brabant) might well belong to the same North Netherlandish tradition.[60] Unfortunately this monument has been so badly damaged, restored, and added to that the style of the sculptor is no longer discernible. But the composition and the manner of the spatial arrangement of the votaries and their patrons below the figure of the Virgin is instructive, since these figures stand in two rows one behind the other in such a way as to fit in with the viewpoint of the spectator (Plate 71B). While at Tonnerre the Entombment is 'scenic' in a naïve sense, here we are already confronted with an attempt to give spatial conviction in a new, conscious way.

The sculpture in the pilgrimage church of Halle (Hal), near Brussels, is particularly interesting. The font dates, according to its inscription, from 1446 and was cast by Guillaume Le Fèvre at Tournai. It has reliefs and groups of figures on shaft and lid, made from models by 'Hubrecht de schildere'. They introduce a completely new style of anecdotal narrative, such as we find also in the corbels with figure work in relief, dating from *c.* 1440–50, on the town hall at Louvain. This increase in sharpness and precision of form and of thematic interpretation is to be seen even more clearly in the corbels of the Church Fathers in the Trazegnies Chapel of the church at Halle. It is seen too in the Crucifixus and the reliefs of the Church Fathers on the beam-ends of the large pendant rood in the same church.[61] Once again the strongly emphasized lineaments in the paintings of Roger van der Weyden spring to one's mind. From the mid-century, I think, dates the impressive, solemn figure of the Virgin in Notre-Dame-de-la-Chapelle in Brussels,[62] which still has both volume and sharpness of line.

What survives in the Netherlands from these years in the form of altars and individual pieces of carving cannot adequately represent the high quality that Netherlandish sculpture must have possessed, as is clear from later derivatives. It is true that there are some fine pieces of sculpture on choir stalls and in fragments of oak carving. The character of the style emerges most clearly in the choir stalls of St Martin at Zaltbommel (Holland) and in the realistic grotesques and drolleries on those in St Pierre at Louvain (Leuven) of 1438/42, carved by Nicolas de Bruyn and Gerard Goris (Plate 71A).[63] The oak Virgin from Ankeveen, near Hilversum, now in the Centraal Museum at Utrecht,[64] reveals a new, terse monumentality. At the same time it is clear that the fame of Netherlandish carved and painted altars had led to their being exported far and wide – to the Lower Rhineland, Westphalia, Lower Saxony, the German Hanseatic towns, Scandinavia, Finland, and also to Swabia, France, and Spain; and this remained the case up to the end of the Late Gothic period.[65]

The extent to which this export was carried on and the mobility of the artists themselves make it difficult for us to judge a group of alabaster carvings from the first half of the fifteenth century, which from their common formal traits clearly belong together and which are yet to be found widely dispersed in the Netherlands, France, Germany, and Italy. It is clear that the marble-like, matt, luminous quality of alabaster was held in particularly high regard at this time,[66] and that from the fourteenth century onwards it was used in France, Spain, and Germany, especially for monuments which were meant to perpetuate the memory of persons of importance. England[67] produced – almost mass-produced – religious statues and reliefs in alabaster which, used either individually or in altars, were disseminated throughout the then known world.

In 1431 the abbot of the Sandkloster at Wrocław (Breslau) bought from a Parisian merchant an alabaster Crucifixion. A section of this group representing the Mourning Women is preserved in the Silesian Museum at Wrocław (Plate 74).[68] In 1432 the Abbot Jean du Clercq of St Vaast at Arras bought alabaster statuettes of twelve Apostles and a Coronation of the Virgin from a German merchant. These were set up in the recesses of an altar which had been coloured and provided with painted wings by Jacques Daret at Tournai in 1434.[69] A further example is the famous alabaster Crucifixion from

Rimini (in the Städtische Skulpturengalerie at Frankfurt; Plate 73B).[70] The non-Italian character of this Georg Swarzenski attempted to explain by ascribing it to the Cologne master Gusmin, who was active in Italy as a goldsmith, and whose great artistry is praised by Lorenzo Ghiberti in his *Commentarii*. To this day a Pietà of the Master of the Frankfurt Crucifixion, called the Madonna dell'Acqua, is held in high veneration in S. Francesco at Rimini.[71] Another very effective alabaster statuette by the same master, the St Christopher in the Museo Civico at Padua, unfortunately disappeared at the end of the Second World War. The multi-figured alabaster altar, originally donated in 1442 to S. Maria Podone in Milan and now in the Palazzo Borromeo on Isola Bella in Lago Maggiore, is clearly the product of several artists who worked in the style of the Master of Rimini.

The Wrocław group of the Mourning Women, brought from Paris and dating from *c*. 1430, reveals a richer impasto in the flow of movement in the drapery than is to be seen in the figures of the Rimini Crucifixion with their sharp, metallic surfaces. Nevertheless there is such a similarity between these two works that we may certainly assume a common source. The Crucifixion is a little later, as is proved for example by its approximation to the style of the Knights on the tomb of Engelbrecht I of Nassau at Breda. But on the other hand the Rimini group is clearly older than the figures in the Humilitas Retable on Isola Bella. Thus a relatively definite date may be established for the Rimini Crucifixion, and this is confirmed by its similarity to the stylization in the imitation sculpture and the grisailles on the paintings of Roger van der Weyden dating from the 1430s.[72] Further small works in alabaster by this master and from his workshop are to be found *inter alia* in Flanders, Holland, and Germany (Plate 73A). The South Netherlandish or Flemish provenance of the Rimini Master has also been proved by the reconstruction of the type to which his multi-figured Crucifixion retable belongs.[73]

I regard the alabaster relief of Christ on the Mount of Olives in the Ashmolean Museum in Oxford (from the Henry Oppenheimer Collection)[74] as an early work of the same master and as directly related to the illuminated-manuscript style of the silver reliefs from Maestricht (1403, Hamburg Museum), and the Rimini altar as an organic continuation of it. A continuation of the Rimini altar on the other hand, by its master himself and pre-dating the alabaster altar of 1442 in the Palazzo Borromeo, is the alabaster group (2 ft high) of the Entombment in the Hermitage in Leningrad. This is a triumph of dramatic tension and precise accentuation. Compared with its boldness, even the Tonnerre Entombment seems posed. The lines are drawn as to a magnet, whereas in the Oxford relief it is the volumes of landscape and figures that dominate. Space in the Hermitage group is no longer a mere imaginary expansion, it is a functional part of the expression. Thus it is not a demonstrative naturalism which is here communicated to us, but a new kind of reality, which lends, to the faces especially, an as yet unknown intensity, without in any way destroying the sublime delicacy and beauty of the whole. Here we have a tangible proof of the European rank of Netherlandish sculpture in the early part of the fifteenth century. Certainly the so-called Master of Rimini knew Italy, as did Roger van der Weyden (who went in 1450).

It is noteworthy that the one piece of miniature sculpture which, from the point of view of outward motivation, has most in common with the Mourning Women of the Wrocław alabaster group should also come from Paris – that is, the gold-enamel Calvary already mentioned which is kept in the treasury of Esztergom Cathedral (Plate 75).[75] This piece of goldsmith's sculpture is the boldest work that survives from this time. The two-tiered structure reminds one of Sluter's Calvary in the Chartreuse of Champmol. In the tabernacle Christ is portrayed at the scourging pillar; prophets stand at the surrounding piers, and narrowly rising above it all is the Crucifixion. The individual figures are incredibly precise in their form, spare and austere, and filled with a strange inexorability of emotional expression; but at the same time – particularly through the warmth of the exquisite colouring – they are sublimated into a realm of idealized beauty. The *verismo* of this work anticipates the 'style rustique' of the sixteenth century. This radical expressionism enables us to assess to the full how much had been achieved at this time that was fundamentally new and how many stimulating inventions from the realm of sculpture have been lost and destroyed, so that we can now only conjecture about them. Even if this piece of goldsmith's work originated in Paris, it can only be understood by presupposing a contact with that Netherlandish art whose significance we can today most clearly measure in the surviving paintings of this period. It would seem too – as is the case with the era which produced the Goldenes Rössel – that for reasons of social structure, the goldsmith's craft at this moment of development was still the most receptive and consequently the most characteristic reactor to the sculptural possibilities of the epoch.

CHAPTER 5

GERMANY: 1430–60

GERMAN sculpture of the second third of the fifteenth century is remarkable for its regional variety. The vast number of works left to us from this period compels me to confine myself to a brief selection of significant examples. It is easier in this period than in the earlier part of the century to recognize individual masters – sometimes we even know their names – and the sphere of influence of local workshops and particular schools.

At the beginning of the period stands a series of monumental statues in the choir of Aachen Cathedral, completed in 1430. They are clearly the work of several masters; the earlier of them carry on the style of the corbel figures of prophets in St Andreas in Cologne, which were completed about 1420, while the later ones (eight Apostles marked with a mason's mark) exhibit that vigorous individualization of form and multiplicity of surface which we have encountered in the more advanced examples of Netherlandish sculpture.[1] This new and powerful sense of life is most clearly visible in the St Matthew (Plate 76B). It has a grave, monumental dignity which is in strong contrast to the intimate charm of the noblest works of German sculpture from the beginning of the century.

In Cologne we find an example of this new style in the magnificent Annunciation in St Kunibert,[2] donated in 1439 by Canon Herrmann von Arcka, who kneels at the feet of the Virgin (Plate 77, A and B). The 'Colognesque' element, which in the St Gereon Madonna was to be seen in the radiant serenity of the 'fair style' of the period round 1420, is here transformed into a new tectonic firmness. The elements accessory to the figure of the Virgin – the image of God the Father at her head and the powerfully concentrated and elongated form of the kneeling angel – combine to give a new graphic objectivity to the whole. Here again there is a development which took place a little earlier in the neighbouring western regions already discussed. The mastery of the statue of the Magdalen in the Louvre from Ancemont (Meuse) is an immediate parallel.

Another work of the same type is the stone altar with the Death of the Virgin in Frankfurt Cathedral, donated by Ulrich von Werstadt in 1434. Beneath a tall stepped canopy, open at the sides, one sees – under the image of God the Father receiving the soul of the Virgin – the apostles clustered round her death-bed as if on a stage. The figures are still closely packed together, as in early-fifteenth-century painting, not separated into individual entities, as in contemporary Netherlandish art. Nevertheless the Frankfurt Death of the Virgin is intensely expressive and individualized in its way, especially in the grief of the Apostles and in the touching episode of the angel closing the eyes of the Virgin. Here a lyrical note is added to the epic narrative, a note which finds even more moving expression in the Death of the Virgin in Würzburg Cathedral, carved in stone by another hand though under the influence of the Frankfurt altar (Plate 78).

Among the works which can be ascribed to the Master of the Frankfurt Altar the most remarkable, on account of the almost sinister gloom of expression, is the stone St Bartholomew dating from about 1438 from the cathedral cloister, which is now in the Historisches Museum in Frankfurt.[3] The stone Madonna of the Deutschordenskirche in Frankfurt, dating from about 1435, transforms the iconic dignity into a joyous humanity,[4] and it is at this point that one is most strongly reminded of Netherlandish painting. From the following decade we have the group of figures in the Augustinian church of Hirzenhain by a pupil of the Master of the Frankfurt Altar, dating from about 1448. Of these, a pillar-like figure of the Virgin is remarkable for the impressive linework of its articulation. Perhaps these figures at Hirzenhain are a late work of the Master of the Würzburg Death of the Virgin.

This Frankfurt master has been identified – though I do not find the identification convincing – with the cathedral architect Konrad Kuene, who was living in Cologne from 1443 until his death in 1469. The Cologne sculpture which can be certainly attributed to Kuene is clearly rooted in the style of the works of *c.* 1430-40 from the region of Aachen–Frankfurt–Cologne which I have just mentioned.[5] The possibilities inherent in these are here developed into a style of differentiated movement. This already applies to Kuene's earliest known work, the portrait-like statuettes of the masons' saints, the Quattro Incoronati, from the monument to Nikolaus von Bueren, cathedral architect, who died in 1445. They are the German bourgeois counterparts of the feudal mourning figures of the Netherlandish metal tombs, realistic in so far as the sacred representatives of the various architectural crafts are portrayed in their working clothes and with their tools. They are notably accentuated in the surface movement, but at the same time firm and concentrated in form. The goal to which this development led is shown by the succession of further works by Kuene: the realism of the sepulchral effigy of Count Friedrich IV von Moers (d. 1448) in St Pantaleon, Cologne; the multi-figured votive representation, full of painterly movement, on the monument to Archbishop Dietrich von Moers in Cologne Cathedral (1460; Plate 79, A and B); the statue of St Cornelius in the abbey of Cornelimünster, with charmingly supple relief figures on the high base; and the angular hardness of the kneeling donor figures, Johann Hardenrath and his wife, beside the choir screen of St Maria im Kapitol in Cologne (*c.* 1464).

Most surprising of all is the monument to Archbishop Dietrich von Moers, erected at his own behest. No doubt the absence of the usual tomb-chest or canopy and the decision to represent the devotional effigy in fully detached figures on the unadorned tomb lid (Plate 79A) was the personal decision of Dietrich von Moers himself. Out of this Konrad Kuene created a composition culminating in the loftily placed figure of the Virgin (Plate 79B), on either side of which the figures press towards this central 'trumeau' figure as on the sides of a portal. But since the group is not part of an architectural setting and the only framework, as it were, is the surrounding space, we are confronted with an entirely new sculptural dynamism. It is a very striking example of sculptural emancipation in the work of the masons' lodges.

Konrad Kuene was the head of the Cologne Cathedral lodge. The origins of his peculiar style should not be sought, it seems to me, in either French or Netherlandish sculpture, but in contemporary Netherlandish painting, so rich in new poetic inventions, in which Stephan Lochner of Cologne also had his share. In this field discoveries of the boldest sort were made at this time, and we shall frequently find that the painting of the fifteenth century gave birth to ideas which had a stimulating significance for sculptors and carvers also. In Kuene's sculpture we also find an echo of the Saarwerden monument, which the same Dietrich von Moers had caused to be executed for his predecessor forty years before. It is the Cologne tradition of a pronounced emphasis on form, which found fulfilment in the charming group of the enthroned Virgin flanked by seated angels bearing coats of arms in the Moers monument.

There is a boxwood statuette in the Städtische Skulpturengalerie in Frankfurt which may have originated in the circle of Stephan Lochner. The individual perfection of this piece makes it so difficult to assign it to any particular region that one is tempted to see in it, as it were, the sum of all the potentialities of its particular period.[6] It represents a Virgin – carved in the round – with a Child nestling close to and looking up to its mother, the whole instinct with that radiant charm and intimacy which prevailed in the early years of the century, but at the same time stamped with a new vigour and firmness of form – an image of experienced reality. Swabia has been suggested as its provenance, and it is true that Stephan Lochner came from Lake Constance; but he developed his atmospheric style of painting in Cologne, and one may well ask why the statuette should not after all have originated in the same sphere as the oak carving of the Virgin from Ankeveen (now in the Centraal Museum at Utrecht), which has been mentioned before, and the Virgin of the Annunciation of St Kunibert in Cologne. The statuette is also of great significance as an early instance of indigenous small-scale sculpture.

A remarkable feature of the sculpture of these decades in North and Central Germany is the way in which, with loving persistence, the figures typical of the so-called 'fair' style of the early years of the century appear side by side with examples of the new realistic and linear style. In the case of the latter, it is usual to assume Netherlandish influence. The sandstone Madonna from the Haus zum Rebenstock in the museum at Erfurt[7] is a typical example of the conservative tendency. It probably dates from as late as the middle of the century, and yet retains the supple rotundity of form which was fashionable fifty years earlier. Nevertheless, a certain compactness of proportion and hardening of the surface bears witness to the later date. Another example of such retardation is provided by the reliefs of the Evangelists on the sides of the font in Lübeck Cathedral,[8] which, according to the inscription, was cast in 1455 by Laurenz Grove in Hamburg. These reliefs were carried out in the strictest tradition of the 'fair' style. In this case the retardation can be explained by the use of earlier prototypes and moulds, of which there are many examples in Late Gothic sculpture in bronze and gold. Equally typical is the St Brigitta Altar in the abbey of Vadstena in Sweden, which was begun in 1456 by the Lübeck master Hans Hesse. This followed the old type of retable with a division into compartments, but a close survey reveals that in some of the figure groups a younger talent (Johannes Stenrat of Lübeck, 1459) has attempted a new realism of a ruthlessly unconventional type.[9] It is moving to witness how these younger talents have wrestled with the problem of creating a new image of the phenomenal world. The magic aura of beauty has been sacrificed; in its stead there has been gained an austere objectivity, of whose stimulating power one can now scarcely have any conception.

The most impressive work of this period from the North German coastal area is certainly the stone Virgin in Lübeck Cathedral (c. 1460; Plate 76A): radiant in its majesty, and with all 'anecdotal' factors and all elaboration of the surface merged into the block-like total effect. The same master was responsible for the stone retable of Albert Bischop in Lübeck Cathedral, dating from before 1459. Here the affinity with Kuene's figures on the monument to Dietrich von Moers is clear enough. It is the same conception of the votive image seen from close at hand: immediate in its human appeal, firm in the lines of its composition and modelling, eloquent and vivid to the last degree. Involuntarily we are reminded of the Tournai relief of 1436 or 1437 in St-Omer Cathedral.

Yet another work by the same master, who was probably resident in Lübeck, is the somewhat later stone Virgin in the Petrikirche in Hamburg. This shows us even more convincingly than the Virgin in Lübeck Cathedral that the prototype of these pieces was developed in the Netherlands – and possibly at Utrecht, as I shall hope to show subsequently on the strength of extant later examples. This Netherlandish type also predominates in contemporary Scandinavian sculpture, in which connexion it is not clear whether there were direct contacts between Scandinavia and the Netherlands or whether they were made via Lübeck.[10] The most important example for these connexions is a Fair Virgin in the convent at Vadstena, which is one of the most beautiful South Netherlandish works of about 1450–60; however, we do not yet know where it was made.

Central Germany also supplies us with an important offshoot of Netherlandish sculpture in the bronze monument of the elector of Saxony, Friedrich der Streitbare (d. 1428; Plate 82A), erected in the middle of the so-called Fürstenkapelle in Meissen Cathedral which was built by the elector as a burial place.[11] On the lid of the tomb lies the figure of the deceased draped in brocade; it is almost completely in the round and is invested with the insignia of the electorate, to which he acceded in 1423. On the sides of the tomb-chest bronze figures of mourning noblemen alternating with figures bearing coats of arms are enclosed by arcading. The style of these figures is precise and realistically severe. In contrast, the recumbent figure of the deceased is all the more full of suggestive power: not a portrait, but the symbol of a ruler, equipped with cap, ermine collar, and a cloak whose folds flounce out at the hips and on contact with the ground. At his feet are two lions. Stylistically there is no relationship to the – partly surviving – sculptural decoration of the chapel, which keeps the soft and gentle forms of the period at which it was built (c. 1425). On the contrary, the masterly quality of the sepulchral figure and the perfection of the casting make it probable that the tomb was imported from the Netherlands. Its formal character indicates a date between 1440 and 1450. It is a known fact that the Elector Friedrich der Sanftmütige did a great deal after 1443 for services in, and the artistic embellishment of, this Fürstenkapelle, the construction of which had come to a halt in 1428 on account of the Hussite wars. Thus this work takes its place in the series of South Netherlandish funerary monuments of the fifteenth century which began with the lid of the Saarwerden tomb in Cologne.

Such imports and derivatives of Netherlands sculpture are sharply divided from the products of an organic development of native German traditions. The most outstanding examples of the latter are to be found in South Germany. The most impressive instance of the possibilities of development inherent in the 'fair' style is the gigantic figure of St Christopher with the coat of arms and name of the donor Heinrich Schlüsselfelder, originally in St Sebald in Nuremberg and now in the Germanisches Museum (Plate 80).[12] It is dated 1442. In this case the harmony of soft and supple forms has been translated into an almost Baroque rhetoric. It presents a voluminous undulation, in which the surface chiaroscuro serves to emphasize the emotional content of the theme. Even the Holy Child seated on the shoulder of the saint has assumed gigantic proportions. We have here a dynamism in the modelling which is reminiscent of Sluter in the degree of its sculptural independence, but now this is more fundamentally realized in a figure of full three-dimensional force. There is much in this figure which is related to the older Virgin in the halo of rays at St Sebald. If both these works were by the same master, then he must be accounted the most brilliant representative of that new realism which distinguishes German sculpture of this period from the idealized style of the early years of the century. The same intensity and intimacy of expression is to be seen in the contemporary painted panels of the Tucher Altar in the Frauenkirche in Nuremberg. Nevertheless, this Nuremberg sculpture from the middle of the century is not altogether lacking in Netherlandish elements. In the Wolfgangskapelle of the Egidienkirche there is a stone group of the Entombment, dated 1446, set in a recess enclosed by the typical basket arch, in which the manner of representation and the forms of the surround are typically 'western'. It is not by chance that this is accompanied by that new linear stylization in face of which the spatial volume of the St Christopher seems like the culmination of an older sculptural tradition. The destiny of the German sculptors of this time lay in the attempt to reconcile these two traditions, in which connexion it should be noted that in the case of the Nuremberg Entombment the new element was again probably conveyed by means of paintings.[13]

In Lower Franconia and on the Middle Rhine we may observe the same process at work, especially in some important funerary monuments.[14] Among them are for example the monuments of canons in the Stiftskirche at Aschaffenburg. We see the way leading from the monument of Schenk von Weibstadt already mentioned (d. 1437) to the narrowly compressed figure of St Christopher on that of Johannes von Kronberg (d. 1439), which depends on linear effect. In Würzburg the way proceeds from the monument of Martin von Seinsheim (d. 1434) in the Marienkapelle, with its display of 'painterly' chivalric features, to the new monumental qualities in the effigy on the tomb of Bishop Johann von Brunn (d. 1440) in the cathedral. The scene of Christ bearing the Cross in a tympanum in Speyer Cathedral is very characteristic of the development at this time; originally this was in the cloisters and belonged to the St Goarskapelle, erected by Dean Nikolaus Burgmann in 1433. Here one may see particularly clearly how, out of a 'painterly' treatment, linear features come to the fore and lend a new expressive power to the whole.

In the area of the Upper Rhine there is a striking likeness between the exquisite gold St Christopher from the treasury of Basel Cathedral[15] (now in the Historisches Museum) and the St Christopher on the monument of Johannes von Kronberg, canon of Aschaffenburg, and this also probably dates from *c.* 1440. There is the same restrained strength of expression, and in the features a similar melancholy and severity. So much likeness of type can be generated by the 'atmosphere' of a particular age.

But in the sculpture of the Upper Rhineland the most striking embodiment of the tendency of the age to reject all *joie de vivre* is the large, ponderous stone figure of a seated man wearing a tall hat in the Musée de l'Œuvre at Strasbourg (Plate 81).[16] This work is an enigma from the point of view of both content and style. The cast of the grief-laden features is so individual that we are led to assume that this is a very personal 'confession', the outcome of a desire for a votive self-dedication. The style of presentation is just as personal, just as masterly, infinitely rich and forceful in its carefully graded surface, remarkably realistic by virtue of the absence of any stylization, and yet at the same time it possesses an admirable monumentality in which the autonomy of the sculptural form is revealed. It is in a way almost a parallel to the Schlüsselfelder St Christopher, but of somewhat earlier date (1430/5) and not without Netherlandish affinities, although it is difficult to find parallels or sources among the diminished number of monuments which still exist in the Netherlands themselves. Is it a work from the generation that succeeded the master of the figures on the Strasbourg Octagon? The closest resemblance is to be found in the stone figures, also of secular provenance, from the Tudot Collection in the museum of Moulins.

The monumental sculpture of Western Switzerland (and Lorraine) occupies a strange halfway-house between the Upper Rhine and Burgundy.[17] Influences from both regions alternate. Perrin Morel of Lyon had been active in Notre-Dame in Geneva, and the Flemish sculptor Prindal, earlier a colleague of Sluter at Dijon, had erected in 1414 the monument (now lost) of the Cardinal Jean de Brogny in the Makkabäerkapelle and later the choir stalls in the cathedral there. The Holy Sepulchre in the cathedral of Fribourg, erected at the instance of Councillor Jean Mossu in 1433, is of Burgundian provenance; it is somewhat crude in style and exaggerated in the dramatization of expression (e.g. the bizarre attitude of the watchmen cowering by the tomb), but at the same time the types represented are so conventional that certain individual figures remind one of corresponding arrangements in the Calvary from the Netherlandish altar in the Reinoldikirche in Dortmund, or of St John the Evangelist in the cycle of figures from the rood screen of the Marienkirche in Lübeck. The wall-monument of Bishop Andreas von Gualdo (d. 1437) in Sion (Sitten) Cathedral, with its Crucifixion and two patrons above a surmounting ogee arch, also belongs to this group of rigid imitations of Burgundian prototypes; alongside this may be placed too the carved figure of Christ at the Scourging Pillar, dating from 1438 and bearing the coat of arms of the Mossu family, in the Franciscan church at Fribourg, and the wooden St Sebastian, dating from 1450, in the church of St Valeria above Sion; whereas the stone figure of the Apostle Simon, dated 1438, and again bearing the arms of the Mossu family, on the wall of the main entrance to Fribourg Cathedral has more in common with the large stone angel of the cathedral lodge at Strasbourg and would appear to be of Upper Rhenish extraction. There is such a plethora of artists here that we do not know which of these works we should ascribe to the sculptor Peter, mentioned in the records of Sion in 1438 and in those of Fribourg in 1459.

The lapidary naturalism in the statue on the monument to Count Konrad von Fribourg at the entrance to the choir in the collegiate church at Neuchâtel is significant. Konrad von Fribourg died in 1424, and the commission for the statue was given to the Bernese master mason 'Mastre Matheus', who may probably be identified with the cathedral architect Matthäus Ensinger, summoned from Strasbourg to Bern in 1421. This figure, with its deep gravity of expression, its compressed proportions, and its feeling of violent movement, reminds one particularly forcibly of the works of the Upper Swabian painter Konrad Witz. The statue of Count Konrad's son, Johann von Fribourg (d. 1458), was modelled on this figure and set up as its counterpart.

The Upper Rhineland, which was very receptive to western influences, produced in 1438–46 that remarkable showpiece of architecture and sculpture, the so-called Schnegg in the cathedral of Constance.[18] If formerly sculpture had played second fiddle to architecture, now we have the Late Gothic reversal of the roles. Clearly here architecture has to comply with the demands of sculpture and painting. The delicate character of this spiral staircase depends entirely on non-material, i.e. visual, factors. Attempts have been made to trace the ancestry of the Schnegg back to the Grande Vis du Louvre of Charles V and to the Grande Vis du Palais du Duc de Berry in Bourges – both, as their name implies, spiral staircases. However, it is my belief that the strange Recevresse of the early fifteenth century in the pilgrimage church of Avioth[19] near Arlon (South Belgium) proves the former existence of similar delicate architectural works in the Netherlands, where they play so important a role in the background of illuminated manuscripts and panel paintings at this time. This is where we must look for our link with the Schnegg, and also for the style of its sculpture (Plate 89A), translated here into the language of the Upper Rhine and Upper Swabia. The flat backgrounds behind the figures in the reliefs resemble blank windows, while the figures themselves, jutting out over the framework, give the impression of being three-dimensional, so ardent is the sculptor in his attempt to achieve the maximum verisimilitude – a parallel to the slightly later architectural sculpture on the house of Jacques Cœur at Bourges (Plate 100).

Records give us the name of the 'Werkmeister' of the Schnegg: Antoni was 'ain priester' who died when the building 'rose from the ground'. This Werkmeister therefore is certainly not the sculptor. Another work by the sculptor is the recumbent effigy on the recessed funerary monument of Bishop Otto III of Hachberg (resigned 1434; d. 1451) which seems to date from 1445, the date on the frescoes belonging to it.

The beautiful stone sign on the former guildhall Zum Rosgarten and some examples of wood carving testify to the high quality of sculpture at Constance at this time, i.e. the time of Konrad Witz, the painter, who must be given special mention, since the parallel development of painting and sculpture is particularly important at this time. A further example of this is a small walnut Virgin from an Annunciation, poignant with feeling. This was originally at Rufach (Alsace) and is now in the Historisches Museum at Basel.[20]

The true incarnation of Swabian sculpture between *c.* 1430 and *c.* 1460 is Hans Multscher. A native of the Allgäu, he was appointed sculptor at Ulm in 1427, and although he is called merely a 'Werkmann', this designation had wider connotations. The inscription on the wing-paintings of the Wurzach altar proves that Multscher was also a painter. His career gives us once again tangible proof of that overlapping of artists' competences typical of the early fifteenth century. Multscher's career is typical too in that his early statues at Ulm (princes with pages as shield-bearers at the state window of the town hall (Plate 83B); a Man of Sorrows, dating from 1429, on the central pier of the west portal of the minster (Plate 85); an altar in a niche inside the minster, donated by the Karg family in 1433) indicate clearly that from his travels in the west, Multscher was familiar with that new conception of sculptural form which had developed in the areas of Bourges, Dijon, and Tournai.[21] In the figures of the town hall and in the Man of Sorrows one senses the sculptor's direct, personal experience of what the new emancipation from traditional canons of form meant; it is visible in the deeply felt graduations of the surface and in the freedom of the spiritual expression. There is a similar dynamism of form to that we have met in the most outstanding of the large statues of the Apostles in the choir of Aachen Cathedral.[22]

In 1435 Multscher, at the instance of Duke Ludwig the Bearded of Bavaria-Ingol-stadt, made in stone from Solnhofen the model of a tomb lid which is now in the Bayerisches Nationalmuseum in Munich (Plate 84) which the duke wished to have erected in red marble for himself and his family in the large Marienkirche which he had founded at Ingolstadt and in which the finest of the gold-enamel works which he had brought with him from Paris were preserved. On account of the unhappy career of the duke, this ceremonial monument was never executed. The so-called model remained in the treasury of the Wittelsbach family, a proof that it was not a model in the modern meaning of the word, that is to say a mere workshop sketch, but a faithful reproduction on a small scale of the envisaged *opus perfectum*, and destined for the duke. Here we have a supreme example of Multscher's treatment of surface. Even the background is full of incident, since the heraldic emblems of the duke are displayed, as indeed he had requested. They are like embroidery in thick raised materials on a curtain. In the lower foreground the duke is presented as an *eques Christianus*, i.e. with the features not at all life-like,[23] but equipped with all the insignia of his rank and looking up to an image of the Trinity in the upper part of the relief. This is an astonishing spatial arrangement whose magic is enhanced by the fact that the composition juts out beyond the narrow projecting frame, thus deepening the latticed background and lending the maximum vividness to the whole presentation. The work shows what fields of possibility of three-dimensional presentation had now been opened up to the sculptor's imagination. Alongside this so-called 'model' we should place the small alabaster relief of the Trinity from Schloss Sandizell (Upper Bavaria), now in private possession. Here the undercutting is so deep that this extremely compressed composition has the effect of being in the round. We must imagine the lost figures on the 'stage' of the Karg niche in Ulm Minster as being equally 'true' by means of clarity of articulation and accentuation. The next step towards the autonomy of sculptured form was to be taken by Nicolaus Gerhaerts of Leyden.

Among Multscher's wood carvings, place of prominence must be given to the seated Virgin (now in the Bayerisches Nationalmuseum in Munich)[24] probably from Brixen (Bressanone; South Tyrol), whose splendid volume is magnificently animated and articulated. Perhaps this figure was originally one of a devotional group in an altar predella, and the role it played in the group would explain the violent movement of the Child. Next come the Mary Magdalen supported by angels in the Staatliche Museen in Berlin; the Virgin in the parish church of Landsberg; and the Holy Virgins in the Lorenzkapelle at Rottweil, which were originally part of an altar group in the abbey of Heiligkreuztal. As early as 1430 the influence of Multscher's sculptural style is visible in the works of other Swabian and Austrian masters, ranging from the attendant figures from a Crucifixion from Überlingen now at Staufen, near Freiburg im Breisgau, the altar figures from the Scharenstetten Triptych originally in Ulm Minster, a Virgin in the Deutsches Museum in Berlin, to the wooden figures on the high altar of St Jakob at Rothenburg (dating from 1466) and the monuments to Friedrich V Schenk von Limpurg (d. 1474) and his wife Susanna von Tierstein at Grosskomburg.

Immediately after 1450, Multscher made the monument to the Countess Mechthild of the Palatinate,[25] which was transferred in 1554 to the family vault in the choir of the Stiftskirche at Tübingen (Plate 86B). This monument was originally in the Charterhouse of Güterstein in a recess with a basket arch and corresponded to the monument of the countess's first husband, Count Ludwig, which latter, however, is no longer in existence. In the flowing movement of this dignified figure, Multscher has pursued the manner of representation which we met for the first time in Jan Delemer's Annunciation of 1428 at Tournai.

The large altar in the parish church of Sterzing (Vipiteno; South Tyrol) dates from 1456–8 (Plate 87, A, B, and C). The rear wall of the shrine is draped like a stage, as in the Karg niche. There is a change discernible in the proportions of the figures, in that the verticals are stressed here, giving the fluctuating surface an increased sense of direction. Edges of drapery pour over the corners of the bases. I have repeatedly emphasized how the corporeality of sculptural figures now tends to break through the frame in which they are set. With this aim in view Multscher – and I know of no earlier example – has placed in the Sterzing Altar on each side of the shrine a knight, St George and St Florian, carved fully in the round and standing against no back wall. Originally a Christ of Pity was placed in the canopy at the top (today in the Museum Ferdinandeum at Innsbruck).[26] In this group the change of form due to the emphasis on verticality and on line is most marked, but the same is true also of the paintings on the wings, whose 'modern' style is in such sharp contrast to the older Wurzach panels that we may assume that Multscher was assisted here by a younger painter on whom Roger van der Weyden had exercised his influence.

About 1460 Multscher must have made the bronze model for a bust of St Catherine, now in the Frick Collection in New York (Plate 86A).[27] This figure is said to have come originally from a church in South Poland, and this fact has contributed to its erroneous ascription to Veit Stoss. Perhaps contacts with the Netherlands had contributed to the prestige and popularity of works in bronze. The bronze statues on the tomb of Konrad von Weinsberg and his wife Anna von Hohenlohe in Schöntal Abbey[28] were cast in Nuremberg in 1424–8. In 1447 Bishop Peter von Schaumberg donated the magnificent bronze retable for the high altar of the west choir of Augsburg Cathedral – a lavishly articulated piece which culminates in a balanced and harmonious Crucifixion in the round. Hermann Vischer the Elder established his foundry in Nuremberg in 1453. But Multscher's bust of St Catherine is by virtue of its common ancestry, so to speak, the German counterpart of the French reliquary head at Ste-Fortunade (Corrèze), which is also cast in bronze: monumentally severe and objective, filled with a radiant vitality but so 'calligraphic' in the details that its ancestry in the art of 1400 is still discernible (Plate 103B).

Multscher died in 1467. In 1455 the panel of the Holy Cross for the Fronaltar in St Ulrich and St Afra at Augsburg was commissioned in Flanders. In Schwäbisch Hall and district there are still several Netherlandish altarpieces in existence which were imported between 1440 and 1470. Thus contacts with the west remained, and acted as a steady source of inspiration.[29]

Contemporary sculpture in Bavaria and Austria remained longer faithful to modes of expression which were current at the opening of the century. A characteristic example of this is the translation of compositions of slightly older paintings (in the style of the St Lambrecht tablet of Hans von Tübingen) into the multi-figured, closely packed reliefs in the portal tympanum (dating from 1438/9) of the pilgrimage church of Mariazell (Styria).[30] The monument in red Salzburg marble to Friedrich von Pettau (d. 1438) in the castle of Ptuj (Oberpettau; Yugoslavia) is outstanding in quality; the type of presentation is still completely traditional, but the animation of the image and the interweaving of figure and surrounding space are a monumental testimony to the new feeling for realism.[31]

The over-life-size enthroned Virgin from Hallein (formerly in the Hessisches Landesmuseum at Darmstadt; destroyed in the Second World War), in all the harmony of her stately amplitude, is typical of Salzburg sculpture around 1430.[32] In the next decade one notices a hardening of the surface and the development of crystalline sharpnesses; the homogeneous flow of the drapery folds turns into restless tendrils, seen at their most impressive in the voluminous carved attendant figures of a Crucifixion from the neighbourhood of Wels, which was formerly in the Darmstadt Museum and, like the Hallein Virgin, was destroyed during the war.[33] Among the smaller figures in the little gilded silver altar from Mariapfarr near Tamsweg, which was given to the church in 1443 by the Salzburg chamberlain and priest, Peter Grillinger, the reliefs of the Life of the Virgin follow Augsburg models in the late 'soft style', whereas the attendant figures in the Crucifixion are already severely linear in outline. From about 1440 until after 1460 a carver was active at Salzburg in whose works, as far as they still exist (e.g. fragments of altars given to the church of St Leonhard at Tamsweg and to Salzburg

Cathedral by Burkard von Weisspriach), we can see the gradual sloughing off of weight and amplitude, the elongating of the proportions of the figures, and the increasing importance of the new linear articulation.[34] The slender Virgin from St Severin at Passau is stylistically akin to these works and is of outstanding quality.[35] A new block-like character is achieved by a tautening of the surface; the drapery lies in small, broken folds, but the facial features have something reminiscent of the sublimity of the Fair Virgins.

As a further example of the way one generation merges into the next I would quote the remodelling of the triptych from the abbey of Viktring (Carinthia),[36] now in St Stephen in Vienna. This was undertaken under the auspices of the Emperor Frederick III. The reliefs on the wings of the Adoration of the Child and the Death of the Virgin were added at this time – sculptural compositions which are full of movement and in whose freshness we may sense the sculptor's discovery of the new naturalism.

The most important Viennese master at this time was Jakob Kaschauer, whose records prove him to have lived from 1429 to 1463. Masons by the name of Kaschauer are repeatedly mentioned in the records of the lodge of St Stephen in Vienna. Perhaps Jakob Kaschauer was a member of one such family. (The lodge of St Elisabeth at Kaschau was closely associated with that of St Stephen in Vienna.) At the instance of Bishop Nicodemus della Scala of Freising, Jacob Kaschauer executed as 'pictor' the high altar for the cathedral of Freising, and this was dedicated in 1443.[37] From the shrine of this altar the central figure of the Virgin (Plate 88), the side figure of St Corbinianus, and the small figure of the donor still survive in the Bayerisches Nationalmuseum in Munich; a fragment of the other side figure, a St Sigismund, is in the Württembergisches Landesmuseum at Stuttgart. Kaschauer was no doubt a wood carver as well as a 'pictor', like Multscher. The Freising figures have an almost Baroque closeness of movement which runs rocking over the surface. The Child is no longer held up by the Virgin for the gaze of the spectator, but appears to be making a wayward gesture to grasp the drooping corner of the Virgin's kerchief, an anecdotal feature which provides an optical link with the donor kneeling at the Virgin's feet. Their three-dimensional weight is what dominates in these figures. A richly apparelled (somewhat cruder) figure of the enthroned St Peter in the Österreichische Galerie in Vienna resembles them in this, and so too does the (perhaps slightly earlier) group of St Anne with the Virgin and Child on the high altar of the pilgrimage church of Annaberg near St Pölten, a piece spreading far out.[38]

I do not think that Jakob Kaschauer the painter can be identified with the master of the painted Altar of the Virgin commissioned by Albrecht II, duke of Austria, for the Carmelite church in Vienna and now in the Stiftsmuseum at Klosterneuburg. The style of painting in this work presupposes contacts with Netherlandish art, whereas in the sculpture we have mentioned one has a strong sense of an indigenous rejuvenation which is not an adaptation of Netherlandish prototypes – though perhaps the sign of an affinity with contemporary works of painting.

Perhaps at this stage the intentions of the painters did indeed exercise a formative power on the style of sculpture altogether. This seems to be the case for example in the Altar of the Crucifixion from St Wenceslas at Znojmo (Znaim) in Moravia, now in the Österreichische Galerie in Vienna,[39] which strikes one as particularly massive. Its shrine, which is stepped at the top in the Netherlandish style, and its wings are filled with intertwining, closely packed reliefs of the Passion. The Austrian master of this altar employed similar models to those used by the painter active in Munich about 1440, who was responsible for the panels of the Passion at Tegernsee.[40] The stage-like space in these Tegernsee panels, which is derived from Netherlandish sources, is supplanted in the Znaim reliefs by the violent projection of the action into the forefront. This gives rise to a sculptural power which is almost bizarre – an anticipation of the Danube style of the mid fifteenth century. The Znaim altar by this rather naïve master is a parallel to Kaschauer's altar of Freising, in so far as the use of volume in both works is essentially opposed to Multscher's conception of art.[41]

In addition, there is a further highly individual work in the court style of the period: the sandstone figure of Duke Frederick V of Styria in the central niche of a fine heraldic wall (dating from 1453) on the front of the church of St Georg at Wiener Neustadt (Plate 89B).[42] This Frederick was crowned emperor in 1452, i.e. became the Emperor Frederick III. Consequently the statue, which shows him wearing his Styrian duke's hat – at least in its design – must be of earlier date. The abstract autonomy of the figure is astonishing. Sheet armour and cloak do not bring about that contrasting tension between core and envelope which is usually an essential feature of Late Gothic sculpture, but they are here homogeneous component parts of one organically constructed form. In this figure and the surrounding heraldic wall I can see no borrowings from Multscher or from Italian sculpture. It appears to use the finest flowering of that courtly and heraldic funerary sculpture which was so much cultivated in Austria in the first half of the fifteenth century. The figure of the Virgin, which stands in a shallow niche in the gable of this heraldic wall and which has flanking figures on either side, is still reminiscent of Kaschauer's type of Virgin, but it translates the bulging breadth and depth of Kaschauer's figures so completely into the new linear style that a remarkable similarity – missing in Kaschauer – to contemporary Netherlandish sculpture, the sculpture of Utrecht especially, and to their derivatives is discernible.[43]

In Bohemian sculpture the types to which the masterpieces of about 1450 belonged remained valid down to the middle of the century.[44] Proof of this are the so-called Steinerne Jungfrau, the bust of a woman with a wreath of glorious curls, the sign of a house in the Altstadt of Prague (now Muzseum mešta Prahy, Prague), and even more the splendid wooden angel bracket in the Altstadt Town Hall. These are pieces in which the so-called 'Soft Style' is translated into a close, heraldically rigid idiom. They must indeed be as late as *c.* 1450-60. The crisis of this tradition occurs only later, by the entry of completely new, younger masters coming possibly from Franconia. The result is a linear style whose most monumental example is the Crucifixion in St Bartholomew at Plzeň (Pilsen).

Italian sculptors too were active at this time at the courts of Budapest and Cracow. Perhaps the most striking example of their influence is the red marble monument (standing free under a canopy restored during the Renaissance) of the Polish King

Vladislav II Jagiello (d. 1434) in the Cathedral on the Wawel in Cracow (Plate 82B).[45] Each of the long sides of the tomb-chest is divided into three panels of relief, and in each of them two representatives of one of the lands united under the crown of Vladislav sit holding his scutcheon. These figures at the same time fulfil the role of *pleureurs*. The relief panels are gently hollowed out. Most striking is the stylization of the recumbent effigy of the king on the tomb lid: a relief without any restricting border. The features of the deceased are uncannily striking – almost as if done from a death mask. The figure is rigid. Apparel and royal insignia are rendered with harsh realism. This realism is continued in the sharply chiselled beasts on the projecting base of the tomb, hunting dogs and also falcons, allusions to the royal chase. Is there not a contact here between the types and emblems of Franco–Netherlandish court art and impressions of the Italian Early Renaissance?

CHAPTER 6

THE ACTIVITY OF NICOLAUS GERHAERTS AND THE SCULPTURE OF HIS TIME IN THE NETHERLANDS AND FRANCE

IF I venture to place at the head of this chapter the name of one artist – that of Nicolaus Gerhaerts of Leyden – my reason is that he is the outstanding exponent of the movement which, at the beginning of the second half of the fifteenth century, opened up fundamentally new possibilities of expression to sculpture north of the Alps. We have already discussed the formative influence on sculpture which radiated – directly or indirectly – from Netherlandish painting, especially from that of Roger van der Weyden. Robert Campin and Jan van Eyck were also associated with sculptural commissions. We have always to bear in mind that the widespread devastation has had its greatest effect upon sculpture, and that this is why it must seem to us as though continuity of development exists more in the parallel field of painting.

Nicolaus Gerhaerts' work reveals most clearly that new inner dynamism in sculpture which became one of the decisive features of the stylistic development during the second half of the century. I shall be able a little later to show that this dynamism is not a characteristic only of German sculpture at this time. Similar tendencies were active also in France. The fact that Nicolaus Gerhaerts as well as Sluter was of Dutch origin tempts us into a look back from the one to the other. But I could not have put Sluter's name in the same symbolic way over the chapter on Central European sculpture about 1400, because in the fourteenth century, in spite of many points of contact, the development of monumental sculpture in the west (Beauneveu) was very different from that in the sculptors' lodges in the German lands (Parler). This fact is best demonstrated if we set Sluter's majestic Madonna from the *trumeau* of the Chartreuse of Champmol against the introspective, lyrical beauty of the Krumau Virgin (Plates 2B and 39).

But by the middle of the fifteenth century among the progressive talents there existed a greater assimilation of style. The common bond between the arts of Northern Europe, which reaches its apogee in the powerful gesture of the French panel painting of the Pietà from Villeneuve-lès-Avignon in the Louvre (*c.*1455), is at this point all the more evident, since in both sculpture and painting later in the century the regionalism of local schools once again predominates. In 1442–50 Roger van der Weyden painted his Altar of the Last Judgement with its inexorable clarity of presentation which was given by Chancellor Nicolas Rolin to the Hospital at Beaune.

When we ascribe such importance to the name of Nicolaus Gerhaerts, the hazards of what has been preserved and handed down to us may well play a part in our judgement. And, since so much has been destroyed, it is not possible, either, to trace the origins of Nicolaus Gerhaerts' work in his Netherlandish home district. We can only assume that there existed parallel phenomena, even if we may now only guess at them. In any case, in the context of the sculpture which still exists from this period, Gerhaerts marks more clearly than anyone else the decisive turning point to the dynamic Late Gothic of the second half of the century. The degree of regional variation within North European sculpture at the end of the fifteenth century makes it all the more necessary to stress the fundamental significance and the collective character of the most out-standing creations of the years round 1460–70.

The profound significance of the old European 'Middle Kingdom' in which the art of Nicolaus of Verdun was rooted, is visible in the stages of Nicolaus Gerhaerts' career. One notes his ancestry as 'nicola gerardi' or 'Gerhaert soen' from Leyden in Holland,[1] and recalls that Sluter was a native of Haarlem. Before critics came slowly to the con-clusion that these places of birth were inexorable facts, the opinion was held that the North Netherlands were certainly one of the places of origin of modern painting, but that they were not predestined for sculpture. One cause of this erroneous judgement lay in the extent of the destruction of sculptural monuments in the Netherlands. I consider it therefore expedient to give an account of the works of Nicolaus Gerhaerts that survive in Germany[2] before examining the few contemporary objects and frag-ments that remain in the Netherlands and France.

The earliest work of his that remains, authenticated by his signature, is the lid, dated 1462, on the tomb-chest of Archbishop Jacob von Sierck at Trier (formerly in the Liebfrauenkirche; now in the Bischöfliches Museum; Plate 91). The tomb was of the two-tiered type frequently used in France, with the lower lid presenting the decaying corpse of the deceased and the upper his effigy. The upper lid is all that survives, and the figure is in very high relief, almost detached, with undercutting of such depth that a rich interplay of light and shade is brought about. Suggestive realism, as for example in the rendering of the pontifical robes, whose flow is broken by the recumbent position and the gesture of prayer, goes hand in hand with an idealization of facial features which is reminiscent of traditions of the earlier years of the fifteenth century.

Then there follow the Strasbourg works of 1463–7 with their excitingly novel themes: the demi-figures of the monument set in a niche to Canon Conrad von Busnang (signed and dated 1464; Plate 90A) in the minster, which is an astonishingly realistic 'ex-voto' figure, the same motif to which Jan van Eyck gave such monumental sig-nificance in his portrait of Canon van der Paele (1436); then the busts, unfortunately only in fragmentary form, in the Musée de l'Œuvre Notre Dame in Strasbourg, and in the Städtische Skulpturengalerie at Frankfurt, of Count Jakob von Hanau-Lichtenberg and of the so-called Bärbel von Ottenheim (Plate 92), both made in 1464 for the portal of the Neue Kanzlei in Strasbourg, above which the almost detached demi-figures were fixed with such a degree of realism that one must have felt they were human beings looking out of the window.[3] Further, in the Musée de l'Œuvre Notre-Dame at Strasbourg there is another bust, also originally no doubt in an architectural setting, of a man deep in meditation, where the features are so inexorably realistic that we may safely regard it as a self-portrait (Plate 93); and there is also the strange fragment of the head of a paralytic cripple. This group of the most important of Nicolaus Gerhaerts' works ends with the (signed) over-life-size stone Crucifixus of 1467 in the Old Cemetery at Baden-Baden (Plate 90B).

The group shows Nicolaus Gerhaerts' immense development in the course of five years. His aim is to emancipate and establish the autonomy of the figure, and this aim is fulfilled in the glorification of the body and the spiritualization of the expression in the Crucifixus of 1467. When we consider the head, we are undeniably reminded of Sluter's Christ at Champmol. In any case, the amplitude of the head of the Baden-Baden figure, with its crown of thorns and the soft moulding of the features, is in complete contrast to the linear, abstract, ideal type which is the general presentation of Christ at this time, for example in the works of Roger van der Weyden. We know how much the succeeding generations admired Sluter's Calvary in Dijon; even the soft-modelled features of the busts from the Strasbourg Kanzlei are 'Sluteresque'. In Nicolaus Gerhaerts we are therefore confronted with something astonishingly new: in his work we meet not so much a tradition as an individual's attempt to come to terms with his art, and this, based as it is on an attitude of self-searching and self-recognition, became a symptom of the intellectual freedom of modern art. The sculptural verisimilitude of the busts from the Strasbourg Kanzlei reminds us of the similarly inspired figures above the gateway into the house of Jacques Cœur in Bourges (Plate 100), and certainly the source of these inventions was Netherlandish.

Already in Nicolaus Gerhaerts' earliest known work, the monument at Trier, the main impression is of a personal approach to art. The increased feeling of volume, the way the figure stands out from the lid, the deep furrowing of the surface in order to render the pontifical robes halted in their flow is tremendous. The monument to Elizabeth, daughter of Duke Johann III of Straubing-Holland, in the Dreifaltigkeitskirche at Trier[4] presents a more difficult problem: here we have a spatially magnificently conceived relief of an angel (with immense pinions) bearing a shield, and below it an elegantly stylized scroll held by angels (Plate 116A). Everything is Gerhaertesque here, but not so austere and pregnant as in his authenticated works. Is it possible that Gerhaerts made a design which a Trier master then executed? But then our main question is one of date. Elizabeth died without issue in 1451. With the death of Duke Johann in 1425 the Wittelsbach line in Holland died out. It is therefore not very likely that the relief in the church of the Minorites at Trier, where Elizabeth was buried, would date from ten years after her death, and, in order to give Nicolaus Gerhaerts any part in this memorial, we would have to assume that he was active at Trier before 1462. Archbishop Jacob of Sierck died in 1456; perhaps Gerhaerts began his work on this monument as early as that.

In the twisted contours of the presumed self-portrait of Nicolaus leaning, brooding, over a parapet, the dynamism of the organic form has become a completely new sculptural experience (Plate 93). Neither Netherlandish nor French sculpture of the time can offer, as far as I can see, any parallel. Moreover, nothing previously had attained that deepening of the anecdotal quality through an almost daemonic element which constitutes the character of the busts from the Kanzlei, together with all the enigmas of their interpretation. And the terrifying realism in the features of the Cripple opens up a vista on to Leonardo's physiognomical studies.

Nicolaus had been active at Strasbourg from 1463 onwards. In the same year he received an invitation to Vienna from the Emperor Frederick III to enter his service. But he did not comply until he was summoned a second time in 1467 to 'carve some monuments'.[5] His fame lay then in his stone carving. All the more galling is it that, owing to the loss of the wood-carved high altar of Constance Minster, done by Nicolaus in 1465/6, we are deprived of the opportunity of forming an idea of his talent in wood.[6]

The migration to Vienna completes the arc of Nicolaus's career from the extreme north-west of the Reich to its Eastern limit. Vienna and Wiener Neustadt, where he now set up his workshop, had become bastions against the Turkish menace. The emperor's great commission was for his own ceremonial monument in red Salzburg marble, as we now have it in the Apostles' Choir in St Stephen in Vienna (Plate 95A). When Nicolaus died in 1473, the lid with the effigy of the emperor must certainly have been completed; the majestic figure of the emperor, rising from the shadowy depths of the deeply undercut relief, arrayed in all the insignia of his rank, surrounded by the highest heraldic emblems, is a work of the greatest austerity of composition and of the maximum subtlety in the animation of the surface. Work on the monument began already in 1469,[7] and by then the general design must have been clear. Only seven years had elapsed since the completion of the bishop's monument at Trier, but what a transformation had taken place in Nicolaus's mastery of the sculptural form, through the gathering of all the stresses into a new monumentality. The pillar-like stone figure of a Virgin (Hamburg, Museum für Kunst und Gewerbe) seems also to have been made in Vienna; this figure too reminds one of Sluter, but at the same time it proclaims a new discipline.[8]

Before trying to show the manifold influences of Nicolaus Gerhaerts' work on German sculpture in the 1460s, and the nature of contemporary work by other masters in Germany, it may be important for an understanding of the situation of European art at this juncture to point out the western ingredients in Nicolaus's early work.

The search must start among works in Nicolaus's Dutch homeland. Here it is the episcopal town of Utrecht which at this time possessed more than any other place a character of its own and which exercised a formative influence on sculptural activity. The monumental sculpture still in existence in Utrecht is, however, only an echo of what was. Not even the evocative force of the equestrian sandstone figure of St Michael with four statues of patrons (Plate 96A) on each side, originally in Utrecht Cathedral (now Centraal Museum), which dates from c. 1455–60, can leave us in any doubt about this.[9] The mural tablets at Utrecht[10] are merely a faint shadow of more significant works no longer in existence. Nevertheless, inside the striking frames of these tablets under their basket arches there is a 'painterly' atmosphere in the relief which later comes to full effect in Nicolaus's sculpture. A sensitivity of touch comparable to Nicolaus's can perhaps be discerned in the pronounced naturalism of the effigy of the cathedral prebendary Dirk van Wassenaar (d. c. 1465) in St Jan at Utrecht,[11] but it lacks the mark of Nicolaus's genius.

The only monumental figure in the austere 'statuesque' style which is akin to the works I have mentioned from Utrecht, which is also no doubt of North Netherlandish extraction and which dates from about 1460, is the St Bavo in the Metropolitan Museum in New York (Plate 96B),[12] but its similarity to Nicolaus's style is superficial. The figure lacks the inner movement which in Gerhaerts' works expresses itself so essentially in the writhing of the form and which expands into the surrounding space.

I see the essential character of Dutch sculpture in the years from 1450 to 1460 expressed most vividly in an oak figure of the Virgin from Ijsselstein, now in the C. van Straaten Collection at Utrecht.[13] Here in a closely compact form a charming fusion of tension and naturalness is achieved. I would also assume that the large ivory Madonna[14] in the parish church of Colleville (Seine-Inférieure) is of Netherlandish origin. This figure seems to me to be the probably Netherlandish prototype of the monumental (Erfurt?) alabaster Virgin in the Städtische Skulpturengalerie at Frankfurt.[15] Utrecht was no doubt also the source of the large stone Virgin in St Columba in Cologne,[16] and it was the source too on which the master of the monumental stone Virgins in Lübeck Cathedral and in the Petrikirche at Hamburg drew. I shall have to show later how this sculptural activity continued in the following decade in the Northern Netherlands. But it always remains a style lacking the special spatial expansion which Nicolaus's genius developed in his work.

The Southern Netherlands can throw some light on the genesis of his style. There is in the Musées Royaux in Brussels a figure of St Adrian (from the Vermeerch Collection; Plate 95B) which has been ascribed to him,[17] but which is so relaxed and so far removed from any hard sculptural severity that it cannot possibly be an early work of Nicolaus's, that is to say, not from the period before the Trier monument. But we should be wrong if we failed to see how Gerhaertesque is the style of this South Netherlandish figure, and how much similarity it shows to the stone sculpture at Trier by Nicolaus's successors. So I think that we certainly have here an important testimony to the part the South Netherlands played in the development of Nicolaus's style.[18] Alongside the St Adrian we should place as an example of the stone sculpture of Brabant the magnificent figure of the Angel of the Annunciation in the Louvre.[19]

There is no connecting link, either, between the South Netherlandish bronze sculpture from Jacques de Gérines's foundry and Nicolaus Gerhaerts' statues which appear to reach out into the space around them. And when we compare the bronze effigy of Isabella of Bourbon on her monument at Antwerp with the monument of Frederick III in Vienna, we see how tradition-bound, in spite of an undeniable developmental affinity, is the effigy at Antwerp, and how boldly 'modern' are the works of Nicolaus, which are in fact ten years older. In the same way the reliquary group of Charles the Bold, made by the goldsmith Gérard Loyet of Lille in 1467, with its charming figure of St George (Liège, St Paul, treasury)[20] remains confined within the courtly elegance and quiet delicacy of a ceremonial style.

I know of only one solitary work, probably of South Netherlandish provenance (and characteristically small in size), in whose picturesque richness and restrained pathos we may sense those impulses of sensitive movement which are so vital to the 'dynamism' of the earliest works known to us of Nicolaus Gerhaerts: this is the alabaster Pietà from Salamanca in the collection of R. Koeber at Hamburg.[21] It again sheds light on the continuous contacts between the Netherlands and Burgundy, since it is closely affiliated to the somewhat cruder 'Vierge de Pitié' in the chapel of the Château of Epoisses (Côte d'Or). The close links between the *inventio* of the alabaster Pietà and Roger van der Weyden give us, I think, a hint of where we should seek the roots of Nicolaus Gerhaerts' style. Here once more we get some idea of the imaginative power of what has been lost and so, in my opinion, it must be assumed that the revolutionary significance of Netherlandish painting of this time was equalled by that of sculptural work. But too much has been destroyed to enable us to show Netherlandish sources for Nicolaus's art, and it is therefore useless to attempt to identify him with a Brussels Master called Nikolaus, mentioned in records of Tongerlo in 1436, or with a Nikolas de Brune, active in St Pierre at Louvain (Leuven) in 1441.[22]

Can sculpture from France help us in our attempt to explain the basic premises and the effects of Nicolaus Gerhaerts' art? In general French sculpture from the mid-century onwards is dominated by traditional types of representation, and as yet no works are known which would embody the impulses towards three-dimensional expansion that we see in Nicolaus Gerhaerts. There is generally an increasing emphasis on line. Characteristic North French examples of this emphasis are the monument to Jean de Frétin (d. 1459) in the museum at Douai and the stone Virgin from St Sauveur at Lille, now in the museum there. Nevertheless there are in France some decisive achievements of the same tendency as Nicolaus's, and they are all the more striking because they sound a very personal note. To be sure, on account of the number of works destroyed, any attempt to gain an idea of French monumental sculpture after the mid-century is once again confined to heterogeneous statues and to fragments which have remained *in situ*. Some of these statues possess indeed that peculiar autonomy of volume which can be regarded as a parallel to Nicolaus Gerhaerts' art. The slightly older architectural sculpture on the house of Jacques Cœur at Bourges, with its high degree of illusionism, had already testified to the new dynamism.

The new passion, probably emanating from Netherlandish sculpture, for conveying transitory movement reaches a climax in the fragments preserved in the museum at Troyes, taken from the Franciscan library there.[23] Special mention must be made of a corbel with a radiantly beautiful curly-headed youth sitting with one leg across the other, surrounded by broad, lobate, sharply serrated Late Gothic foliage. Here we have the same interweaving of the buoyant human figure with its surroundings that we meet in Nicolaus Gerhaerts' works. This corbel, incidentally, bears the inscription 'Jubert', which may well be a signature, since there was a sculptor of that name at Troyes in the early sixteenth century, with the Christian name of Jacques.

Affiliated to this corbel at Troyes is the beautifully preserved stone figure of St Barbara in the Metropolitan Museum in New York (Plate 102B).[24] Unfortunately its provenance is not known, but it is, I think, typically South Netherlandish,[25] though translated into the different sculptural language which is generally that of France. Even the detailed rendering of the dress is French. I would suggest that it is North French and date it *c.* 1460–70. In its surface, which shows great beauty of movement, we sense most keenly the stresses of contrast which, after the mid-century, became in Netherlandish sculpture synonymous with sculptural dynamism.

Of Burgundian works of the mid-century mention should be made firstly of the monumental stone figure of the pilgrim St James from Semur-en-Auxois (Côte d'Or), now in the Louvre (Plate 101A).[26] This figure is extremely impressive by reason of the violence of its deep articulation of the massive block and the sharpness in the drawing of the features. Two angels in flight, also from Semur and now in the Louvre,[27] are similar in tone and perhaps were part of an Entombment formerly in the Carmelite house at Semur. They are only a little later, but already there is a hardening of the linear features of the kind we know from Netherlandish art. One is reminded of the stylization of the charming angels on the limestone relief of a Virgin in the Rose Bower (Berlin, Staatliche Museen; Plate 94B)[28] which, in spite of its Netherlandish echoes, is probably French and whose lyrical charm of expression corresponds to the gracious beauty of the St Barbara in the Metropolitan Museum.

The sculptural decoration of the Chapelle de Bourbon at Cluny,[29] undertaken at the instance of Jean de Bourbon around 1465–70, is still rooted in the Burgundian tradition of Antoine Le Moiturier. Unfortunately only the prophet corbels in the chapel are still in existence (Plate 99); originally there were also figures of the Virgin, St John the Baptist, and the Apostles. When we observe the volume with which these closely set corbels emerge from the wall, we realize that the displacement of space in the original sculptural decoration was something completely novel. The precision of these corbels conveys the impression of a vehement force striving to burst its bonds.

This naturalism is translated into an abstract monumentality in the immensely expressive male head from Châlons-sur-Marne now in the Louvre,[30] to which five equally striking fragments of heads, still in Notre-Dame-en-Vaux, are related (Plate 98, A and B). The features are sharply chiselled, lending the maximum individualization to these reflective, tense faces which present an extraordinary feeling of spatial depth. Probably these are fragments from a monumental Entombment. If so, they are a parallel to the figures of the Tonnerre Entombment, though they lack the calligraphic features and the stiff rigidity of the latter and approximate more closely to the intellectual climate of Nicolaus Gerhaerts' early works, even if they betray nothing of his gift for free self-expression. However, in the treatment of the surface the same methods have been employed as were used by Nicolaus.

Apropos the elements of Burgundian tradition which dominate in the corbels at Cluny, I must mention a fragment of a St Christopher in the museum of St Louis (Missouri) which is supposed to come from Dijon and is of slightly later date (Plate 97A). The head bears a fillet and the face is framed with wisps of hair which merge into a thick beard. All the features in the face are permeated with an objectivity closely akin to that of Nicolaus Gerhaerts' work, and they reveal a similar intensity of creative power. The similarity springs more from the spirit than the technique.

I should like to add also the fragment of a man's tonsured head with eyes almost closed, in the Metropolitan Museum in New York (Plate 97B). This is no doubt the head of the effigy of a priest or friar, taken from his monument.[31] The spiritualized features are of an almost uncanny realism, both noble and majestic. The cheeks are deeply furrowed; veins stand out on the temples. Once again there is a striking likeness to Nicolaus's works, for example to his 'Thinker' at Strasbourg. On the other hand, there is also a similarity to the pronounced characterization in the painted portraits[32] of the so-called Master of 1456. Even though in this and in the other works mentioned we are dealing with examples chosen more or less at random, it is nevertheless evident how deeply involved the French sculpture of this time was in that new spiritual analysis which is so strikingly visible in Nicolaus Gerhaerts' works.

Further, there is the stone figure of Nicodemus, unfortunately badly damaged, from an Entombment, also in the Metropolitan Museum in New York (Plate 102A).[33] This is an impressive figure whose striking naturalism is of a definitely bourgeois character. This distinguishes it from the series extending to and including the Entombment at Tonnerre, whose character is still determined by Burgundian feudalism. On the other hand, the Nicodemus is not yet dominated by the linear stylization typical of the second half of the century. In this triumphant presentation of human physique and in its emphasis on volume, I see certain parallels to portraits by Jean Fouquet of the years 1450–60 and also to the solidity and poignancy of his Pietà at Nouans. In the first half of the century such impressive naturalism is perhaps met only once – in the large seated portrait figure in the Musée de l'Œuvre Notre-Dame at Strasbourg. At the same time the Nicodemus seems to me to be pre-eminently French, comparable in physiognomy to the St James from Semur-en-Auxois in the Louvre, or to the figures from the Tudot Collection in the museum at Moulins. There can, however, be no doubt that the pedigree of the Nicodemus goes back to the Netherlands. We have only to remember Roger van der Weyden's Nicodemus of his Descent from the Cross from the Escorial.

It is important at this point to stress the fact that in French sculpture, after the midcentury is passed, regional character makes itself more strongly felt. From this point of view, the cycle of figures in the Sainte Chapelle in the castle of Châteaudun (Eure-et-Loire) seems to me to be typical.[34] These figures were commissioned by Jean d'Orléans, Vicomte de Dunois and Comte de Châteaudun, and the chapel was consecrated in 1464. As I have already pointed out, from this series of fifteen figures, we can assume that the Virgin is of somewhat earlier date. The remaining figures of patrons (Plate 101B), together with the statue of the lord of the castle, are of a uniform character, tall and towering, their drapery keeping close to their sides, so that they give the impression of an unbroken block. The folds and hems of the garments follow, like lines, along a flowing, winding course. Head and features are firmly and clearly formed. There is no trace of any splitting up of the block into deeply undercut, shadow-filled grooves, which was to become an increasing tendency in German sculpture from now on. The serene beauty of the Châteaudun figures will have to compensate us for all that we have lost.

The destruction has been greatest among altar sculpture and carved wooden statues. The most important examples that remain are two walnut attendant figures from a Crucifixion: the mourning figure of St John from the abbey church of Beaugerais (Indre-et-Loire) in the Louvre (Plate 103A), and the lamenting Virgin in the Metropolitan Museum of Art in New York.[35] These are generously proportioned figures with strongly marked, precise articulation of surface, and with deep sincerity of feeling.

In their monumental humanization they are akin to the painted prophets by the Master of the Aix Annunciation (dating from soon after 1442). The mood of these wooden figures is continued in the more slender and delicate, also wooden, figure of a mourning Virgin in the Musée des Antiquités at Tours.[36] The stone retable made at the instance of Archbishop Jean de Bernard of Tours between 1455 and 1464 and erected in the chapel of the archiepiscopal palace of Tours at Vernou (Loir-et-Cher) bears a close resemblance to this figure by virtue of its restraint and quiet solemnity of expression.[37] Is the tripartite composition of the relief reminiscent of painted or carved triptychs? In the central panel is a harmonious image of the Pietà with the *arma Christi*, and kneeling in prayer on either side are the donor and his nephew. A similar serenity and harmony of form is to be found in the effigy of Jeanne de Montejeau (d. before 1456) from Bueil (Indre-et-Loire).[38]

Echoes of Jean Fouquet confirm the opinion that we are here dealing with works which can give us an idea of the peculiar character of Touraine. Similar in type and stylistically akin are the sculptural unity and animation in the figure of a Virgin in the church of L'Hôpital-sous-Rochefort (Loire).[39] The bronze reliquary head of St Fortunade in the treasury of the church of that name in Corrèze doubtless belongs to the same orbit (Plate 103B). This is a work of the greatest sculptural power, revealing the features of the human face with a tautness which is both charming and clear.[40] Again we are reminded of Jean Fouquet, and in particular of the poignant immediacy of the Virgin of Melun.

At the end of this chapter I want to place a particularly magnificent wood carving, certainly of slightly older date, which by virtue of its incomparable mastery will serve to reveal the strength of tradition and also, though in a new style, to arouse memories of Sluter. It is the walnut mourning Virgin from a Crucifixion in the Staatliche Museen in Berlin (Plate 104A).[41] The motif of this figure, as also that of less good figures of the type, links up with Sluter's Dolorosa in the Crucifixion group from the Chartreuse at Champmol, and yet from the same formula a completely new image has emerged, as austere and as expressive as the Pietà of Villeneuve-lès-Avignon. This Dolorosa in Berlin has been declared to be a South Netherlandish piece, a judgement rightly based on the feeling that it is in the Southern Netherlands that one can most readily assume these particular conventions of style. However, as far as I can see, there are no comparable works to be found there. So we are left with the supposition on the one hand that the wood-carvings from Touraine and the statues from Châteaudun are of later date, and on the other, that the translation of Sluter's art into the language of the younger generation bore no connexion with the style of Roger van der Weyden (i.e. Tournai). May not this therefore be a last flicker of the Burgundian style?

CHAPTER 7

THE NETHERLANDS: 1460–90

WE open our survey of North Netherlandish sculpture after the middle of the fifteenth century – and it is from this time onwards that there is a general increase in the number of examples that still survive – with the monumental carved figure of a gigantic St Christopher from Oud-Zevenaar in the Archiepiscopal Museum in Utrecht.[1] This figure demonstrates how at this stage of sculptural development a feeling for the structure of the human form claimed precedence over a regard for conventional beauty. It is also the most eloquent proclamation of a new pictorial realism in sculpture. This work is followed by two groups of figures whose style is of significance but in which the possibilities of expression are not quite equal to their task, and which must therefore no doubt have been influenced by works of higher quality no longer in existence. The first of these works is the relief of oak representing the Adoration of the Magi and preserved in the Episcopal Museum in Haarlem.[2] This was copied in one of the limewood side reliefs of the high altar in the Chartreuse in Strasbourg (c. 1470).[3] In Strasbourg too are the corresponding side reliefs of the Birth and Circumcision of Christ. We may presuppose Netherlandish models in the style of the Haarlem relief for these two also. But the influence of the Haarlem master can hardly have radiated thus far. It is more likely that the Haarlem relief itself was influenced by a more important North Netherlandish piece of c. 1450–60, presenting scenes from the Life of the Virgin in cyclical form, which were then copied – in France too, as is proved for example by the relief of an Adoration in the church of Vert-St-Denis (Seine-et-Marne). These scenes at the same time found a strong echo, either directly or indirectly, in engravings (for example in those of the Master E.S.), which in their turn served as models for sculpture. The feeling of concentrated strength and clearly articulated composition which is discernible in the Haarlem relief may be regarded as typical of the style of these assumed originals.

A decisive step leads onward from the Haarlem relief to the oak groups of the meeting of Joachim and Anna (Amsterdam, Rijksmuseum; Plate 105B) and of the Birth of the Virgin (Berlin, Staatliche Museen),[4] both works, no doubt, of 1460/70. They are highly evocative through their urgent austerity, poignant in their sensitive rendering of content, permeated with the strongest inner movement, striking in both outline and internal articulation, and at the same time achieve the maximum of effect through severity of composition and delicate treatment of surface. They provide us with our strongest argument in support of the claim, which is so often and so wrongly denied, that Dutch sculpture at this time held parity with the contemporary masterpieces of Dutch painting.

The other relatively early group of works (i.e. of 1455/60) is the stone statues from the cathedral of Utrecht at the centre of which is an equestrian figure of St Martin.[5] There is an archaic breadth about these figures, noticeable especially in that of St Paul.

Decades later the type of composition of the St Martin was still repeated.[6] Thus we may assume that the composition of the whole Utrecht group was derived from a pre-existing formal convention.[7] The important point is that in this case a definite locality is clearly discernible, i.e. Utrecht. In the field of applied art there is much evidence to prove that Utrecht sculpture, at any rate from the mid-century onwards, exercised a formative influence. It is worth remembering in this context the reliefs in pipe-clay which are typical of Utrecht[8] and the sculpture on the choir stalls in the Vrouwenkerk in Breda (after 1468), where the Utrecht style springs from a tradition which can be traced back unbroken to the earliest parts (e.g. the relief of St Dymphna) in the choir stalls of the cathedral of St Jan in 's-Hertogenbosch (Bois-le-Duc) of after 1427.[9]

Then in 1470 a radical tautening of the figure and a linear abstraction of surface appears in the oak figures of the Master of Coudewater Abbey (near 's-Hertogenbosch) in the Rijksmuseum in Amsterdam.[10] These figures are almost rigid in their block-like character and yet at the same time they are graceful, and, especially from the point of view of physiognomy, full of charm. This style blossoms out into a radiant vividness in the noble oak Virgin in the Louvre and in the charming St Ursula in the chapel of the Begijnhof in Amsterdam.[11] Deep undercutting reveals a strong feeling for the spatial values of sculpture, and the sharpness of the linework brings about an almost metallic precision of form. We also have to remember that originally colour added to the effectiveness of such figures. The characteristics which have just been emphasized are all general features of sculpture at this time, but, as far as we can see, nowhere else are they combined with such a sense of clarity as we find in the Northern Netherlands. It is still not possible in the sphere of sculpture to differentiate localities and masters in the way we are able to do in painting. But the degree of individual variation within Late Gothic Dutch sculpture is yet apparent when we observe the subtle differences between the oak Madonna from the collection of J. Böhler in Munich[12] and the examples I have discussed. Did this figure have its birth-place in a border district near the South Netherlands?

The most striking example of this clarity of sculptural structure is the painted reproduction of an altar group showing the sacrifice of Abraham on a panel painting of the Holy Family by Geertgen tot St Jans in the Rijksmuseum in Amsterdam (Plate 105A).[13] This is the most suggestive evocation of North Netherlandish sculpture and the most beautiful example of the feeling that then prevailed for spatial effect.

The outstanding importance of Utrecht is also revealed by the fact that here for once a master is known by his name, one whose influence reached far beyond Utrecht itself and of whom we have documentary evidence from 1447 until after 1499 or 1500. He is Adriaen van Wesel. His main work was the Altar of the Virgin which he executed in 1475–7 at the instance of the Fraternity of the Virgin Mary of 's-Hertogenbosch for their chapel in St Jan there. Parts were later found at 's-Hertogenbosch, in the Rijksmuseum in Amsterdam, and in private collections.[14] Between 1488 and 1489 Hieronymus Bosch painted the wings of this altar. The two wing-reliefs preserved at 's-Hertogenbosch with the representations of the Emperor Augustus and the Tiburtine Sibyl and of St John on Patmos are set in astonishingly deep, architecturally articulated box-like shrines, from the shadowy space of which the groups of figures emerge with tremendous sculptural power. In order to do justice to the full sculptural possibilities of the other statues which belonged to this altar and which are now dispersed, we must always provide them in our imagination with a similar deep shrine. The tripartite group of the Adoration of the Magi, with angels playing various musical instruments, shows the astonishing intensity of expression achieved. It represents at one and the same time the fulfilment of a great tradition and the liberation of sculpture from the conditions of painting. The block-like nature of the reliefs and the basic features of the composition serve to show the North Netherlandish affinity between the works of Adriaen van Wesel and those of the master of the (slightly older) group of Joachim and Anna and of the master of the St Ursula in the Begijnhof in Amsterdam. But the works of Adriaen van Wesel gain their effect not by virtue of the wealth of their abstract contours, but through the fine balance of their volumes. A delicate feeling for form and for scenic action in space distinguishes this master, shown most effectively in the psychological subtleties in the Virgins (private collections at Valenciennes and at Forest (Vorst) near Brussels) and in the group of angels with musical instruments (Amsterdam, Rijksmuseum; Plate 108) from which the name of the sculptor was taken before he was identified as Adriaen van Wesel. Documentary evidence conveys the impression that he was the most important exponent of North Netherlandish sculpture in the late fifteenth century. In 1480 he was responsible for three statues for the high altar of Utrecht Cathedral; between 1484 and 1486 he was engaged on the high altar for the Nieuwe Kerk in Delft. In 1487 came the commission for the high altar of Agnetenberg Abbey, near Zwolle, followed in 1487-8 by sculpture for the Burkeerk and in 1489 by work for Utrecht Cathedral. I regard the wooden group of the Mourning of Christ in the Staatliche Museen in Berlin as a late work from his hand.[15] Here the restrained lyricism of his earlier style has acquired an almost rhetorical note, which shows clearly the difference in the North Netherlandish style in comparison with the South Netherlandish Entombment formerly in the Arenberg Collection (Plate 110A).

This group of works provides us with a tuning-fork for our analysis of the character of Late Gothic sculpture in the North Netherlands. The difference between it and contemporary Lower Rhenish sculpture is unmistakable but difficult to define. If we place alongside the works by Adriaen van Wesel the St Lucia and St Oda in the parish church of Venraij and the St Catherine and St Agnes from St Aldegundis at Emmerich (near Cleves, in the Lower Rhineland),[16] the spiritual superiority of Adriaen van Wesel's works, their vividness and formative power, is apparent. While the dignity of the works of the Emmerich master, which are especially outstanding by virtue of the precise expressions of the features and the radiant abundance of the hair that frames them, owes much to immediate contact with Utrecht sculpture, in the beauty of movement of the Venraij figures one may well sense an affinity with Cologne.

At the same time there are individual statues in Holland whose austerity and severity give rise to a remarkably harsh realism of expression. This is seen for example in the four wooden figures of rulers of the past, preserved in the Rijksmuseum in Amsterdam, which come from the old town hall (c. 1475),[17] and in the wooden figures from churches in Gelderland which are permeated with deep religious feeling; further, in two figures of St Roch in the museums of Amsterdam and Utrecht, both dating from *c*. 1480–90, and a Trinity from Baarn in the Archiepiscopal Museum in Utrecht.[18] From the end of the century dates the wooden Pietà from St Nicholas at Eemnes,[19] where naturalism is given a new tectonic monumentality. All these works have in common a great intensity.

Owing to the wealth of material, it is more difficult to appraise the significance of the sculpture of the Southern Netherlands in the second half of the century. Charles the Bold, true to Burgundian tradition, by cutting across the frontiers between the German Empire and France, reunited parts of the former Middle Kingdom. The prince bishops of Liège, Utrecht, and Cambrai were brought under the Burgundian protectorate, and Flanders, Artois, and Picardy were reckoned for a time as Burgundian territory. The hub of this circle lay in the Southern Netherlands. We have already seen what a decisive part for Europe was played by the inventions and traditions emanating from this district. The increasing development of maritime trade now added to the established economic importance of the area. The flourishing of trade resulted in the commercial prosperity of the towns, which in its turn stimulated the arts and crafts, and this accelerated the mass production of works of art.

Regional peculiarities and iconographical traditions now emerged, permitting us to differentiate not merely between Brabant and Flanders, but also between definite types within the ramifications of local workshops, e.g. those of Brussels, Antwerp, Malines, Louvain, and the Pays de Liège.[20] But we are still far from possessing a clear knowledge of the objects in question and of the regional, local, and individual products. As yet too little has been done towards a systematic assembling and examination of the works that survive in the Netherlands and elsewhere, such as was undertaken long ago for corresponding works of painting.

The style of presentation is dominated by the wish for illustrative vividness. This is clear if one looks at the choir stalls in the churches and at the anecdotal treatment of architectural sculpture. The finest examples are the stone reliefs from the old town hall of Brussels, portraying Flemish proverbs, and the corbels in the town hall of Louvain (Leuven; 1448–59). The choir stalls by Philippot Viart in Rouen Cathedral[21] appear to have been particularly rich in sculptural decoration. Flemish sculptors – beginning with Paul Mosselmann from Ypres in 1458 – seem to have been mainly responsible for this. The work was completed in 1469. Only parts of it survived the Revolution, and these are of a strong and concentrated expressive power.

The more wooden altarpieces with many small figures assume primacy in the total production of sculpture, the more vital it is for us to study large individual figures which enable us to judge the monumentality of which South Netherlandish sculpture was all the same capable. The oak figure of a nobleman – perhaps it is St Adrian; it is certainly not, as has been assumed, a portrait of Philippe le Beau – seems to me to be of importance here. (It was originally in a private collection in Lille, and is now in the John Herron Art Institute at Indianapolis, Indiana.)[22] A certain similarity to the wooden St Michael in the museum of Oudenaarde (Audenarde)[23] will help us to determine its possible provenance. It is an abundant figure, and in this it resembles the St Barbara[24] which is slightly older and which passed from Maaseyck into a private collection in Germany. In its statuesque tautness the nobleman from Lille presupposes the linear style of the stone St Adrian in the Musées Royaux in Brussels.[25]

The stylistic similarity between the Virgin from Ijsselstein, almost statuettish in its tautness, and the oak figure of an upright Maria Lactans, now at Oscott College, Sutton Coldfield (probably of Brussels provenance and dating from a decade later), appears to me to shed interesting light on the relationship between the art of the Northern and Southern Netherlands.[26]

Such works as these enable us to form an idea of the background of the bronze effigy of Isabella of Bourbon (d. 1465; Plate 106). This work was originally in the abbey of St Michel and is now in Antwerp Cathedral. Bronze statues were the most monumental achievement of Late Gothic sculpture in the Netherlands, and indeed they represent an achievement which no country other than Italy could rival at this time. We have no Italian prototypes for the life-size bronze statues that the Emperor Maximilian commissioned for his tomb in the Hofkirche in Innsbruck, and it was no doubt his intention to follow the traditions of that Burgundian and Netherlandish court art which in the Late Gothic decades had substituted bronze for marble and alabaster – a reaction at the same time against the increasingly bourgeois character of the widespread wood carving of the time. Bronze – in spite of all that poets may say of its timelessness – is an even more transient medium. Thus very little indeed remains of Late Gothic bronze sculpture in the Netherlands.

The main work surviving is the effigy of Isabella of Bourbon just referred to. It was erected at the instance of her daughter, Mary of Bourbon, in 1476. In all the discussions on the provenance of the smaller bronze figures of members of the family on this tomb (preserved in the Rijksmuseum; Plate 107, A, B, and C),[27] I think we have neglected to emphasize sufficiently what immense power radiates from the effigy itself. This figure combines austerity of structure with a wonderful melodious flow of draperies. The metallic sharpness of accentuation of surface is subordinated to the noble harmony of the majesty of the figure as a whole. Here we have for once a surviving Late Gothic piece of the very highest rank. The striving after the truth of the ideal 'imago' is combined with a splendid amplitude. It is assumed that a model cast by Jacques de Gérines of Brussels was used for the figure. But Jacques de Gérines died in 1463. Was it his successor, Renier van Thienen, known to be active in Brussels between 1465 and 1494, who cast the effigy? We may assume this; Renier van Thienen died before June 1498.

Two sketches[28] in the Kupferstichkabinett in Dresden, one for a double tomb and the other for the tomb of a feudal lord, characterized by two angels holding scutcheons with lozenges, give us an idea of the appearance of the 'patrons' which figure so frequently in the contracts concerning the erection of tombs at this time. We have repeatedly emphasized the great importance attaching to the designs made by influential painters (court painters) in the stylistic development of Late Gothic sculpture. These Dresden drawings show us on the other hand how much the peculiar stylistic character depends in the end exclusively upon the sculptor who carried out the work. The similarity in the sketches between the angels holding the scutcheons and the figures on the sides of the tomb-chests makes it seem unlikely that the effigies were meant to be cast in bronze. It is more probable that we have here 'patrons' of two stone monuments. The style is Netherlandish and approximates most closely to that of the stone St Adrian in the Musées Royaux.

The other work still in existence which enables us to see the importance of South Netherlandish bronze sculpture at this point of development is the Paschal Candelabrum of 1482-3 by Renier van Thienen in St Leonard at Zoutleeuw (Léau). We do not know who was responsible for the model for the founder, but we do know that the founder was commissioned to follow the pattern of a candelabrum in the choir of St Pierre at Louvain. There is no connexion between it and the style of the wooden altarpiece in St Leonard, which is of the same date (Plate 109B). We are also unable to judge whether designs by Aert de Maelder were used. But we may certainly sense that in the expressive gesture of the attendant figures of the Crucifixion from the candelabrum (Plate 107D) there still lingers a distant echo of the deep moral rhetoric that fills the paintings of Roger van der Weyden.[29]

On the other hand, the fifteenth century in the South Netherlands saw the flourishing of wooden altars with painted wings, of individual religious figures, and of small works of sculpture. It is works such as these which demonstrate most clearly the almost incredible extent to which mass-production was carried on. Such works were not produced merely on commission; there was a supply ready to meet the commercial demand. In certain towns it now became usual to mark wares with a sign burnt or stamped on them as proof of their being the carver's good handiwork and as guarantee of the colours used. Such was the case from 1455 in Brussels, from 1471 in Antwerp, and slightly later in Malines. We do not know to what extent this was generally compulsory or under what conditions unmarked statues were produced and supplied. Further – and this too is something new – such stamps were used as the personal seals of individual masters. The number of names and items of which we have documentary evidence proves the extent of the demand and supply of such works.[30] France, Germany, the Scandinavian countries, and Spain were also customers in this trade.

The oldest completely surviving carved altarpieces with wings from the Netherlands are those donated by Philip the Bold to the Chartreuse at Champmol. These were meant to be constructed like altars which the duke had observed in Bijloke Abbey at Ghent and in the church at Dendermonde (Termonde): i.e., they followed an established style. The Hakendover altar was doubtless made in Brussels. The possibilities of stage-like and spatial representation contained in these types of altar are realized in the sculpture of the high altar in the Reinoldikirche at Dortmund (after 1421; Plate 19). The lyrical isolation of two groups side by side in the Dortmund altar is contracted into one common image in the Calvary from the neighbourhood of Angers, now in the Schwartz Collection at Mönchen-Gladbach (c. 1440-50). There is a considerable enrichment in this group by genre accessories. Whether it is a work from the Southern Netherlands exported to France or a French replica is not certain.[31] The altar representing the Death of the Virgin in the church of Ternant near Autun (Nièvre) is an important work, displaying on its painted wings the donor, Philip of Ternant (with the insignia of the Golden Fleece, *c.* 1449), and his wife.[32] The middle part of the centrepiece is much taller than the sides, which became typical of Brussels altarpieces in the second half of the century. A second (slightly later) altar at Ternant, carved in Brabant, has scenes from the Passion reminiscent of Roger van der Weyden.

The altarpiece in the parish church of Rheinberg [33] near Xanten dates from *c.* 1440–50 and was also probably made in Brussels. The same is true of the altarpiece at Grieth near Kalkar, which is slightly later. Both these works are rigid in style, but nevertheless they provide important testimony to the tradition which was obviously developing at this time in altar sculpture from workshops in Brabant and especially in Brussels itself. The extent to which these altarpieces, already about the middle of the century, herald the spatial and linear characteristics of the second half of the century is shown most clearly by the painting of an altarpiece, or 'portrait' of an altarpiece,[34] in the background of the Seven Sacraments, a picture from Roger van der Weyden's workshop, probably of 1453, which provides a vista into the interior of the church of Ste Gudule. So altarpieces were produced in Brussels round 1450 (i.e. in the later years of the great painters who, like Roger van Weyden, discovered the new possibilities of three-dimensional representation) that gave concrete embodiment to the dynamic interweaving of sculpture, painting, and architectural setting which was to become general in the second half of the century. The representation of the altarpiece in the background of the panel painting of the Benediction in the Museum of Antwerp, a work made no doubt in Brabant too, shows effectively the painterly, three-dimensional nature of such a *Gesamtkunstwerk*. The preference for a severe, box-like, right-angled shape for the centrepiece, reaching up higher than the rest, is typical of the style of Brussels, whereas Antwerp developed the altar in which compartments within the shrine have more than one tier.

In churches at Schwäbisch Hall and in the neighbourhood, as it happens, a whole group of Netherlandish altarpieces and indigenous imitations of them have been preserved. The oldest is from Rieden and dates from *c.* 1450 (Stuttgart, Württembergisches Landesmuseum; Plate 109A). The latest is the magnificent high altar in St Michael at Hall (*c.* 1470) which is built up like the stage of a Passion Play. Thorough examination of the style of this group of altarpieces [35] has revealed how much even such late examples owe to the inventions of Roger van der Weyden and his school, and how firmly established certain formal conventions were. It is therefore scarcely possible – and this applies to the mass-produced altarpieces as well – to distinguish individual achievements from the general background. An exhibition of Ancient Ecclesiastical Art, held at Strängnäs in Sweden in 1910, has thrown much light upon the Late Gothic altarpiece of the Southern Netherlands and has produced an excellent survey of Netherlandish altarpieces in the Scandinavian countries.[36]

At the head of my list of outstanding individual examples I would place the Altar of the Passion of 1466 in the church of the Benedictine priory of Ambierle (Loire; Plate 111B), donated in his will by Michel de Chaugy, Chamberlain of Philip the Good, and by his wife, Laurette de Jaucourt. This piece bears no mark of origin, but from the style of painting in the wings it has been assumed that it was made at Beaune by a sculptor from Brabant. There appears to me in any case to be no doubt of the Brussels character of the walnut carvings.[37] The Altar of the Virgin at Ternant is a precursor of this work, and its sculptural style is continued in the altarpiece of Zoutleeuw (Léau; Plate 109B) and the Altar of the Passion in St Dymphna at Geel (Gheel; Plate 110B).

Next in chronological order is the tripartite Altar of the Passion, made in Belgium and reacquired from Italy in 1891 by the Musées Royaux in Brussels (Plate 111A). This altarpiece bears the Brussels town mark and is characterized by the portrait, name, arms, and motto of its Italian donor, Claudio de Villa, and his wife, Gentine Solaro. Claudio de Villa was a merchant at Cinzano who had business dealings with Flanders and Brabant, as is shown by documentary evidence, for example in 1448. His brother Pietro was similarly placed. There are also paintings from the wings of another Brussels altar with portraits of Claudio de Villa and his wife, in the Schnütgen-Museum in Cologne. External evidence makes it likely that the Brussels altarpiece dates from c. 1470. The total ensemble, as far as figures and structure are concerned, gives an astonishing spatial illusion; it is precise in outline and at the same time highly evocative. The flamboyant style of the latest phase of Gothic in the Southern Netherlands seems already to have dawned in this work.

Among altarpieces in the Netherlands which today are still *in situ* we must first mention the Altar of St Leonard in the church of that name at Zoutleeuw (Léau; Plate 109B). This is perhaps by the same Brussels master responsible for Claudio de Villa's altarpiece. The relief groups on the side panels are separated only by the surmounting canopies, and there is consequently in the body of the work a continuous 'drama' taking place, rich in figures. The closely knit unity of the whole is enhanced by the sharpness of treatment of the individual figures. These are tall and slender; the folds of drapery flow generously and present a very emphatic system of lines. Contacts with Dirk Bouts's style of painting are evident. According to its mark, the altarpiece was made in Brussels in 1479.[38] Alongside this work should be placed the fragment of an Adoration of the Child in the Louvre from a Brussels altar presenting scenes from the Life of the Virgin.[39] An Altar of the Virgin, made according to its stamp also in Brussels (1480) for the house of the Poor Clares at Megen in North Brabant, is now in the Staatliche Museen in Berlin.[40] This work has a great wealth of figures and of architectural decoration but, notwithstanding, it is of a brilliant precision in the tautness of the sculptural surface of all its details.

There follows the main item in this group of works, the magnificent Altar of the Passion in St Dymphna at Geel (Gheel; Plate 110B).[41] This also bears the Brussels town mark and dates from c. 1480–90. Here also the central portion is clearly articulated and raised, and in it is presented the scene of the Crucifixion. The continuation of the scene into the lower side sections is achieved so successfully by the abundance of little figures at the sides and by architectural decoration that the total effect is one of triumphant unity. Here for the first time we meet with the realistic exploitation of the altarpiece as an architectural microcosm. The density of impression produced by these many figures creates an immense sculptural tension. Form and colour unite in a radiant whole, reminiscent of the goldsmith's art. Movement is intensified into a violent expressiveness. The addition of tiny sculptural groups in the mouldings of the frame is important, resembling the use of voussoirs in church portals. This employment of very small figures – seen first perhaps in the Netherlands – produced a Late Gothic sculpture of small format, which was to become of great significance when, at the beginning of the Renaissance, the monumental, all-embracing architectural style of altar carving lost its cohesive force.

We do not know the name of the master of the altarpiece at Geel. The high altar in the cathedral of Strängnäs (Södermanland) also bears the Brussels town mark, and comes from the same workshop, and it too is an Altar of the Passion.[42] It was made at the instance of Bishop Conrad Rogge, who held office from 1479 to 1501, but it does not appear to have been carved by the same hand as the Geel altarpiece. A second Altar of the Passion in the cathedral of Strängnäs bears the Antwerp town marks. This, too, was commissioned by Bishop Conrad Rogge, but at a slightly later date.

Again and again we find echoes of Roger van der Weyden's circle in the multi-figured sculptural compositions of these altarpieces.[43] In the latter years of the fifteenth century these reminiscences became increasingly liberated from the linear style and achieved more depth. We can see this if we set in juxtaposition two outstanding works from Brabant, the Descent from the Cross from the collection of the Duke of Arenberg now in the Detroit Institute of Arts (Plate 110A) and the Mourning of Christ from the collection of Baron von Decker at Forest (Vorst) near Brussels.[44] The Descent from the Cross shows the change in style; the cohesion in the composition of Roger van der Weyden's pictures is here loosened – as in an epic narrative – into a series of character types. Reminiscences of Roger still cleave to them, but they are made autonomous and concrete in a new way. This explains the mastery in the elaboration of detail, and pre-eminently in the new significance of the details of the faces. Thus there develops a new 'Late Gothic' expressionism which has the dramatic quality of an action on a stage.

It is impossible to illustrate the history of altar sculpture in Antwerp[45] in the latter part of the fifteenth century from examples that are equally well preserved and of comparable artistic significance. Documents show (for example those of 1432 and 1444 in St Jan at 's-Hertogenbosch) how much demand there was for Antwerp altar sculpture already before 1450. But probably Antwerp did not reach its highwater mark until after the turn of the century. Carved altar fragments and altarpieces, stamped with the Antwerp town mark, from the late fifteenth century prove that we have here a parallel development to that of Brussels, but it appears that the quality at this time was higher in Brussels.

The high altar in the pilgrimage church of Clausen near Trier would appear to date from c. 1480.[46] This tripartite altarpiece presents a multifigured Passion in realistic high relief. There is no break in the scenes, which culminate in the elevated centre in the Crucifixion itself. This is carved with the greatest expressiveness and filled with a splendid vividness of detail. The surrounding tabernacles and towering canopies are not abstract in character, but act as a supple, melodious accompaniment to the whole. The formal language of the (second) Altar of the Passion in the cathedral of Strängnäs is harsher; this is certainly the product of another (Antwerp) workshop. The tripartite Altar of the Passion, dating from the beginning of the sixteenth century, in the Staatliche Museen in Berlin,[47] also marked in several places with the Antwerp stamp, seems like the later replica of a Brussels altarpiece in the style of the master of Geel. There appear to be no altarpieces with the Malines mark before the early years of the sixteenth century.

Surviving individual statues from the Southern Netherlands dating from the later fifteenth century are many in number. The stone Virgin and Child in the Musées Royaux d'Art et d'Histoire in Brussels indicates most clearly the traditional powers still at work in the middle of the century.[48] This figure possesses the fullness and breadth of style of the previous decades, but at the same time its cohesive linear features give it decisive articulation by means of a new grouping of sculptural stresses. The next step is shown in the wooden Virgin at Braine-le-Comte ('s-Gravenbrakel) in Brabant. This figure has the kind of structure which became universal in the latter part of the century. In general the feeling for the expressive power of volume seems to have been more marked in South Netherlandish sculpture in the second half of the century than it was in contemporary work from the Northern Netherlands. An example of this is the fine St Anne with Virgin and Child in the Musée des Antiquités in Antwerp. The structure here has both weight and a sinuous, rippling movement. These pre-eminently spatial stresses of movement lose their linear character around 1500 (cf. e.g. the Pietà – 'Maria ter Noodt' – in the church of Merchtem).[49]

After observing this difference, it is all the more important to emphasize that in the development of Late Gothic sculpture of the Southern Netherlands the same stylistic tendencies in general are to be observed as in North Netherlandish works. We have proof of this for example in Brabant, where the way proceeds from the austere sculptural concentration in the figures of the saints in the church of Hasselt to the elegant, slenderly towering figure of St Margaret (from the collection of J. Frésart at Liège and now in the Gruuthuse Museum in Bruges)[50] and to the mature, conscious beauty and stylish dignity of the St Barbara from Maaseyck.[24] Between 1480 and 1490 this development culminates in a statuesque type of representation, austere and almost intellectual in the clear arrangement of the drapery. Examples of this style, bearing the Brussels mark, were very widespread. The St Barbara in Notre-Dame du Bon Secours in Brussels[51] would appear to be an early example of the type.

With regard to the carved stalls which still survive from this time in the Netherlands,[52] I would like to direct attention to the later parts of the choir stalls of St Jan at 's-Hertogenbosch (Bois-le-Duc), dating from c. 1475 (e.g. the impressive reliefs of St Michael and St Anthony), and to the novel anecdotal development of genre motifs on the stalls of St Sauveur at Bruges (c. 1478).

CHAPTER 8

GERMANY: 1460/70–90

WE begin our survey of German sculpture between 1470 and 1490 with the districts bordering on the Netherlands. The bishoprics of Utrecht and Liège belonged to the archdiocese of Cologne, and those of Verdun, Metz, and Toul to the archdiocese of Trier. This fact alone – and we can disregard any historico-political changes of the years in question – makes it clear that at the end of the Middle Ages, as far as ecclesiastical art was concerned, the frontiers created later by the development of national states were of no significance. It is astonishing how hard it seems to be for both scholars and others to discard the blinkers that have been fashioned by later political history.

In 1469 Konrad Kuene, whose work shows many contacts with sculpture in the Netherlands or with Netherlandish sculpture in France, died in Cologne.[1] Cologne's traditional style is perhaps seen most clearly in the beautiful life-size wooden figure of St Michael in St Andreas, in so far as this figure has its prototype in a similar statue in St Aposteln in the same city,[2] modified by the more or less exact adaptation of an engraving by Israel van Meckenem (G.309) which itself was derived from an engraving by the Master E.S. dating from 1467 (L.154). Thus varied were at times the sources of Late Gothic sculpture: on the one hand, the local or regional character, springing from traditions of the workshops; on the other, its translation into a contemporary idiom through the use of formulae taken over from engravings, in their turn already 'secondhand'. Our admiration therefore for the remarkable spatial quality in this towering figure of St Michael, which probably dates from the 1470s, and the force of its expansive gesture is all the greater. The representation of St Christopher was another influential motif; we have its basic expression in the linearly clear figure of c. 1470–80 in St Andreas in Cologne,[3] and this is then translated in the gigantic St Christopher in the choir of Cologne Cathedral[4] into a new and tremendous rhetoric. The power of the almost life-size wooden figure of St Jerome from the parish church of Lövenich near Erkelenz (Cologne, Schnütgen Museum)[5] is just as astonishing. In these works we feel their new expressive power to issue from a turn of the naturalistic style into tectonic austerity.

In the midst of these traditions of Cologne, the master of the stone figures of a Virgin (Plate 113A) and of a Salvator Mundi in the Salvatorkapelle of St Maria im Kapitol in Cologne, donated by Johann Hardenrath in 1466, strikes an alien note. The amplitude and freedom of his sculptural style reminds one of Nicolaus Gerhaerts,[6] and in it clarity of structure goes hand in hand with a delicate elasticity of surface. Basically, however, there is no connexion with the work and personality of Gerhaerts, and the similarity of style springs no doubt from the fact that both artists drew upon common Netherlandish sources, though even here one may see that the ancestry of the Cologne figure of the Virgin rather goes back as far as the Virgin of the Annunciation in the Madeleine at Tournai (Plate 69B). On the other hand we must remember how wide a range of derivatives had already sprung from these early examples of the new sculptural style.

A further such early example is offered by the attendant figures of a wooden Crucifixion group from the demolished rood screen in the parish church of St Nikolaus in Kalkar, probably corresponding in date with the consecration of the church in 1469 (Plate 112, A and B).[7] These figures are filled with a new expressive naturalism, but at the same time in their voluminous weightiness still cling to the style of the middle of the century. On piles of clods at the foot of the Crucifix lies the skeleton of Adam – an expression of a macabre realism whose antecedents we know already from Netherlandish–French funerary sculpture. But we have to interpret this not merely as an expression of a new naturalism, but also of a new religious feeling, which radiated at this time from Deventer. The striking breadth of surface in the drapery of the attendant figures shows a genuine richness of 'painterly' values that do not come our way again in the development of sculpture during the late fifteenth century, when linear sharpness grows increasingly marked. Hence my reason for dating this Crucifixion group to c. 1470. Among the variations of Netherlandish prototypes, which are not easily distinguished, this work represents a typically Lower Rhenish parallel to the carved French Mater Dolorosa in the Staatliche Museen in Berlin. The reliefs on the choir stalls of 1474 in the Minoritenkirche at Cleves[8] help us to determine our date. Here the brilliant sharpness of form is certainly to be ascribed to contacts with the not so distant city of Utrecht, but at the same time a Lower Rhenish feeling for volume and solidity is paramount, such as we do not find in contemporary Dutch sculpture. It is not always easy to differentiate clearly between the character of Lower Rhenish and Dutch works, and certainly genetically we know them to be closely related. After all, Kalkar was the see of a Utrecht suffragan bishop. But in the Calvary at Kalkar and in the choir stalls at Cleves it seems possible to distinguish the Lower Rhenish element beyond any doubt. They serve as a veritable touchstone in the evaluation of works of a slightly later date preserved in great numbers in the lower reaches of the Lower Rhineland.

In the Aldegundiskirche at Emmerich[9] we find a group of St Agnes and St Catherine whose resemblance to typical Utrecht works of the years round 1480 is so striking that we are bound to ask whether they were actually imported from Utrecht, or whether they are by a Utrecht master who had settled in Emmerich. There is the same stateliness of form conveying an impression of corporeality not usual in Lower Rhenish sculpture; also the abundance of hair is more in the Utrecht style, where Lower Rhenish sculpture tends to render it with greater linear stylization. Moreover, the deanery of Emmerich, together with a few other Lower Rhenish towns, was under the immediate jurisdiction of the bishop of Utrecht. Closely akin to these, but revealing a more definitely Lower Rhenish character in their block-like style, are oak figures of St Catherine in the Louvre and in private ownership in Milan (Plate 104B); also figures of St Ursula from Erle (Westphalia) in the Diocesan Museum at Münster, and of St Agnes from Rheine (Westphalia) in the Staatliche Museen in Berlin – so fluid are the gradations from North Netherlandish to Lower Rhenish style. In any case, the charming silver statuette of a Virgin with the coat of arms of the donor, Moritz von Spiegelberg (d. 1483), in the treasury of St Martin at Emmerich is Lower Rhenish.[10]

Cleves and Wesel were the main centres for the production of such works; it is worth remembering that both these towns were the seats of courts, so that one can assume that feudalism still played a certain part in the furthering of talent. The stone figure of St Victor in Bannita Square in Xanten was made at Wesel in 1468, and so were the figures of St Jerome, St Gregory, and St Christopher on the piers of Xanten Cathedral,[11] which are two years later in date. In 1486–8 followed the statues of St Ambrose, St Victor, St Martin, and St Augustine, and here we know from documentary evidence that the Master was Wilhelm von Wesel. The deeply ridged, block-like shapes of these figures exhibit a certain rigidity which is typical of the Lower Rhineland and differs essentially from the more supple linear idiom of Dutch works.

The only surviving wooden altarpiece of any significance from this region is the Altar of St George in the Nikolaikirche at Kalkar, donated by Peter Gisen (d. 1493), burgomaster of the town. In this altarpiece the scenic relief extends uninterruptedly over its three sections and teems with small figures, arranged before a realistic landscape complete with vistas of castles and cities – the kind of tribute to landscape that is familiar in later cribs. The vividness and the epic quality of the legendary action lend the work great charm; we see a painting translated naïvely into sculpture, without any of the formal severity or calculated grouping that we met in Netherlandish altarpieces. At the same time, however, there is a clear and striking sculptural distribution of emphasis. The work can be dated round 1480, but there is not enough evidence to ascribe it to Arnt von Zwolle, though he is known to have been active at Kalkar at this time. We may assume that the carver of this altar was also responsible for a domestic altar, now in the Musée de Cluny, Paris,[12] donated by a Carthusian monk from (or for) Kranenburg, with a representation of the Mourning of Christ. The same epic style of presentation occurs in both works.

It is remarkably difficult to form any clear idea of the quality of Cologne sculpture at this time. The most important work that survives is without doubt the stone figure of the Virgin in St Columba. Here we have the nobility of form and delicacy of feeling that make the work pre-eminently Colognesque. The figure has a taut economy of line, but nevertheless there is a painterly richness in the harmonious movement of the inner forms. A distinct squatness in the proportions suggests that we have here a somewhat older style than that of the strangely alien group in the Hardenrathkapelle in St Maria im Capitol.[13] But apart from certain links with late paintings by Lochner, there is no formal tradition in the sculpture of Cologne which can explain the origin of this Fair Virgin in St Columba. A certain similarity to Netherlandish works is therefore all the more important, as for example with the St Mary Magdalen from the St Martin group at Utrecht.

Apart from the examples just referred to, one would seek in vain for outstanding large sculptural works in Cologne at this time, though from contemporary panel painting as it flourished in Cologne one might be led to expect impressive carved altarpieces as well. Where, for instance, is a sculptor corresponding to the Master of the Life of the Virgin? Or is it perhaps characteristic of this phase of development in Cologne that artistic talent expressed itself in painting rather than in sculpture? This would be in marked contrast to the contemporary state of affairs in the Netherlands, where it is easy to find impressive sculpture in the style of Dirk Bouts. Do we have Cologne's equivalent to the Dirk Bouts style in such wooden figures as the Virgin and St John from a Crucifixion group formerly in the Germanisches Museum in Nuremberg (destroyed in the War), and from Cornelimünster near Aachen, now in the Suermondt-Museum in Aachen? A similar pair of figures (of somewhat later date and with less individual characterization) in the Szépművészeti Muzeum in Budapest proves, I think, that this Dirk Bouts style may have existed in the sculpture of Cologne and the Lower Rhineland.[14]

A search in Cologne for works of small format meets with better fortune, and here one is reminded of the delicate 'Virgin in the Sun' of c. 1400 in the Schnütgen Museum. There is, for example, the small walnut Virgin of c. 1470, also in the Schnütgen Museum, from a convent near Siegburg, and the limewood statuette of a seated Virgin and Child in the Deutsches Museum in Berlin.[15] The 'Virgin with the flowing Cloak' of c. 1480, again in the Schnütgen Museum,[16] is perhaps by the same hand as a seated Virgin in the Diocesan Museum in Liège – another proof of that community of style which makes nonsense of existing frontiers. These are all works which already exemplify the qualities in its own right of small-scale sculpture. We shall return to this later. The growing autonomy of sculpture and the condensation of the motifs into a self-contained sculptural 'picture' is already clear.

Since we are dealing with districts bordering on the Netherlands, it seems appropriate to include here the most important contemporary works from the archdiocese of Trier. First, we have monumental statues which appear in a very peculiar way to carry on Burgundian traditions. The impressive Entombment at Pont-à-Mousson leads the way, along with figures of the Magdalen at Nancy and from Ancemont now in the Louvre.[17] From here it is a short step to the ample Virgin[18] in the parish church of Vic-sur-Seille near Château-Salins (Lorraine). The delicacy of surface in this figure in the Netherlandish manner of the mid-century anticipates the style of the Virgins in St Columba in Cologne and in Lübeck Cathedral. There follows somewhat later the tomb of Count Johann III of Nassau-Saarbrücken and of his first and second wives in the collegiate church of St Arnual near Saarbrücken.[19] Count Johann died in 1472, and it was at the instance of his second wife that the tomb was erected. The angels at the head of the effigies remind one of the style of the angels in the Pont-à-Mousson Entombment. But the realism in the heads and in the sheet-armour and dress is new. This epic vividness is typically German. I am unable to accept the repeatedly asserted connexion between this work and the portrait figures (preserved only in fragments) from the ceremonial tomb of the lords of Heinsberg (dating from round 1446) in the parish church of Heinsberg in the district of Jülich. The sharpness in their presentation seems to me to be South Netherlandish.

The works mentioned so far are proof of the existence of an indigenous sculpture in the Meuse and Moselle districts, and perhaps, as we saw, the Annunciation in St Kunibert in Cologne may also fit in here. Dating from about 1470 there is one group which united the older Burgundian element with the more modern style: the attendant stone figures of a Crucifixion in the Diocesan Museum in Cologne,[20] originally from the Eifel. Here the Virgin is conceived in the same block-like amplitude as the figure of the Virgin at Vic, whereas in the St John an effective contrast between body and drapery is already visible.

Alongside these works, in Trier we have Nicolaus Gerhaerts' tomb of Bishop Sierck (1462) and the mural monument to Elizabeth of Straubing-Holland (d. 1451; Plate 116A), which was carved either under Gerhaerts' influence or after his design. An echo of this boldly three-dimensional style of Nicolaus Gerhaerts in Trier is to be sensed in the stone predella of a (lost) Altar of St Sebastian in St Gangolf, erected to the memory of Junker Nikolaus von Nattenheim (d. 1467). Here no doubt Peter von Wederath,[21] known to have been active in Trier from 1463 to 1478, was responsible for the design. Did Peter von Wederath take on Gerhaerts' mantle in Trier? The finest parts of the surviving lower tier of this altarpiece are the reliefs, densely packed with scutcheon-bearing angels. They do not, however, possess the mastery of the angel bearing the scutcheon of Duchess Elizabeth. The evocative power of the new potentialities of sculptural presentation as revealed by Gerhaerts is seen more strikingly in a further armorial relief in Trier, dating from c. 1465. Here a knight in armour and a naked lady with pointed hennin and veils reaching to the ground hold a shield surrounded by leafy tendrils.[22]

For a long time the beautiful stone Virgin standing on an elegant angel corbel in the cloisters of Trier Cathedral, donated by Dean Edmund von Malberg before his death in 1478, was regarded as an early work of Gerhaerts'. Although we now know this work to date only from 1475, it is a typical early example of the Late Gothic presentation of the Virgin in South German sculpture. It is probably a combination of the style of Nicolaus Gerhaerts' successors in Strasbourg[23] with, I would say, certain Franconian features (Franconian influence reached westwards as far as Trier; a fact confirmed again and again up to the time of Balthasar Neumann and Ferdinand Dietz). Doubtless the master of the Malberg Virgin was also responsible for the wonderful stone group of St Anne with the Virgin and Child[24] from the neighbourhood of Wissembourg in Alsace (Berlin, Staatliche Museen; Plate 114A) which has also erroneously been ascribed to Gerhaerts. Here among Gerhaerts' successors we find a stress on the beauty of the facial features which is so essentially German in character that the Netherlandish elements disappear. It would seem to me that by removing these two works from Nicolaus Gerhaerts' œuvre, we increase our opinion of his genius and do more justice to its western origin. But at Trier the peculiar style of the master of the Malberg Virgin is continued in the wooden Virgin from Wasserliesch near Trier, now in the Diocesan Museum at Trier. In this work we can see already the style of the 1480s – i.e., a vigorous contrast of body and drapery and an almost metallic sharpness of outline and inner forms developed with dramatic intensity.

When we remember too that a carved triptych of the Passion, bearing the town mark of Antwerp and dating from c. 1480, was once in the former abbey of Pfalzel near Trier (later in the Ambras Collection and now in the neo-Gothic Votivkirche in Vienna) and also that the limestone figures of the three Magi in the Benedictine abbey of St Matthias outside Trier,[25] probably of the same date, are of South Netherlandish provenance, our picture of the outstanding significance of Trier as a meeting-place of western and Rhenish sculpture is complete.

The tremendous seated stone figure of an unknown municipal officer in the Musée de l'Œuvre in Strasbourg (Plate 81)[26] is evidence that already about 1430–40 there was artistic interchange between the Upper Rhineland and the most advanced artists of Burgundy and the Netherlands. Perhaps the most important item in the monumental sculpture of Alsace that greeted Nicolaus Gerhaerts when he arrived in Strasbourg was the Holy Sepulchre in the church of the former convent of the Beguines at Vieux Thann.[27] According to the chronicle of Thann, this tomb was of the same date as the church itself, i.e. not much later than 1455. The type of representation resumes an Upper Rhenish tradition which is continued until the later years of the century (cf. the Holy Sepulchre of 1478 in St Peter and St Paul at Neuwiller-lès-Saverne). The sculptural style, in its impressive, concentrated tension, with the crystal-clear lines of drapery and in the gentleness of the facial expression, is Upper Rhenish. But at the same time the similarity between the figures of the standing angels here and those at Pont-à-Mousson shows the affiliation between this Upper Rhenish sculpture and advanced developments in the north-west.

I must mention at this point the fragment of a head from the tomb of a bishop, found under the floor of the Nikolauskapelle of Basel Minster and now in the Klingenthal Museum in that city (Plate 83A). This is an astonishingly precise piece of chiselling with the greatest individualization in the facial features; austere in surface, and yet at the same time, especially in the decoration on the mitre, of great delicacy and subtlety. R. Riggenbach, who discovered this fragment, was of the opinion that we had here a piece from the tomb of Bishop Hartmann Münch, who died in 1424.[28] If this is the case, it would prove the existence in the Upper Rhineland of a talent equal to that of Nicolaus Gerhaerts in the individualization of the sculptural portrait, and preceding the Master of the Strasbourg Municipal Officer with his demonic melancholy. I find this hard to believe. The delicacy of surface in this head would suggest to me that it is of even later date than the statues on the Schnegg in Constance Minster. I think the head from the bishop's monument is a most impressive indigenous parallel to Nicolaus Gerhaerts' art of portraiture in Strasbourg and may indeed even be influenced by him.

The other magnificent reminiscence of Gerhaerts in Basel is provided by the Calvary group on the Hallwyl Reliquary in the treasury of the minster, acquired in 1470.[29] Is this piece of goldsmith's art by Georg Schongauer? He married Nicolaus Gerhaerts' daughter, Apollonia. The painter and engraver Martin Schongauer was his brother.

It appears that in addition to Nicolaus Gerhaerts, another Netherlandish sculptor was active in Strasbourg c. 1465–70. The three wonderfully preserved limewood reliefs with scenes from the Life of the Virgin (Musée de l'Œuvre Notre-Dame; Plate 115A) are his work; originally they flanked a central figure of the Virgin in a triptych in the Chartreuse of Strasbourg.[30] In 1591 the altarpiece was removed to Molsheim; hence these reliefs are now generally known as the Molsheim Reliefs. The Adoration of the Magi resembles the oak relief in the Episcopal Museum in Haarlem (p. 88) so strongly that we must assume that they were originally fitted into a similar box-like altarpiece. The Netherlandish relief is more severely stylized. The Molsheim Reliefs are richer in three-dimensional contrasts, and the facial expression has been transmuted into a gentler and more charming mode. One might assume from the delicacy of the workmanship that the artist had in mind closer scrutiny on the part of the spectator. The echo left by the carver of the Molsheim Reliefs accounts for a certain fairy-tale atmosphere in Alsatian art. We find it, for instance, in the Nativity formerly in the Spetz Collection at Colmar, now in the Rijksmuseum in Amsterdam (Plate 115B), with its compositional development deep into space; in the fragment of another Nativity in the museum at Saverne (Zabern); and in the charming group of three singing angels[31] in the Staatliche Museen in Berlin.

The works of the Master of the Molsheim Reliefs have a forerunner in a walnut figure of a kneeling Virgin from a Nativity in private ownership. This figure, block-like in shape, probably of slightly earlier date than the Haarlem relief, is doubtless an imported work of South Netherlandish provenance.[32] The groups of mourners in a Calvary[33] (Strasbourg, Musée de l'Œuvre Notre-Dame) dating from c. 1475 and exe-cuted in what is called 'alabâtre de la Meuse' were probably also imported from the Southern Netherlands, or else were the work of an itinerant artist. Such works as these, coupled with the influence of Nicolaus Gerhaerts, furthered the production in both Strasbourg and the Upper Rhineland of stone and wood carving of the highest order. The tradition and the character of this sculpture is responsible for the fact that for more than half a century outstanding works followed on each other in quick succession. This makes it all the more remarkable that around 1475 the immediate in-fluence of Netherlandish talents appears to cease in the Upper Rhineland. On the other hand, the influence of engravings in providing ideas for sculptural compositions and also for stylistic innovations remained current. It had been firmly established by the Master E.S., who had practised the art of engraving so widely in the Upper Rhineland between c. 1440 and 1467. Is it possible e.g. that the strangely precious style of the beautiful St Catherine in the Musée de l'Œuvre Notre-Dame in Strasbourg[34] had a Netherlandish engraving as its prototype?

The reproduction of such engravings established a new quantity production and answered a demand that was by no means purely regional; in the same way and in the same area reproductions of small-scale sculpture sprang up, and the wide distribution of these reproductions was the source of various artistic innovations. We have already encountered this phenomenon in Utrecht around 1460–80,[35] and the Upper Rhineland did not lag behind in the production of such works. I would cite as a dated example the small limewood relief of 1468 of the Adoration of the Magi from the Imperial Hohen-zollern Collection at Sigmaringen, now in the Städtische Skulpturengalerie in Frank-furt.[36] Its formal character is definitely Netherlandish, but judging by its inscription it is doubtless of German and probably Upper Rhenish provenance. In the same collection in Sigmaringen was the cartapesta version of a relief of the Annunciation; the Upper Rhenish hardwood original of this is in the Carrand Collection in the Museo Nazionale in Florence. There are cartapesta and stucco versions of reliefs of the Nativity and of the

Adoration of the Magi belonging to the same cycle (e.g. in the Staatliche Museen in Berlin and formerly in the Sigmaringen Museum). The walnut original of the relief of a demi-figure of the Virgin (now in the Staatliche Museen in Berlin) came from Detzem on the Moselle, while its stucco replica, originally from Strasbourg, supplemented by the addition of a realistic spatial background, is in the Colmar Museum.[37] It is astonishing to observe how widespread, even in Northern Italy, are such small-scale Upper Rhenish reliefs and their replicas in clay and cartapesta.[38]

But wood carvers on a larger scale who had moved to North Italy from the Upper Rhineland also received important commissions there at this time; this is the case, for instance, in Venice, as is proved by the decisive share these German carvers had in the relief decoration of the choir stalls of 1468 in the church of the Frari (see p. 107). The naturalistic and yet formally severe and vigorous style of Upper Rhenish carving must have been a real discovery for Early Renaissance patrons in Italy.[39] This Upper Rhenish small-scale relief work presupposes Netherlandish sources. The triptych in the Musée de Cluny with terracotta reliefs of the Life of the Virgin,[40] dating from the mid fifteenth century, and certainly of Netherlandish provenance, proves this fact.

Among the representatives of the advanced style of Upper Rhenish sculpture at this time, the artists whose work is immediately derived from Nicolaus Gerhaerts stand out. This is most clear in the sphere of stone sculpture. Nicolaus Gerhaerts' Crucifix in Baden-Baden was the prototype of the stone Crucifix on the rood screen in the church of the Cistercian abbey of Maulbronn. This bears the date 1473 and is signed with the initials CVS, which were identified as those of Conrad von Sinsheim, i.e. Conrad Sifer,[41] who became master mason to Strasbourg Minster in 1491. I shall return to him in a later chapter. Here we are more concerned with pointing out Gerhaerts' fundamental significance. In this connexion it is interesting to note how strong the impression of certain works was. They were obviously at once considered typical examples. This is clear for example from the fact that the painter and carver Clemens von Baden received firm instructions when commissioned to do the Crucifixion on the rood screen in St Georges at Haguenau (Alsace) that he was to follow the pattern of a similar rood screen in the church of St Thomas in Strasbourg.[42] Clemens von Baden had an assistant called Hans von Coblenz. All that has survived in the church of St Georges at Haguenau is the gigantic cross, dated 1488. The uninterrupted influence radiating from these Strasbourg models explains the reappearance of Nicolaus Gerhaerts' type of Crucifixus in the fragment of a stone Christ in Pity in St Georges at Sélestat and in the (later) wooden fragment of a head from the triumphal cross in the same church.

In Strasbourg the most important work of the Gerhaerts succession that survives is the minster pulpit of 1485; the design for this work (in the Musée de l'Œuvre Notre-Dame) was made by the master mason to the minster, Hans Hammer,[43] in 1484, but Hammer was certainly not the sculptor who executed the work; for the drawing itself and the execution of the architectural part are austere compared with the bubbling vitality of the sculpture, with its wealth of brilliant inventions, and its indirect contacts with Burgundo-Netherlandish art are not merely by means of the legacy of Nicolaus Gerhaerts. This is true especially of the noble form and masterly rhetoric of the St John the Baptist[44] and the St Catherine. Their execution is typically Upper Rhenish. One senses the artist's immense delight in the deep furrowing of the volumes and in the truly inexhaustible play of the drapery. Here for the first time one meets figure types which in Late Gothic sculpture became current throughout the whole of South Germany, in the same way that the innovations of Nicolaus Gerhaerts and the engravings of the Master E.S. had done.

The most important work by Nicolaus Gerhaerts' successors on the Middle Rhine is the stone relief of the Annunciation in Speyer Cathedral (Plate 114B).[45] Originally this was part of the tomb of Bishop Siegfried III von Venningen (d. 1459) and his brother Canon Nikolaus von Venningen (d. 1483), which was erected in the cathedral cloisters. The master took as his model the three-dimensional style of the Busnang monument at Strasbourg, and it is fascinating to observe how the bold and yet remarkably intellectual figures of the great Netherlander, in the hands of a native German release a still stronger emotion in the composition and vibration in the surfaces. There is a conscious contrast between the meditative quiet of the Virgin on the one hand and the movement of the angel rustling his fine towering pinions on the other. Here one is made keenly aware how 'Niklas von straspurgk brought to light the new style' in German sculpture.[46] The stone fragment of the head of a monastic saint (Heidelberg, Historisches Museum of the Palatinate), which was discovered in Speyer Cathedral when the imperial vault was opened, is by another pupil of Nicolaus Gerhaerts.

If we now return to the sphere of wood carving, we find that in 1465 Nicolaus Gerhaerts appears to have complied with a request from the chapter of Constance Minster to carve a high altar for the church.[47] In any case, we have the bill, dated 1467, for extra charges for the altar panel delivered to the minster a year earlier. Gerhaerts had been temporarily resident at Constance to carry out the work. Payment for work on the choir stalls was included in this bill, and by it he was absolved from any further work on them. He appears to have brought Heinrich Iselin as a collaborator with him from Strasbourg, and the latter then married the daughter of the Constance master carpenter, Simon Haider, with the result that the Haider–Iselin workshop continued the work begun by Nicolaus Gerhaerts on the minster choir stalls. The high altar has not survived, but we know it to have been an Altar of the Virgin. Knowing Gerhaerts' genius and the position occupied by Constance Minster – it was the see of the largest German diocese – we may assume that its influence was extensive. When we remember what refinement was introduced into spatial sculpture from Nicolaus Gerhaerts' monumental reliefs, we may conclude that his altar sculpture would have been distinguished by the same ability to make of it a piece of architecture in miniature. This was to become the essential element in South German altar carving of the Late Gothic period.

The extensive choir stalls in the minster, for whose design Gerhaerts was no doubt responsible,[48] have survived. Something of Gerhaerts' freedom and inventive genius still clings to the more important parts of the carving (1467–71). We may identify the carver of the north ends as Heinrich Iselin. The fully mature individuality of this artist is seen in the busts from the choir stalls of the Benedictine abbey of Weingarten (preserved in the Berchtesgaden Castle Museum), on which we know him to have been engaged in 1478 (Plate 124, A and B). Here we have Nicolaus Gerhaerts' image of man translated into terms of the voluminous, rhetorical, and sentimental – magnificent in conception, but in execution lacking both subtlety and precision.

There is one work which gives us some idea of what Gerhaerts' wood carvings must have looked like: the relief of the demi-figure of a Virgin under a tent canopy, hung with curtains, which are drawn aside by angels caught in steep descent (Munich, private collection; Plate 94A). Beneath are two angels holding a scutcheon. The whole magic of Netherlandish–Burgundian goldsmiths' craft clings to this work,[49] together with an echo of Roger van der Weyden. A subtle play of light and shade is created, which in the South German statues of Gerhaerts' successors is translated into much less delicate alternation of light and dark. In addition, there is the lyrical elegance of the taut form which distinguishes all Gerhaerts' works, from the bishop's tomb in Trier to the imperial tomb in Vienna. I am inclined to believe that this relief comes nearest to supplying us with an idea of the vanished beauty of the main figure in the Altar of the Virgin in Constance Minster. At the same time, in style this relief has something of the serene quality we see in the lid of the Viennese tomb.

Important in this connexion are the reliefs of the choir stalls erected by Marco Cozzi in 1468 in the Frari church in Venice (cf. p. 105).[39] The chief carver here came from Nicolaus Gerhaerts' field of influence in Strasbourg and Constance. In these reliefs and in the relief of a demi-figure of the Virgin carved by the same hand for a small Venetian altarpiece (now in the Wadsworth Atheneum at Hartford, Conn.) the first steps are taken towards a striking new linear style. It has been recognized that the reliefs were added to the choir stalls at a later date; on the other hand, the space intended for them cannot have remained empty for long, so that we may assume them to date from c. 1468–70. Immediately related is the handsome Virgin now in the Benedictine abbey church of Downside (Plate 119B).[50] From this Virgin and the connexion between it and the Frari Master, the transition is easy to the carved altar sculpture which from this date onwards assumes increasing importance in the artistic output of the Upper Rhineland. Owing to the large number of surviving examples, we shall have to restrict ourselves to a small selection.

First we must mention the almost pain-wracked demi-figure of a poor man leaning on his elbows (from Wissembourg in Alsace) and the two so-called older busts, revealing an equal degree of violent inner tension, from the Hospital of St Marx in Strasbourg, probably representing two prophets (Plate 118B). All are now in the Musée de l'Œuvre Notre-Dame.[51] By another hand are four busts of Holy Virgins from the abbey of St Peter and St Paul at Wissembourg. Two of these, St Barbara and St Catherine, from the collection of J. P. Morgan, are now in the Metropolitan Museum in New York; another, St Margaret, from the Buckingham Collection, is now in the Art Institute of Chicago.[52] I would date these works c. 1470. In them one senses a new elegant sharpness of both outline and inner forms, and in addition a new realism in the treatment of the themes. A seated figure of St James in the parish church of Kaysersberg[53] presents the same union of dignity with veracity of portraiture. The Kaysersberg figure is again closely related to the Virgin at Downside.

The next stage in this development, which probably took place mainly in Strasbourg itself, leads us to a medium-sized limewood figure, no doubt of the Virgin, with a book; originally in private ownership at Colmar, it is now in the Staatliche Museen in Berlin.[54] Here the body emerges with such clarity from the block of drapery that the contrast between core and envelope is experienced to the very full. A similar treatment of body and drapery is achieved with even greater mastery in the Virgin from Dangolsheim (Alsace), now also in the Staatliche Museen in Berlin (Plate 120). This piece, by another hand, is said to have been found originally in the church of the Benedictine abbey of Schwarzach near Baden-Baden.[55] No work shows better than this with what noble resonance the art of Nicolaus Gerhaerts reverberated through the Upper Rhineland. The Virgin of Dangolsheim is in walnut and is executed entirely in the round and with goldsmith-like precision. On the lavishly worked back an abundance of beautifully carved hair hangs down. It is characteristic that this work, which marks the border of the sphere of influence of Nicolaus Gerhaerts, the last monumental sculptor comparable in stature to Sluter, should at the same time open up a vista on to the realm of the most delicate sculptural subtleties of the early sixteenth century, subtleties appearing at their triumphant best in small-scale works quite independent of altarpieces. However inexhaustible these sculptural effects may seem in the Dangolsheim Virgin, emanating from the magnetic relationship of body and drapery, the figure is nevertheless meant to be viewed from the front. Only when thus viewed do we see what might be called a new linear order, such as is not yet visible in Nicolaus Gerhaerts' work. The question arises how far this mode of presentation is dependent upon engravings and in its turn spread by means of engravings.[56]

There is a close affinity between the sculptural style of the Dangolsheim Virgin and that of the four busts of the Holy Virgins from Wissembourg. The latter appear to be of only slightly earlier date and to be closer to Nicolaus Gerhaerts. The affinity is such that it is impossible to envisage the provenance of the Dangolsheim Virgin as anywhere other than Strasbourg. In addition, there is its close connexion with the Virgin from Colmar in the Berlin Museum. Compared with the painterly full-blown beauty of the Dangolsheim Virgin, the Berlin figure has a more austere structure and is therefore probably also of somewhat earlier date. I regard the St Mary Magdalen in the parish church of Biengen near Freiburg[57] as a work of the same master. Judging by its broad folds of drapery, this figure too is of earlier date than the Dangolsheim Virgin. The exaggeration of the proportions and the brilliance of the play in the details show that in the Dangolsheim figure the possibilities of representation, inherited by the post-Gerhaerts generation in the Upper Rhineland, are realized to the full. Other works from the orbit of the Dangolsheim Master which still survive in the Upper Rhineland are as charming in the delicacy of their physical content as they are polished in expression.[58] I would cite as examples the St Sebastian from Altsimonswald in the Augustiner-Museum at Freiburg and associated figures in the parish church of Altsimonswald near Freiburg; the Coronation of the Virgin in the parish church of Honau near Offenburg;[57] and the ample and charming kneeling Virgin from a Nativity, originally in the monastery of Wonnenthal near Kenzingen, and now in the Staatliche Museen in Berlin (Plate 119A).[59]

Unfortunately, all attempts to discover the leading talents in Strasbourg and Alsace after Nicolaus Gerhaerts' departure lead, in spite of a mass of records, to very little.[42] In 1467, the year of Gerhaerts' departure, Barthel Widitz from Meissen gained the rights of citizenship. We may assume that he founded a sculptural tradition which was continued in Freiburg in the work of his son, Hans Weiditz, at the turn of the century. The sculptor Hans Kamensetzer from Ulm bought his citizenship in 1471, and from 1477 records show Lux Kotter to have been resident in Strasbourg.

More than by documents, we are helped by the influence radiating from Strasbourg sculpture. The most impressive items here are the figures from the high altar in St Georg at Nördlingen (Plate 117A); they comprise a Crucifixion group in which the Crucifix itself is more dependent than the engraving (L.31) by the Master E.S. could have conveyed on the Baden-Baden Crucifix of Nicolaus Gerhaerts. The attendant figures are suffused with the lofty rhetoric and ethos of Netherlandish painting. The side figures of St George (Plate 121) and St Mary Magdalen seem immediately affiliated in style to the Magdalen in Biengen. They are elegant in armour and drapery respectively, as was popular at the time, and of extreme agility in gesture and movement. The wing paintings are the work of the town-painter of Nördlingen, Friedrich Herlin, and date from 1462–6. They presuppose an acquaintance with Roger van der Weyden's altarpiece in St Columba in Cologne. Documentary evidence to the effect that in 1477/8 the Burgomaster of Nördlingen, prompted by Herlin, demanded from the town council of Nuremberg the delivery of 'some statues' which the Nuremburg carver, Simon Lainberger, had undertaken to 'cut' for an altarpiece by Herlin,[60] has been connected with these figures. However, it is not possible to recognize any connexion between the highly individual Upper Rhenish style of these statues and Nuremberg sculpture at the same time.

The triptych in the parish church of Bopfingen in the immediate vicinity of Nördlingen bears the date 1472. The sculpture here, while not of the same quality as that at Nördlingen, already shows the complete transposition of the Upper Rhenish spirit of Nicolaus Gerhaerts' successors into the local style, which is full of movement, and which, in regional variations, is ubiquitous in South German sculpture from 1470 to 1490. We may therefore safely assume that the sculpture on the Nördlingen high altar, which is so intimately connected with the Upper Rhineland and which represents such a vigorous and individual achievement, pre-dates the Bopfingen figures only by a few years. The Crucifix with the beautiful little angels in flight in the centrepiece of Friedrich Herlin's high altar in the Jakobskirche at Rothenburg (Plate 117B),[61] which is also derived from Upper Rhenish sources, cannot be much later than the date signed upon it, i.e. 1466. (It is worth noting that a painter of the outstanding quality of Friedrich Herlin apparently employed different carvers for different altars.)

It will be clear from this that the Virgin from Colmar and the Magdalen from Biengen, with their impressive fullness and breadth, must have preceded these statues from Herlin's altarpieces, whereas the sublime maturity of the style embodied in the Dangolsheim Virgin followed later. The Upper Rhenish wooden figure of St Agnes in the Bayerisches Nationalmuseum in Munich,[62] with its coquettish little head set above the gigantic volume of the drapery, provides a parallel, and in its stress on the optically important features it is already a forerunner of later developments. I would therefore date these two pieces c. 1480.

According to documentary evidence, in 1478 Count Wolfgang von Öttingen applied to the town council of Nördlingen for the cancellation of an order, issued two years previously, forbidding Hans Kamensetzer to reside in the town. Unfortunately, however, no profession is cited for Hans Kamensetzer in this document. If he can be identified with the sculptor of the same name who in 1471 came to Strasbourg from Swabia, then a connexion between him and the altar-figures in St Georg at Nördlingen would appear likely, especially since Kamensetzer's son-in-law became a citizen of the town in 1479. The Strasbourg Hans Kamensetzer, like Nicolaus Gerhaerts before him, received shortly before 1487 a summons to the imperial court in Vienna, where he died in the ensuing spring.

The next influential works in Upper Rhenish sculpture are the figures for the high altar in the parish church of Lautenbach near Offenburg. The date of this altarpiece has been associated with the dedication of an altar in this church in 1483, but scholars were then led away from the acceptance of this date by the character of the wing paintings. In the architecture and in the style of the statues the spatial factor is so stressed that I have no doubt that the whole work really dates from the 1480s. All three figure niches are constructed in a truly architectural way, i.e. as chapels [63] – with real windows at the back – and are coordinated under the elastically overlapping arches of the framework, which itself is decorated with serrated leaves and vine foliage, offset by the shadows of the depths of the niches. The whole is extremely graceful. Grace lingers too round the figures themselves, half emerging from the shadow. This is tantamount to saying that in the function of these carved figures the microcosm of the altar assumes the same dominating role that the macrocosm of the whole building played in relation to the subordinate architectural sculpture in the epoch of the Gothic cathedrals. The chiaroscuro of the composition lends the linear movement a new spatial significance. The stresses reveal the dynamic forces which are at once the source of the statues themselves and of their finely proportioned framework. The complexity in the drapery folds, for example in those of the Virgin which stands at the centre of the Lautenbach shrine, point forward already almost to Mannerism. The figures of a triptych from the abbey of Lichtental near Baden-Baden are related to those in the Lautenbach high altar. They are the three Magi in the Metropolitan Museum in New York,[64] the seated Virgin and Child from a Nativity still in the abbey of Lichtental, and the wing paintings dated 1489. The most magnificent of the carved figures is the Virgin, in the rich abundance of her drapery and her beautifully braided hair.

Of slightly later date is the splendid Virgin in the pilgrimage chapel of Arlange near Wuisse in Lorraine,[65] impressive through its size and weight. Here the drapery surfaces are not subject to Mannerist linear display, but are deeply furrowed in a painterly way, though dominated by generous, flowing lines. The Upper Rhenish premises upon which this style depends are clear, but it deserves yet another word of admiration. To what heights the legacy of Nicolaus Gerhaerts' art could ascend!

From the innumerable pieces belonging in this context, I can only single out two:

the remarkable rhetorical group of Joachim and Anne, probably from a church in Strasbourg and deriving from the style of the minster pulpit; and the wooden Virgin on a crescent moon in the Frauenchörle of Freiburg Minster,[66] a work already characteristic of a peculiar Freiburg style which became increasingly evident towards the end of the century.

Constance and Ulm were next in order of importance for the diffusion of the new style in South German sculpture. We have already discussed Nicolaus Gerhaerts' work at Constance, and especially the significance of his lost altarpiece in the minster. We have mentioned too the Netherlandish altarpieces in Franconian Swabia – Schwäbisch Hall belonged to the diocese of Würzburg – and also Nördlingen's connexions with Strasbourg.

Acquaintance with Hans Multscher's bronze head of St Catherine (Plate 86A) can leave no doubt that the magnificent decorated bronze lid of the monument to Count Jörg von Waldburg (d. 1467) in the abbey church in Waldsee was also cast at Ulm.[67] It is the style of the late works of Multscher and the Netherlandish style of his assistant at Sterzing which is continued here. The armoured figure of the duke bears no trace yet of the dynamism of the new style. The work is raised to monumental quality by its austerity and by the juxtaposition of heraldic emblems to fill the remarkably large background. The character of the late works of Multscher is also reflected in some of the sculpture of the tabernacle for the Holy Sacrament in Ulm Minster, erected in 1467.

Thus it is understandable that in the almost incommensurably rich sculptural decoration of the choir stalls of Ulm Minster,[68] carried out by the elder Jörg Syrlin between 1469 and 1474 (Plates 122 and 123), we should meet among his assistants sculptors who clearly come from Multscher's workshop. They provide us with evidence of the strong local tradition which existed in Ulm. The tremendous significance of these choir stalls, however, does not reside in the fact that many traditional talents participated in their creation, but in the new intellectual quality they present, in the boldness of their inspiration, and in the sharp delineation of facial features. These qualities appear just in those sculptural elements which differ sharply from the local tradition. They are derived from contacts with the new vision of sculpture possessed by Nicolaus Gerhaerts. In the contract concerning the work Jörg Syrlin is expressly named as a joiner. His name appears among the records of Ulm for the first time in 1449, and he was the son of a carpenter from a village in the vicinity of Ulm. His earliest known work, the prayer-desk from Ottenbach, dated 1458 and now in the Ulm Museum, gives us no indication of the exceptional things that were to come. But the new spirit is certainly visible in the ornamental gesture of a vast cupboard (also in the Ulm Museum) signed and dated 1465, and this almost abstract quality is fully revealed in the sedilia in the choir of the minster. These were carved, according to the inscription, by Syrlin in 1468 and were no doubt a 'try-out' for the choir stalls themselves.

I feel that the picture has been distorted through the attempt to explain the magnificence of the carvings on the Ulm choir stalls by branding Jörg Syrlin just as a joiner, and declaring him to have had as partner in the work some outside sculptor of genius. It is certain that in order to get the vast work accomplished in the short time stipulated in his contract, Syrlin did need a large number of collaborators. And it may be that we owe the most impressive of the choir-stall carvings to some such anonymous genius. Later sculptural work known to be that of the elder Syrlin – like the stone knights on the fish trough from Ulm Town Hall, dating from 1482 – in no way possesses the same liberated and liberating creative power. But the signed and accredited joiner-work of the elder Syrlin does prove that between 1458 and 1465 he assimilated the abstract formal language and beauty of Burgundo-Netherlandish carving. The boldest sculptural achievements of the Ulm choir stalls have their roots in this Western art, and the question whether the genius behind them may or may not be identified with the elder Syrlin, who in any case bore the responsibility for the whole undertaking, is of secondary importance. This problem proves once again that North European sculpture, even in Nicolaus Gerhaerts' day, was still affected by the tradition of communal author-ship, and that it is impossible for the scholar to apply to this field the criteria of indi-vidual authorship which are a matter of course in Italian fifteenth-century sculpture. Nicolaus Gerhaerts himself is perhaps an exception to this rule. But even when we consider his immediate successors at Constance (Heinrich Iselin?), the question of the master's identity is as vexed as when we examine the Ulm choir stalls. We cannot, for example, identify one single work by Heinrich Multscher, known to have been a wood carver and the brother of Hans Multscher, and the same is true of the sculptor Jörg Stein, though his name is repeatedly mentioned in the records of the most important commissions in Ulm from 1455 until his death in 1491.

What are the specific qualities of these choir stalls? I think they are the abstract austerity of the architectural arrangement and the controlled clarity of the far-reaching spatial dispositions. In this case we are presented with the apparent paradox that the sculptural parts possess the maximum freedom and are yet completely subordinated to the architectural whole. They are full of strength, and are yet not as expansive as is usually the case in German sculpture. A remarkable power of judgement is evident in the architecture of the stalls, in the combination of architecture and sculpture, and in the balance between figure and ornament. Late Gothic here speaks the language of Early Humanism. Alongside the representatives of the Old Testament and of the Christian doctrine of salvation, heathens who foresaw man's redemption, wise men and sibyls, are portrayed, it seems to us, with special intensity. It may be that Heinrich Steinhövel, doctor to the city of Ulm, exercised his influence here; for he had trans-lated Terence and Boccaccio and he belonged to the leading lights in the art of book-printing which flourished at this time in the city. The connexions between wood carving and the woodcuts of contemporary Ulm book illustrations are close.[69] The carving on the choir stalls, however, takes precedence in both time and quality as the expression of a new human type. The main star in the constellation which led to this, I must insist, bears the name of Syrlin.

Most stupendous of all are the busts on the lower stall ends. They are symbolical and visionary, raised from the objective into the spiritual sphere, and of metallic sharpness in both outline and inner structure. Everything is permeated by a luminous clarity and at the same time by an astonishing spatial power. Wilhelm Vöge has described the psychological content of these carvings and pointed out their sources. But what does it help us to know that in all probability a series of woodcuts, reproducing an older cycle of painted panels, acted as prototypes? The astonishing thing remains their serene mastery of sculptural form. These busts are calculated parts of a trigonometrical scheme, resulting from the skill of the basic architectural arrangement.

They are Germany's most amazing echo of the new sculptural possibilities first revealed in Nicolaus Gerhaerts' art. But in reality there is only an indirect connexion between the Ulm choir stalls and Gerhaerts' sculpture. Probably Syrlin's sedilia in Ulm Minster[70] presuppose an acquaintance with the choir stalls at Constance. To the same extent we may assume that the carver of the Ulm stall ends also had contact with the world of Nicolaus Gerhaerts. But the differences in the sculptural feeling are so marked that the individuality of the Ulm master only emerges more strongly when we compare him with Nicolaus Gerhaerts and his circle. We have here a highly individual and characteristically German solution of the new possibilities of representation which had been opened up by the most advanced talents in Netherlandish art at this time. We know Netherlandish engravings to have been one source, but we have no proof that the Ulm master had any personal contact with contemporary painting or sculpture in the Netherlands. May one assume that, via the extremely individual treatment of Netherlandish prototypes in Multscher's late works, this 'arte moderna' had penetrated so deeply into the native soil of Ulm that now, under the auspices of Early Humanism, it produced this translation of human and spiritual worlds into a new sculptural presence? Apropos of Syrlin's indebtedness to Nicolaus Gerhaerts' art I can only quote the striking and pithy phrase of Pinder: 'It is just in the finest of the busts that he thinks differently from Gerhaerts, although he knows him.'[71]

Even in that most magnificent bust which bursts through its confines and which is doubtless a self-portrait (Plate 123B), and where we see the artist relinquishing the abstract harmony of the portrait for a circling movement inside the figure, I feel that we are confronted, not with an approximation to Gerhaerts' type of representation, which always derives from spatial depth, but with a proof of the great Ulm master's originality and range.

This is all the clearer when we compare the Ulm busts with those on the stall ends from the Benedictine abbey church of Weingarten, known to have been carved by Heinrich Iselin around 1478 (see pp. 106–7; Plate 124). Iselin appears to have been a member of Gerhaerts' workshop already in Strasbourg. Around 1466 he probably joined the workshop of his father-in-law, Simon Haider, at Constance, and shared in the carving of the choir stalls there. Of all the Late Gothic carvers at Constance Iselin was the most talented. His delight in sculptural fullness and painterly movement, as seen in these Weingarten busts, mirrors the influence of Nicolaus Gerhaerts. We meet this exuberant amplitude already in the busts of the prophets on the spandrels of the Constance choir stalls. The list of items to be carved on the Weingarten stalls may well have been determined by those at Ulm: all the more marked is the difference in style. Iselin's work is naïver and lacks the formal and spiritualized eloquence which is the hallmark of the Ulm carvings.

From Weingarten we have the busts only, and no evidence as to what the original

choir stalls were like. This is regrettable; for at both Constance and Ulm the architectural character of the original plan and its effect upon us today cannot be sufficiently
stressed. At Constance[72] the spatial composition was originally meant to culminate in
Nicolaus Gerhaerts' high altar. Research has shown that this was not an Altar of the
Cross, but, as we have seen, of the Virgin. At Ulm Syrlin was commissioned in 1473 –
already before completion of work on the choir stalls – to carve the shrine, also within
eight years. The altarpiece was destroyed by the iconoclasts. A magnificent parchment drawing (from Ulm) in the Württembergisches Landesmuseum at Stuttgart[73]
shows what the original plan may have looked like. It is a drawing about 7 ft 7 in. (231
cm.) in height, and looks like the product of a masons' lodge. At the same time it lets
us, in an exemplary way, into the entire secret of the woodcarvers' workshops of the
Late Gothic period. There is much reason to suggest that we have here a plan of the
erstwhile high altar of Ulm Minster; but may it also be that this delicate, transparent
drawing with its remarkably shrewd disposition of sculptural stresses represents the
personal handiwork of the master who was responsible for the Ulm choir stalls – or is
it the invention of another great anonymous artist, destined to be carried out by joiners
and woodcarvers? The Ulm character is clear. The composition of the figures, standing
in front of a curtain held by angels, may have a connexion with Hans Multscher's altar
at Sterzing (Vipiteno; 1456/8). At the same time the architectural articulation of the
canopy in the drawing is reminiscent of Syrlin's sedilia. On the other hand, the type
of the altar in the drawing has an immediate antecedent in the high altar of the church
at Tiefenbronn,[74] which according to its inscription was made in 1469 by the Ulm
painter Hans Schüchlin. It is true that the Tiefenbronn altar has none of the magnificent spaciousness or the delicate ramifications of decoration that we find in the Ulm
drawing. The type of representation in the statues, too, appears to lack any connexion
with the individualized style of the most outstanding of the busts of the Ulm choir
stalls. In 1474 the sculptor Michel Erhart, whom records show to have been active in
Ulm since 1469, was commissioned to carve 'some figures' for the shrine of the high
altar of the minster, and between 1499 and 1503 he was still engaged in carving busts for
the predella of this altar. Here is one more outstanding example of the extent to which
work was distributed in such a case among a number of important collaborators, and
also of the length of time taken to complete it.

The Ulm stalls, the high altar at Tiefenbronn, and the drawing at Stuttgart all bear
testimony, together with information we have for the decade following Multscher's
death, to an astonishing wealth of artists at Ulm. Among these the activities of the more
traditionally minded and the first beginnings of the next generation (Michel Erhart,
Jörg Syrlin the Younger) are inseparably interwoven. To the carver of the magnificent
busts on the stall ends may perhaps be ascribed a male bust in the Bayerisches Nationalmuseum in Munich, two demi-figures of prophets in the Städtische Skulpturengalerie
at Frankfurt, and a female reliquary bust in the Ulm Museum.[75] The stone figures,
signed by Syrlin, on the fish trough formerly in front of Ulm Town Hall (now in
the Museum) reveal the same style in its penetration of body and space. The elder
Syrlin died in 1492. The problems surrounding his personality continue to mark the

work of his successors – however clear the significance of the entire group may be.

The large carved wooden Pietà from the Dominican house of Weil near Esslingen (now in the Württembergisches Landesmuseum at Stuttgart; Plate 125) occupies a special place. It is dated 1471 and is signed with a cross and the initial P, which may possibly refer to a master Peter Köllin, known to have been active at Esslingen between 1479 and 1502.[76] We realize once again the significance of the monumental realism of Multscher's late works in Ulm; there is a magnificent assurance and a block-like quality in the form, and at the same time a deep sensibility in the facial expressions. This Pietà is of significance too in that it was probably never part of an altarpiece, but was an independent piece of sculpture, somewhere in the abbey precincts. The features of the face are reminiscent of Multscher's Sterzing Virgin.

The work of the younger Jörg Syrlin[77] is relatively clear within the Ulm school, and is recognizable from the time of his drawing for a vespertolium in Ulm Minster which is dated 1475. Thus the work of the son, too, had its origins in the joiner's sphere, and we know of several commissions to him for joinery work in Swabia. Along with these there were drawings for altarpieces (Ulm) and for altar shrines, e.g. the high altar (1496–9) of the former Benedictine abbey of Ochsenhausen (statues now in the parish church of Bellamont), and also monuments, e.g. that of Hans von Stadion (dated 1489) in the parish church of Oberstadion. Once again we get the impression of a remarkable variety. In the sculptural field the individual is subordinated to the type. The detailed agreement for example between the Ochsenhausen altar figures and those at Biengen prove how strong certain formal conventions were within the framework of this prolific output. The reliefs of the Passion carved between 1509 and 1516 by Jörg Syrlin, together with Christoph Langeisen, for the abbey of Zwiefalten (now in the Württembergisches Landesmuseum at Stuttgart) are formally, apart from certain variations of dress, still in the Late Gothic convention. What is impressive in the works of Syrlin the Younger is the perfection in the handling of the surface and the brilliant coloured decoration it receives. The problem of the division of labour in the altar workshop is complicated in the Late Gothic period by the supplementary activities of the painters of the sculpture and of the painters of the pictures on the wings. Through them arose that 'painterly' opus completum which – in situ – fitted in with its surrounding architectural setting. Syrlin the Younger died about 1521.

The development of Michel Erhart is of much greater significance.[78] He was resident at Ulm from 1469, the year of Syrlin's commission for the choir stalls. We have already referred to his first known and highly honourable commission, dating from 1474. He was asked to produce statues for the high altar of the Minster, whose 'sarch' (i.e. coffin) – which we should probably interpret not only as the predella but as the whole altar shrine – had been entrusted to Syrlin the Elder. This high altar became the centre-piece of Syrlin's great choir-stall design. The result must have been an optical unity in the arrangement such as still strikes us today when we enter the choir of the abbey of Blaubeuren. If the retention of the elder Syrlin seemed a guarantee for the success of the undertaking, may we not assume from Michel Erhart's commission for the statues on the high altar that he too was one of the carvers of the choir stalls?

Michel Erhart's name is mentioned more frequently than any other among the records of Ulm craftsmen during these decades. In 1485 he was entrusted with preparing an altarpiece 'carved in the raw', i.e. unpainted, for the chapel of St Dionysius outside St Ulrich and St Afra at Augsburg. This altarpiece, which has not survived, was erected in 1487, and it was painted and gilded by the Augsburg painter Gumpold Giltlinger in 1490–2. Michel was responsible in 1489 for statues for the church of the abbey of St Katherine at St Gallen. An inscription on the frame of paintings by Hans Holbein the Elder from the abbey of Weingarten, now in Augsburg Cathedral, bears the date 1493 and the name of the sculptor. We have a signed work of the master dated 1494 in the wonderfully carved monumental wooden Crucifix at the entrance to the choir in the Heiligkreuzkirche at Schwäbisch Hall. The high altar of the former abbey church of Blaubeuren is dated 1493–4, and this is the joint work of Michel and his son Gregor. As late as 1516–18 he was responsible for the stone figures of the prophets for the Mount of Olives designed for Ulm Minster by Matthäus Böblinger in 1474.

Attempts have been made to identify Michel Erhart with the master of the most important of the end busts of the Ulm stalls. But I do not think that we can sense the same reflective and spiritual quality in Erhart's later works – even apart from the themes treated – nor is there that newer demonstrative insight into character which endows a carving like the Cimerian Sibyl with an almost Netherlandish character. On the contrary, Erhart's later statues are imbued with a vigorous, refined, and purified naturalism, free from the trelliswork of linear ornamental dynamism. Through the extension of Michel Erhart's work via his son Gregor, this serene naturalism became the path which led from the Late Gothic style into a new world.

To Michel Erhart has also been attributed the Virgin of the Misericord from Ravensburg, now in the Staatliche Museen in Berlin (Plate 126).[79] The towering stance and the linear precision of surface suggest a date about 1480. By the same hand are two magnificently preserved reliefs from a carved altarpiece representing the Mass of St Gregory and the Martyrdom of St Catherine in the Berlin Museum.[79] The connexion of these pieces with those which have been attested as works by Michel Erhart seems to me evident. At one time the apocryphal story that the high altar of the parish church of Ravensburg was 'carved by Friedrich Schramm (from Ravensburg) and painted and coloured by Christoph Kelltenhofer' in 1480 was connected with the Virgin of the Misericord from Ravensburg. 1482 is the date on the partly gilded silver statuette of the Virgin, now in the Berlin Museum,[80] made by the Augsburg goldsmith Hainrich Hufnagel. Is it possible that Michel Erhart was the master of the model for this goldsmith-work? Was the Virgin on the high altar of the former Premonstratensian abbey of Weissenau perhaps originally the central figure of the altar, completed in 1493, for the neighbouring abbey of Weingarten, of which the wings, now in the cathedral at Augsburg, bear the names of Hans Holbein as painter and of Michel Erhart as sculptor? In this case the Virgin at Weissenau would be a work by Michel Erhart and not, as generally assumed, by his son Gregor.

Further, we must consider the rich native traditions of the workshops in the flourishing mercantile towns in the neighbourhood of Constance. I would mention here a charming little wooden Virgin in the Staatliche Museen in Berlin which is of slightly later date.[81] This statue, based on an engraving by the Master E.S. – and taking into account the surviving statues from the high altar and choir stalls of Constance Minster – shows vividly that in Upper Swabian sculpture at the end of the fifteenth century an increasing autonomy of the statue had been achieved, parallel to that in the works of Michel and Gregor Erhart.

The neighbouring districts of Bavaria did not, as far as we can see, produce works of equal quality at this time. Here sculpture of a conventional character predominates, such as the altar figures of an Enthroned Virgin with attendant Benedictine saints in the former Cistercian abbey of Fürstenfeldbruck near Munich.[82] The only work which can be compared with the Upper Rhenish and Swabian sculpture just discussed is the enigmatic red marble monument to the Emperor Ludwig of Bavaria of c. 1480 in the Frauenkirche in Munich (Plate 128, A and B). This is a magnificently impressive figure; it is accompanied by various narrative scenes, as was popular at the time, for example the reconciliation of Duke Albrecht III with his father Duke Ernst – impressive in the way the content has been translated into the abstract monumentality of the red marble.[83] It was once thought to be the work of the wood carver Erasmus Grasser, who was responsible for the burlesque Morris Dancers of 1480 in the town hall in Munich (Plate 129, A and B). Actually the connexion between the dynamism in the reliefs on the tomb lid and the tension of movement and the spatial quality of the morisco dwarfs is but slight. These dancing figures are the most outstanding examples of the astonishingly expressive sense of movement characteristic of South German sculpture round 1480; they have the gaiety of the bizarre and are in composition closely linked one with another, each being fired by the violence of gesture and mime of the other. Their silhouettes moreover form the most fantastic linear ornaments.

Three fragments of limewood reliefs from a Crucifixion altar now in the Berlin Museum are South German translations of a Netherlandish altar in the style of Roger van der Weyden.[84] Such works as these exercised a formative influence upon the style of Grasser's altar sculpture (e.g. the Holy Cross Altar at Ramersdorf and a little monstrance altar in the Bayerisches Nationalmuseum in Munich),[85] whereas for Grasser's red marble monuments at St Peter in Munich the large-scale disposition of the imperial tomb in the Frauenkirche in Munich probably served as model. But the Morris Dancers and the attendant figures from a Crucifixion at Pipping[85] (Munich, Bayerisches Nationalmuseum; Plate 127) serve to show how in this phase of development certain tendencies of the time were translated into a highly individual style possessed of movement, strength of feeling, and clarity. In Grasser's work, too, near the turn of the century there was a sloughing off of abstract ornamental qualities, and a new endowing of the linear conventions with energies derived from approximation to nature. We shall have to refer to this phenomenon repeatedly in the works of Late Gothic wood carvers at the end of the century. The apex of this style is reached by Grasser in his enthroned St Peter on the high altar of St Peter in Munich, donated by Duke Albrecht IV in 1492 (Plate 174B). The drama of surging movement in the massive block of the figure is here yet further increased. From the wealth of rich vestments the monumental image emerges majestic, with its human and spiritual qualities transcendent.

In South-East Bavaria we encounter an echo once again of Nicolaus Gerhaerts' art in the impressive figure of St Martin from Zeillarn (Lower Bavaria) now in the Bayerisches Nationalmuseum in Munich, which is remarkable for the striking modelling of the features. The stride forward is expressed with an elegant breadth, but in terms of the flat surface, as it pleased the style of 1480.[86] Probably this statue originated in Passau and may be an early work of the Master of Kefermarkt, of whom we shall have more to say later. Two works at Passau deserve special mention: the stone figures on the portal of the old town hall[87] and the wooden figure of St Aegidius in Niedernburg Abbey. Both are works whose vitality of expression and clarity of inner structure can be explained only through contact with the art of Nicolaus Gerhaerts. Moreover, one cannot sufficiently emphasize the inseparability of these Bavarian districts from neighbouring Austria. It was only in 1468 that the bishopric of Vienna was severed from the diocese of Passau, which up till then had extended as far as the river Leitha. Salzburg was the seat of the archdiocese. Records show that the same masters were frequently active in both Salzburg and Passau. Salzburg was the centre of a highly developed monumental sculpture in a splendid red marble, of which we still have examples in both Bavaria and Austria. I would cite as the finest of these the monument to Marx von Nussdorf and his wife in the abbey church of Laufen, dating from 1478-9.[88]

In Vienna and Wiener Neustadt the successors of Nicolaus Gerhaerts, who died in 1473, again occupy the foreground.[89] According to a payment made in 1478, work on the imperial tomb was continued first by Max Valmet and then by the Salzburg stonemason Michael Tichter, known to have been a member of the St Stephen's lodge from 1467 onwards. More interesting works arose from the attempt of native sculptors and carvers to come to terms with the spatially expansive ideas of Nicolaus Gerhaerts; for example, the monument of Empress Eleonora of Portugal (d. 1467) in the Neuklosterkirche in Wiener Neustadt, a work where traces of the impressive magnificence of a Netherlandish prototype are still visible, but in which the details of execution are jejune and finicky; and also individual statues in St Stephen in Vienna (in particular those in the nave), where emphasis on linear features has led to the development of a consistently abstract style of presentation.

In 1478 there followed the magnificent bust of an over life-size Man of Sorrows, signed 'Thomas Strayff pictor', in the parish church of Wiener Neustadt (Plate 118A). This is a work of masterly clarity, closely related in the subtle treatment of the surface to Upper Rhenish works by the immediate successors of Nicolaus Gerhaerts. (Its greatest similarity is to the stone fragment of a head of Christ in St Georges at Haguenau in Alsace.) Records show Thomas Strayff to have been active at Wiener Neustadt from 1466 to 1483. The red marble font by the Salzburg master Ulrich Auer in St Stephen in Vienna dates from 1476-81, but its over-richly decorated cover was perhaps added slightly later. The choir stalls in St Stephen, with their rich sculptural decoration (destroyed in the Second World War), dated from 1476-86. It is certain that several carvers were engaged on these, but the name of Wilhelm Rollinger alone is known to us.

One meets the local character of an expressly Viennese style of sculpture most definitely, I think, in the relaxed and colourful beauty of the series of carved figures, presumably of the same date, in the Burgkapelle in Vienna. There is here a highly individual charm, independent of influences from contemporary engravings and also of allegiance to any definite school; whereas in the sculpture on both the font and the choir stalls in St Stephen one senses a certain dependence upon Salzburg or Swabia.

Is the sculpture of the majestic high altar in the choir of St Elizabeth at Košice (Kaschau), in formerly Hungarian and now Slovakian territory, of the same time (Plate 131)? Additions made during the Renaissance and, still more, unhappy restorations made in the nineteenth century have very much changed the character of this altarpiece.[90] There is, however, no doubt that among the original parts which have been preserved may be counted not only the brilliantly coloured wing-paintings, but also the three main figures of the altarpiece, representing the Virgin flanked by the two Sts Elizabeth. We have documentary evidence of money spent on work for this 'tabula magna' between 1474 and 1477. The wing-paintings stand, I think, in close stylistic relationship to the Viennese 'Master of the Schottenstift' (1469-75). The sculpture of the Košice altarpiece also has Viennese affiliations. The work which bears the closest resemblance to the Košice figures is the wooden Annunciation in the Burgkapelle, with its elegant charm of facial expression and its delight in the almost metallic clarity and dynamic vibration of the forms. Similarities to the Swabian sculpture of the school of Michel and Gregor Erhart have been unduly stressed, and also the sculpture on the Košice altarpiece has been dated too late; the figures must have been carved soon after the wing-paintings were made. In reality the slender, upright figures, the contrasting of body and drapery, and the broad swirl of the latter on contact with the ground are typical of the years round 1480, and any links with Swabian works (e.g. with the Magdalen on the Nördlingen altar) only serve to prove that the ideas which we first met in the Upper Rhineland and Swabia find an echo here. Probably the fine wooden relief of the Nativity from the castle chapel at Hlohovec-Galgóc in the Slovakian National Gallery at Bratislava is by the same master. The origins of this relief extend back to the magical fragment of a similar scene in the Historical Museum at Saverne in Alsace. This Košice Master is thus of outstanding significance.[91]

The most eloquent expression of Austrian carving at the time is to be found in the large figures of the Apostles in the nave of the parish church (cathedral) of Wiener Neustadt (Plate 130). In their spatial function they possess monumental character. Within the framework of the church interior they are meant to play the part of the stone statues which it had previously been the task of the lodge to produce. Here the tragedy of the Late Gothic becomes apparent: in the sphere of the altar it could achieve marvels, but it was no longer capable of realizing the architectural function of sculpture. Thus, by means of passionate expression, it is the sense of movement which predominates in these Apostles, and the extent to which this sense of movement is conveyed to the surrounding space is indeed astounding. In the faces too there is a spiritual fire which exceeds anything in contemporary statues from the Upper Rhineland, Swabia, or Bavaria. The turmoil of the drapery of the Annunciation at the entrance to the choir is just as magnificent. There is no doubt that the dynamism seen here presupposes an acquaintance with the most advanced contemporary examples of Upper Rhenish sculpture. The nearest approach is in the carvings on the pulpit in Strasbourg Minster. But I feel the Austrian quality in the expression of these carvings to be so strong that the master responsible – perhaps Lorenz Luchsperger – probably knew these Upper Rhenish examples only at second-hand, i.e. that he had received his impression of them from works in Austria or Bavaria; for the feeling for movement in the sculpture of Nicolaus Gerhaerts' successors had by then already exercised its influence over the whole of South Germany. The wood carving of the Death of the Virgin in the museum of the abbey of Herzogenburg shows in its turn the wide extent of the influence of the Master of Wiener Neustadt.

Two further examples, especially characteristic of Austrian sculpture, are of somewhat later date, i.e. of *c.* 1490. First, the highly expressive Crucifixion on the high altar of the parish church of Murau (Styria). This is related to the Munich sculpture of Erasmus Grasser, but it is harder in cut, sterner in sentiment, and filled with a deep religious feeling.[92] Owing to the serenity of its form, this Crucifixion is usually dated about or after 1500; but I think that there is such a spontaneous immediacy about the figures that they must have arisen out of direct contact with the engravings of the Master E.S. The Virgin's cloak in particular spreads out at her feet in opulent breadth and depth in a way we no longer meet at the turn of the century, when such fold-work becomes rather applied to more block-like figures. From the same Eastern Alpine area during the Late Gothic epoch I would place alongside this Mount Calvary from Murau a wooden Virgin from St Johann in den Tauern, now in the Städtische Skulpturengalerie in Frankfurt.[93] The sharpness of the surfaces here shows what marvels were achieved even in apparently remote districts in the presentation of majestic and yet charming figures at that particular moment.

All the masters of Late Gothic sculpture in Austria are left behind by Michael Pacher, known to have been a citizen of Bruneck (Brunico, in Val Pusteria or the Pustertal in South Tyrol) from the early 1460s and to have died presumably at Salzburg in 1498. In Pacher's workshop were created large altarpieces in which the art of the 'altar architect', the carver, and the painter were inseparable. From the altarpieces which have survived *in situ* one may trace with amazement his increasing boldness. The development goes from the altar in the old parish church of Gries near Bozen (Bolzano; 1471–5) to the miracle in the pilgrimage church of St Wolfgang in the Salzkammergut (1471–81; Plates 132 and 133). The composition of the altarpiece at Gries is still additive in the traditional way, and we have indeed proof of its traditional character, since Pacher was commissioned by his contract to follow, as far as the centre scene was concerned, the pattern of the high altar in the parish church of Bozen, which was presumably the one made by Hans von Judenburg in 1422–3. Pacher may well have seen from Multscher's Sterzing (Vipiteno) altarpiece how the shrine of the altar could be given a greater illusion of depth by the use of painted angels in the background holding a curtain. But in the Gries altarpiece all the figures are still symmetrically arranged. The St Wolfgang altar instead is a mysterious microcosm: a deep recess from whose shadowy spaces the web of canopies and pinnacles emerges which then continue in the openwork pinnacles and canopies of the framework of the altarpiece and finally seem to merge into the vaulting of the choir itself. The sculpture is raised to a magical monumentality and is also more clearly coordinated and at the same time subordinated to the architecture of the altar than at Gries. At St Wolfgang the painted wing-panels are doubled. They therefore have to be opened twice before the fortissimo of the sculpture itself is revealed. On the outside on each side of the shrine are wooden figures of St George and St Florian, only visible when the outer wings are closed, an arrangement first met with in Multscher's Sterzing altar.

In the individual figures at Gries and St Wolfgang no such differences are visible. In both cases their structure is of a stupendous static clarity. The contrast of core and envelope time and again produces new effects of form and colour, as though the surface were charged with life. This reaches its climax in the rich variations of the serene features of the figures. The sculpture at St Wolfgang is suffused with the greatest sense of movement and inner tension. The folds of drapery have an opulent rhetoric, which however is never excessive: on the contrary, each figure is instinct with deep gravity. All the movements are controlled, so that the total effect is one of serene harmony, transfigured by the gold and the noble luminosity of the colours.

If we try to trace back Michael Pacher's development as a carver, it seems that before the work at Gries he was responsible for the altarpiece in the parish church of St Lorenzen (S. Lorenzo in Pusteria) near Bruneck, of which the centre figure, an Enthroned Virgin, still survives *in situ*. Here a block-like character still prevails. The lines of the drapery folds are tauter and lack the gentle gradations which already characterize the surface of the figures at Gries. If we take in addition the older figure of St Valentine from Pfalzen (Fálzes) near Bruneck,[94] we can watch how Pacher's carving grows out of a regional tradition which is closely associated with works in Salzburg dating from the middle of the century. Pacher also exploited numerous ideas drawn from contemporary engravings by the Master E.S. But all this does not really suffice to explain the creative contacts between Pacher and his environment.

Pacher was just as brilliant as a painter. His paintings on the outer sides of the wings of the Gries altar have not survived. It is nevertheless remarkable that the paintings on the back are by another hand and are indeed the work of an Upper Rhenish master.[95] So, if we are going to confine ourselves to altarpieces whose authenticity is assured, we have to depend entirely on the magnificent wing-paintings at St Wolfgang. These paintings show in how sovereign a manner Pacher came to terms with contemporary Italian painting, and especially that of Mantegna – and this in an altarpiece whose architectural arts and whose carving are an unprecedented peak in South German Late Gothic art. If we examine the carvings in both Gries and St Lorenzen from this point of view, we must stress the fact that in them neither style nor character of the figures shows any contact with Italian art. Documentary records suggest that the St Lorenzen altarpiece was donated in 1462-3. The execution of course – as the case of the St Wolfgang altarpiece proves – may have extended over a longer period. It is assumed that the wing-paintings by Pacher, representing scenes from the lives of the Virgin and of St Lawrence (now Munich, Bayerische Staatsgemäldesammlungen, and Vienna, Kunsthistorisches Museum) were originally part of this altarpiece. These paintings already presuppose a knowledge of the spatial autonomy of the Italian Early Renaissance, though a knowledge superficial compared with the deep penetration that one senses in the St Wolfgang paintings. In the paintings from St Lorenzen there appears to be as yet no personal experience of Italy, so that we can assume that this decisive contact – the contact with Padua – only took place later.

The connexion between Pacher's altar carvings in the years before the St Wolfgang masterpiece and the most recent innovations in the Upper Rhineland, i.e. from Nicolaus Gerhaerts' circle, is therefore all the more important. The squat, voluminous figure of St Valentine at Pfalzen is in the local tradition. More difficult of interpretation is the style of the Seated Virgin at St Lorenzen and of her (supposed) attendant figures, St Lawrence (Innsbruck, Landesmuseum) and St Michael (Munich, Bayerisches National-museum).[96] Influence from the most advanced ingredients of the Sterzing altarpiece is possible, but cannot be regarded as a sufficient explanation of the style of these figures. Probably the St Lorenzen altar is actually later than 1462-3, and it may be assumed that before this Pacher had already had personal contact with the Upper Rhenish circle of Nicolaus Gerhaerts – perhaps at Constance. This encounter led to a radical change in his sculptural ideas. Already in the figures of the Gries altar the similarity of the En-throned God the Father and Christ to St James in the parish church of Kaysersberg in Alsace is of greater significance than any inherited local tradition. Moreover, in the carving on the Gries altar one cannot overlook the influence of the engravings of the Master E.S.

Thus we may say that Pacher's experience of Italian art only bore fruit when he began to prepare the *opus perfectum* of the St Wolfgang altar. Even if he possessed in-directly a knowledge of the mastery of composition and of the convincing power of the representation of the human body as achieved in the Italian painting of the Early Renaissance – living where he did it would be unlikely for him to escape such knowledge – it was only his personal contact with the work of Mantegna that opened up for him the secret of the spatial possibilities of painting and sculpture. The wing-paintings of the St Wolfgang altar and the panels of the Altar of the Church Fathers are a striking proof of this. When one looks at the carvings in the St Wolfgang altar, there can be no doubt that the power of the human form and the deepening of the psychological and spiritual facial expressions presuppose an acquaintance with works of the Italian Early Renais-sance. The only question is: what kind of works were they? I would suggest that they were works of painting and not of sculpture. For ready as the painter Michael Pacher was to surrender himself at Padua to the impression of Mantegna's works and to study the possibilities of achieving a new truth in the presentation of man and space, the carver Michael Pacher was incapable of drawing any such applicable conclusions from any encounter with the works of Donatello at Padua. Referring to the differences between their respective sculptural tasks – the carved triptych on the one hand and the bronze altarpiece on the other – is not a sufficient explanation. I incline rather to the belief that the deep, inborn affinity between North Italian sculpture and the heritage of the ancient world was at that time so strong that a Late Gothic carver was unable to follow into this realm. Yet it is patent that the immense transformation in Pacher's painting called forth a similar transformation in his sculptural ideas. In Pacher's work, more clearly than in any contemporary art in Northern Italy, painting and carving led together to a common end: the creation of a microcosmic altar architecture to which both were subordinated and with which both were coordinated. It is worth observing that Pacher's carving, which, as we have seen, presupposes an indirect acquaintance with the radical change that had taken place in sculpture in Nicolaus Gerhaerts' work, was yet incapable of a similar fructifying interchange of ideas with the sculpture of the Early Renaissance in Northern Italy, while Pacher's painting on the other hand could achieve this with contemporary North Italian painting.

All the more stupendous then is the experience of the sculpture of the St Wolfgang altar. I assume that the decisive preparations for this work were begun even before the Gries altar was completed, and that in the execution the composition of the carving of the central shrine ante-dated the addition of the painted wings. There is in fact no better introduction to the great golden age which began in South German sculpture in the second half of the 1470s than the carvings of St Wolfgang. In Nicolaus Gerhaerts the image was still stone – as it had been in the triforium of Prague Cathedral. But now, out of a harmony of carving and painting, was born the magic world of the *theatrum sacrum*, still suffused with the fire of the deep religiosity of the Late Middle Ages and yet at the same time expressive of a new realistic presentation. Hence the emphasis on three-dimensionality. In the Sterzing altar one still felt the confinement of sculpture in a plane and an abstract tectonic order, and this is also true of all those figures mentioned so far which, for the sake of establishing a certain *consenza*, I have connected with Roger van der Weyden's name. But now this whole conceptual world takes on a new concrete, corporeal reality, though the gold paint still lends it a magic, most lovely enchantment. However much profusion there may be in the decorative framework of the St Wolfgang altar, this is only of secondary importance compared with the rationally considered central composition and the piety of the attendant patron saints. A vital step has been taken which already leads beyond the expressionism of, say, the Nördlingen altar to the qualities of the epoch of the young Dürer. At the end of Pacher's career stands his triptych in the Franciscan church at Salzburg, but to this we can refer only when we come to deal with sculpture at the end of the century.

Pacher's work exercised an extensive influence over workshops at Bruneck, Brixen, and Bozen.[94] I will mention only Hans Klocker, active at Brixen (Bressanone) and documentarily recorded there from 1482 onwards. Probably payment of a bill dated 1481 from the cathedral in Brixen refers to him; it is 'pro formulare', i.e. for the design of the beautiful silver reliquary bust of St Agnes, which was then completed by the goldsmith Valentin Schauer in 1489 (now in the cathedral treasury). This work is the finest proof of the close alliance between the gold-painted German Late Gothic sculpture in wood and the actual art of the goldsmith. The alliance shows that it is wrong to regard the painterly character of the wood carvings as an expression of realism. The *accedens* of their being gilded removes the *opus perfectum* of these carvings into a world of magic. The bust of St Agnes at Brixen is the most beautiful example of this *legenda aurea* of Late Gothic art. In 1486–90 Hans Klocker was responsible for the altar in St Leonhard im Passeiertal (Vienna, Kunsthistorisches Museum) and between 1495 and 1500 for altarpieces in Bozen and its immediate vicinity.

In making our survey of the most important artists and works of German sculpture in the decades immediately succeeding Nicolaus Gerhaerts, which were so clearly defined in character and of which so many examples still survive, we had to arrange our material according to regions of origin, since sculpture at this time far more than previously is marked by the innate peculiarities of each individual district. In any appraisal of these works, distinguishing epithets like 'Swabian', 'Franconian', 'Rhenish' occur, as it were, automatically, but we must always bear in mind that generally speaking the impulses of development were released by supraterritorial forces. I think I have made this fact clear by discussing first of all sculpture in the Lower, Central, and Upper Rhineland and then in Swabia, Bavaria, and Austria.

In proceeding to Franconia I must first emphasize the fact that these geographical terms do not tally with historical data – for example, the subdivisions of Germany at the end of the Middle Ages. There were far too many such subdivisions of rulership to make it possible for them to assume regional meanings; and this is so not merely on account of the sizes of these innumerable political units, but also on account of the differences between secular and religious powers. Apart from these considerations, there is also the increasing extent of trade relationships (e.g. between the Free Imperial city of Nuremberg and both the Southern Netherlands and Northern Italy). Thus, while on account of the growing strength of the middle class we have to take into consideration the development of regional and local character, we must at the same time reckon with the emergence of supra-regional individual forces.

If we are looking for *incunabula* of Franconian sculpture at this time which can be dated with certainty, the foremost example is the high altar in the Jakobskirche at Rothenburg of 1466 (Plate 117B). There is a distinction in the carving between the figures in the central shrine,[97] which are clearly by a pupil of Multscher, and the Crucifix (together with its attendant angels), which has an affinity with the circle of Nicolaus Gerhaerts' successors. The general similarity of such figures permits us to date the carved Fair Virgin in the Frauenkirche at Nuremberg to *c.* 1460.[98] This figure is preeminently in the Franconian or Nuremberg tradition; for its genealogy reaches back to the Fair Virgin with the Halo of Rays at the entrance to the choir of St Sebald, with which it shares the fusion of solidity with delicate charm. On the other hand, the epic breadth and fullness of Middle Franconian sculpture is continued up to the carved altarpieces from Michael Wolgemut's workshop. Here a marked continuity of local style is apparent.[99] An example immediately succeeding the Fair Virgin from the Frauenkirche is the wooden Virgin from a canopied altarpiece from Weissenburg, near Nuremberg, now in the Bayerisches Nationalmuseum.[100] What, one asks oneself, may the lost carved figures of the large painted altarpiece, dated 1465, by Hans Pleydenwurff in the Trinitätskirche at Hof have looked like? The paintings are in the Alte Pinakothek in Munich.

Other *incunabula* of the Franconian style are the massive tombstone of Bishop Gottfried Schenk von Limpurg (d. 1455), perhaps by Lienhard Romer, and that of Bishop

Johann von Grumbach, both in Würzburg Cathedral. They derive their dignity and monumentality from their massive volume and the austerity of the linear articulation of their surfaces. On the other hand, the monument to Georg I Schenk von Limpurg (d. 1475) in the Schenkenkapelle at Grosskomburg already exhibits the whole sleekness of the new style which corresponds to the expressive engravings of the same years, with its increased mobility in the interweaving of figure and surrounding decoration. Thus at this moment the beginnings of new important traditions are visible in the Main-Franconian as in the other regions.[101]

Alongside the carvings just discussed, we have a group of alabaster statuettes which extends from the Middle Rhine via the borders of the Main to Thuringia and Magdeburg.[102] On account of the material used and the fact that they were easily transportable, it is very difficult to ascertain the provenance of these statuettes. I regard the Virgin from Heerberg in the Kerner-Haus at Weinsberg (Württemberg) as a work imported from the Netherlands about 1460. There follow a large relief of St Michael, dating from 1467, in the Severikirche in Erfurt (Plate 116B); the statue of St Maurice of 1467 in Magdeburg Cathedral; a Virgin with surrounding angels in the Andreaskirche at Halberstadt; a Pietà in the Marienkirche at Mergentheim; and an Annunciation of 1484 from Würzburg, now in the Bayerisches Nationalmuseum in Munich.[103] These – and I am making only a selection of the most important – are Franconian or Central German 'translations' of Netherlandish works of a similar kind. They do not show such virtuosity as the latter, but they exhibit a true understanding of the special potentialities of the noble material employed. The same applies to the less linear and more painterly alabaster Virgin in the Städtische Skulpturengalerie in Frankfurt.[104] I have inserted at this point this group of works, whose probable provenance is Erfurt, to show that – quite apart from the widespread influence of engravings – there were regional products which reveal actual contacts with Western sources.

If we continue our chronological study of Franconian sculpture, we are confronted with the enigma of Veit Stoss's life work. In 1477 he surrendered his Nuremberg citizenship and moved with his family to Cracow. Records of the date of his birth vary between 1438 and 1447, and this apparently small space of time is in reality of importance if we wish to assess clearly how far Veit Stoss was already a Nuremberger before he moved to Cracow. We now know from the researches of a Polish scholar[105] that Horb in Swabia and not Nuremberg was his home town. It was from there that his brother Mathias (Matis Schwab), a goldsmith, also emigrated to Cracow.

Two altarpieces characterize the artistic situation in Cracow before Veit Stoss arrived there. One is the Altar of the Trinity, dating from 1467, in the chapel of the Holy Cross of the Cathedral on the Wawel. This triptych continues the architectural style of altarpiece which we have been able to trace back to the beginning of the century. In the shallow centre is a carved Trinity; on each side of this and horizontally subdivided into two tiers are two niches with a female saint in each; in the top canopy are three reliefs. The figures of the Holy Virgins are the most interesting, because they preserve a style which appears to be linked with prototypes of the mid fifteenth century and which in its economy of composition has great sculptural power.

Of Franconian, perhaps indeed of Nuremberg, origin is the Altar of Pity in the Cathedral on the Wawel, dating from *c.* 1470–5. In the central section (unfortunately very much restored) are the Man of Sorrows and the Mater Dolorosa, turning to face each other; above them and against the back wall are six demi-figures of angels bearing the Instruments of the Passion. The scene reveals the greatest sincerity of feeling, and is restrained in expression and still free from that ornamental exuberance which developed so boldly under the influence of the engravings of the Master E.S. The same is true of the style of a contemporary example of Silesian sculpture, the Altar of the Nativity marked with the arms of the Prockendorf family in St Elizabeth at Wrocław (Breslau).

We must look for the influences which acted upon Veit Stoss's art in his years as apprentice and journeyman to the general heritage left by Nicolaus Gerhaerts in the South German lands. The fact that obvious points of similarity are few will not cause surprise, since we are dealing with an artist whose genius has produced the exceptional at almost all stages of his career. 'Uno miraculo di legno' said Vasari of Veit Stoss's St Roch in Florence. Nicolaus Gerhaerts' artistic sphere and the Netherlandish influences of the generation following Roger van der Weyden are left behind. We are faced with something completely new.

In Cracow Veit Stoss was commissioned to construct the high altar for the church of St Mary, and the work began in May 1477 (Plates 134 and 135). Money for this undertaking had been collected previously, and one may assume that it was this commission that had attracted Stoss to Cracow. At that time commercial relations between Nuremberg and Cracow were so close that the path chosen by Stoss was by no means unusual. Veit Stoss's masterpiece at Cracow is of unheard-of proportions: it is 40 ft high and 35 ft wide, when the wings are open. The theme is the Life of the Virgin, and scenes from the Passion are included in the reliefs on the outside of the double wings. The outer wings are not movable, so that when the inner doors are closed we have twelve reliefs arranged in three tiers. The central section and the figures are magnificently coloured and gilded (now excellently restored), and the backgrounds are exquisitely painted and give a great illusion of depth. Thus painting contributes largely to the total effect of the altarpiece, although the wings are not actually paintings.

The choice of the Death of the Virgin as the theme for such a monumental altarpiece is unusual. Gigantic figures of the Apostles surround the kneeling Virgin as she dies. Above them is seen her ascent into heaven. This is a scenic composition as powerful as Roger van der Weyden's Descent from the Cross in the Prado, and in its union of natural and supernatural it heralds Raphael's Transfiguration. It is a 'theatrum sacrum' in the sense of Asam's Assumption of the Virgin in the abbey of Rohr.

The gamut of sculptural form is inexhaustible, and arises in each case from the contrast between body and drapery, a tension, as it were, between core and envelope. We are filled with admiration for the drama of the flowing drapery, the trenchant truth of the faces, and the wealth of human expressions. Of even greater suggestive power is the entirely new function allotted to movement and gesture. The composition of the Death of the Virgin reaches its apex in the grief-stricken figure of one of the Apostles, who stands at the back wringing his hands. It is impossible to describe how, even taken from their context, these hands manage to convey the essence of the whole work.

The Cracow altar was completed in 1489. In 1482 Veit Stoss's brother, the goldsmith Matis Schwab, had moved to Cracow. He probably had a part in this great work, for at about this time the gilders and painters began their task, though normally the gilding of carvings was not really part of the goldsmith's craft. In any case Veit Stoss had collaborators in his pay to whom he was able to give a free hand; for in 1486, when his father-in-law died in Nuremberg, he left Cracow for two years to return there.

During the time he was working on the Altar of the Virgin, Stoss was responsible for two pieces of stone sculpture which still survive at Cracow: a relief of the Mount of Olives in St Mary's Cemetery (preserved in the Museum Narodowego, Cracow) and a Crucifix, now part of an altarpiece on the end wall of the south aisle in the church of St Mary there. In both these works the delicate modelling of the surface and the wealth of 'painterly' movement in the folds of drapery are astonishing. Then followed the most distinguished commission that Poland had to confer, the tomb of King Casimir Jagiello in the old burial church of the Polish kings, the Cathedral on the Wawel. The tomb here was originally the counterpart of the slightly older one of King Vladislav (Plate 82B), and corresponded to it in its character as a canopied funeral monument. The lid bears the name of Veit Stoss, his master's mark, and the date 1492. As the king died in the same year, the commission must have been given during his lifetime. The effigy of the dead monarch is of dark red Hungarian marble which is almost disfigured by veins of lighter colour (Plate 136). It is deeply furrowed; the linear sharpness of the outlines invites one to read it in an abstract way, and it achieves a depth of intellectual and spiritual power hitherto unprecedented in the realm of sculptural portraiture. The marble tomb lid of Archbishop Zbigniew Oleśnicki (d. 1493) in Gniezno (Gnesen) Cathedral also bears Veit Stoss's master's mark.[106] Documentary evidence proves that Veit Stoss was responsible as well for the red marble tombstone to Bishop Peter von Bnina in the cathedral of Włocławek on the Vistula (with a dedicatory inscription of 1493).

The sum-total of these works – without mentioning the numerous products of the workshop – is so great and so varied that any judgement on the origin of the particular style of presentation is problematic. One incontrovertible connexion is that between Nicolaus Gerhaerts' monument of Frederick III and the tomb lid of King Casimir. There is a similar arrangement of the monarch's figure, though at Cracow the symbol of Majesty is turned into a moving image of the royal personage as a human being. The bold figure of the Pectorale – a woman in labour, presumably as an allegory of immortality – has its roots in the small-scale sculpture[107] of Strasbourg at the time of Nicolaus Gerhaerts. This connexion gains in conviction when we recognize that in the deeply felt realism and the purified rhetoric of Veit Stoss's stone Crucifix in St Mary at Cracow there is an echo of the lofty ethos of Gerhaerts' Baden-Baden Crucifixus. The capitals of the canopy on the tomb of King Casimir, which are chiselled in brilliantly lucent marble, are, according to their signature, the work of the sculptor Jörg Huber of Passau, and show stylistic contacts with the Austrian successors of Nicolaus Gerhaerts.[108]

It is much more difficult to assess the stylistic origins of the carvings on the Cracow altar, which account for the early fame of Veit Stoss. If we are seeking for anything comparable, I do not think we shall find it in Nuremberg sculpture of before 1477. But there are points of contact with Upper Swabian works in the presumed style of Michel Erhart, although these – for example the Virgin at Weissenau – are of later date. Thus we may assume that before Veit Stoss settled in Nuremberg, he had been decisively influenced by certain Upper Swabian sculpture, the formal character of which we are only able to deduce from later works.

In Nuremberg itself sculptural development may be traced from the compact figure of St Paul in the Euchariuskapelle adjoining St Egidien, via the St John the Baptist who seems to be striding out in space (c. 1470) in the Johanneskirche,[109] to the St Michael in St Lorenz, whose style was influenced by the Master E.S. The stone Virgin, dating from 1482, originally on a private house and now in the Germanisches Museum,[110] belongs to the typical Nuremberg style, which we have discussed already apropos the Fair Virgin from the Welser altar in the Frauenkirche. The linear clarity and austere grace of the Altar of St Peter of c. 1480 in St Sebald[111] is also an embodiment of the Nuremberg tradition with which Veit Stoss had to vie when, at the beginning of 1496, he reassumed his citizen's rights in the town. From Heinrich Deichsler's chronicle we learn that between 1488 and 1491 no less than twenty-three altarpieces were made in Nuremberg. The basis of this productivity was the cooperation of carvers and painters. Especially in altar carvings from the workshop of Michael Wolgemut (independently active from 1472 onwards), a common Nuremberg tradition is embodied.

Syrlin's choir stalls at Ulm (1469–74), Pacher's altar at St Wolfgang (1471–81), and Veit Stoss's altar at Cracow (1477–89) provide us with the most striking evidence of the heights achieved by, and the tremendous and highly individual character of, German sculpture in these two decades. This was the full flower of the seed sown by Nicolaus Gerhaerts. These great achievements found a full echo in almost all regions, but it is impossible to appraise here the special features of the products of the various districts. Late Gothic altar sculpture extends from Switzerland to Hungary and Poland and from the Lower Rhine to the Baltic provinces, Scandinavia, and Finland.

In the north, the formative power was concentrated at this time especially in Lübeck. The last name from the sphere of Lübeck sculpture mentioned in this survey was that of the Master of the Stone Virgins of c. 1460, when the Netherlandish sources of his type of figure were stressed. It is important to recognize that the beautiful monument to Albert Bischop in Lübeck Cathedral must have come from Bruges, and that its inscription was not added until after Bischop's death in Lübeck in the year 1468.[112] This same Flemish source, it seems to me, once again exercised a direct influence on the beautiful oak figure of the Virgin and Child at Vadstena (Plate 138B). This serene figure is connected with a slightly later stratum of Netherlandish sculpture, and it is characteristic of the radius of influence of such works that the nearest parallel to it is a painted wooden figure of St Agnes by Lorenzo Mercadante on the portal of the Convent of S. Inés in Seville.[113] The monumentality of this figure – almost Burgundian in character – dates it not later than 1470. It is still free from the remorseless realism visible even in the earliest works of Bernt Notke, who represents the apotheosis of Late Gothic sculpture in Lübeck.

Side by side with the Master of the Stone Virgins, from about 1455 onwards we have evidence of altar-carving with strong traditional Lübeck roots. First, there is the relief of the Death of the Virgin in the Great Guild Hall at Riga;[114] this is a vivid narrative composition with rich 'painterly' qualities. The sculpture, dating from 1458-9, on the Altar of St Bridget in the abbey of Vadstena, begun by Hans Hesse and completed by Johannes Stenrat, radiates the same atmosphere.[115] In 1460 there followed Hans Hesse's charming Altar of the Miller Lads in Lübeck Cathedral; in 1468 the former high altar of the Storkyrka in Stockholm (now in the Statens Historiska Museum), which, according to its inscription, was made in Lübeck. The paintings on this altarpiece are by Hermen Rode, and the carver may perhaps be identified with Master Bertil, whom we know from documentary evidence to have been active in Lübeck.[116] Further works from Lübeck include the two carved altarpieces by Johannes Stenrat dated 1471 in the churches at Bälinge (Uppland) and Sorunda (Södermanland); an altarpiece from the church of Tuna (Södermanland) now in the Strängnäs museum;[117] and a further altarpiece dating from 1481 in St Nicholas at Tallinn (Reval) in Estonia.[118] It must be emphasized that in all three altarpieces the wing-paintings by Hermen Rode are artistically strikingly superior to the carved portions. The carved work has a jejune, but none the less impressive character. The high-water mark reached by these conventional talents is, it seems to me, the unadorned but beautiful clarity of the high-relief figures on the Altar of St Luke from the Katharinenkirche in Lübeck, now in the St Annenmuseum. The wing-paintings are again by Hermen Rode, but I would not like to identify the carver with either Johannes Stenrat or with Notke's pupil, Hinrik Wylsnyck.

Bernt Notke was a native of Lassan in Pomerania, and evidently came of a distinguished Hanseatic family. In Lübeck archives he is mentioned for the first time in 1467 as a painter,[119] apropos of some trouble concerning the legal standing of apprentices serving in his workshop. So even at that time he exercised an influence about which the guild had qualms. From this date one may deduce that Notke belonged to the same generation as Pacher and Stoss. It is also significant that he too was both painter and carver.

His earliest authenticated sculptural work, the wing-reliefs from an Altar of the Passion at Kirke Stillinge on Zeeland (Denmark), dates from c. 1475, and already shows Notke's characteristic and radical transformation of the illustrative style of Netherlandish prototypes into an austere, monologue expressionism. In the Triumphal Cross from Lübeck Cathedral (1477) his talent reaches unexpected heights.[120] The facial features of the Crucifixus and the mourning figure of St Mary Magdalen (Plate 138A) achieve deep sincerity of emotional expression. There prevails in all the figures of this Calvary a sparse and bitter simplicity of form, which comes near to the monumentality of earlier architectural sculpture. The gravity here is of a profoundly religious, sombre kind. It strikes an epic and not a dramatic note, such as was the case in contemporary Netherlandish sculpture. Notke's emphasis on the spatial effect of gesture and movement made it technically impossible for him to find one block of wood adequate for his purposes, and so he added on pieces in a way not permitted by the rules of his craft. The very range of expression, even in the technique of sculptural representation, thus begins to make it impossible for the Late Gothic sculptor to keep within these rules. It is worth observing that in this work Notke enjoyed partnership with a donor, Bishop Albert Krummedieck, who was just as outstanding a personality as the artist himself. In 1478–9 there followed Notke's high altar for the cathedral of Aarhus, and in 1483 the high altar for the Church of the Holy Ghost at Tallinn (Reval) (Plate 139A). The figures of the Pentecost in the central section of the Tallinn altar are markedly finer in workmanship; Notke now began to liberate himself from the harshness of his early works. This central section is not merely a box-like space but is built up in depth like a stage, giving an illusion of space such as had not before been seen in the carved altarpieces of Lübeck. This opened the way to the three-dimensional *fortissimo* of the more than life-size group of St George in the Storkyrka in Stockholm, which was to be Notke's greatest feat (Plate 137).

In 1471 the Swedish Regent, Sten Sture, freed Sweden from alien rule by his victory over the Danes. He owed this victory to the assistance of St George. As a monument to his triumph, he caused to be erected at the entrance to the choir in the main church in Stockholm, where he had prayed before the battle, an Altar of St George, which is dominated by the carved group of the saint's fight with the dragon.[121] This intended monument is the most magnificent votive image that has survived from the Late Middle Ages. The tomb of the donor was meant to be incorporated in the base, which is rich in architectural articulation and which has been recently restored. The Gattamelata in Padua bears the most eloquent testimony to the fact that in the Early Renaissance in Italy the same transition from funereal to equestrian monument took place.[122] In Stockholm, St George's horse is a portrait of Sten Sture's horse, and the same is true of the sheet-armour of the saint. This is therefore a unique combination of pious votive offerings.

Notke was summoned to Stockholm in 1483, and he was not resident again in Lübeck until 1498. The monument of St George was solemnly dedicated in 1489. Because it was placed under the arch of the entrance to the choir, the architecture of the church interior became its encompassing setting. The group was not a monument like the Gattamelata, but part of a larger setting, comparable to the Late Gothic altarpieces which extend up to the vaulting of the choir.

The saint appears victorious as the ideal embodiment of the *eques christianus*. The horse rears up over the monstrous dragon rising from the ground. The beast is vested with an uncanny intensity. Details from the legend of St George are displayed with the objectivity of an epic: remnants of human victims (a large bust of a dead man, a small death's head, a skull) and smaller portions of the dragon's meal. Exquisite colouring ennobles the whole. Yet realism goes so far that the dragon's horns and wings are made of real elk antlers – 'style rustique' of the Late Gothic epoch!

The second main figure of the group – the princess – kneels in intercession at the side, elevated above the rest, as she watches St George's fight with the dragon. This manner of arrangement underlines once again the architectural discipline and the spatial tension of the composition.[123] If one compares the magnificent volume of this figure with the expressionistic hardness of St Mary Magdalen in the Triumphal Cross from Lübeck Cathedral, one realizes Notke's astonishing evolution towards a complete mastery of the monumental in the ten years that separate them. It is not easy to point out the influences that might have helped him in this evolution. It has been suggested that contact with Pacher, or perhaps even an acquaintance with Italian art, were contributory factors. But I am not convinced of this. Any similarity of features in Pacher's sculptural work seems to me to arise from the general concatenation of circumstances, and, as far as Italy is concerned, I would think that such a contact – as we have seen so characteristically in Pacher's case – would primarily have had an effect on Notke's painting; for his work as a painter and engraver is by no means inferior to his carving. But of this it seems to me there is no trace in the 'decorative lavishness' (Paatz) of the panel of the Mass of St Gregory in the Marienkirche in Lübeck, which represents Notke's masterpiece as a painter.

Thus, when considering the stylistic significance of the St George group in Stockholm, we can, I think, only emphasize the distance which divides it from Netherlandish sources. There is just one point of comparison which perhaps gives some idea of the experiences undergone by Notke while he was preparing for the Stockholm monument, namely a reminiscence of the Strasbourg sculpture of Nicolaus Gerhaerts' immediate successors. The sophisticated figure of St Catherine, dating from c. 1470–80, in the style of the Master E.S. in the Musée de l'Œuvre Notre-Dame approaches more closely to the princess in Notke's group than any works of contemporary Netherlandish sculpture. Even more striking is the similarity between the wooden demi-figure of a 'poor devil' at Strasbourg[124] and the large bust of the dead man in the Stockholm monument.

In the same way Notke's silver reliquary of St George for the Fraternity of St George at Elbląg (Elbing; formerly West Prussia), now in the Museum für Kunst und Gewerbe in Hamburg,[125] is instructive (Plate 139B). This is a small-scale work permeated by the same imaginative power as the monumental work in Stockholm. It maintains the greatest sculptural tension throughout, and epic vividness into its minutest detail. The features are more angular, and the stance of the silver figure is somewhat more rigid than that of the dynamically perfect Stockholm group. I would thus assume the Elbląg figure to date from the early 1480s, and to be the actual work of Notke himself, not that of a goldsmith after a model by him; for Notke came of a goldsmith's family, and Sten Sture bestowed the highest recognition upon him by making him Master of the Swedish Mint in 1490. Now there existed at Elbląg itself a prototype of the Stockholm group, namely a very similarly inspired reliquary of St George (since 1870 in the possession of the Kunstgewerbemuseum in Berlin), in a sharply linear style and of a slightly earlier date and probably of Lower Rhenish provenance; so that here once again light is cast upon the significance of Lower Rhenish sculpture. As is proved by an engraving by Israel van Meckenem, who was using a drawing by the Master E.S. dating from 1467, this reliquary was based upon a Netherlandish invention. Thus Notke's indirect contacts with Rhenish and Netherlandish art round 1480 appear to have given him new inspiration.

The radical transformation which came about in Notke's work has its parallel in the rejuvenation of style in the Netherlandish wooden altars imported at this time into Scandinavia. We can observe this rejuvenation in work from Lübeck and from the German and Scandinavian Baltic provinces, but with a certain time-lag – so very established and adequate had the austere style of the middle of the century become in these districts. It appears that for his work on the wooden sculpture of the high altar in Aarhus Cathedral in 1479, Notke had a collaborator, to whom we owe the St Thomas of Canterbury from an altar in Skepptuna (Uppland), now in the Statens Historiska Museum in Stockholm. At about the same time (between 1481 and 1484), Notke's workshop took on another collaborator, the so-called Imperialissima Master, perhaps to be identified with Henryk Wylsnyck,[126] whose further activity it is possible to follow. He was responsible for the altarpiece from Thurø, now in the Copenhagen National Museum, and in 1488 for the figure of the Virgin in the Great Guild Hall at Riga.[127] To all these there cleaves a certain heaviness and rigidity of expression. They lack the extensive spatial quality which finds such supreme manifestation in Notke's St George and the Dragon.

CHAPTER 9

FRANCE: 1470–90

THE quality and the quantity of Netherlandish and German altarpieces that have survived from the years 1470–90 prove that in these two decades the altarpiece had stepped into the forefront of artistic creation and that the increasing splendour of the altar structure had lent a new function to sculpture. We shall observe a similar phenomenon in Spain. On the other hand, sculpture which survives in France from this epoch does not reveal how far this development of the altarpiece into a monumental, three-dimensional structure had had a similar effect upon French sculpture. It may be that this is due not only to the fact that so much has been destroyed, but also that France did not participate to the same extent in this new sculptural embellishment of the altarpiece. If this is so, then the great difference in the situation of sculpture in France and that in the Netherlands and Germany, which is apparent at the beginning of the sixteenth century, existed already in the preceding decades. French sculpture at this time is conservative and traditional. Violent feelings are seldom permitted. This conservatism sheds its influence also upon the future, and the crisis which occurred in Germany at the turn of the century, when the last product of the Late Gothic epoch came face to face with the Early Renaissance, never appeared in French sculpture. I do not think that it is just because examples have been destroyed that one gets the impression that the interaction of carving and painting in the altarpiece played a smaller role in the history of French sculpture, although naturally here too works did exist which were imported from the Netherlands and whose style had an influence on the products of the various regions. One may, however, claim that it is because of destruction that outstanding personalities cannot easily be distinguished and the interchange of talents between different regions is to be much more rarely observed. Developments of the Burgundian style are evident in Burgundy, Auvergne, and Languedoc. But it is not clear in which regions of Central and Northern France lay the most important centres of production. Even recent exhibitions and research have failed to fill this gap in our knowledge. The sculpture of Northern France appears to correspond with that in the adjacent Southern Netherlands. But 'schools', with the one exception of Troyes, are not clearly discernible until the following period.

Michel Colombe, the last French 'imagier gothique', appears to have been a native of Bourges, where his father Philippe Colombe was active as a sculptor. It is known that Michel Colombe studied the tombs of the dukes of Burgundy in the Dijon Chartreuse, 'mesmement par maistre Claux et maistre Anthoniet, souverains tailleurs d'images'. So these works retained a very great significance for French sculptors even in the second half of the century – an astonishing example of artistic retrospection. There is indeed French sculpture of the late fifteenth century which is stylistically dependent on works of the early years of the century. Characteristically, they are always works of monumental stone sculpture.

A fine example is the charming little marble votive figure of Duke Jean II de Bourbon (d. 1488) kneeling in prayer, from the crypt of the Nouvelle Sainte-Chapelle of Bourbon-l'Archambault and now in the Walters Art Gallery, Baltimore (Plate 140A).[1] In its precision and its aristocratic delicacy of touch, one senses an echo of Jacques Morel's style. This retention of a harmonious charm of expression is even clearer in statues of the Virgin dating from c. 1470–80, as for example in the Maria Lactans in the church of Villebret near Montluçon (Allier), and the charming Education de l'Enfant from Longvé (Allier) and the Virgin and Child from Moulins, both in the Louvre.[2] These delicately chiselled works are monumental by virtue of the severe, block-like compactness of their contour and inner form. Their style is still reminiscent of the large Virgin Enthroned from Poligny in the Metropolitan Museum in New York. The emphasis on the depth of the block is striking. The expression of face and gesture lack the vivacity of works from the beginning of the century, and there is no trace of that expressive dynamism which Nicolaus Gerhaerts and the Netherlanders had released into sculpture two decades earlier.

Mention must be made at this point, as coming from the same region, of the Pietà in Notre-Dame at Montluçon and the relief of the Entombment in the church of Souvigny.[3] Both are outstanding proofs of strength of feeling and formal restraint in French Late Gothic sculpture. Perhaps one may assume that their style was influenced by that of contemporary French painting. The stone figure of St Mary Magdalen[4] in the church at Limeray (Indre-et-Loire) in the neighbouring district of Touraine represents the full perfection of this style.

From Burgundy I would select as examples of my argument the marble St Catherine in the Musée Rolin at Autun (Plate 141A) and the stone St Barbara in the Hospital of Seurre (Côte d'Or).[5] These are characteristically Late Burgundian, with their oval-shaped heads and the softness of their facial features, set in a framework of sharply drawn tresses, which fall well below shoulder level and end in a delicately curled roll. We know what the antecedents of these figures looked like. The Musée Rolin provides us with excellent examples: firstly the generous breadth in a figure of the Magdalen from the beginning of the century which embraces a wonderful amplitude of space within its soft delicacy of line; and secondly the more economical precision in a tall, slender Virgin, tenderly pressing the swaddled Child to her breast. I have already emphasized the fact that the deep sincerity of feeling in the figure of St Jean de Reôme at Asnières-en-Montagne (Plate 59C)[6] represents a similar aspect of this second phase of Burgundian sculpture; here the almost impasto modelling of the surface is still very painterly in style. Now the St Catherine at Autun and the St Barbara at Seurre show that in the late fifteenth century Burgundian sculpture loses this painterly character. The structure becomes essentially linear. The tendency towards a more austere objectivity is paramount, but – because it is Burgundian – the sculpture for all that retains its engaging quality. The marked emphasis on the details of the elegant dress and on the attributes of the saints is typically Burgundian too. These outstanding examples from the last years of Burgundian sculpture prove its undiminished creative power.

To the same period belong two stone figures in this 'linear style' from Avignon: a Pietà from the Dominican house and a St Martha from the monastery of the Célestins, both now in the Musée Lapidaire. From these two works may be judged the widespread validity of this style.

At Aix-en-Provence too there is a group of statues which throws much light on regional developments in the second half of the century. Of outstanding importance is the large, three-figured votive group in a wide mural recess with an arch of the type the French call *anse de panier*, in the north aisle of the cathedral, originally in the Carmelite church (Plate 141B).[7] In the centre are St Anne and the Virgin and Child; they are placed above a box-like shrine with a deeply undercut relief of Christ in Pity, surrounded by the *arma Christi*, and they in turn are flanked on either side by figures of St Martha and St Maurice. The three-dimensional weight of the figures within the stage-like space of the wall-recess is an essential feature. The drapery flows in generous lines, which are broken only at the ends of the sleeves and where the garments touch the ground to turn into rope-like curves. The dragon at Martha's feet is huge, and the ground beneath him already suggests the future 'style rustique'. The antecedents of the monumental naturalism of this group are again to be found in the style of the early fifteenth century, where a similar epic explicitness in the presentation of the *ambiente* characterizes small-scale pieces of goldsmiths' work. As is evident from the allusion of the Christ in Pity to the holy sacrament, this entire ensemble was an altarpiece. It was donated by Urbain Aygosi in 1470,[8] and this date provides us finally with the most cogent proof that for French sculpture of the second half of the century ideas from the early years of the century still held good, though they were translated into a new and hard objectivity.

I would ascribe to the Master of the Aygosi altar the stone figure, kneeling in prayer, of Jeanne de Laval, second wife of René of Anjou, count of Provence and titular king of Naples, in the Musée de Cluny in Paris.[9] Aix-en-Provence is the provenance of this figure, and it is likely that Jeanne was originally shown as the donor in an Annunciation group. Once again one is struck by the way in which a new realism is apparent in the traditional monumental block-like quality of the figure. Deep shadows supply new sculptural stresses; there is however no furrowing of the form as a whole, such as is characteristic of contemporary Netherlandish and German sculpture.

The equestrian stone statue of St Martin from the tomb of Martin du Puyloubier[8] in Aix Cathedral, supposedly dating from *c.* 1457, is stylistically akin to the Aygosi altar, and so too is the marble figure of a monk kneeling in prayer in the museum of Aix. Finally, mention must be made in this context of two outstanding stone Apostles in the chapel of the château of Caderousse, near Orange. Here the pillar-like compactness of the figure and the calligraphic movement in the lines of the surface are even more emphatic.

Was Étienne Audinet, native of the district round Cambrai and after a period of activity in Marseille resident from 1450 in Aix, the master of these works? In fact the special interest of these statues – just as of that of Jean II, duke of Bourbon, from Bourbon-l'Archambault – lies in their specifically French character. This shows itself in a monumentalizing of Late Gothic naturalism such as is not to be met with in German sculpture of this time, and also in an austerity of outline and a radiant beauty of the material employed. We have already observed these features in the Virgin from l'Hôpital-sous-Rochefort and in the St Fortunade (Corrèze).

As a late document of the merging of Burgundian traditions in a typically French canon I can refer to the stone Entombment donated by Jacotin Ogier to the Carmelite house of Semur-en-Auxois[10] in 1490. To this group also belongs the magnificent walnut figure of a Mourning Virgin from a Crucifixion group in the Staatliche Museen in Berlin.[11] The similarity of the Semur Entombment to the older one at Tonnerre (1451–3) and also to the St John the Baptist (1457–60) in the church at Châteauneuf-en-Auxois[12] is obvious. The bodily weight which creates in the Tonnerre Entombment so convincing an illusion of a scene on a stage is now translated into linear planes. The group is monumental in the severity of its composition and arrangement. It is harmonious in the balance of the silhouettes, abstract by virtue of the validity of certain transitory lines, and it possesses a quiet restraint of facial expression. Two pairs of angels in flight, one in the museum at Semur-en-Auxois, the other in the Louvre, are similar in character.[13] The master of this Entombment was also probably responsible for the stone Virgin of the Annunciation in the Hospital of Semur-en-Auxois.[14] But I think that the Man of Sorrows with two attendant angels in Notre-Dame in the same town,[14] with the bodily weight seeming to emerge from the pillar-like rounding of the contours, the 'painterly' wealth of its spatial quality, and the soft nuances of gentle emotional expression, comes nearer to the Burgundian source of this style and should be dated somewhat earlier. The Entombment of 1496 at Solesmes (Plates 190–1),[15] and works like the Moissac Entombment, which dates from the early years of the sixteenth century, prove the persistence of Burgundian conventions in the treatment of this theme.

The great final achievement of late monumental sculpture in Burgundy was the monument erected at the instance of Philippe Pot, Lord High Steward and subsequently Grand Seneschal of Burgundy, in the Chapel of John the Baptist in the abbey of Cîteaux (Côte d'Or). Since 1889 this monument has been in the Louvre (Plate 143B).[16] We have already seen how in the Burgundian ducal tombs in the early part of the century the ceremonial spectacle of the funeral procession was developed out of what had been separate mourning figures. Now, in the peculiar treatment it received in Philippe Pot's monument, we witness the translation of this motif into the vivid realism of the late fifteenth century. The spectator meets the funeral procession 'in corpore'. Eight hooded figures, differentiated one from another only by the heraldic shields they carry, bear upon their shoulders the tomb lid on which Philippe Pot lies with hands folded in prayer. He is clad in sheet armour and accompanied by the insignia of his house. At his feet sits a lion. This monument represents the grand finale of Late Gothic Burgundian funerary sculpture.

Philippe Pot died in 1493, but the compact proportions of the figures and the blunted quality of the formal stresses would suggest a somewhat earlier date for the monument. The style has none of the generosity of outline and inner form which arouses our admiration in the Semur-en-Auxois Entombment of 1490. Philippe Pot had probably already commissioned this work when he made arrangements for the building of his burial chapel in the abbey of Cîteaux between 1477 and 1485. At that time Antoine Le

Moiturier, the master of the tomb of John the Bold, was still active in Dijon.[17] We may assume that Pot gave him the commission. But it is difficult to be certain about this, since in the general style of the work the individual peculiarities of the artist completely recede behind the general traditional character of Late Burgundian sculpture – a situation typical of the time. The new spirit of extreme realism is all the more striking, but here too the solemn atmosphere of Burgundian feudal art still lingers.

Perhaps the purest example of this Late Burgundian style is the stone Virgin in the Louvre which is from Montigny-sur-Vingeanne (Côte d'Or).[18] The sculptural autonomy and the perfect display of this figure show most clearly how Late Burgundian sculpture – without concessions to the decorative dynamism of Late Gothic – already approximates to certain essential features of Renaissance sculpture. Thus the structure of Burgundo-French sculpture in the late fifteenth century had a completely different character and a completely different significance from contemporary works in the Netherlands and Germany, whose extrovert quality opened so deep a cleft between the Late Gothic and the Renaissance.

May we ascribe the stimulating contacts with Netherlandish art enjoyed by Late Burgundo-French sculpture at this time to the supra-territorial interests of the feudal lords? René d'Anjou had collected works by Flemish masters,[19] while the art of Nicolas Froment, who was active at René's court, was influenced by Netherlandish painting. Therefore it is not surprising that the bronze figure from the top of the tower of the Château du Lude (Sarthe; Plate 145c), representing an angel which according to the inscription on one of the wings was made by 'Jehan Barbet dit de Lion' in 1475 for Jean Daillon, lord of the said castle, should be in the austere style which, round 1490, in the work of such men as Renier van Thienen and Jan Aert van Maastricht, led to the golden age of South Netherlandish decorative metal sculpture.[20] This figure is now in the Frick Collection in New York.[21] The date 1475 of the Lude angel is symptomatic of a parting of the ways between the traditional style and Late Gothic innovations. We shall see how in sculpture of the last quarter of the fifteenth century in France contacts with Italian works soon produced their effects. Barbet was a bronze-founder at Lyon. But where might the modeller and the model of this Lude angel have come from?

The carvings on the choir screen in Albi Cathedral are also generally regarded as representative of Burgundian sculpture (Plate 145A). They date from the time of Bishop Louis I of Amboise, who was installed in 1473. But I fail to see any specifically Burgundian character[22] in either the form or the expression of these carvings. The Nostre-Dame de Grasse and the St Michael in the Musée des Augustins in Toulouse showed the heights attained by the sculpture of this region in the middle of the fifteenth century. The decisive formative influences in the last years of the century were, I believe, still local ones. There appears to be a close link between the carvings in the choir of Albi Cathedral and the tympanum relief on the portal of St Nicholas in Toulouse.[23] The remarkable spatial freedom in this very fine relief and the strongly three-dimensional nature of the individual figures suggest, together with the fact that the building was completed in 1458, that this tympanum predates the very much harder stylization of the screen at Albi. If we begin with the Nostre-Dame de Grasse (certainly originally part of a similarly three-dimensional composition which, in this case, probably represented the Adoration of the Magi), we gain the idea of a regional production which doubtless owed its inception to contacts with Burgundy, but which gradually went its own way. The fragments of an Entombment from Toulouse Cathedral in the Musée des Augustins and small-scale goldsmith's pieces of the second half of the fifteenth century in the treasury of Conques (Aveyron) are abundant proof of this.

The terracotta figures of prophets and sibyls from the ambulatory of St Sernin in Toulouse (now in the Musée des Augustins; Plate 145B) are of the same date. Terracotta is not often employed in French Late Gothic sculpture, and the figures have an unusual violence of expression, particularly by means of the structure of the faces. They are of a compact, block-like character, and the drapery is deeply furrowed. This gives rise to a strange monumentality which, it seems to me, is not to be explained as deriving from Spanish influences, however likely contacts are between one side of the Pyrenees and the other.

In this survey I have deliberately placed works of Burgundian style and works from Southern France in the forefront in order to stress continuity as a dominant feature of French sculpture. Examples like the Virgins at Azat-le-Riz (Haute Vienne)[24] and at L'Hôpital-sous-Rochefort, the St Agnes at Jaligny (Allier), and the St Mary Magdalen at Limeray (Indre-et-Loire)[25] demonstrate the continuity of sculptural types in the southern part of France whose Frenchness is apparent at once in the peculiarly stylish drapery. From the northern provinces a representative example is the dressed-up stone St Barbara[26] at Rampillon (Seine-et-Marne). This slender statue is of an austere linear articulation, but – as the emphasis on the horizontal lines of the square neck opening of the dress proves – dates from as late as *c.* 1490.

Northern French sculpture maintained unbroken contacts with workshops in Flanders and the Southern Netherlands, so that their styles are virtually identical. Records concerning the sculpture of this area offer little help in an attempt to gain an idea of the formative influences at work, or of the local schools. So much Late Gothic sculpture in both Northern France and the area that was later to become Belgium has been destroyed that it would require a systematic survey of all that has survived in both monumental sculpture and documentary records to reveal the quantity, the peculiar local character, and the significance of these regional products, which so far have remained a matter of conjecture. As yet we have not been able to estimate how much significance is to be ascribed to the local traditions of the sculptural crafts in the most important centres, e.g. in Rouen. We know of Simon Marmion's altarpiece in the Abbey of St Bertin at St-Omer (1453–9); we know of the leading talents in Amiens panel-painting. But what did the carved parts of these altarpieces look like, which stood side by side with paintings whose importance has long been acknowledged? The choir stalls of Rouen Cathedral date from 1457–69. We see from sporadic examples[27] how carving on choir stalls developed, and we can also see how striking each surviving example is. But we can form no conception of the function which sculpture fulfilled in the *opus completum* of the altarpiece.

Funerary monuments will serve as our surest guide. This branch of sculpture remained typologically relatively conservative, though it often provides us with surprising revelations in the individual effigy. The most distinguished tombs, however, have been destroyed. Surviving documentary evidence, as for example in the case of the monument of King Louis XI (d. 1483) in Notre-Dame at Cléry,[28] shows how complex the genesis of such works can be. In 1474 Jean Fouquet made a parchment sketch and Michel Colombe 'en pierre un petit patron en façon de tombe' for the king. It may have been a derivative of Fouquet's sketch which eight years later was sent to the sculptor Colin d'Amiens as a basis for the bronze monument he was to make. The actual execution of this monument was entrusted to the founder Laurent Wrine and the goldsmith Conrad of Cologne.

From the monuments which survive, attention may be drawn to two, which seem to shed special light upon the development of sculptural style at this time. First, the monument to Charles d'Artois (d. 1471) in the crypt of St Laurent at Eu (Seine-Maritime; Plate 140B). This presents us with a portrait of the greatest individuality from the point of view of the features, figure, and armour of the deceased. It is economical – one might almost say abstract – in form and sharp in outline. It is a highly rational presentation, such as we encounter neither in French sculpture under Burgundian influence nor in that of the Netherlands. There is a *verismo* here which opens up a new kind of close-upness. Sculptural form is the handmaiden of clarity – an essential feature in French sculpture in the latest phase of Gothic. We have already seen a similar style in the effigy of Jeanne de Montejeau (d. before 1456) from the abbey of Bueil-en-Touraine.

More difficult of assessment is the tomb of a feudal lord in the church of Malicorne, south of Le Mans (Plates 142 and 143A). The recumbent figure is of immense size, the hands are raised in prayer, the features of the face noble and of a highly personal quality. The movement on the surface of the stone has a certain tenderness. In spite of its realism there is an aura of the ideal about the whole. It is assumed to be the tomb of Antoine de Sourches (d. between 1485 and 1487), Seigneur of Malicorne,[29] and it was originally thought that there was a connexion between it and the sculpture of Solesmes, which we have yet to discuss. However, it is more likely to be the work of a master of another kind, upon whose provenance the much weaker mourning figures of Late Burgundian type on the walls of the tomb shed no light. More important is the fact that this effigy awakens a memory of the style of Nicolaus Gerhaerts' epoch, and it is possible that the relatively late date of the Malicorne figure casts further light upon the continuity of style in French sculpture during the second half of the fifteenth century. The Entombment at Solesmes, dating from 1496, demonstrates the triumph of a new style.

At this point two wooden figures of female saints must be added, originally in the Chabrière-Arlès Collection and now in the Metropolitan Museum in New York (Plate 144A). They were clearly once part of a multi-figured Lamentation of Christ, but their provenance is not known. I believe that their compactness of form and clarity of structure prove them to be French and not Netherlandish. They are suffused with a strong inner tension, but are not expansive. Similar is the coloured stone St Michael from the abbey of Ferrières (Loiret) in the museum of Montargis.[30] Such figures of the

1480s demonstrate, I think, a peculiarity of French Late Gothic sculpture which has as yet received too little attention.

Documentary records suggest that there existed a very intensive artistic activity in the years between 1470 and 1490 in the large towns of Northern France such as Rouen and Amiens. Unfortunately, however, it is impossible to form any clear conception of the work of the masters whose names occur in these records. In the years round 1500 and at the beginning of the new century sculpture in a markedly regional style occurs, which obviously presupposes local traditions round 1480. I think, for example, that the rhetoric of movement in the drapery of the St Margaret in the church of Noyelles-sur-Mer and of the same saint in the church of Méru is characteristic of the style of Picardy [31] and suggests the existence of prototypes dating from *c.* 1480.

A tripartite retable with reliefs from the Life of the Virgin from the chapel of St Éloi near Bernay, now in the Musée de Cluny, is a relatively early example, dating from *c.* 1470, of the diffusion of small-scale objects from Brabant and Flanders.[32] Two significant works imported from Brabant are the carved triptychs which were made between 1478 and 1498 for the Chartreuse of St Honoré at Thuison near Abbeville. One of these, with scenes from the Life of the Virgin, is now in the church of St Wulfran at Abbeville and the other, containing scenes from the life of St Honoré, is in the church at Le Crotoy.[33]

A work which reflects the whole situation of sculpture at the time is the wooden Virgin on a large crescent moon in Amiens Cathedral (Plate 144B).[34] The ample folds of drapery upon this tall and slender figure, which still retains its original colouring, are traversed by a network of angular, deeply cut lines in a style similar to that seen in contemporary Netherlandish sculpture. The same may be said of a stone figure of the Virgin from Quaiant now in the museum of Arras (Plate 144C). The stone Virgin in the choir of the church at Folleville (Picardy),[35] which on the basis of the dating of the church itself has been assigned to the period between 1513 and 1519, is a replica of the type of the Virgin at Amiens, which is thirty years older. Equally, a South Netherlandish prototype of *c.* 1480 may be assumed for the charming stone Virgin turning over the pages of a book in the church at Luat, Fresnoy-le-Luat (Oise).[36]

The stylistic origin of such figures can be recognized in some splendid stone mural tablets with wonderfully three-dimensional reliefs which date from *c.* 1470-90. The finest surviving fragments, unfortunately in very poor condition, are in the museums of Amiens, Arras, and Douai. Foremost among them is the tablet to Canon Jean Lamelin (d. 1470) in Tournai Cathedral, where the masterly composition calls up memories of the art of Roger van der Weyden and Hugo van der Goes.

The absence of any more outstanding examples of sculpture in Northern France at this time makes it worth while to mention a very vivid relief in oak of St Crispin and St Crispinian, formerly in the collection of Dr Figdor in Vienna. This comes from Ypres, but the two pairs of donors with their patron saints, which belong together with it, are from Amiens.[37] In such carvings as these, the type and style of Brabantine workshops, e.g. that of the Brussels Master of the Claudio de Villa retable, has found an echo.[38]

In the last decade of the fifteenth century there follow the Virgin in the Chapelle de la Mère Dieu of Notre-Dame at Évreux and the earliest parts of the reliefs on the choir screen (from 1490 on) of Amiens Cathedral, representing scenes from the Life and Passion of St Firmin (Plates 186B and 187).[39] These are works in a magnificent impasto style, inspired with a rich inner vividness and almost inexhaustible in the epic charm of the narrative. A wealth of artistic skill is perceptible in such works, which must reach back to a local tradition of the preceding decade.

CHAPTER 10

SPAIN AND PORTUGAL IN THE SECOND HALF OF THE FIFTEENTH CENTURY

THE most famous Netherlandish painters of the fifteenth century – from Jan van Eyck and Roger van der Weyden to Hugo van der Goes – painted altarpieces for Spain, and the best of the Spanish painters were quick to assimilate these new influences. It would be wrong to describe the direction of this development simply as realism; for that leaves out of account the magical element which the Spaniards added to the new realism. Hence for instance the differences between the Netherlandish and Spanish use of colour.

Just as close were the contacts between Spanish Late Gothic sculptors and France, the Netherlands, and Germany, beginning with the work of Enrich Alamán and Johan de Valenciennes (1397) for the Puerta del Mirador of the cathedral of Palma on Mallorca. In 1422 Guillermo Sagrera added to this portal statues of St Peter and St Paul of a Netherlandish type, closely related to the Portuguese statues of the same saints in the Ernesto de Vilhena Collection in Lisbon. Sagrera was in charge of the cathedral lodge of Perpignan. He was also responsible for the Lonja (Exchange) at Palma, which dates from 1426–46; in the portal tympanum there is an exquisitely beautiful figure of an angel (Plate 146B), whose bold 'painterly' abandon most impressively demonstrates how decisively the Burgundo–Southern-French type of representation had been changed in Spain. Janin Lomme of Tournai, who carved the double monument for King Charles the Noble of Navarre and his wife in the cathedral of Pamplona in 1425, also had his roots in Burgundian sculpture. The fact that he too was 'maestro mayor' of Pamplona Cathedral is another indication of the extent to which this type of sculpture was connected with the lodges. His closest collaborator was called Juan de Bruselas. All of which goes to show that it is in Spain that we are most likely to be able to fill in the lacunae in our knowledge of events in Northern France and Belgium. Burgundian influences are also strong in the reliefs of the mourners on the tomb of Bishop Escales by Antonio Canet in the Capilla de la Santísima Trinidad in Barcelona Cathedral, and these are followed about 1420–30 by the Netherlandish wooden altarpiece and the monumental figures of the apostles in Netherlandish style in the Capilla de López de Saldaña in the abbey of S. Clara at Tordesillas (Valladolid).

Thus there is a recognizable tradition of contacts in the early fifteenth century, and this tradition was to have a decisive influence on the style of Spanish sculpture in the second half of the century too. Indeed one gets the impression, both from documentary evidence and from the works themselves, that the contacts became still closer. Some of the works in question may be said to give us our first true idea of the significance of the sculptural heritage of Northern France and the Netherlands at this time – a heritage which, as we have seen, has almost entirely disappeared.[1] Instances of what I mean are the stone Virgin and Child, dating from *c.* 1450–60, in the Old Cathedral of Salamanca, the terracotta Virgin in the church of Prádanos de Bureba (Burgos), which is one of the earliest and finest surviving examples of Utrecht terracotta sculpture, and the South Netherlandish or Flemish wooden Virgin and Child in S. Pedro Zumaya (Navarre), dating from *c.* 1460–70.[2] In the composition of the fragmentary wooden group of mourners (Plate 147B) and a Magdalen from a Calvary of *c.* 1460–70 in the abbey of Guadalupe we seem to have a sculptural translation of a picture in the style of Roger van der Weyden.[3]

In Portugal we find a similar development. Here too the imported objects are less interesting for us than the works of visiting artists from abroad whose style has taken on a partly Iberian flavour. An outstanding example of this is the magnificent wooden retable in Sé Velha Coimbra, executed between 1498 and 1508 by Olivério de Gand and João d'Ypres.[4] However Flemish the figures in this work may be, the colour and decoration are predominantly Iberian. Even isolated wood carvings like the Virgin at Funchal or the angel in the Charola dos Templários at Tomar prove the degree to which Portugal shared in these South Netherlandish influences.[5]

In the following survey of the most important Spanish works of sculpture from the second half of the fifteenth century we shall frequently encounter the names of artists from the Netherlands, France, and Germany; it is therefore all the more necessary to stress at the outset the special direction taken by Spanish altar architecture and sculpture in the fifteenth century. In this development the visiting artists from abroad also took part, which makes it possible to distinguish their work from objects imported from the Netherlands[6] or England. Late Gothic altarpieces in Spain assumed gigantic proportions, compared with the traditional prototypes, and are as much *sui generis* as the vast contemporary triptychs in Germany. It is a pity that, apart from some penetrating studies by theologians,[7] there has been very little attempt to investigate the peculiar characteristics of these Spanish altarpieces.[8]

The type of altarpiece most favoured in Spain is the *retablo*, i.e. a retable in a wall recess, the retable itself being reminiscent of an iconostasis in the division into horizontal and vertical panels of equal value, generally filled with high relief scenes or groups of figures. The origin of this additive arrangement is in conventions of Trecento retables. The sculpture of the panels, apart of course from their illustrative religious significance, is predominantly decorative, as is the emphasis on larger-scale recesses and the introduction of central compositions which – like stained glass in a rose window – fill a large tondo. Thus these retables tower up, relief after relief, to the very vaulting, enclosed between shafts which are embellished with little statues. The only emphasis by size is certain principal figures such as the Virgin or patron saints, or certain dominant figure groups, such as the Crucifixion. We do not get the complex, large-figured scenes of the *theatrum sacrum* of the Netherlandish and German altarpieces: on the contrary, the multi-figured sculpture of the Spanish retables is always and everywhere subordinated to an architectural scheme, though with the increase of Flamboyant elements the architecture loses its abstract character and becomes ever more smothered by decorative *accessoires*.

Another striking contrast to the Netherlandish and German altarpieces lies in the fact that the Late Gothic Spanish retables have ceased to be *corpora mobilia* in space. For the most part they are attached to the wall, as a result of which the sculpture, which is almost always carved in wood and brightly coloured and gilded, is remarkably similar to architectural sculpture, as far as function and style are concerned. And so in the following survey we can treat the wooden altarpieces along with the stone sculpture of the portals and monuments. The number of people involved in the creation of the *retablos* was necessarily large, beginning with the designer (*trazador*), who might be a painter, but who was not necessarily the person in charge of the execution of the work. Then there were the *talladores* and other specialists: namely the *encarnadores*, the *estofadores*, and the *doradores*, all of whom played their part in the work. This fact makes the attribution of particular pieces to individual masters almost impossible.

What is particularly impressive in Spain is the reflection of the various historical situations in the characters of the individual landscapes. However, pressure of space makes it necessary to confine this survey to a summary of the leading centres. At the same time the reader must be referred to the admirably full and scholarly treatment of the subject by Ainaud de Lasarte and Duran Sanpere in the eighth volume of *Ars Hispaniae* (1956).

From 1448 Hanequin de Bruselas was *maestro de la obra* at Toledo Cathedral,[9] and it was under his supervision that the Puerta de los Leones was erected in the south transept, the figures in the jambs and the inner tympanum of which were carved by Juan Alemán and his collaborators after 1465 (Plate 146A). They are beautiful in line, noble in design, clear in silhouette, and sharply defined in the subdivision of the surface. In particular, the relief of the Tree of Jesse in the tympanum is directly reminiscent of Lower Rhenish sculpture and of the graphic style of the early works of Israel van Meckenem, which suggests that the home of this 'Alemán' was the Lower Rhineland. The relief tells of the carver's pleasure in the clear linear forms; it is an early example of the 'graphic' style of Lower Rhenish Late Gothic and culminates in the seated Virgin, at the top of the Tree of Jesse.

The sculptor Egas Cueman (of the masons' family of Coeman in Brussels) was a brother of Hanequin de Bruselas. According to a contract dated 1454, both brothers were commissioned to carve the choir stalls of Cuenca Cathedral (now in the abbey church of Belmonte). Then in 1458 at Toledo Egas Cueman carved the monument of Gonzalo de Illescas, bishop of Córdova, for Guadalupe Abbey; in 1463 he made three figures for the Puerta de los Leones in Toledo; and from 1467 he was engaged on the double tomb of Alonso de Velasco and his wife at Guadalupe, which, including the painting, was not finished until after 1480 (Plate 150B). It is a wall monument with two kneeling patrons and two pages in the background. Today this work seems austere, sombre, almost hard, but originally it was richly embellished with colour. Completely Netherlandish in character is the delicate filigree of the high pinnacles against the wall above, where pairs of singing angels flank the central figure of an enthroned Virgin. In its South Netherlandish manner this latter figure forms an instructive contrast with the Lower Rhenish character of the Virgin from Juan Alemán's Tree of Jesse. On the basis of such distinctions I believe that the group of three angels with musical instruments under a canopy on the Puerta de los Leones in Toledo can be ascribed to Egas Cueman.

Toledo became a centre for both native and foreign sculptors. A significant product of these Toledo workshops is, I think, a group of mourners in wood, a fragment of a Calvary from Guadalupe Abbey,[10] which is movingly grand in its restraint and at the same time thoroughly Spanish in its impasto style. In the rich modelling of the surface and the depth of feeling expressed in the gesture a wooden Mater Dolorosa (probably from the last decade of the century),[11] in the Museo del Greco in Toledo, which is a fragment from a Crucifixion, is strikingly Spanish too, and this Spanish spirit was so strong that even the works of foreign artists active in Spain are notably different from those produced in their countries of origin. Altogether it can be said that the works of Netherlandish, German, and French carvers in Spain between 1470 and 1490 have a decidedly expressive abstract character.

The number of works commissioned was enormous. One familiar example is the immense number of carvings on the screens of the capilla mayor of Toledo Cathedral. In charge of the works under Hanequin from 1463 to 1479 was Lorenzo Martínez. His brother Martín Sánchez Bonifacio was the leading master in the cathedral lodge from 1475 to 1493. Probably their family too came from the north, and more precisely from Tournai. From 1472 to 1475 Martín Sánchez Bonifacio was engaged, along with Juan Guas, whose father came from Lyon, on the capilla mayor of the abbey of El Parral in Segovia.

After the victory of the Catholic Kings in 1476, Juan Guas was entrusted with the design for the collegiate church in Toledo, which was planned both as a memorial of the victory and as a burying place. The church, called S. Juan de los Reyes, was begun in 1477. Some very interesting drawings by Juan Guas, also for altarpieces, are preserved in the Prado.[12] The interior of the church is encrusted with a positive forest of statues, some of which were not completed till 1495. Few of them possess any very individual character, but in the best of them (e.g. the stone figure of St James; Plate 147A) the foreign influence is completely subordinated to the native, neo-Castilian element.

Psychological factors bestow upon Spanish tomb sculpture and the position it occupies in the church interior a special significance. In the sculptural decoration of these monuments during the Late Gothic period Spain developed a style of its own which was just as individual as her altar architecture. Therefore a group of funerary monuments may be considered at this point. The group seems to have much in common with the art of Toledo. An early example of the type of monument usual in the second half of the century is that of Caballero Pedro de Valderrábano (d. 1465) in Ávila Cathedral. The armour-clad effigy lies on the tomb lid, and at its feet the small figure of a page crouches by the knight's helmet. Of the same type and style are the mural monuments of the first Count of Tendilla, Don Inigo López de Mendoza (d. 1479), and his wife from the abbey of St Anne at Tendilla, now in the church of S. Ginés in Guadalajara. In these works the connexion with the sculptural tradition of Toledo, in so far as it was determined by the activities of Egas Cueman and Juan Guas, is evident enough.

Sebastián de Almonacid (from Torrijos near Toledo) also had his roots in this tradition. He was responsible for the tympanum statues of the doorway to the cloisters of Segovia Cathedral (1486–7). They represent the Pietà with the Magdalen and St John and are impressive by virtue of the restraint in the gestures. The same master was responsible for the monument to Cardinal Alfonso Carrillo de Acuña (d. 1482) in the Iglesia Magistral at Alcalá de Henares, and for the ceremonial marble tombs of the Condestable Álvaro de Luna in the full dress of the Order of Santiago and his wife (d. 1488), carved in Guadalajara in 1489 and now in the Capilla de Santiago in Toledo Cathedral (Plate 151). It is in the precision of form and picturesque richness of these sculptures that their Spanish nature becomes evident. The name of Sebastián de Almonacid recurs in the records relating to sculptural activity in Toledo as late as 1527.

In this phase of Spanish sculpture, Flemish realism was able to inspire works of a power and vigour greater than any to be found in the Netherlands themselves. A similar phenomenon is to be observed in contemporary Spanish painting. It seems to me that sufficient attention has not been paid to this fact. It is in the 1480s that we meet the most striking examples of this unmistakably Spanish element, culminating in the splendid alabaster tombs of Gil de Siloe[13] in the Cartuja de Miraflores. In their sharp realism and luminous radiance, these works are so impressive that the exact provenance of their creator is of only secondary importance.

In this context, two monuments in New Castile are of outstanding significance. One is the mural monument erected in S. Clara at Toledo by Juan de Morales (d. 1490) to his parents Juan Fernández de Morales and Maria Fernández Sedeña (Plate 149). The style of the alabaster portrait figures goes back to the tomb of Alonso de Velasco by Egas Cueman at Guadalupe (Plate 150B). But now all the features are imbued with a new precision. It is true that the faces are realistic, but this is a realism of a new intellectual subtlety. In their harmonious compactness there is an affinity with portraits of the Florentine Early Renaissance, such as we have not so far met with anywhere in Spain, France, or the Netherlands.

The same is true of the portrait figure of a Knight of the Santiago Order who fell before Granada in 1486, Martín Vázquez de Arce (Plate 148). This is part of a monument in a recess in the Capilla de S. Catalina in Sigüenza Cathedral. The father and brother of the deceased erected the monument in 'alabaster marble'; it was in course of construction in 1488. Once again the connexion with Toledo sculpture is clear. But what a transformation has taken place in the type of recumbent effigy which we know from the Valderrábano tomb at Ávila and the Mendoza tomb at Guadalajara! Here is no longer a representation of the dead, but an immortalization of the living. The effigy is magically transfigured in a way that is totally different from the realism of the Netherlands. A new type of portrait has been realized – the portrait of Humanism and the Renaissance.

The next name we meet in Toledo sculpture is that of a German, Rodrigo Alemán, who carved the lower choir stalls in the cathedral between 1489 and 1495. He was a vivid illustrator, evidently from the Lower Rhineland, and we also owe to him the choir stalls in the cathedrals of Plasencia (after 1497) and Ciudad Rodrigo (Plate 150C).

The apogee of the surviving works of this Late Gothic School of Toledo is the wooden high altar in the cathedral, which was executed from a design of Peti Juan (1498-1504) in collaboration with Diego Copin and Cristiano from Holland, Felipe Vigarny from Burgundy, Rodrigo the German, and Sebastián de Almonacid, together with the painter Juan de Borgoñia, who coloured the altar. It consists of four tiers, and the individual niches are filled with scenes from the Passion, in the centre of which stands the pyramidal 'Custodia'. It is the culmination of the type of altar in which the individual personalities of the artists concerned are completely lost in common service to the decorative splendour of the work as a whole.

Late Gothic sculpture in Andalusia[14] presents the same features as we have met in Toledo and New Castile. Here too it is preceded by a remarkable vacuum, so that one gets the impression that a local tradition was lacking. Consequently when production did start on an increasing scale after the middle of the century, it was again foreign carvers and sculptors who were chiefly responsible. In Seville, for instance, Lorenzo Mercadante from Brittany was active from 1454 to 1467. He is the master of the alabaster sculpture on the tomb of Cardinal Juan de Cervantes (d. 1453) in the Capilla de S. Hermenegildo in Seville Cathedral and also of the terracotta sculpture on the Puerta del Nascimento in the cathedral (1466-7) and on the portal of the baptistery. In the treasury of Gerona Cathedral too there is a series of alabaster saints by Mercadante (Plate 150A). All these works have a precision and tautness of linear form in which the austerity of expression and the unemotional treatment of the subject matter is characteristic of the mid century, and perhaps also of Mercadante's Breton origin. His wooden St Agnes on the portal of the abbey of S. Inés in Seville looks like the sister of the Lübeck Virgin at Vadstena – so complex is the problem of the diffusion and local variations of the Netherlandish style in Late Gothic Sculpture. Another illustration of this is the beautiful wooden 'Nuestra Señora de la Antigua' in the cathedral of Granada. No doubt this is the work of a South Netherlandish master; it is characterized by the tall stature and the clarity and austerity which are typical of the period round 1470.

The next artist working in Seville to whom we must direct our attention is a certain 'Dacart pieter sayn', who is probably identical with Pieter Dancart, a carver who was active at Lille in 1468. In 1478-9 he completed the choir stalls by Nufre Sanchez in Seville Cathedral, and from 1482 he was engaged on the stupendous high altar of the cathedral (Plate 154A). After his death in 1489 his work on the altarpiece was continued by his countryman Maestro Marco, but it was not completed till 1505. The parts which can be ascribed to Dancart are typically Flemish in their linear precision of form and in the convincing spatial relations of the reliefs. However, the architecture of the altarpiece is so commanding and the scenes depicted so numerous that the sculptural elements are totally subordinated to them.

Lorenzo Mercadante's work in Seville was mainly in terracotta and seems to have been continued chiefly by Pedro Millán, who was active in Seville in 1487-1506 and died before 1526. Millán made numbers of coloured terracotta pieces for the cathedral and other churches in Seville – e.g. the apostles and prophets in the dome of the cathedral (1506) – in which the Spanish manner of dealing with the types and style of northern Late Gothic is most clearly visible. The treatment of the body is different, less linear and more three-dimensional. Their psychological type is different too: gentler, though not subtler, but more homogeneous than their northern prototypes. It must be enough to give four examples of such painted terracottas, all signed by Millán: the 'Virgen del Pilar' in the Capilla de Nostra Señora in Seville Cathedral, a draped figure in sharp-edged Late Gothic stylization; the St Michael from the nunnery of S. Fiorentina in Ecija, elegant in his feudal accoutrement and the boylike charm of his expression; a tightly packed group of the Lamentation of Christ from the abbey of Aracena, near Seville, of great intensity of expression (both the latter now in private collections);[15] and the magnificent Christ in Pity with two attendant angels and donor in the church of El Garrobo (Plate 153B). Here, in Late Gothic terms, a new type of sculptural autonomy has been realized – not only a symptom of the artistic situation at the turn of the century, but at the same time a beacon of Spanishness in sculpture.

The essentially Spanish mode of expression, violent in its intensity of emotion, but at the same time tied and incapable of a truly liberating gesture, is most clearly perceptible in wood carvings of the early sixteenth century. An example is the figures of a Dolorosa and St John the Evangelist, kneeling on the ground in a distraction of sorrow, from a Crucifixion group in Cordova Cathedral.[16] This is a Spanish echo of Late Gothic, at a time when the Renaissance had already introduced a new and alien Latin note into Spanish sculpture. In this respect the situation in the early sixteenth century in Spain is remarkably similar to that in Germany: the arrival of the '*stilo nuovo*' produced the most violent – and at the same time the most magnificent – reactions among the last of the Late Gothics.

Both Catalonia and Aragón had particularly vigorous sculptural traditions in the late Middle Ages; but here too it appears that these traditions had become exhausted before the middle of the fifteenth century.[17] A good example is in the Seo of Zaragoza, where the Archbishop Dalmau del Mur commissioned the Catalonian sculptor Pedro Johan to undertake the carving of the high altar in 1444. All he achieved, however, was the predella, and in 1467 the Chapter signed a contract with Master Hans of Schwäbisch Gmünd.[18] The result was one of those enormous Spanish *retablos* which are so crowded with figures and architectural embellishments that it is almost impossible to distinguish the individual contributions of particular artists, especially since the situation has been further obscured by ruthless nineteenth-century restorations. The work was completed in 1480, but already in 1482 the original design was modified by the introduction of a central roundel by Gil Morlanes. Of the three large multi-figured compositions by Hans of Schwäbisch Gmünd, the central one of the Nativity and the Adoration of the Magi (Plate 152A) would appear to be the best preserved. The episodic narrative style of these reliefs is very German. But it is quite difficult to be precise; for we shall find nothing of about 1465–70 quite comparable in Master Hans's homeland on the Swabian and Franconian border, unless it be perhaps the reliefs on the choir stalls of Constance Minster – and here we are again in the sphere of influence of Nicolaus Gerhaerts, the great Netherlander. The only really Swabian element in these reliefs is their narrative style; for the figures are mainly Netherlandish in character, and the decorative detail (e.g. the bejewelled hems of the garments) Spanish. One may compare, for instance, the alabaster figure of the Virgén Blanca in the Seo of Zaragoza, which according to documentary evidence was carved by the sculptor Juan Dusi of Bruges between 1498 and 1504.[19] From all this I would conjecture that on his way to Spain Master Hans spent some time in the Netherlands, and that he learnt a lot there; later, after his long and successful sojourn in Zaragoza, he adopted in some measure a Spanish idiom.

The monument of Archbishop Juan de Aragon (d. 1473) in the Seo at Zaragoza, which – apart from some later additions and alterations – was carved by Juan de Salazar, shows to how many stimuli immigrants were exposed. Both the treatment of the relief and the expression are simplified and rigid, whereas Master Hans's work is diversified by a fascinating display of height and depth, of light and shade.

Another German who was working at this same time in Barcelona was Miquel Luquer (Michael Luger or Locher?). From 1483 until his death in 1490 he was in charge of a workshop, to which his pupil Juan Frederic de Alemania succeeded. To Luquer is ascribed the wooden relief of a Pietà in the tympanum of the south-east portal of the cloisters in Barcelona Cathedral, whose austerity of line and form and intensity of expression are reminiscent of Rhenish and North German art.[20] But here too the exact provenance of the sculptor is obscured for us by the extent to which he – like all his fellows – had become integrated into his Spanish environment. Luquer and his pupil Juan Frederic were also responsible for the carvings on the upper choir stalls in Barcelona Cathedral.

To these pieces an imported work ought to be added whose significance, it seems to me, has not been sufficiently recognized. It is the life-size bronze equestrian statue of St Martin and the Beggar over the portal of S. Martín at Valencia. This group was cast in 1494 and was handed over to the church in 1495 by the heirs of Don Vicente de Peñarroja, Knight of Santiago.[21] It is an early example of that autonomy of the statue which was something new and in contrast to Late Gothic sculpture and which we have already mentioned in connexion with Pedro Millán's Cristo de Piedad at El Garrobo. Horse, rider, and beggar are no longer fused into one 'picture' in the traditional way, but are equal ingredients of a balanced rational composition. As far as we know, Spain did not at this time possess foundries of sufficient experience to undertake the casting of such a monumental group. Such foundries did however exist in the Southern Netherlands, especially in Brussels. The nearest parallel to our work, on account of its monumentality, is indeed the bronze monument of Mary of Burgundy which will be discussed later. So the St Martin is most probably an imported work from the Southern Netherlands or Flanders.[22]

Northern Spain, as far as we can see, is the area in which Late Gothic sculpture is most richly represented, and also the area in which a regional development can most easily be traced. As we have already dealt with New Castile, we can now turn to the sculptural achievement of León, Asturias, and Old Castile.

At the beginning stand the choir stalls of León Cathedral (Plate 153A). In 1467 the cathedral chapter spent a considerable sum of money on them. Now we know that at that time the sculptor Jan van Mecheln was active at León. Work on the choir stalls seems to have continued until 1481. If, however, the stalls go back to a design by Jan van Mecheln of 1467, then this relatively early date would be one of the most important in the history of Late Gothic sculpture in the Southern Netherlands.[23] It may be, of course, that the astonishingly painterly expansion of the style of these reliefs accrued only gradually during the fifteen years or so before they were completed, and that the original design was more austere. Certainly the compositions of these stalls exhibit a linear sharpness and painterly boldness of which the South Netherlandish sculpture of this time may, as we know from many indications, have been capable, but which we shall look for in vain among actual surviving works in the Southern Netherlands. In the Northern Netherlands the carvings on the choir stalls in St Jan at 's-Hertogenbosch (e.g. the reliefs of St Anthony and St Michael) and in St Martin at Bolsward are comparable in style to the León stalls.

Now we must consider the carved and painted altarpiece in the collegiate church of Covarrubias near Burgos.[24] In the central section, the back of which is articulated architecturally, are the wooden figures of an Adoration of the Magi, arranged additively as in a composition of Roger van der Weyden (Plate 152B). The sculptural style is austere, one might almost say a little stiff; a certain hardness, and especially the elongation of the proportions, make a date c. 1500 probable. This master too certainly came from the Southern Netherlands. To make a comparison with sculptural developments in the Brussels area, the Covarrubias carvings seem to be contemporary with the scenes from the Life of St Leonard in the altarpiece of Zoutleeuw (Léau) – which would mean that the altarpiece at Covarrubias was only a little later than the carvings of Hans of Schwäbisch Gmünd for the retablo mayor of the Seo of Zaragoza. The Netherlandish wooden figure of a King Melchior in the Schnütgen Museum in Cologne (Plate 113B),[25] obviously from just such an altar composition of the Adoration of the Magi, is so closely related to the Covarrubias Adoration that one is tempted to think that they might both be by the same master. The wing paintings in the Covarrubias altarpiece are believed to be by Juan de Borgoñia.

The altarpiece in the Capilla de S. Pedro in S. María at Orduña (Biscaya) of 1504 was – according to documentary evidence – imported from Flanders. From the same year dates a retable stamped with the town mark of Antwerp in El Salvador at Valladolid. There is also an altarpiece from the Brussels school of Jan Borman in the Valladolid Museum. The wooden altarpiece in a mural recess of the Salamanca family chapel in the church of S. Lesmes at Burgos shows the stylistic peculiarities of South Netherlandish workshops in the early years of the sixteenth century in so pure a form that one must conclude that its sculptor had only recently arrived in Spain. Such examples could be multiplied indefinitely, and it is clear that in Northern Spain especially a 'Hispano-Flemish' style developed, which makes it exceedingly difficult to decide in many cases whether it is a question of a native carver working under South Netherlandish influence or of a Netherlander working in Spain.[26]

Some examples in chronological order follow. Outstanding as a document is the high, narrow rectangular altarpiece with a multi-figured wooden Lamentation of Christ against a painted background of Jerusalem, which is now in The Cloisters in

New York (formerly in the B. Oppenheim Collection, Berlin; Plate 186A).[27] This work is a wonderful, typically Late Gothic union of sculpture, painting of sculpture, and panel painting, all concentrated in the narrow space of the box-like frame. This concentration seems to intensify the dynamic peculiarities of the sculpture and also the emotional content of the scene represented. The source of the composition is no doubt a painting by Roger van der Weyden. At the same time the work is imbued with a new fervour of expression which is not to be found in comparable South Netherlandish sculpture. The altarpiece is believed to come from the neighbourhood of Burgos. Is this intensification of expression a sign of Hispano-Flemish origin? In any case the dynamic intensity expresses a reaction against the static monumentality of the composition of the altarpiece at Covarrubias. Related to the Oppenheim altar is a group of the Virgin below the Cross supported by St John and the Magdalen, which is evidently a fragment of an extensive wooden altarpiece, in the Musée de Cluny. Similar too in form and feeling is the walnut figure of a mourning Virgin in the Berlin Museum.[28] If one is looking for connexions with the Oppenheim altar in South Netherlandish sculpture, one must mention first and foremost the Brussels altarpiece in St Dymphna at Geel.

Now for architectural sculpture, which played a comparatively large part in Late Gothic Spain. I have already mentioned the similarity between wooden altar carvings and architectural sculpture, owing to the integration of the altarpiece into the architecture of the building. In Castile we are able to trace through three generations the work of a family of architects, who came from Cologne, and who were also in charge of the sculpture of the buildings on which they were employed. Hans of Cologne, who built the spires of Burgos Cathedral, seems to have entered the service of Bishop Alonso de Cartagena in 1442.[29] He married a Spanish woman, and the issue of this marriage, Simon de Colonia, carried on and completed his father's work in Burgos Cathedral and in the Cartuja de Miraflores after the latter's death (shortly before 1481).[30] As leader of the cathedral lodge Simon, who was perhaps also a sculptor, was responsible for the ever more lavish sculptural decoration there. Thus the almost unbelievably rich figural sculpture of the Capilla del Condestable Pedro Fernández de Velasco (1482–98) is a product of his design and supervision (Plate 154B). To him or his son Francisco and their numerous assistants we owe too the sculpture on the façade of S. Pablo at Valladolid (1486–92) and of the Colegio de S. Gregorio (1488–96) in the same city; also of S. María la Real in Aranda de Duero (after 1500) and on the trascoro of Palencia Cathedral (after 1505).

To these examples we must add the richly sculptured funerary monuments in recesses, which carry on a tradition already well established in Burgos. But however charming individual passages of this monumental sculpture may be (e.g. the relief of the Nativity in the Capilla del Condestable), it is so completely subordinated to the decorative system that it is hardly possible to speak of individual quality. Nevertheless their ubiquity in the region is astounding. Francisco de Colonia[31] even applied this decorative system to wooden altar sculpture, in the retablo mayor of the little church of S. Nicolás at Burgos, where all the details, including of course all the sculpture, are swallowed up in the stupendous effect of the whole. This retable was completed, though perhaps not yet painted and gilded, in 1505 – a very late date for a piece which had grown out of cathedral Gothic; for the tondo of the Coronation of the Virgin, which surmounts the whole, attempts to realize once again the principle of composition of the rose window – already an anachronism – though now for purely decorative purposes.

A more individual significance attaches to the monument to Bishop Alonso de Cartagena (d. 1456), the patron of Hans of Cologne, in Burgos Cathedral (Plate 155). According to documentary evidence, the monument was completed in 1447 or 1449. This is an enigma; for the formal character of the sculpture is so closely allied to the works of Gil de Siloe dating from the 1480s that it seems impossible to suppose that forty years lie between them. The style of the figures is without doubt South Nether-landish. But if we compare them with the known *incunabula* of this style in the Nether-lands themselves, then the date 1447, i.e. fifteen years before Nicolaus Gerhaerts' monu-ment to Archbishop Sierck at Trier, is scarcely credible. For this reason some scholars have ignored this dating,[32] and have assumed that the Cartagena monument was a later creation, either by an immediate predecessor of Gil de Siloe, or the earliest recog-nizable work (*c.* 1480) from his hand. The figures of the apostles and saints on the sides of the tomb-chest follow in their linear articulation the stylistic type which was usual in Netherlandish art at home and abroad in the 1470s, though they include such magical creations as the figure of St Casilda. At the feet of the recumbent effigy of the bishop the sculptor has placed his acolyte holding open the pages of a Bible. This is an astonishing piece of sculptural inspiration, deeply moving in both volume and gesture.

For the Cartuja de Miraflores, which was built by Hans of Cologne and his son Simon in 1454–88, Gil de Siloe[33] designed in 1486 the free-standing monument of King John II, the founder of the abbey, who died in 1454, and his second wife Isabella of Portugal (Plate 156B), and also the wall monument of the Infante Alfonso who died in his youth in 1468 (Plate 157A). They were commissioned by the successor to the throne, Isabella the Catholic. The monuments were actually built between 1489 and 1493. The tomb-chest of the double monument is octagonal and corresponds to the shape of the surrounding space, from which one may conclude that sculptor and architect were jointly responsible for the design. It is lavishly studded with alabaster figures, and the robes and insignia of the royal effigies are worked with the highest degree of subtlety. The reproduction of goldsmiths' work, pearls, and embroidered textiles create a magical *diatetron* of the surface, as do the canopies and framework decoration. The same exaggerated realism is to be seen in the wall monument, where the richly robed Infante kneels before a prie-dieu covered with a fine cloth and cushion, whereas the framework and wall are a web of openwork ornamentation. It is un-necessary to stress how many artists and craftsmen must have shared in the execution of such elaborate works.

It would be easy to demonstrate the close affinity between the style of Gil de Siloe and that of Lower Rhenish sculpture. But at the same time the statues have the same elaboration and intensification – at times approaching the bizarre – that is characteristic of the architectural decoration surrounding them. Hence his works have a more Spanish quality than is usual with other foreign artists working in Spain: one is involuntarily reminded of the extent to which the architecture of Simon de Colonia, whose mother was a Spaniard, had already acquired a regional character in contradistinction to that of his father Hans, who had emigrated from Germany. This incidentally brings us back to the monument to Bishop Alonso de Cartagena. For its style is certainly more closely related to South Netherlandish than to Lower Rhenish sculpture. And so its creator may after all have been someone other than Gil de Siloe, though doubtless he employed the same assistants as Gil himself was to do slightly later.[34]

Gil de Siloe's sculptural masterpiece is the wall monument to Juan de Padilla, who fell outside Granada in 1491 fighting against the Moors (Plate 157B). He was the favourite page of Queen Isabella, and she was no doubt responsible for the erection of the monument to his memory in the church of Fresdeval (now in the Museo Provincial de Burgos), which is so similar to the one she caused to be erected to her brother at Miraflores. Wethey, the authority on the work of Gil de Siloe, has convincingly shown that the monument of Fresdeval must be a late work of Gil's, dating from *c.* 1500–5. In the greater width and openness of the recess and in the perfected mastery of the portrait, we are confronted with a new style of representation which we no longer feel to be Late Gothic – though the vocabulary of the accompanying ornament is. At the same time it is evident that younger artists, who had already learnt the language of the French Early Renaissance, have had their share in the work. This is most clearly seen in the new three-dimensional quality of the figures in the background relief of the Lamentation of Christ. It is true that the design for this relief probably came from Gil, but it must have been executed by a sculptor who was under the influence of Felipe Vigarny (born in the neighbourhood of Langres) who had been active at Burgos since 1498.[35]

Gil de Siloe was also active as a wood carver for *retablos*. In these a certain 'Diego de la Cruz pintor' always seems to have been his partner. The earliest surviving example (*c.* 1486–92) is the multi-figured altarpiece with the Tree of Jesse in the Capilla de S. Ana in Burgos Cathedral. This was followed about 1488–9 by the now destroyed altar in S. Gregorio at Valladolid; in 1496–9 by the vast high altar of the Cartuja de Miraflores (Plate 156A); and *c.* 1500–5 by the Altar of St Anne in the Capilla del Condestable in Burgos Cathedral. In these works the dimensions are so large and the number of scenes represented so immense that it is scarcely possible to distinguish the individual contribution of Gil de Siloe from those of his collaborators, especially as we have to reckon with the equalizing effects of restoration as well. And, incidentally, was Diego de la Cruz perhaps more than a painter?

Nevertheless, among the works mentioned there is one – the Altar of St Anne in Burgos Cathedral – whose delicate, slender-limbed figures enable us to gain a close insight into Gil de Siloe's work as a wood carver. This is the latest, and also the smallest, of the works just mentioned, and therefore it is a relatively homogeneous work. It is also the best preserved of them all. Here the figures are sublime, draped in close-fitting robes, and so linear in style that it is immediately perceptible when an outside collaborator who is an exponent of the new three-dimensional style (e.g. in the *imago pietatis* in the centre-piece of the lower compartment) has had a share. In his larger works, such as the high altar at Miraflores, Gil's personal style is somewhat obscured. Nevertheless these vast altarpieces cannot be sufficiently admired, both on account of their architectural composition and their sculptural achievement. Finally we must mention as wood carvings from Gil de Siloe's workshop the doors of the Puerta del Claustro in Burgos Cathedral donated by Bishop Acuna.

On the basis of such figures by Gil de Siloe I once attributed to him the figure from Burgos of a seated saint reading a book, in the Museum of the Instituto Valencia in Madrid.[36] A special significance does indeed attach to this little figure, admirably preserved in its original colouring; for on the one hand it shows affinity with Gil, but on the other, in its flowing linear style, it is certainly older than, for example, the alabaster seated Virgin and Child on the monument of the royal couple at Miraflores which, as we have seen, has such close similarities to Lower Rhenish sculpture. So the figure in Madrid serves to illustrate anew that there was a sculptural tradition at Burgos which was not created, but only adopted, by Gil de Siloe.

CHAPTER II

THE NETHERLANDS: 1490–1500

OF the century which forms the subject of this book, only the last decade remains to be dealt with. It may well be unnatural to project transitory events in art on to the rigid grid of decades; nevertheless I believe that it has certain advantages to try and obtain from such an abstraction of set limits a total picture. The method highlights that *coincidentia oppositorum*, which by means of a struggle between different forces at the same time often produces artistic progress.

On the other hand the method reduces to its proper proportions the significance of territorial frontiers, which have been for the most part over-emphasized. These frontiers, many of which have in any case changed in the course of history, actually get in the way of a true understanding of organic artistic developments. Roussillon (on this side of the Pyrenees) belonged in the Late Middle Ages to the kingdom of Aragón, and not to France; the county of Hainault and the dukedom of Brabant were parts of the Holy Roman Empire: the bishoprics of Liège and Utrecht were subject to the archbishop of Cologne – to give only a few examples. Thus in considering the art of the Late Middle Ages, divisions by date are more helpful than divisions by place.

Whereas Italian art in the fifteenth century was dominated by the Renaissance, Central European Late Gothic – for which in Italy, apart from imported works of art, there are very few parallels – was dominated by the Netherlands. But thorough as is our knowledge of Netherlandish painting in the fifteenth century, our knowledge of Netherlandish sculpture in this period is woefully inadequate. So much so indeed that for the first half of the century the path that extends from Claus Sluter to Nicolaus Gerhaerts is for long stretches merely a matter of guesswork. When Gerhaerts' influence ceased to be effective, the international dominance of the Netherlands in the sculptural sphere was succeeded by an astonishingly rich and varied regional activity (especially in Germany), which in its turn gave way suddenly about and after 1500 to the radiating influences of the Italian Renaissance.

At the end of the fifteenth century the export of art and artists from the Netherlands extended from the Iberian Peninsula as far north as Scandinavia. The turn of the century did not in itself bring about any sudden stop of this, though then a certain Renaissance Italism crept in, which, however – at least as far as sculpture is concerned – was more a matter of externals than of inner structure. Nevertheless it must be remembered that as early as 1506 the brothers Mouscron had presented the marble Madonna by Michelangelo to Notre-Dame in Bruges.

When one comes to consider the wealth and variety of Late Gothic sculpture in the Netherlands at the end of the fifteenth century, it might well seem that the subject should be divided into two sections, one dealing with the North and one with the South; for North Netherlandish sculpture at this period is often indistinguishable from the products of Lower Rhenish workshops, whereas that of the South Netherlands has the closest affinities with the art of the neighbouring towns of Northern France. But such a division into North and South – just in the case of this pivot of Europe – would obscure what the two areas of Netherlandish sculpture have in common. It would lead to serious distortions; for Lower Rhenish sculpture, for example, also has close connexions with Westphalia, Lower Saxony, and the Hansa cities. Thus, if we wish to remain faithful to the facts and to make clear the persistence of great traditions, we can only, it seems to me, proceed as we have done so far – namely, by first considering Netherlandish sculpture in all its most important examples, and then turning to North Germany and afterwards to South Germany and Austria, both so rich in talents. Only then can we deal with French and Spanish sculpture, which was open to the revolutionary influences of Italian art round 1500 to such an extent as if Late Gothic had never been.

The greatest achievements of Late Gothic sculpture in the South Netherlands in the decades following the middle of the fifteenth century were figures and groups of figures whose composition was influenced by paintings from the time of Roger van der Weyden; altarpieces (especially from Brussels and Antwerp); and bronzes in an impressive three-dimensional display. These kinds of sculpture were still flourishing at the end of the century with undiminished vigour. Examples of the persistence of compositions and types of representation from the time of Roger van der Weyden are the multifigured group of a Lamentation of Christ – from an altarpiece – carved in oak and stamped with the hall-mark of Brussels in the de Decker Collection at Forest (Vorst) near Brussels; a Crucifix in the de Beule Collection at Ghent; and a mourning St John and a mourning Virgin from a Crucifixion, formerly in the Demotte Collection in Paris.[1] In these works the linear sharpness of the prototypes has been translated into a new impressive breadth and subtle atmospheric effect. The violence and expressive gesture has been toned down, and has given place to a restrained but deeply-felt religious emotion.

Typical of the period is also a certain technical brilliance. Examples of this are the fine statue of St James in St Jacques at Louvain (Leuven)[2] and the formally perfect carvings on the beautiful choir stalls of St Sulpice at Diest,[3] which date from about 1493 (Plate 161B). But the end of the century is mainly notable for the quantity of carved and painted wooden altarpieces, though their wide dispersal through export and the lack of any systematic investigation of the subject make it difficult to form a clear idea of the most outstanding examples. The majority of surviving Netherlandish altarpieces of high quality belong already to the early years of the sixteenth century.

The outstanding wood carver in Brussels at this time seems to have been Jan Borman the Elder. The earliest known work by his hand is the Altar of St George, dated 1493, from Ons-Lieve Vrouw van Ginderbuyten at Louvain, now in the Musée du Cinquantenaire in Brussels (Plate 163).[4] This type of altarpiece, with the arrangement of the scenes side by side in box-like compartments, hollowed out to look like a chapel and rich in architectural ornamentation, is already familiar to us from slightly older altarpieces, e.g. that at Strängnäs. Evident as this convention is, just as striking is the novel perfection of the fully three-dimensional details, so that the throng of figures creates an evocative theatrical effect, without expressive tension, and as rational as it is naturalistic. The use of figures in the foreground of the composition with their backs turned to the spectator serves to concentrate his gaze on a central point. There is an immense wealth of detail in the often fantastic costumes. The technique has an element of routine in its skilfulness, and there is a degree of realism which excludes any hint of the mystery so potent in medieval art. Thus it would seem that in this case, despite the retention of traditional conventions, a notable step has been taken across the threshold of the new age. The altar is the forerunner of those mass-produced altarpieces and fragments which have survived in almost embarrassing plenitude from the first quarter of the sixteenth century.[5]

Jan Borman was active as a wood carver in Brussels from 1479 onwards, together with his sons Jan Borman the Younger and Pasquier Borman. He seems to have done particularly much for Louvain after 1489. On the other hand most of the surviving examples of altarpieces from his workshop or from Brussels workshops, who employed his style, but in an independent way, are to be found in Sweden.[6] The latest date that can be associated with Jan Borman is on the altarpiece of 1522, signed by him, in the parish church of Güstrow in Mecklenburg[6] – so much of his mature work belongs to the new century.

The same development in the direction of technical brilliance is to be found in the Antwerp altar sculpture of the same time. Here too traditional types of figures undergo a metallic sharpening of the forms and an exaggerated realism attained by overstressing the expression of the features and the decorative details of clothing and armour. Examples are the oak fragment from the relief of a Calvary, signed with the hallmark of Antwerp, now in the Rijksmuseum in Amsterdam; the fragment of a wooden Christ carrying the Cross in the Victoria and Albert Museum in London; and the reliefs of an altar of the Passion in the church of Hulshout (Province of Antwerp), together with allied works.[7] In Antwerp there was a liking for the employment of anecdotal illustrations. Yet these altars are three-dimensional compositions of great dramatic tension and realistic vividness. Instances from the period 1490–1500 are the group of a swooning Virgin supported by St John and the Magdalen from a Calvary in the Deutsches Museum in Berlin,[8] and the particularly effective group of dicing soldiers, doubtless from the same altarpiece, signed with the hallmark of Antwerp, and now in a private collection in Munich (Plate 159B). These groups lead directly to the free painterly sculpture of Antwerp altarpieces in the flamboyant style of the early sixteenth century, such as the Altar of the Lamentation by Laureys Keldermans (1511) from the abbey of Averbode, now in the Vleeshuis Museum in Antwerp,[9] and the majority of the Antwerp altarpieces in Sweden and Denmark.

But there is another aim – and it cannot be sufficiently emphasized that from about 1490–1500 on we find ourselves at a crisis of style and have to reckon with many possibilities of sculptural expression – that of trying to establish a harmony between the originally expressive and expansive style of Late Gothic sculpture and a new emphasis on statuesque and representational images. This endeavour meant that traditional types were given a revived, retrospective validity. We shall have to deal with this tendency when we come to speak of contemporary sculpture in Germany.

The complexity of this situation is most clearly illustrated by the wooden Crucifixion in the collegiate church of St Pierre at Louvain (Leuven; Plate 158, A, B, and C),[10] where a new harmony and compactness has become the means of expressing deeply felt emotions. The connexions with painting are obvious: both mood and composition derive from Roger van der Weyden. The only questions that arise are: when was the group carved, and who carved it? Traditionally it is ascribed to the elder Borman; more recently it has been ascribed to Nicolaus Gerhaerts. This uncertainty as to whether such a work dates from 1480–90 or from forty years earlier illustrates vividly the difficulty of distinguishing the final creative phase of Late Gothic from the *incunabula* of this particular type of sculpture. However, in this case, so it seems to me, the painterly qualities of the carvings and the sensitive movement of the surface of the drapery indicate a date round 1490 as unequivocally as does the muted rhetoric of the sentiment. I would assume that the Calvary in St Quentin at Louvain[11] precedes this group in date, and also that it translates more literally into sculptural terms the paintings which also were the source of inspiration for the sculptor of the Crucifixion.

But this is only one side of the problem. The other question is the relationship between the figures of the Crucifixion, with their astonishingly self-contained character and their magnificent sense of movement, and contemporary altar carvings. In view of the date I have assigned to the former, the most natural comparison would be with Borman's Altar of St George in the Brussels Museum, which dates from 1493, but as far as I can see there is little resemblance between them. On the other hand it is known that the elder and the younger Borman were commissioned in 1489 to design the bronze door of the choir screen in St Pierre at Louvain. It is also known that 'about 1491' the elder Borman made a model for a bronze figure of the Duchess Mary of Burgundy for her tomb in Bruges, which we shall discuss later. If this model was actually used for the finished effigy – and there is no reason to suppose that it was not – then I am of the opinion that connexions can be established between Borman and the Calvary at Louvain, especially with the figure of the mourning Virgin; so much so that it appears possible that his busy and obviously famous workshop was responsible not only for ingenious and detailed altar carvings, but also for monumental free-standing statues of the highest quality. In any case this phase of development saw the creation of new types of statuary which were to find many echoes in South Netherlandish religious sculpture in the sixteenth century.

Owing to lack of space we must confine our selection from the large number of surviving objects[12] to those which point the way to a new age. Such is the impressive monumental wooden Calvary from St Gertrude at Nivelles, now in the Louvre (Plate 159A).[13] In this work the muted rhetoric of the Louvain Crucifixion has become open and uninhibited. It is instinct with a hitherto unprecedented emotional ardour, and the dynamism of the form is translated into a new type of human gesture. I believe that it is in this type of statuary rather than in the narrative and dramatic scenes of the altar carvings that we feel most clearly what striking achievements this sculpture was capable of even in the new century. At the same time I believe that this type of expression is characteristic of the Meuse and Moselle regions; one has only to think of the artistic achievements of this area in the thirteenth century. Related to the Crucifixion from Nivelles, though less expressive, are the statues of St John the Evangelist and the apostles Peter, Paul, and Andrew, which are still to be found in the church of St Gertrude.[14]

Because of the new sense of the statuesque, individual statues become more important at this time, even if the term is applied to figures belonging to larger compositions but preserved as *membra disiecta*. They possess the same new 'objective' individuality that is characteristic of the autonomous small-scale sculpture now beginning to flourish in the Netherlands. Through this latter a new and independent branch of sculptural activity developed in the sixteenth century.[15]

Already in the relief of the Nativity from a Brussels altar dating from about 1470 and now in the Louvre,[16] a degree of sculptural objectivity has been reached which imparts the greatest possible self-sufficiency to every detail. The next step is two statues of St Mary Magdalen – particularly charming in the austerity of their form – both with the Brussels hallmark; one in the Musée du Cinquantenaire in Brussels,[17] the other in the Musée de Cluny in Paris. Their date is determined by their close relationship to the choir stalls of St Sulpice at Diest of 1491-3. Closely related, too, are two oak carvings of a seated Virgin and Child; one in the Louvre, originally from the abbey of Bethlehem, then in the abbey of Hérent near Louvain, stamped with the Brussels hallmark (Plate 162B); the other in the Staatliche Museen in Berlin.[18] These carvings are notable for the imposing amplitude of the forms, though at the same time they are taut in features and outline. This combination of volume and economy of style led to a type of autonomous sculpture whose rational structure seems already to belong to the new century, although it dates in fact from 1490-1500.

Closely connected with these carvings is the impressively contemplative and formally austere oak St Gertrude in the church of that name at Etterbeek near Brussels, stamped with the Brussels hallmark (Plate 162C).[19] This figure is one of the most monumental achievements before the turn of the century. If we regard it as the culmination of the development of the autonomous wooden statue in Brabant, whose earlier stages extend from the St Margaret in the Gruuthuse Museum in Bruges to the attendant figures of the Crucifixion in St Pierre at Louvain, then the independent significance of Late Gothic sculpture in Brabant, and especially in Brussels, will be more patent than if one only looks at the striking realism of the narrative style of altar sculpture, however much this may be anticipatory of the new century. The inner tension of expression in such works as the Nivelles Crucifixion in the Louvre demonstrates the fact that it was mainly these works from Brabant that served as the source for outstanding contemporary works of the same type in Spain.[20]

A masterpiece of the period round 1490 is the oak statuette of St Ursula in the Staatliche Museen in Berlin (Plate 162A).[21] It is crystal-clear in its sculptural articulation, consistent in its three-dimensional form, and radiant in its charm. It is stamped with the Bruges hallmark.[22] The statuettes from the workshops of Malines have recently been collected by various scholars, but they have not yet been arranged chronologically.[23] Beside the relatively early statuette of the Virgin, with the Malines hallmark, in the Musée de l'Hôtel-Dieu at Beaune I should place the similarly stamped St Catherine in the church of St Quentin at Hasselt and the charming though austere statuettes of St Michael in the Louvre and in the Musée de Cluny in Paris. I believe that these works are *incunabula* of that small-scale sculpture of Malines which in the early years of the sixteenth century apparently overshadowed even that of Brussels.

However, it must always be emphasized that along with the differing styles which we have been discussing, the traditional tasks remained, and that they were fulfilled with an unprecedented wealth of painterly effect. An example is the memorial to Canon Jean de Paeu from Notre-Dame at Courtrai (Kortrijk), in the Musée d'Art Industriel et d'Archéologie in that town. This was executed during the donor's lifetime, between 1495 and 1503, and conveys an astonishing feeling of depth. Even in its fragmentary form, it retains something of its original magic. I am indeed of the opinion that it is precisely in such fragmentary works as these that the fascination of South Netherlandish sculpture from the turn of the century can most vividly be felt.

Around 1500 both Brussels and Antwerp had attained world rank, and the towns in the neighbouring counties of Flanders and Artois were also highly prosperous. However fluid the boundaries of the artistic landscape of the South Netherlands towards the west may have been, they were even more ill-defined towards the south-east. Here the bishopric of Liège was the artistic centre of the Meuse district. In this bishopric and in the County of Namur were situated the most important centres of metalwork, the type known as Dinanderie. It is an essential characteristic of the stylistic situation at the turn of the century that sculpture in bronze played an increasingly important part. This was because the sculptors of Central Europe strove for a monumentality through which they could vie with the Italian sculptors, in whose work bronze had fulfilled a vital function ever since the beginning of the fifteenth century.

To appreciate this tradition, one ought to remember the peculiarly grand character of the bronze effigy of Isabella de Bourbon (d. 1465) from the monument to her erected in 1476 in the abbey of St Michel, which is now in Antwerp Cathedral. This was followed by the bronze monument to the Duchess Mary of Burgundy, who died in youth (Plate 161A). This is in Notre-Dame in Bruges and was cast by Renier van Thienen in Brussels in 1491–8. It is uncertain whether this was the elder or younger Renier; the van Thienen family were active as bronze-founders through several generations. As we have seen, the wooden model for the effigy of the duchess was made by Jan Borman,[24] possibly after the design of a court painter. The effigy itself has taken on a completely new and impressive life, of an astonishing freedom and beauty. Every detail of line is of the highest precision, but at the same time the whole is surrounded by a spatial atmosphere, from which the figure emerges in all its magical corporeality. It is known that the goldsmith Pieter de Beckere was responsible for the gilding of the work. Here is proof indeed of the heights to which Netherlandish sculpture in the last decade of the fifteenth century was capable of attaining. Equally magical in its poetry is the composition of a genealogical tree which extends over the walls of the tomb, in which delicate 'Gothic' angels hold the scrolls of the shields, while traditional apostles and patron saints are posted at the corners under canopies. All this is closely interwoven in a typically Late Gothic manner; but against it the lifelike effigy, with hands folded in prayer, stands out in striking contrast. Here already we have an anticipation of those sepulchral figures which Margaret of Austria commissioned from Conrat Meit for Brou, the point of comparison being the union of beauty and dignity with the accompanying shadows of the macabre. At the same time the splendour of the jewels and embroideries translated into the medium of bronze anticipates the accessories on the statues of the tomb of Maximilian I in Innsbruck – so indicative of things to come are these outstanding works from the last decade of the fifteenth century.

We have already met the elder Renier van Thienen as the founder of the Paschal candelabrum of 1482–3 in St Leonard at Zoutleeuw (Léau),[25] the figures of which remind one in their gestures of the compositions of Roger van der Weyden (Plate 107D). It is clear that Renier took his models from various carvers or painters. His mastery of casting has obscured the fame of those responsible for the designs.

The Paschal candelabrum at Zoutleeuw was followed in 1492 by the font in St Jan at 's-Hertogenbosch (Bois-le-Duc), cast by Jan Aert van Maastricht (Plate 160).[26] Unfortunately this work has suffered considerable damage in the course of the centuries. Nevertheless it is an exciting example of the boldness of which the art of bronze casting in the Netherlands was capable at the turn of the century. The font is divided into three portions: the base with bearer figures, the nobly proportioned sharp-angled basin, and the three-storeyed tapering cover. The latter contains representations of the Baptism of Christ and of the Virgin, accompanied by angels. But it is in the bearer figures on the base that the artist's boldness of invention is most clearly seen. These figures are representatives of the common people, and their realism is no less striking than their tectonic austerity. It is precisely this combination which points to new possibilities of a monumental art of the future.

Once again we do not know who was the designer of this work. But its contribution to the separation of sculpture from architectural framework is clear enough. These apparent bearer figures are in reality expressions of a new autonomy of the human figure; it is not by chance that these earliest identifiable types of the common people – Julius von Schlosser calls it 'Armleutekunst', that is, poor man's art[27] – occurred at the same time as the latest examples of the *imagines* of Burgundian feudalism with their romantic overtones. As late as 1501 Aert van Maastricht added realistic bearer figures to his bronze candelabra balustrade at the entrance to the choir of St Victor at Xanten,[28] which, like the statuettes of the latest architectural sculpture, look upwards according to the demands of their architectural context.

And now a few words about the contribution of the Northern Netherlands. The sculpture of this region in the last decade of the century seems to lack the originality and pioneering quality of the Southern Netherlands. In North Netherlandish painting in these same years we experience the development from Geertgen tot St Jans to the Master of the Brunswick Diptych and the Master of the Virgo inter Virgines, a development towards an ever greater emphasis on colour together with atmospheric effects, which allow the subject matter to appear in a new light. In sculpture the variations on the traditional types of representation are not as rich as in painting. The style of Adriaen van Wesel still kept its validity. His St Martin (Utrecht, Central Museum), for example, seems to have been translated into the anecdotal realism of the early sixteenth century in a group in the Wadsworth Atheneum at Hartford, Conn.[29] Conventional motifs (e.g. the Virgin and St Anne and the Virgin and Child, the Crucifixion, etc.) are completely dominated by a 'Late Gothic' type of presentation; though a charming work like the wooden figure of the Virgin on the donkey with the carefully wrapped Child, from a group of the Flight into Egypt, originally in the town hall of Wijk-bij-Duurstede and now in the Rijksmuseum in Amsterdam,[30] shows most beautifully how this complete mastery of a very concise and yet delicately articulated style could produce a highly painterly effect. Perhaps it is not by chance that the creative talent of the Northern Netherlands made its important contribution to the earlier phase of Late Gothic sculpture.

CHAPTER 12

GERMANY: 1490–1500

We ended our survey of Lower Rhenish sculpture of the years round 1480 with a reference to the style of the reliefs on the Altar of St George in the Nikolaikirche at Kalkar. It is difficult to thread one's way through the maze of documentary evidence concerning the masters from other Lower Rhenish towns who had a hand in the making of the largely surviving altarpieces in this church. From among them I would mention Master Loedewich, who, between 1498 and 1500, was responsible for the high altar.[1] When we consider its size and the wealth of figures it contains, it is not surprising that the records should cite numerous craftsmen as having been engaged on it. We owe the predella to Johann von Haldern (of Wesel). The central shrine consists of a large 'carved painting' of the Passion, embracing a vast throng of more than two hundred figures (Plate 164A). The number of figures involved conceals the visual drama of the Passion scene, and in spite of the excellence of detail, the whole remains purely illustrative in its effect. Nevertheless, Master Loedewich's work is possessed of a weight and a gravity which we normally seek in vain in the multiform technical brilliance of South Netherlandish altar reliefs of the Brussels or Antwerp style, which were obviously his prototypes. The Lower Rhenish characteristic in these reliefs is a certain austere objectivity. Throughout their composition the 'painterly' intentions always dominate, but here we no longer have the common character of the linework such as united painting and sculpture in the time of Roger van der Weyden, but the tendency towards a new spatial illusion.

In the Nikolaikirche in Kalkar we can also admire the serene monumentality of the beautiful wooden group in the central compartment of the Altar of St Anne (Plate 164B).[2] It used to be thought that a panel painting by Derik Baegert (of Wesel), now in the museum in Antwerp and dating from 1492, formed part of this altarpiece. But I fail to see the connexion between these works, since their measurements do not tally. We may date this altarpiece c. 1495, though its firmness and inner tension are reminiscent of the carvings on the choir stalls in the Minoritenkirche at Cleves, which date from 1474. There is no trace in it of the supple fluidity of line to be found in corresponding Netherlandish sculpture. On the contrary, the local character and tradition of the Lower Rhineland and at the same time the new ability of the last decade of the fifteenth century to clarify sculptural structure are apparent in this altarpiece.

An assessment of the carving on the Altar of the Seven Joys of Mary in this same church presents us with certain difficulties.[3] Here we have the clearest example of the transition from the vertical and horizontal division of the altarpiece into separate compartments to a new complex sculptural composition. This is a feature typical of this moment, and we shall frequently return to it. We shall also see how decisive a role was played by painting in the development of the *opus completum* of the altarpiece between 1490 and 1500. At the same time we shall have to watch how certain contrary tendencies towards a new, abstract tectonic independence were also current in this decade. The co-existence of Late Gothic features and the first signs of a new standard of sculptural objectivity is one of the many contrasts apparent in the art of the turn of the century.

The question that confronts us is whether we may associate with this Altar of the Seven Joys of Mary the name of Master Arnt. This man was resident at Kalkar from 1479, and was commissioned by the Liebfrauenbrüderschaft there to carve an altarpiece for them in 1483, and then in 1487, after he had moved to Zwolle, was admonished by them for not having completed his task. After Arnt's death in 1491 Everhard van Monster was entrusted with the completion of the altarpiece. The figure of Christ from a Holy Sepulchre in the Nikolaikirche is the accredited work of Arnt von Zwolle in 1489, but the carvings on the altarpiece do not appear to be in the same style. But in the carving on the Altar of the Seven Joys we are confronted, it seems to me, with a thoroughly homogeneous piece of work whose mature calm is inconceivable before 1490. In the relief of the Annunciation we already catch a glimpse of the importance of 'milieu', which subsequently reached such magic dimensions in the Lower Rhenish sculpture of the early sixteenth century and especially in the work of Heinrich Douvermann, who represents the climax of the Kalkar school.

Cleves was another important centre of sculptural production. Here Dries Holthuys, responsible in 1496 for the tall, slender stone Virgin[4] in Xanten Cathedral, was active. In this statue, comparatively traditional in type, the treatment of the surface shows great delicacy and refinement of touch. The full sculptural power of Late Gothic formal conventions is shown most impressively by the wooden Virgin in the church of the former abbey of Gaesdonck near Goch. In its elegance and self-assurance I would also reckon as late the oak figure of a female saint, formerly in the Schnitzler Collection in Cologne.[5]

The strongly pronounced individuality of these works from the lower reaches of the Lower Rhine is strikingly different from contemporary sculpture in the Netherlands and Cologne. It is also worth observing that altarpieces imported from Antwerp of comparatively normal type and which were produced almost ready-made are to be met with more frequently in the upper part of the Lower Rhineland.

The 'Expressionism' which brought about a striking sharpness in the accents of Lower Rhenish sculpture is met with only rarely in contemporary work in Cologne. Here the types depicted are in the traditional Late Gothic style, but are suffused with an impressive new monumentality. A juxtaposition of the attendant figures from a Crucifixion in St Johannes at Cologne with the wooden Crucifixion groups in Gross St Martin[6] and Königsdorf Abbey throws interesting light on the situation at the time. We are moving from the transparent, luminous clarity of the painting of a Roger van der Weyden to the subdued and muted tones of a Gerard David, just as we do in individual pieces of sculpture from Brabant round 1500.

At this time Heinrich Brabender[7] moved from Brabant to North-West Germany, though the first reference to him in records appears to have been in 1511 at Münster in

Westphalia. His early stone works provide us with proof of his Brabant origin: they are the Crucifix dating from 1490 in Bremen Cathedral and four large reliefs of the Passion (1498–1500) on the parapet of the polygonal apse of the Marienkirche at Lübeck. These works are tauter in form and more restrained in the presentation of their subject-matter than the Nivelles sculpture, which is suffused with a far stronger dynamism of feeling. This tendency towards an objective and cumulative style completely carries the day in Heinrich Brabender's work in the first decades of the sixteenth century. Brabender is typical of the interrelationship between the various regions at this time. In this short survey of the most outstanding talents in German sculpture at the turn of the century, it will best serve our purpose if we follow a line that runs horizontally across the country.

As we leave the Lower Rhineland, we must therefore first move to the Low German districts, where we will find works of the most varied kind. First, there is the handsome wooden Virgin from Soest Cathedral in the Museum für Kunst und Gewerbe in Hamburg.[8] This is an example of the translation, so characteristic of the time, of a work originally conceived as a drawing in the 1480s, into three-dimensional form. As a counterpart I would mention the saints from an altar in the church at Eimke (district of Uelzen), now in the Friderikenstift at Hanover,[9] and originally probably in the neighbouring Augustine nunnery of Ebstorf near Lüneburg. These figures show the highly effective adaptation of South Netherlandish prototypes to the broad and somewhat austere Lower Saxon diction, and their charm resides in the tension between the impressive style of the prototype and the completely Late Gothic sincerity of feeling in the replica. I mention these two examples just to show that at the turn of the century when the lofty style of a new idealism had not yet arrived, we must still reckon with adaptations of older types.

In Lübeck Bernt Notke[10] was still active at the turn of the century. He died in 1509. His later work of both painting and sculpture (e.g. the wooden Trinity in the Heilig-geistspital at Lübeck) shows a remarkable hardening of expression and a deep seriousness, which regarded only the most essential themes as worthy of artistic representation. Notke's formal canon, which derives from the style of the late fifteenth century, was promulgated by members of his school. Among the works of the so-called Imperialissima Master, whom we may perhaps identify with Hinrik Wylsnyck, I would cite the Rese Triptych from the Marienkirche in Lübeck, now in the St Annenmuseum there, which dates from 1499; the central compartment of the altarpiece in the church at Hald near Randers (North Jutland, Denmark); and a wooden altarpiece in the Gardner Museum in Boston. The most magnificent achievement of this conservative tendency deriving from Notke and his school is the Fair Virgin (1509) in Lübeck Cathedral (Plate 165B).[11] This figure is still retrospective in style, but it is a completely free translation of a traditional Late Gothic image into a new and radiant dignity.

The situation in Lübeck sheds light upon the alternative courses which faced the sculptor at the turn of the century. Alongside the late work of Bernt Notke, the personality of a new and younger artist emerges, who, in spite of his apparent early connexions with Notke, reveals himself increasingly as a highly individual character. He is

Henning von der Heyde,[12] of whom we have documentary records in Lübeck from 1487 and who died before 1536. The gentler, mellower tone of his work is already visible in the centre compartment of a Mass of St Gregory in the altarpiece of the church at Rytterne (Västmanland, Sweden) – particularly clear in the figure of St Gregory kneeling in prayer – and it is equally apparent in the impressive St Jerome in the abbey of Vadstena. The Corpus Christi Altar from the Burgkirche in Lübeck, now in the Annenmuseum, dates from 1496, and here again the central figures are possessed of a vivid, delicate, and quiet beauty. This is followed between 1497 and 1500 by the reliefs of the Passion from a church in Zeeland, now in the Kunstindustri Museum in Copenhagen. The very moving Crucifix, astonishing in the masterly treatment of the human figure, in the burial chapel in the Storkyrka in Stockholm must be of the same date. A comparison between this and the wooden Triumphal Cross of 1489 in the Katharinenkirche in Lübeck shows the daring with which Henning von der Heyde has produced a really new image of Christ in keeping with the spirit of the Reformation period.

Lack of space compels me to restrict myself to a mere list of von der Heyde's further works: the silver reliquary statuette of St George in the Schwarzhäupterhaus in Riga (Latvia), which was completed between 1503 and 1507 by the goldsmith Berendt Heynemann in Lübeck from a model by Henning von der Heyde; and the tomb lid of Sophie, duchess of Mecklenburg (d. 1504), in the Marienkirche at Wismar (here the bronze cast by Tile Bruith(?) is based on a model by von der Heyde). We may judge of Henning von der Heyde's reputation as an artist from these important commissions. Of c. 1504–5 is the wooden group of St George, unfortunately surviving only in fragmentary form. It came originally from the chapel of the Hospital of St George in Lübeck and is now in the St Annenmuseum. Here Notke's monumental group in Stockholm is translated into a new, illustrative close-up style. Henning von der Heyde's individual development away from the Late Gothic style of Bernt Notke is manifest most vividly in the sequence of the wooden St John the Evangelist in Roskilde Cathedral, then the St John the Baptist in the Deutsches Museum, Berlin,[13] and finally the spiritually transfixed St John the Evangelist in the Marienkirche in Lübeck, which dates from c. 1505 (Plate 165A). Here is the German answer to the South Netherlandish invention of this type of figure.[14] It expresses itself in a new harmony of form permeated by a great depth of feeling.

Lübeck was certainly not the only town on the Baltic coast with a large output of sculptural works, but in spite of diligent research concerning the works of the Baltic area that still survive, it remains difficult to locate the workshops that continued for any length of time, and particularly those possessed of anything more than local significance. What, for example, is the provenance of the more-than-life-size Crucifixion in St Maria at Ystad (South Sweden), which is an outstandingly fine example of the mature calm of the Late Gothic before the turn of the century and of the rise of a spatial sculpture?

There is much in common between the wooden altarpieces from Antwerp at Strängnäs and Västerås (Sweden)[15] and the charming Altar of the Holy Family, dating from 1490–1500, which was sent from Brussels to the Dominican church at Tallinn (Reval) and is now in the Estonian Museum there. The scene represented is distributed over the three compartments of the altarpiece and is surmounted by a representation of Mount Calvary[16] in a further recess. A similarly constructed altarpiece at Bollnäs (Norrland, Sweden) is affiliated to this Tallinn work. But the Bollnäs altarpiece is further remarkable in that the central compartment appears to be of Brussels provenance, while the groups of figures in the side compartments are reminiscent of works of Ludwig Juppe of Marburg (whom we shall discuss presently). In this area we have therefore to reckon with immigrants and influences from Central and Eastern Germany[17] as well as with the traditional contacts with Lübeck and the Netherlands. Indeed, in the Scandinavian towns and churches the import of South Netherlandish altarpieces appears to have increased after the turn of the century. I would mention as examples the Antwerp altarpieces at Arsunda and Ljusdal (Gästrikland, Sweden); the Brussels altarpieces at Nordingrå (Norrland) and at Ytter Selö; and altarpieces by Jan Borman (at Jäder, Södermanland) and his workshop.

At Marburg on the Lahn, Ludwig Juppe was active as a sculptor and wood-carver from 1486 till his death in 1537.[18] He was responsible in 1493 for the heraldic relief of the Landgrave Wilhelm III on the Neuer Bau of the castle, with the busts of the landgrave and his wife under a canopy shaped like a window – an architectural motif known to us from the Netherlands. Between 1511 and 1514 Juppe carved four altarpieces for the north and south transepts of the Elisabethkirche at Marburg. These were fitted into wall recesses and are derivatives of fifteenth-century Netherlandish altars. The style of the individual figures of these genre-like scenes reveals a new-found delight in the beauty of line typical of Late Gothic sculpture. Thus I have no doubt that the charming figure of St Elizabeth on the sedilia, which used to be dated 1460-70 on account of its linear structure, is in reality a work of Juppe's subsequent to 1490. The Lower Rhenish sources of these works are clear.

A group of statues in Mainz Cathedral will serve to illuminate further the situation at the turn of the century. I refer to the tomb of Adalbert von Sachsen (d. 1484); the relief demi-figure of the Virgin with halo, donated by Dean Bernhard von Breidenbach and Philipp von Bicken upon their return from a pilgrimage to the Holy Land in 1484 (now in the cathedral cloisters, originally in the Liebfrauenkirche); the multi-figured Entombment, dating from 1495 (also originally in the Liebfrauenkirche); and the tomb of Breidenbach (d. 1498; Plate 166A). These are from the hand of a sculptor of a pronouncedly monumental character, who inspired the consistently taut form of his works with a conscious dignity, and produced – free from any Netherlandish prototypes – a new sculptural autonomy, combining maximum vividness with a severely tectonic structure. Thus, in the early tomb of Adalbert, the figure emerges with an almost abstract quality from the wide spatial void of the background.[19] In the late Breidenbach tomb there is a striking 'condensation' of the figure: the surface appears frozen, the folds of drapery metallic, the face assumes a magic, ethereal quality, and the eyes have a visionary look. Here naturalistic form is used to express a new transcendental meaning.

Strasbourg still remained the centre of Upper Rhenish sculptural activity. Conrad Sifer of Sinsheim (a little Palatinate town between Heidelberg and Heilbronn) was in charge of the cathedral lodge from 1491 to 1493.[20] In 1473 he was responsible for the Crucifix on the rood screen in the abbey of Maulbronn, a translation of Nicolaus Gerhaerts' Baden-Baden Christ into a more 'painterly' image (Plate 166B). In 1488, perhaps in collaboration with his brother Hans Syfer, he carved the relief of the Tree of Jesse in the cloisters of Worms Cathedral. In this work, donated by the early humanist, Johann von Dalberg, bishop of Worms,[21] we have an amazing interweaving of figures and foliage, all depicted with a strong feeling for three-dimensionality – an echo once again of Nicolaus Gerhaerts. These works were followed in 1489 by the rood screen in St George's Minster at Sélestat (Alsace) with its rich ornamentation of flowers and branches and probably also by the striking stone fragment of the head of a watchman from the Holy Sepulchre, no doubt originally also from the same church. From Conrad Sifer's work in Strasbourg Minster itself come the mighty branch-work balustrade of the gallery of the south transept and the sundial, dating from 1493, over which the demi-figure of a man is bending under an arch of branches (Strasbourg, Musée de l'Œuvre Notre Dame). This relief emphasizes once again the new tectonic quality in the presentation of the human form. Finally, from an account dated 1501, we know that Master Conrad also carved a martyrdom of St Lawrence for the north portal of Strasbourg Minster, but this was destroyed during the French Revolution.

The career of Hans Syfer, presumably the brother of Master Conrad, proceeded along similar lines. We may discern his hand for the first time in the reliefs of an Entombment and in parts of an Annunciation in the cloisters of Worms Cathedral (1487–8; Plate 169A). Two slightly older male demi-figures of stone in the Staatliche Museen in Berlin, probably originally from Strasbourg Minster (Plate 167A),[22] are so closely affiliated to these reliefs that we may safely assume them to be early works of Hans Syfer, produced under the influence of Nicolaus Gerhaerts. The clarity and decisiveness of the naturalistic style are here coupled with a new kind of fullness and breadth of form, which subsequently led to the impressive sculptural self-portrait in Hans Syfer's high altar in the Kilianskirche at Heilbronn, completed in 1498 (Plate 169B). Once again it is clear that the types represented are derived from the conventions of Rhenish Late Gothic,[23] but at the same time we see that sculpture has attained a new independence in the presentation of individual figures. This fact is brought home to us most forcibly by the masterly head from a stone Crucifixus by Hans Syfer – unfortunately preserved only in fragmentary form – from the former clergy-house at Heilbronn, now in the Städtisches Museum there. I have no doubt that Conrat Meit learnt much from the tautness and spatially 'expansive' power of the Worms Entombment.

Hans Syfer's stone Calvary by the choir of the Leonhardskirche at Stuttgart dates from 1501. Of 1505–12 is his Mount of Olives in the cloisters of Speyer Cathedral, of which only fragments and later drawings survive. These all show how a new conception, deeply rooted in the visual world, now gains importance and how even the minutest details are inspired with a fascinating, radiant force. Hans Syfer appears to have died while engaged on the Speyer Mount of Olives.

The choir of the Kilianskirche at Heilbronn was erected between 1482 and 1487 after Austrian patterns. We may therefore assume that plans for it were brought by

Anton Pilgram (a native of Brno (Brünn) and, according to records, active in the church of St James there in 1502) when he was summoned from Vienna to Heilbronn in 1481.[24] Pilgram was also a sculptor, and his works in St Stephen in Vienna stand among the masterpieces of German art in the early years of the sixteenth century. It has been concluded from these figures that Pilgram was also responsible for the tabernacle with its high canopy which is of the same date as the choir of the Kilianskirche.[25] The small sculpture on this tabernacle demonstrates Pilgram's highly individual style. His stone pulpit-bearers at Heutingsheim near Ludwigsburg, those from the abbey of Öhringen (now in the Berlin Museum),[26] and those in the Lorenzkapelle at Rottweil, are some of the most astonishing products of German sculpture round 1490.

It is interesting to observe the renewed significance of stone at this stage of sculptural development. Its importance has already been brought to our notice by the works of the master of the tomb of Adalbert von Sachsen in Mainz and by those of Conrad Sifer. Other examples are the tympanum of the Scholar Saint in the cloisters of Würzburg Cathedral (Plate 168B),[27] the reliefs of the Passion by Veit Stoss in St Sebald (Plate 181A), and Adam Kraft's tabernacle in St Lorenz in Nuremberg (Plate 182), and the red marble monuments by Hans Beierlein at Augsburg. It would appear that towards the end of the century sculptors welcomed the lapidary monumentality of stone, seeing in it a corrective to the freedom provided by the wood carving of the altarpieces and its combination with painting. The pulpit-bearer from Öhringen (Plate 183) shows very clearly the lines along which sculpture was now to develop: there is a new tectonic quality in the figure, and this gives rise to a more functional approach to what the foot of a pulpit is. We observed a similar feature in Jan Aert van Maastricht's font at 's-Hertogenbosch (Plate 160). The boldest and most consistent expression of this tendency is Peter Vischer's Branch-breaker of 1490 (in the Bayerisches Nationalmuseum in Munich; Plate 185), which we shall discuss later.

The realistic content visible in these functional 'bearers' is just as instructive. They are self-portraits of the craftsmen responsible for the work, and in their features we may observe a menacing expression of dissatisfaction. Hitherto the self-portrait had always depicted the artist with uplifted countenance. Now that is no longer so. I would remind readers, as I did when discussing the font at 's-Hertogenbosch, of J. von Schlosser's phrase 'Armeleutekunst' to describe the folk types portrayed by Riccio. Is it not remarkable that in this latest phase of Gothic sculpture it is virtually impossible in the self-portrait of the craftsman to separate the individual from the social aspects? In the bronze portrait plaque of Peter Vischer the Elder and in the portrait medals of his sons we first see the 'craftsman' elevated to the rank of 'artist', and this reaches its apogee when Conrat Meit places his own portrait bust in the library of Margaret of Austria at Malines.

It is assumed that Pilgram brought the architectural plan for the choir of the Kilianskirche at Heilbronn with him from Austria, but this surely does not apply to the sculptural work in the choir. The similarity between this and a corbel figure dating from 1489 in the Strasbourg Minster treasury,[28] which is no doubt a portrait of the master, shows vividly how the sculptor of these 'bearer' figures on the tabernacle of the

Kilianskirche follows in the Upper Rhenish tradition. Anton Pilgram must also have been deeply influenced by the work of Hans Syfer while in Heilbronn, as his busts of the church fathers (dating from 1514–15) on the pulpit of St Stephen in Vienna serve to show.

Conrad Sifer was followed at Strasbourg[29] by the sculptor Hans von Aachen (a burgher of Strasbourg in 1493), who in 1503 received his payment for the exaggeratedly dramatized figures on the Portal of St Lawrence on the north side of the Minster (now in the Musée de l'Œuvre Notre-Dame).[30] A further successor was Veit Wagner from Haguenau in Alsace (active at Strasbourg from 1492). Probably Veit Wagner was the master of the once famous Strasbourg Mount of Olives (completed in 1498; Plate 167B). The similarity between the surviving parts of this work and the fragments of Hans Syfer's Mount of Olives at Speyer demonstrates with the utmost vividness the close relationship between the various Upper German districts shortly before and immediately after the turn of the century.

Niclaus Hagnower was also a native of Haguenau. He became a full burgher of Strasbourg in 1493, although he had apparently been active there for several years previously. Wilhelm Vöge[31] believed that he was able to recognize certain early works of Hagnower in Swabia, namely the tabernacle of 1471 in Ulm Minster, corbel figures in St Jodok at Ravensburg, and the tabernacle of 1484 in Chur Cathedral. I cannot subscribe to this theory, and think that any similarity between these works and those of Hagnower is due to the wide extent of Nicolaus Gerhaerts' posthumous influence, which found an echo in the immensely rich and varied productivity of Upper Rhenish and Swabian workshops. I would also suggest that any Strasbourg contacts that such Swabian stone sculpture suggests may be due to the influence of Moritz Ensinger, who was in charge of the Ulm Minster lodge and a son of Matthäus Ensinger, master mason of Strasbourg Cathedral in the middle of the century.

From 1486 onwards we can discern the hand of Niclaus von Hagenau in various pieces of sculpture in Alsace. First, there are fragments of wooden altarpieces, commissioned by Albrecht von Pfalz-Mosbach, bishop of Strasbourg, from Niclaus, the sculptor, and his two brothers Veit and Paul, joiners, for the abbey of Saverne (Zabern). But the records concerning the tomb which Bishop Albrecht caused to be erected at Saverne by Niclaus in 1493–4 are of greater significance. The tomb itself has not survived. On it was depicted a 'contrafecten todt', a counterfeit Death, that is a skeleton, of such anatomical accuracy that the Strasbourg doctor H. von Gersdorf had a woodcut of it made – bearing the name 'Nicklaus bildhawer' – while the sculptor was still alive.[29] Perhaps it was the proximity of France that inspired the bishop with the idea of this macabre theme, but in any case by his execution of it Niclaus von Hagenau produced something completely new: that combination of art and science which is a hallmark of the Renaissance.

In 1500–1 Niclaus von Hagenau was responsible for the Corpus Christi Altar in Strasbourg Minster. The appearance of this altarpiece was known from an etching dating from 1617, and thus it was possible to recognize as belonging to it the predella figures of a Lamentation of Christ and the busts of two prophets from the predella at

St Marx in Strasbourg. These busts (now in the Musée de l'Œuvre Notre-Dame)[32] show how penetrating was Niclaus's understanding of the human form. And even if these wood carvings do still speak the language of the fifteenth century, their completely new intellectual content is almost terrifyingly clear. Vöge has accurately analysed and interpreted the background of these figures: the work of art is no longer just the mirror of intellectual and religious experiences; it has become the means of a new analysis of the world of ideas. It is thus not the degree of their intended realism that we admire in these busts, but the way they lay bare their intellectual and psychological content, which up till now had always been gently veiled.

It was by some happy chance that in 1505 Niclaus was chosen to carve the statues for the large altarpiece in the Anthonite church at Isenheim in Alsace (Plate 170); subsequently – between 1512 and 1516 it is assumed – Mathis Neidhart of Aschaffenburg (Matthias Grünewald) was to paint the wings of this same altarpiece (Colmar, Unterlinden Museum). In the predella are demi-figures of Christ and the twelve Apostles; in the central portion is seated the enthroned figure of St Anthony, flanked by St Jerome and St Augustine, together with the kneeling donor. The space above the canopies is filled with exquisite vegetal carving. The figures of two peasants bearing votive offerings (in a private collection in Munich) originally belonged at the feet of St Anthony, the central figure. In these figures wood-carving has attained a new majestic dignity, and at the same time a radiant spirituality has been added to Late Gothic naturalism. Without doubt, in the artistic development of the first decade of the sixteenth century painting took pride of place; it is all the more striking that we feel Niclaus von Hagenau's carvings in the Isenheim altarpiece to be a fit consort for the painting of Grünewald.

We have documentary evidence of Niclaus's activity at Strasbourg until 1526. It was a shrewd hypothesis of Otto Schmitt that the male demi-figure (dating from about 1495) on the balustrade above the portal of St Andrew's Chapel in the south transept of the minster was a self-portrait of Niclaus,[33] looking up in veneration to the Angel Pier with its thirteenth-century carvings (Plate 168A). In fact, a new state of affairs had now arrived, when fidelity to and emancipation from tradition were both possible at one and the same time. Niclaus von Hagenau appears to have been the father of Friedrich Hagenauer, the most outstanding master of German 'Contrefetter', that is, carved portraits, in the early sixteenth century.

We shall follow this appraisal of Niclaus von Hagenau with a short reference to the work of the most outstanding of the later altar sculptors in the Upper Rhineland, Hans Weiditz,[34] known to have been active at Freiburg im Breisgau from 1497 to 1514. He too has his roots in the traditions of Strasbourg, being in all likelihood the son of the sculptor Bartolomäus Weiditz from Meissen, of whom we have documentary records at Strasbourg from 1467 to 1505.[35] The Altar of the Magi in Freiburg Minster, dating from 1505, bears the unusually clear signature 'Joh. Wydyz'. This altar was originally intended for the private chapel of the Emperor Maximilian's chancellor, Konrad Sürzel, in the Baslerhof at Freiburg. This fact sheds light upon the highly intimate atmosphere of the carvings on the altarpiece, which were clearly meant to be seen at close range. Around 1512–14 Weiditz was responsible for the altarpiece donated by Johannes Schnewlin to a choir chapel of Freiburg Minster. The central compartment consists of a carved representation of the Holy Family, based on an etching by Dürer, set against a painted background, whose brilliant colouring has led to the assumption that it is the work of Hans Leu. Here we have an essentially painterly conception, which embraced sculpture with the happiest results. But Weiditz's work also illustrates the new function of small-scale sculpture, e.g. the charming boxwood group of the Fall of Man in the Historisches Museum in Basel (c. 1505; Plate 172B).[36] Weiditz is the first of the many Breisgau woodcarvers who were to achieve fame in the early sixteenth century.

It is more difficult to define the special character of the Basel workshops.[37] Is the striking wooden figure of the seated St Theobald (with two kneeling votive figures) in Thann Minster[38] by an Alsatian or a Basel master? Is there an organic line of development from the work of the master of the lyrically inspired wooden Virgin, dating from c. 1490, from Warmbach near Rheinfelden, now in the Historisches Museum in Basel, with the bold, clear, and decorative energy in the lines of its drapery, to the large imposing Virgin from Isenheim, now in the Louvre (c. 1510), which has been attributed – in my opinion erroneously – to a 'pupil of Veit Stoss in the Upper Rhineland'?[39]

In 1483 the Westphalian-born Erhart Küng succeeded Moritz Ensinger as master mason of the Bern Cathedral lodge.[40] But apart from this, altar sculpture in Central Switzerland, and especially in the dioceses of Constance and Chur, is dominated at the end of the fifteenth century by Upper Swabian influences. These affected even the work of native masters, such as Jörg Keller, who is known to have been active at Lucerne. The export of altarpieces from the commercially organized and developed Upper Swabian cities extended to regions south of the passes of the Alps. Jakob Russ of Ravensburg,[41] the master of the carvings in the town hall of Überlingen (1492–4), was responsible in 1485 for the tomb of Bishop Ortlieb of Brandis and in 1486–92 for the high altar in Chur Cathedral. In 1502 Matthäus Miller from Lindau delivered a carved altarpiece to the church of Brione in Valle Verzasca (Ticino), and the workshop of Ivo Strigel (d. 1518) at Memmingen[42] was the source of about twenty altarpieces imported to the Grisons and the Tyrol. Swabians completely dominated the art of the court at Innsbruck,[43] which was personally fostered by the Emperor Maximilian, and in the mining towns on both sides of the Brenner their influence also held sway.

The centres of this far-reaching Swabian sculpture were Ulm and Augsburg. It is most brilliantly reflected in the monumental altarpiece which Michel Erhart of Ulm, with the cooperation of his son Gregor, carved for the choir of the Benedictine monastery of Blaubeuren in 1493–4 (Plate 171).[44] The interior of this church is unique; for not only is the entire very large altarpiece itself preserved in all the splendour of its colour and gilding, but also statues from the original setting are still extant: the stone Apostles on the piers and the choir stalls by Syrlin the Younger. There is nothing 'wooden' about the carving in Erhart's altarpiece: here we come face to face with a new sublimity of vision. This was the period of Dürer's journeyman years in the Upper Rhineland, for the young Dürer a period full of 'Sturm und Drang'. In the Blaubeuren altarpiece we experience the opposite evolution, i.e. the new serenity overlaying the traditional rugged language of Late Gothic, and producing as a result nobility and solemnity – a harmony of qualities from which a quite new monumentality emerged.

This is also the hallmark of the vast Crucifix over the choir arch of St Martin at Landshut; naturalism, but also a most moving intimate delicacy. This work was donated by the Schönbrun family in 1495. The Crucifix signed and dated by Michel Erhart in 1494 in St Michael at Schwäbisch Hall is so much less sensitive that we cannot accept the Landshut Crucifix as by Michel. Is it perhaps an early work of Gregor Erhart? In any event, I regard the wooden Infant Christ, which is believed to have come from Heggbach Abbey (now in the Museum für Kunst und Gewerbe at Hamburg) and which is so full of radiant vitality, as a work of Gregor Erhart, dating from round about 1495. The self-assurance in the stance excludes the possibility of an earlier dating.

We have a few documentary records which, meagre though they are, help us in distinguishing Gregor Erhart's work from that of his father. We know that in Ulm Michel Erhart was in close contact with Konrad Moerlin, prior and later abbot of the monastery of St Ulrich and St Afra at Augsburg, and that on several occasions he received important commissions from there. In 1490 Michel's son-in-law, the joiner Adolf Daucher, moved from Ulm to Augsburg, and four years later Gregor Erhart too became a burgher there. This fact sheds light upon the relative importance of the two cities.[45] At this time Augsburg – perhaps even more than Nuremberg – was the gateway to a new art in Germany.

In 1499 the lay altar in St Ulrich at Augsburg was erected, and dedicated, like that of Blaubeuren, to the Virgin and to St John the Baptist and St John the Evangelist. Payment for it was made to the joiner Adolf Daucher. Was Gregor Erhart responsible for the carving on the altarpiece and thus the master of the majestic wooden Virgin which still survives in St Ulrich and St Afra? We may assume with certainty that this was the case, since there is so close an affinity between the Augsburg Virgin and that from the Cistercian abbey of Kaisheim (formerly in the Staatliche Museen, Berlin),[46] and this latter figure indubitably formed part of the choir altarpiece for which the joiner Adolf Daucher, the sculptor Gregor Erhart, and the painter Hans Holbein were jointly responsible in 1502. (The mention of Hans Holbein the Elder will show the happy auspices under which Augsburg art flourished at this period.) These two figures of the Virgin have an amplitude and a certain full-blown generosity of form compared with the austere dignity of the Virgin from Blaubeuren, which makes it clear that they come from the hand of a younger generation, i.e. that of Gregor Erhart, and that the Blaubeuren altarpiece is predominantly the work of the father, Michel Erhart.[47]

Around 1510 Gregor Erhart was commissioned by the Emperor Maximilian to carve a wooden figure of an Enthroned Virgin of the Misericord, and this is still today in its original setting in the pilgrimage church of Frauenstein in Upper Austria. Among the kneeling figures seeking refuge beneath the Virgin's cloak are the emperor himself, his wife Bianca Maria, and Wolfgang von Polheim and his wife. It is a work of enchanting harmony and conveys an astonishing illusion of space. It has a close connexion with the wooden St Mary Magdalen in the Louvre, where it is not so much the presentation of a nude figure that astonishes us as the delicate realization of a consistent contrapposto. Doubtless Dürer's engravings had contributed to make such an achievement possible, but this fact is of slight importance compared with the consistent way in which new possibilities of sculptural form are spatially realized here.

Gregor Erhart's career will become clear if we compare the Magdalen with the naked figures in the Vanitas group in the Kunsthistorisches Museum in Vienna (Plate 172A).[48] This group – no doubt dating from the first decade of the century – shows that Gregor Erhart's cautious approach to the possibilities of an autonomous sculptural presentation of the human figure is still indebted to painterly criteria. Another example of the peculiar potentialities of the new genre of miniature sculpture is the wonderful busts of Adam and Eve in the Victoria and Albert Museum in London.[49] These are striking by virtue of their concise roundness of form and an entirely new quality in the modelling of the lower portion of the bust, which presupposes a knowledge of Italian Renaissance sculpture. I am convinced that these particularly important works are from the hand of Gregor, significantly enough an Augsburg man. The contact with Italian Renaissance sculpture is clear again in the bronze casts of the statuette of a standing horse, which appear to go back to a model made c. 1508–9 by Gregor from a drawing by Hans Burgkmair for the equestrian figure of the Emperor Maximilian to be set up in the choir of St Ulrich and St Afra.[50] Once again it is typical of the early stages of Renaissance sculpture in Germany that the sculptor himself had no personal contact with Italian sources, but depended on the mediation of contemporary German paintings or engravings. Mastery of the new monumental style is shown also in funerary tablets.[51] They make clear the supra-personal significance attaching to Gregor Erhart's achievements which extended beyond the turn of the century and created a genuinely German Early Renaissance sculpture.

The Augsburg sculptor Hans Beierlein, older than Gregor Erhart, was responsible for numerous funerary monuments, dating from round 1500, of high church dignitaries. They are in a fine dark red marble, and a large number of them have been preserved. In this series of monuments[52] we can trace the increasing ability of the sculptor to express himself with a new spatial, one might even say 'classical', presentation. In these monumental pieces of stone sculpture is demonstrated most clearly the inner necessity of the development which – doubtless influenced by the achievements of contemporary Augsburg painting, but without contact with the Italian sources of its style – led to an ever greater autonomy of sculpture.

These new possibilities of sculptural representation are expressed even more definitely in the work of the Augsburg sculptor Jörg Muscat, who was more or less a contemporary of Hans Beierlein. The models of the bronze busts of the Emperor Maximilian and his second wife Eleonore (1510),[53] preserved in the Kunsthistorisches Museum in Vienna, are doubtless from his hand and obviously made in the attempt to introduce the bronze-cast memorial to the north in the sense in which it is familiar in the Italian Renaissance. In fact, it had already once been done before – in the bronze bust of Frederick the Wise made by Andrea Fiorentino at Dresden in 1498.[54] If Jörg Muscat was also responsible, as would appear likely, for the model of the bronze bust of Philip, duke of Burgundy,[55] preserved in the Württembergisches Landesmuseum at Stuttgart, it is typical that in this art of portraiture of the Early German Renaissance the problems of historical perspective created by the ancestor cult had already become acute. It is no mere chance that Augsburg beyond all other German cities in this phase of development became the centre for the earliest German sculpture which can be called Renaissance sculpture. The problems inherent in the bronze busts made from models by Jörg Muscat have been resolved in the statues in the Fuggerkapelle in St Anna, donated by Jakob and Ulrich Fugger in 1509. So propitious was the soil of Augsburg for the painless transition from Latest Gothic to Early Renaissance.

The finest reflection of this transition is to be seen in the sculptural work of the Augsburg goldsmiths. And this again is no accident. It was symptomatic of the transition that Martin Schongauer's brother Jörg and Albrecht Dürer's father should both have been goldsmiths. But the greatest master among these craftsmen was the goldsmith Johannes Müller, who in 1470 made the monstrance in St Moritz at Augsburg. The statuettes on this monstrance – some of which were replaced in the sixteenth century – and particularly the mourning figures of the Virgin and St John reveal in their twisted form an unprecedented strength of expression. They show contacts with the sculpture of Upper Rhenish goldsmiths and are parallels to the work of Jörg Schongauer.[56] Of 1482 is the figure of the Virgin, which according to its inscription was the work of the Augsburg goldsmith Hainrich Hufnagel and which is now in the Staatliche Museen, Berlin.[57] Its polished style would appear to anticipate the clear and strikingly articulated parcel-gilt silver Virgin from St Moritz at Augsburg,[58] now in the Diocesan Museum there (Plate 173A). This figure already has something of the wonderful new harmony of style that resulted from the confluence of the art of Hans Holbein the Elder with that of Gregor Erhart in the last decade of the fifteenth century in Augsburg.

The contrast between the 'extensive' Late Gothic style and the new 'intensive' form is seen perhaps at its clearest in the silver statuette of St Sebastian, dating from 1497, originally in the Cistercian abbey of Kaisheim and now in the Wernher Collection at Luton Hoo.[59] The entire magic of the illusory world of Gothic in its decline still clings to this graceful figure – realistic in every detail down to the 'style rustique' of the tree trunk. Fluid in its movement and of a delicacy such as we see in the silverpoint drawings of the elder Holbein, at the same time the figure is filled with a new vitality and idealization. Is this piece of goldsmith's work another example of the transition from the Late Gothic epic style of Michel Erhart to Gregor Erhart's new sense of beauty?

As far as we can see, Bavaria and Austria produced nothing in the last decade of the fifteenth century which would form a comparable transition to the monumental style of the early sixteenth century. Erasmus Grasser was active in Munich till his death in 1518. The figure of St Peter on the high altar of the Peterskirche in Munich, donated by Duke Albrecht IV in 1492, represents the apex of his achievement (Plate 174B). In this figure the ornamental style of the 1480s took on a new weight and rhetoric.[60] The other tendency in Late Gothic sculpture, which aimed at giving the traditional forms a new statuesque structure, is represented in Bavaria chiefly by the master of the cycle of wooden figures (dating from 1490–5) in the chapel of Schloss Blutenburg, near Munich.[61] This tendency is continued in red marble sepulchral sculpture, e.g. by Wolfgang Leb of Wasserburg,[62] until the early years of the next century. The beginnings of a new dynamic style are to be seen in the sculptural decoration on the choir stalls of St Martin at Landshut.[63] This work was begun in the last years of the fifteenth century, and – like the contemporary works of the painter Mair of Landshut and not unconnected with them – through its three-dimensional style of representation and its violence of expression it seems to be a forerunner of the so-called 'Danubian Style' of sculpture.

Austrian sculpture in the last decade of the fifteenth century and at the beginning of the sixteenth has more to offer. We have already made a survey of Michael Pacher's work up to his death in 1498. His last work, the Enthroned Virgin on the high altar of the Franciscan church at Salzburg, shows in its sublime beauty of form the sharp, crystalline precision of structure characteristic of Upper German Late Gothic sculpture in its highest perfection.[64] Pacher's paintings too were of fundamental importance in the development of a peculiarly Austrian style of painting in the new century.

The cost of the large altarpiece (unfortunately now deprived of its paint and gilding) in the parish church of Kefermarkt in Upper Austria (Plates 174A and 175) is said to have been met out of funds left for the purpose by Christoph von Zelking in his will of 1490. Eight years were calculated as necessary for making this large work. There can be no doubt that Passau, the diocesan see, was the place where it was made. It probably came from the workshop of Martin Kriechbaum, although it is true that Kriechbaum is cited in records only as a painter. In 1473 he undertook *inter alia* to carve a large altarpiece, which had originally been commissioned from his deceased brother Ulrich. This was for the abbey of Göttweig in Lower Austria.[65] As a proof I would refer to the slightly older St Martin from Zeillarn (now in the Bayerisches Nationalmuseum, Munich),[66] which may even be by the same hand. What distinguishes the Kefermarkt altar from this St Martin is the firm structure of the figure. Was not the master of this work influenced by Michael Pacher's altarpiece at St Wolfgang? St Wolfgang was so frequented as a pilgrimage church that Pacher's altarpiece there must quickly have become famous. At Kefermarkt we are able to trace the genealogy of a type which goes back to Nicolaus Gerhaerts' Austrian influence and then incorporates Pacher's use of sculptural volume. The development out of these premises is clear: there is an increase of bodily weight beneath the swirling movement of the drapery, a softer modelling of the faces, and, dependent on this last, a stronger conscious individualization.[67] All these are tendencies which produced an abundant harvest in Austrian sculpture of the early sixteenth century.

The third outstanding Austrian piece is the wooden altarpiece in the chapel of the Cistercian abbey of Zwettl, near Kefermarkt, in Lower Austria. According to the inscription, in 1500 Jörg Breu the Elder of Augsburg did the paintings on the wings. In these wonderful representations of scenes from the life of St Bernard, the whole of the so-called 'Danubian Style' may be seen in embryo.[68] Though the paintings are by an Augsburg master, I do not think that the same is true of the carving. The difference from the harmonious style of Gregor Erhart's Virgin of the Misericord at Frauen-stein (Upper Austria) is too marked. I would suggest rather that here again we have an echo of Pacher's St Wolfgang altar, and that thus the extremely fluid, painterly style of these carved figures is once more an expression of regional development.

The fourth Austrian work is the life-size wooden St Sebastian in Wiener Neustadt Cathedral. This figure was thought to have so much in common with the Apostles in the nave of the same church, which date from *c.* 1490, that it became the custom to ascribe it to a 'pupil of Lorenz Luchsperger'.[69] My impression is that this 'pupil', active round 1500, was greater than his so-called master; for here the martyr's fate is experienced for the first time absolutely and entirely from a human point of view, and at the same time the sculptural figure has acquired a self-contained and supple beauty. These are symptoms – like the 'emancipated' physiognomic interest in the Upper Rhenish busts of Niclaus von Hagenau – of the rapprochement between the indigenous sculpture of Upper Germany round 1500 and the idealizing tendencies of the Renais-sance. But we must note that this attempt to come to terms with Italian models, introduced in the first place through the medium of engravings, led initially (e.g. in Lucas Cranach's woodcuts, which originated in Vienna in 1502–3), in both the painting and sculpture of the so-called Danubian Style, to a period of veritable 'Sturm und Drang'.

Finally, we once again encounter Anton Pilgram, the last representative of monu-mental cathedral sculpture. His last signed work in Swabia was an angel on the corbel of the chancel arch in the choir (rebuilt in 1495) of the parish church of Schwieber-dingen near Ludwigsburg.[70] In the same church a wooden Crucifixion, closely affiliated to the style of Hans Syfer, was set up in 1500. An affinity with Hans Syfer's style still characterized Pilgram's work when he returned to Moravia. His master's sign is to be found in the north wall of the nave of St James at Brno (Brünn), with the date 1502. The stone carvings on the Jews' Gate (1508) and the Town Hall Gate are also from his hand. In 1511 Pilgram appears to have become the master mason to the cathedral of St Stephen in Vienna. If I include in this survey his monumental stone figures in this church, his self-portrait dating from 1513 on the organ bracket, his busts of the Church Fathers, and another self-portrait on the pulpit, I do so only because it seems to me that the legacy of late-fifteenth-century Upper Rhenish sculpture – indeed of Nicolaus Gerhaerts himself – extends even as far as this.[71] Anton Pilgram died in Vienna five years later.

In Hungary – e.g. at Buda and Esztergom (Gran) – buildings were erected by Italian workers in the style of the Italian Renaissance as early as the reign of King Matthias Corvinus (1458–90), and at the court the sculptors and painters of both frescoes and illuminated manuscripts were of Italian extraction.[72] We also meet early evidence of Italian Renaissance influence in both Prague and Cracow. Such infiltrations form part of the background of that remarkable 'Danubian Style' which – in sculpture too – produced a kind of Gothic Survival in the early years of the sixteenth century.

In our survey of Franconian sculpture at the end of the fifteenth century, the figure of Tilman Riemenschneider must take pride of place. His work, more than that of any-one else, acts as a bridge between the two centuries. If Riemenschneider's latest works (he died in 1531) still bear witness to the inexhaustible imagination of the Late Gothic, the language they speak – compared for example with the Italianism of Augsburg or the Romanism of Antwerp – had already become an outmoded tongue – 'altfränkisch' in German is a nicely ambiguous term, meaning, as we have seen, both ancient Franconian and old-fashioned. The modernity of Riemenschneider's earliest accredited works is thus all the more astonishing.

Riemenschneider, who was the son of a mint-master of the same name from Osterode in the Harz Mountains, is mentioned for the first time in the records of Würzburg in 1478 or at the latest in 1479. As a journeyman Riemenschneider probably went farther afield, but we can only guess at the extent of his travels from their reflection in his works. These betray, for example, the stimulating influence of the most progressive products of the Trier–Strasbourg–Ulm area, though this influence has been transformed into a new and highly personal style by Riemenschneider.[73] He settled at Würzburg in 1483, and two years later became a citizen and master there.

It has been said that the masters then active at Würzburg were unable to offer him any work. Be that as it may, the alabaster Annunciation (1484) from Würzburg, now in the Bayerisches Nationalmuseum in Munich,[74] which translates the style of Netherlandish grisaille painting into a finely polished but very solid piece of sculpture, is, in my opinion, very like those early works of Riemenschneider which evidently accounted for his rapid rise to fame. Alabaster works from Riemenschneider's prime[75] still betray such Netherlandish echoes, and it is interesting to observe that he participated in the general tendency of the west at this time to return to the use of alabaster rather than bronze for important commissions of sepulchral sculpture.

Riemenschneider's reputation stood so high that, while he was still a journeyman at Ulm, he was engaged as a 'fully qualified carver' for altar sculpture in Wiblingen Abbey. On the other hand, round several of Riemenschneider's early works at Würzburg – e.g. the tomb of Eberhard von Grumpach (d. 1487) in the parish church of Rimpar, and the painted stone Virgin in the Neumünster at Würzburg, with the date 1493 on the bracket – there clings a certain degree of Late Gothic convention, which even in later authentic works occasionally makes it difficult to be sure of the master's genuine handwriting. This is a proof of the outstanding quality of Late Gothic Franconian sculpture.

In the restoration of Würzburg Cathedral after the Second World War, a splendid, deeply cut tympanum, hitherto walled up, was brought to light above the portal of the cathedral school (Plate 168B). The demi-figure of a scholar saint (or Evangelist?), its original uniquely beautiful colouring still preserved, emerges from the shadows of the surround, proffering an almost disproportionately large opened book. The effect is one of astonishing verisimilitude, transfigured by a muted peace and harmony; the form is austere and taut, and this applies even to the one 'accessory', the strip of cloth that fills the left-hand corner with a Late Gothic swirl. There can be no doubt that this work dates from the late 1480s, and it has been stressed that in Würzburg at this time no master other than the young Riemenschneider was capable of such an achievement.[76] But do we not feel here a different human quality and a harder atmosphere than in the rest of

Riemenschneider's early works at Würzburg? My impression is that this tympanum has more in common with the austerity of form in the Adalbert von Sachsen (d. 1484) in Mainz Cathedral than with Riemenschneider.

In 1490 Riemenschneider was commissioned to carve the high altar in the parish church of Münnerstadt, and the work was completed in 1492. Parts of this altarpiece are preserved at Münnerstadt itself, parts are in museums[77] – they are all works of delicate, gentle beauty, naturalistic in style, intimate, and free of all rhetoric (Plate 177, A and B). In particular the Evangelists of the predella show the stylistic advance which has taken place since the Würzburg tympanum, and the same may be said of the John the Baptist in the parish church of Hassfurt. It is worth observing that Riemenschneider delivered the Münnerstadt altar uncoloured, something that only the Netherlanders had done hitherto, obviously relying for the full aesthetic effect of the work on the beauty of the material.[78] But this innovation does not appear to have met with approval, for in 1503, when Veit Stoss was staying at Münnerstadt during his exile from Nuremberg, he was commissioned 'to colour, paint, and gild' the altarpiece.

The same careful treatment of the surface distinguishes the stone figures of Adam and Eve, which Riemenschneider did in 1491 at the expense of the Würzburg city council for the south portal of the Marienkapelle (Plate 176, A and B). The work was ready two years later. These figures are characterized by tenderness and shyness. Our recognition that the exquisite delicacy of the surface arises from qualities resident in the sandstone itself, and that the sensitive modulations in the Münnerstadt altar figures spring from the natural appearance of the limewood, proves that the sculptor himself had adopted a conscious aesthetic attitude[79] towards the material he was employing, which we have scarcely encountered hitherto. It is true that we do not know what the wood carving of the high altar at Constance by Nicolaus Gerhaerts – that greatest of magicians – looked like. But we must certainly recognize in this perfection of surface an outstanding feature of Riemenschneider's work.

The Marienkapelle at Würzburg was also the original home of Riemenschneider's sandstone Virgin, which was acquired a few years ago by the Mainfränkisches Museum there.[80] This exquisitely harmonious statue is the most perfect expression of the idealized image of the Virgin characteristic of Late Gothic sculpture, the manifold variations of which (generally in wood) made Riemenschneider the most famous of all German Late Gothic masters. The Virgin probably represented the climax of the sculptural furnishing of the Marienkapelle. (Figures from portal and buttresses are now in the Mainfränkisches Museum.)

The development of Riemenschneider's funerary effigies is just as impressive. The monument to Prince Bishop Rudolf von Scherenberg in Würzburg Cathedral, in whose weighty pontifical dignity there is a new undercurrent of intellectual and spiritual nuance, dates from between 1496 and 1499. This is followed by the memorial erected by the city council of Würzburg in the Marienkapelle to Marshal Konrad von Schaumberg, who died at sea in 1499 while returning from the Holy Land. In spite of all its delicate beauty there is a bitter, elegiac austerity about this figure; it represents very much the 'waning' of the Late Gothic period. Between 1499 and 1513 Riemenschneider was responsible for the monumental memorial of the Emperor Henry II and his wife Kunigund in Bamberg Cathedral. The reliefs on the sides of the tomb, illustrating legendary events from the lives of the imperial pair, reveal a new human understanding.

During the first and second decades of the sixteenth century Riemenschneider was responsible for the famous altarpieces in St Jakob at Rothenburg of 1501–5 (Plate 178); in the small church of Creglingen; in the parish church of Windsheim (now Heidelberg, Kurpfälzisches Museum);[81] in the parish church of Dettwang (originally in St Michael, Rothenburg); in St John's chapel at Gerolzhofen (now Munich, Bayerisches National-museum); and, finally, the very late Altar of the Holy Family, parts of which are today in several collections.[82] The wealth of figures in these altarpieces proves the unbroken vitality of the Late Gothic, and at the same time they show how Late Gothic traditions have been lent a new visual harmony and beauty. By his masterly treatment of the surface Riemenschneider introduces a new quality into the traditional canon of Late Gothic forms. We realize keenly what intense empathy was involved in this when we study the late stone Mourning of Christ in the high altar of the Cistercian abbey of Maidbronn, which dates from between 1520 and 1525. This work testifies to the fact that the will to fathom the meaning of the Gospel, which led to the religious contro-versies of the period, was also reflected in the artistic sphere by the attempt to solve the equation 'verbum est carne'.

In Riemenschneider's works we see the culmination of traditions that were now fading out, traditions which stretch back in German and Netherlandish Late Gothic sculpture to Tournai. They bear upon them the imprint of the secret tragedy of their time. Does one not feel in the sensibility inherent precisely in Riemenschneider's most formally perfect works that they come from the hand of a man who, as a Würzburg councillor, was to come into conflict with the Church authorities during the Peasants' War and to pay a bitter price for his boldness?

Out of Riemenschneider's vast œuvre only a few objects can be dealt with here, especially as the completely preserved altarpieces all belong to the sixteenth century and show in their 'altfränkisch' character a significance beyond the individual one. In addition, we must consider the wide repercussions of the school of Riemenschneider. The register of the Fraternity of St Luke at Würzburg, which goes back to 1501, has records of no fewer than twelve pupils of Riemenschneider's. We may imagine that the numbers were similar in other centres whose output led to the creation of a definite local style. The influence of Riemenschneider and his workshop was especially strong in Thuringia and Saxony. Mention can be made as an example of Peter Breuer, registered as an apprentice at Würzburg in 1492 and then active at Zwickau from 1500 on.[83] His chief work is the highly expressive Mourning of Christ (1505–10) in St Mary at Zwickau.

The radical difference between Tilman Riemenschneider's career at Würzburg and that of Veit Stoss at Nuremberg cannot be sufficiently emphasized, if one wants to appreciate fully the variety of character in art around 1500. Stoss, of whom we have records from 1477 on, was certainly the older of the two. Only two years separate the dates of their death: Riemenschneider died in 1531, Stoss in 1533. Neither master was a native of the town where he made his name; Stoss, a Swabian by birth, came to the Free City of Nuremberg after he had already won fame and honour at Cracow; Riemenschneider came to the prince-bishopric of Würzburg after having travelled in the Rhineland and Swabia. Stoss became so completely a Nuremberger that his true place of origin was forgotten. In the same way, Riemenschneider, who was born at Heiligenstadt in Thuringia, became completely identified with Würzburg. It is a paradoxical fact that in the work of Riemenschneider, who was to become a rebel in the Peasants' War, we sense a leaning towards a new harmony from early on. Stoss, who throughout his life appears to have been the victim of personal legal conflicts, was one of the perfecters of the 'expressive' Late Gothic style in his Cracow high altar. In his late work at Bamberg he became the master of a new abstract perfection. But there was no future for this type of altar sculpture; it was given the death-blow by the Reformation, by Humanism and the Renaissance. There was also the strange chance that these two masters with obviously very different tendencies should both have worked on the Münnerstadt altar.

Veit Stoss – now a man of means – resumed his citizenship in Nuremberg in 1496. His first accredited works there after his return, the three stone reliefs of the Passion in the choir of St Sebald, signed and dated 1499, are of enormous power and formal concentration (Plate 181A). These reliefs and the wooden figures above them were donated by Paul Volckamer in connexion with the decoration of the church undertaken by the Nuremberg patriciate. The deeply-cut, 'painterly' reliefs fit into an enclosed area of the wall, and on each side of the tall windows above them the wooden figures of the Man of Sorrows and the Mater Dolorosa, standing on corbels beneath canopies, form part of a clearly calculated architectural composition. The figures in the stone reliefs are of a strong physical presence, but at the same time the reliefs are suffused by a dynamic linear abstraction, in keeping with the secret tendency of the Late Gothic towards ornamental background patterns. This combination of body and temperament shows very strikingly the multiplicity of the rational and sensuous forces which were active in German sculpture round 1500. The two wooden figures above the reliefs are, by virtue of the position they occupy, very late 'architectural sculpture', but at the same time they are self-contained and pillar-like to such an extent that even the swirling movement of the draperies takes on a monumental quality.

Veit Stoss's power as a wood carver is seen even more clearly in the Virgin and Child, of more or less the same date as the St Sebald composition, which he made for the house he purchased in 1499, intending it to serve partly as a trade-sign (Nuremberg, Germanisches Museum; Plate 180B). Here we feel none of the gentle dreaminess of Riemenschneider's works. There is instead a bright astringency and a violence of inner compulsion. The wooden Crucifix from St Sebald, now on the high altar in St Lorenz, dates from the same period (Plate 179). In this piece, it is the anatomical realism that astonishes us, but this is sublimated by Stoss's severe tectonic discipline. His knowledge of the human figure achieves sculptural autonomy and supreme clarity. The indispensable ornamental enrichment is not lacking, but the whipped-up curve of the loincloth does not billow out, but is concentrated in front of the body itself, once again emphasizing the growing feeling for three-dimensionality. This quality is seen most vividly in the large wooden St Andrew in St Sebald, donated by the Tucher family. This figure, about six feet in height, is a descendant, as it were, of the gigantic breed of Apostles in the central compartment of the Cracow altar, but now all expressionistic exaggeration is absent, and even the cascading drapery folds are carefully controlled.

Then came Veit Stoss's conflict with the legal authorities of Nuremberg, which finally culminated in his being publicly branded on both cheeks. He fled to Münnerstadt to the house of his son-in-law, whose recklessness involved him in yet further suffering. At Münnerstadt, as we have seen, he painted the figures on the high altar of the parish church, which had been carved by Riemenschneider ten years earlier, and added the paintings on the wings (completed in 1504). These latter are translations into strangely hard, pale colours of the violently dynamic, flat style which had characterized the ten engravings he made at Cracow. These late works prove that even at this stage in the history of Late Gothic sculpture, the gifts of sculptor and painter could be effectively combined.[84]

In 1505 Stoss was allowed to return to Nuremberg, but he had to atone for his flight by a period of imprisonment. Then came the years of loneliness for the 'quarrelsome fellow'. We sense that the works produced during this period were not the outcome of workshop activity, but a kind of personal confession – both artistic and human. Among them are the wooden Mourning Virgin and St John above the high altar of St Sebald (these we can probably identify with the 'two figures below the Cross' in the Frauenkirche, for which the Council of Nuremberg provided Stoss in 1506 with 'a lime-tree from the forest'), and also the Crucifix, formerly in the Heiliggeistspital, now in the Germanisches Museum. The deep undercutting in the drapery of the attendant figures lends added emphasis to the contrast of light and shade, but at the same time the modelling of the surface appears softer and gentler, and this gives the facial features of Christ Crucified a new tenderness. Stoss must have been in his sixties at this time. The limits of our survey do not permit the inclusion of his works from the second and third decades of the sixteenth century. In 1512 the Emperor Maximilian honoured the dishonoured master, to whom he had already given a written pardon six years earlier, by commissioning him 'to cast some statues'.

In his old age Veit Stoss had actually evolved a style where the 'measured' human form – in Albrecht Dürer's meaning of the word – in spite of all the creative immediacy which characterizes his work, achieves a new autonomy. The process is thus not as rational as that of Dürer's development.

The Renaissance concern for the autonomy of the arts, as opposed to the *opus completum* of the Late Gothic, makes the transition from coloured to uncoloured sculpture an instructive symptom. In Renaissance sculpture the natural character of the material employed is a contributory factor to the treatment of the surface. At Münnerstadt in 1504, to say it yet once more, Veit Stoss coloured the unpainted altarpiece carved by Tilman Riemenschneider. Riemenschneider's early refusal to use colour is perhaps due to the influence of Lower Rhenish and Netherlandish oak and walnut carvings which he had seen during his years as a journeyman. On the other hand, Stoss's St Andrew, which probably dates from 1503, shows such sophisticated treatment of the surface that it too must have been meant to be left uncoloured. At the end of Stoss's career – I am passing over the intermediate stages, including the superbly coloured Salve Regina of 1517–18 in St Lorenz (Plate 180A), which had to be painted to achieve the full optical effect, and the statuette of the Virgin in the Victoria and Albert Museum, which, being a piece of Renaissance miniature sculpture, is naturally uncoloured – we have the miraculous carving of the Bamberg altar of 1520–3, representing the culmination of Stoss's art, and here, by the express wish of the master, the figures were 'never to be thoughtlessly coloured'. The Carmelite prior Andreas Stoss, at whose instance this altarpiece was made, was a son of Veit Stoss's first marriage; he decreed that it was to be opened only on the highest feast days, and no large candles were to be placed in front of it 'on account of the smoke'. Thus we see that the altarpiece by this time had become so much a work of art that its use for liturgical purposes had to be correspondingly limited. So ends the Late Gothic epoch.

The Nuremberg of Dürer's day was the most impressive centre of Late Gothic sculpture in Germany, because the heterogeneity of the leading masters and of their pupils was more pronounced there than at Augsburg, Strasbourg, Cologne, or Lübeck. The genius of Veit Stoss was indeed so strong that it was impossible for any forceful individualities to develop in his 'school'. An example of this is the large high altar in the parish church of Schwabach, commissioned from Michael Wolgemut in 1507 and erected a year later. But Wolgemut himself was responsible for scarcely anything beyond the paintings on the wings of the predella – all else is work given out on contract. This applies also to the figures in the central compartment of the altarpiece, whose style unites the traditions of the Wolgemut workshop with the customary traits of the Stoss school.

On the other hand, Stoss's influence did produce strong talents in Galicia, Poland, Silesia, Slovakia, Hungary, and Rumania. This is mainly the result of his twelve-year sojourn at Cracow. It is also interesting to note that not only Stoss's brother, the goldsmith Mathias, who settled at Cracow in 1482, probably at Veit Stoss's request, but also later his own four sons emigrated from Nuremberg to the east. Of Stanislas Stoss, the painter, there are records at Cracow from 1505, of Florian, the goldsmith, at Görlitz from 1513, of the painter and carver Johann at Sighişoara (Schaessburg), while Veit the Younger was a carver at Braşov (Kronstadt), both in Transylvania, from 1522 to his death in 1531. It is true that we cannot attribute with certainty any particular work to any one of them, but the works which survive testify in general to the artistic fertility of Veit Stoss's progeny.[85] I would mention specially the Altar of St Luke in the church of the Magdalen at Wrocław (Breslau), the silver figure of St Stanislas in the treasury of the abbey on the Skałka at Kazimierz, the Altar of St Stanislas in St Mary at Cracow, and the works of Master Paul at Levoča (Leutschau; after 1508).[86]

Side by side with Veit Stoss, Adam Kraft worked at Nuremberg. He is known to have been active there from 1490 up to his death in 1509. This short span of time is filled with stone carvings of a pre-eminently Nuremberg character. In the tabernacle in Ulm Minster, dating from 1464–71, and in the pulpit by Hans Hammer in Strasbourg

Minster (1485), the premises of Adam Kraft's sculptural style have been seen, and attempts have been made to trace his personal development from them. Indeed, Kraft did incorporate impressions of this kind in his work when, in 1490-2, at the instance of Sebald Schreyer and Mathias Landauer, he rendered in stone on the outside of the choir of St Sebald the paintings above the burial place of these two families (Plate 181B); a strange commission which sheds light on the causal link between sculpture and painting. The extensive area covered by the reliefs indicates their genesis in painting. But in them the focal points of the compositions emerge with a new clarity and produce what one might almost call an anecdotal emphasis; this is especially true of the masterly psychological interpretation of the reactions on the faces. There is a peculiar ethos in these reliefs – perhaps one would be right in feeling it to be Franconian – such as we see in Nuremberg panel paintings from the time of Pleydenwurff up to the early works of Dürer – but not in the works of Stoss.

Between 1493 and 1496, at the instance of Hans Imhof the Elder, Adam Kraft erected the towering tabernacle in St Lorenz in Nuremberg. This is perhaps the most magnificent embodiment of Late Gothic ecclesiastical art on the eve of the Reformation. The master and two apprentices kneeling at the foot support the base of the structure – figures still in terms of Gothic architectural sculpture (Plate 182). They are functional, but at the same time they represent a human presence and are, in fact, true portraits. Reliefs and groups of the Passion, along with statuettes of prophets and angels, are incorporated into the individual tiers of this spire, which tapers upwards to reach the vault. It is as mysterious as a monstrance, but at the same time possessed of a lapidary clarity in its construction and in the style of all the details.

This Kraft followed by pictorially conceived reliefs, as for example those of the Municipal Weigh-House (1497), and the monuments to the Pergenstörffer (1498-9) and Rebeck (1500) families in the Frauenkirche, and that on the tomb of the Landauer family (1503) in the Tetzelkapelle of the Egidienkirche. Between 1505 and 1508, probably at the instance of Heinrich Marschalk von Rauheneck, Adam Kraft was responsible for sandstone reliefs in the Johannisstrasse and Burgschmietstrasse in Nuremberg. The harmony of these works conveys to us the feeling of the purified ethos of Franconian sculpture. A fine objective clarity pervades them, and it is their intellectual more than their artistic aspect which lends them so great a significance.

Peter Vischer the Elder is the next sculptor whom we must discuss. Neudörfer, the authoritative historian of Nuremberg, tells us that Adam Kraft the stonemason, Peter Vischer the bronzefounder, and Sebastian Lindenast the coppersmith (some statuettes cast by him have been preserved) all 'grew up together like brothers and went about together on feast-days even as old men and always behaved together as though they were still apprentices'. This is no mere 'artist's fairy tale', but a remarkable proof, first, that in the Nuremberg of Dürer's day a new community of like-minded artists had grown up over and above the traditional workshop life, and secondly, that the branded Veit Stoss played no part in this circle.

Peter Vischer's father, the bronzefounder Hermann Vischer the Elder, had become a citizen of Nuremberg in 1453 and had established his foundry there. Tomb lids cast by him have been preserved. Of particular importance is the bronze font, dated 1457, in the parish church of Wittenberg, in which we may trace a contact with Netherlandish traditions, but whose austerity of form is unequivocally German. In 1488, soon after his father's death, Peter Vischer began to prepare the work which was to qualify him as a master, and in 1489 he was inscribed in the masters' roll. Peter Vischer's signed parchment sketch for the reliquary shrine of St Sebaldus in the church of that name in Nuremberg is dated 1488 and measures 5 ft 10 in. in height. This sketch, made at the instance of two Nuremberg patricians, is now in the Akademie der bildenden Künste in Vienna, and the delicacy and wealth of detail in the clearly articulated architecture of this Late Gothic canopy with its host of pinnacles are amazing. The organic quality of his transparent structure reveals a new artistic standpoint, even though the sculptural details may appear conventional. This work, more than any other, anticipates the tectonic framework of Adam Kraft's tabernacle. The life-size figure of Otto IV of Henneberg (d. 1502), which Peter Vischer cast in the round for his monument in the Stadtkirche of Römhild (Rhön), must also date from about this time. It is a striking figure whose sharpness of outline is still reminiscent of the style of the 1480s, but the tension in the presentation of the body, the natural way it occupies its position in space, and the penetrating quality of the outstandingly individual features raise it above what was then usual.

The bronze figure of the so-called 'Branch-breaker' in the Bayerisches Nationalmuseum in Munich[87] bears the (original) date 1490 (Plate 185). Its traditional title is meaningless, since the figure does not represent an activity but carries an attribute, as is the case with the figures of workmen at the foot of the tabernacle in St Lorenz. The subject is therefore 'Armleutekunst' (see p. 169 above), as in the Netherlandish bronze fonts (e.g. the one of 1492 by Aert van Maastricht at 's-Hertogenbosch). The 'Branch-breaker' has so much in common with the bearer-figures of Adam Kraft that it has even been attributed to him, in the belief that in this and other of his accredited works, Peter Vischer was responsible merely for the actual casting. But it can be proved from contemporary records that Peter Vischer was in reality the creator and not merely the caster of this and other bronze statues. The very fact that such a problem should exist at all [88] is part and parcel of the mystery surrounding the workshops at the end of the Middle Ages, as we have already witnessed in the case of Syrlin's choir stalls in Ulm Minster. The really exciting new element in the 'Branch-breaker' is that in it we witness the discovery of the body in this last phase of the Late Gothic, before either artist or patron had had actual experience of the world of a Pollaiuolo. Adam Kraft, on the other hand, tarries in the world of traditional architectural sculpture. I think that in attributing the 'Branch-breaker' to Kraft, one fails to recognize an essential feature in the sculptural situation at the turn of the century, just as one would if one attributed Conrat Meit's Entombment of 1496 (Munich, Bayerisches Nationalmuseum; Plate 192A) and his so-called 'Falconer' in the Kunsthistorisches Museum in Vienna to Anton Pilgram, who was responsible for the pulpit-carrier in the Berlin Museum (Plate 183) and who was the master of the stone-carvings in St Stephen in Vienna.

It was an ingenious idea to propose the 'Branch-breaker' as a test-piece cast prior to

O

the casting of the Sebaldus shrine, although in the parchment draft in Vienna no such upward-looking bearer-figure was included. Following on this figure, which broke all conventions, came the monumental bronze tomb of Archbishop Ernst von Sachsen in Magdeburg Cathedral (Plate 184). Here again we see two things simultaneously: conventional apostles in the typical style of the cathedral lodges and then, alongside them, excitingly novel inventions of the greatest sculptural energy (e.g. St Maurice and St Stephen), culminating in the effigy of the feudal prince of the Church, whose imposing dignity and weighty presence outshadow everything that we have witnessed in the way of contemporary sepulchral sculpture north of the Alps. Here, out of the Late Gothic draped figure, a new, deeply felt creation of monumental dignity has developed, sustained by an objective view of man. No comparison with the faces we have met in Adam Kraft's work or in that of other contemporary Nuremberg sculptors will help us to understand this change, and, when we compare it with the works of Veit Stoss,[89] we are faced with a chasm – which tells us a great deal about the divergences within contemporary art round 1500, especially in the art of the greatest masters. In the Magdeburg effigy, as in Peter Vischer's early work at Römhild, the decisive quality is its detachment from the background and the way in which the figure occupies the frontal plane. The spatial quality of this Magdeburg figure, the way the archbishop's head is bedded on the pillow, and the manner in which the shading canopy protects him are among the most magnificent achievements of German sculpture round 1500.[90]

Foundry products tend to possess a certain ready-made character; thus, alongside these first elements of a new approach to the human body, there are also certain conventional features in Peter Vischer's work, e.g. the tomb lid, dating from 1496, of Bishop Johannes IV Roth in Wrocław (Breslau) Cathedral. The naked shield-bearers on the relief slab of Canon Bernhard Lubranski (d. 1499) in Poznań (Posen) Cathedral show on the other hand how great were the imagination and power of this German sculpture when, for various reasons, it was forced to come to terms with the Early Italian Renaissance.

Peter Vischer's design of 1488 for the reliquary shrine for St Sebaldus in St Sebald in Nuremberg was not carried out. In 1507 a further decision to commission a shrine was made. Again the commission was given to Peter Vischer, but according to the records of payment, which have been preserved, the work soon came to a standstill. Only from 1514 are there records of regular payments for delivery of work, and in 1519 the undertaking was completed. What was the reason for the crisis that evidently occurred?

Quite contrary to the architectural nature of the sketch of 1488, the shrine (which is only a quarter of the height originally planned), with its rich ramifications, resembles a portable canopy culminating in three cupolas, above which rise the tabernacles of goldsmith's filigree work. Thus, since the Late Gothic Magdeburg tomb, a radical change had taken place in Vischer's ideas. This may probably be attributed to the influence of the younger generation, that is to say to the collaboration of his sons, Hermann Vischer the Younger and Peter Vischer the Younger, in the foundry. Scholars are still unable to distinguish between the work of the various hands engaged on the shrine.[91] Does the fact that work on it progressed so slowly – and after all, this undertaking must have represented to Peter Vischer the Elder the fulfilment of a lifetime's dream after the failure of his first commission – point to the difficulties involved when the Old Franconian style tried to come to terms with completely new ideas and feelings? In any case, we are faced with what might be called a marginal phenomenon of Quattrocento sculpture.

No doubt progress on the Sebaldus shrine was adversely affected by the fact that at this moment the Emperor Maximilian asked 'the most skilful and most famous coppersmith in Nuremberg' – such were the words used to describe him in 1506 – to participate in his great monument in the Innsbruck Hofkirche. In fact Peter Vischer the Elder was commissioned about 1512 to cast two of the ancestral statues for this monument, those of King Arthur and Theodoric, and both were completed a year later. These statues are life-size, free-standing figures in poses of easy contrapposto, and they draw the ultimate consequences from the ideas of sculpture already visible in Vischer's bronze figures at Römhild and Magdeburg. Doubtless, sketches by Dürer[92] helped Vischer to achieve the freedom they embody, and if there is still anything tentative in them, this too may be ascribed to the master's hesitant approach to the new ideals of the Renaissance. Peter Vischer died in 1529, predeceased by both his sons.

As Peter Vischer's 'Branch-breaker' opens up the way to the German bronze statuettes of the sixteenth century, so the pearwood Entombment in the Bayerisches Nationalmuseum[93] and the statuette of the Falconer in the Kunsthistorisches Museum in Vienna, which are early works of Conrat Meit, lead on to the small-scale German Renaissance sculpture in different materials. The career of Conrat Meit of Worms at the opening of the new century, by taking us to the Wittenberg of Lucas Cranach and later to the court of Margaret of Austria at Malines,[94] where he received the commission for the marble and alabaster 'Burgundian' tombs at Brou, completes the cycle of Netherlandish and German Late Gothic sculptural achievement.

CHAPTER 13

FRANCE: 1490–1500

IF we accept the date 1500 as the time limit of this book and relate it to stylistic phenomena such as Late Gothic and Early Renaissance, we will be struck by the discrepancy
in the dates of works of decisive importance. This is indicative of the astonishing wealth
of talents and of the varied character of the regional reactions upon which the stylistic
development of sculpture during the new century was based.

In the sphere of Netherlandish sculpture, a work such as the wooden figure of St
Gertrude in the church of that name at Etterbeek near Brussels (Plate 162C), to which
I have already referred, may demonstrate how a growing sense of the body and a new
idealized human quality in the individual expression combined with the perfection of
the linearly conceived Late Gothic altar figures. We encounter this sovereignty of form
only during a short span of time, the time we call 'circa 1500'. There followed in the
Netherlands – both in altar and funerary sculpture and in the increasing number of
isolated statues, some small in size – a certain Romanism, deeply influenced by contemporary Netherlandish painting.

German sculpture of 1500 on the other hand is very much less homogeneous. On the
one hand we feel that Gregor Erhart of Augsburg is a 'Late Gothic classic', but alongside him in the Fugger Chapel in St Anna at Augsburg, donated in 1509, we have an
Italianism in the sculpture, whose beauty and harmony already presage that new order
which became an accepted doctrine in Dürer's *Kunst der Messung*. Examples of how
violent were the contradictions in the situation round 1500 are the fact that Veit Stoss's
Salve Regina in St Lorenz in Nuremberg, dating from 1517–18 (Plate 180A), still, as it
were, translates the medieval hymn of Marian worship into the magic of the cathedral –
objectively considered the Salve Regina is nothing other than a monumental chan-
delier – sensibly covered with a piece of Genevan cloth to protect it from the dust; and
that in 1532 Stoss was forbidden by the City Council of Nuremberg to sell his wares on a
stall in front of the Frauenkirche after the Protestant faith had been introduced into this
church. In our appraisal of German sculpture round 1500 we may consequently be
tempted to go beyond the beginning of the new century in a search for a decisive turn-
ing-point in the style. But we shall find that we need not go far; for the Austrian woodcuts of the Franconian Lukas Cranach the Elder which constitute the first decisive
examples of the passionately dynamic and painterly Danubian Style, which was a
typically German feature of the new century and for which there were parallels in other
German districts, date from as early as 1502–3. On the other hand, Peter Vischer's
'Branch-breaker' (Plate 185) and Conrat Meit's Munich Entombment (Plate 192A),
dating from 1490 and 1496 respectively – though outwardly they fit in with the
traditional Late Gothic formal canon – already exhibit the new comprehension of the
relationship between body and space, along with a vital energy which also pro-

claims the future. They have left the sphere of Late Gothic linear or painterly sculpture.

In France, we are tempted to draw the line between Late Gothic and the beginnings of the Renaissance at an earlier date. Hence our chapter on French sculpture in the last decade of the fifteenth century will contain relatively few examples, for the character of the most outstanding sculptural works of this time in France was already completely that of the Renaissance of the new century. It is true that when surveying the various regions of France at this period, we find co-existing at one and the same time examples of the latest phase of Gothic, of sublimations of this Late Gothic into a new and vigorous monumental style, and of the first expressions of a Renaissance sculpture resulting from contacts with Italy and from the work of immigrant Italian artists. Nevertheless in France one is more aware of the decline of the Late Gothic mode of expression, while in sixteenth-century Germany it still flares up spasmodically like a dying candle.

I would place at the beginning of the survey, as an example of a relatively traditional style, the misericords from the choir stalls of the abbey of St Lucien at Beauvais, now in the Musée de Cluny in Paris.[1] These misericords illustrate anecdotally the activities of the crafts. The art of wood-carving is represented by a master at his bench working on a crucifix. The figures are taut in outline and full of dramatic vigour, and their illustrative character is very Netherlandish. Executed at the instance of the titular abbot Antoine du Bois between 1492 and 1500, they demonstrate the wealth of a vivid narrative vocabulary, whose appeal resides in a naturalism and close-range vision which still lay at the disposal of the conventional carver at this phase of very late Gothic.[2]

At the same time, in Northern France we find sculpture which lends to the diction of Late Gothic a new dignity and harmony. A significant example of this is the Virgin in the Chapelle de la Mère-Dieu in Notre-Dame at Évreux, and this tendency prevails in the North French districts which belonged to the Burgundo-Netherlandish territory, i.e. Picardy and Artois. We have already referred to the magnificent reliefs of the life and martyrdom of St Firmin on the south choir screen of Amiens Cathedral (Plates 186B and 187).[3] Work on these reliefs was begun in 1490 and extended into the new century. (The corresponding reliefs of the story of St John the Baptist on the north choir screen are dated as late as 1531.) The St Firmin reliefs are closely packed with figures, severely linear in detail, and by virtue of the arrangement of the figures in layers they are derivatives of a tradition which is clearly developed in Late Gothic sculpture and panel-painting at Amiens.[4] The first carver to be known by name at Amiens is recorded only at the beginning of the sixteenth century. In 1508 Antoine Ancquier (or Avernier) was commissioned to carve seventy-two misericords for the cathedral choir stalls[5] – a gigantic task which was executed by the joiners Arnould Boulin and Alexandre Huet and took until 1522 to complete. The monumental altar-pieces (e.g. that in St Wulfran at Abbeville) were also early-sixteenth-century products of a local school; their austere Late Gothic clarity distinguishes them fundamentally from the flamboyant style of the contemporary altar carving carried out in the workshops of Flanders, Brabant, and the Walloon territories. The relief of the Last Judgement in St Wulfran at Abbeville is probably the work of a member of the Lheureux family. We have records of several masters of this family from 1473 on. They were active at

Amiens, Arras, Beauvais, Rouen, and Abbeville – all then prosperous towns – of whose common regional character in the sculpture of the years round 1500 we can today glean only a faint impression.

It is at Troyes[6] and in the adjacent district of Champagne that we have the clearest example of a definite school. Late Gothic echoes are most perceptible in a Lamentation of Christ in the ambulatory of St Jean at Troyes: traditional in composition and religious character, it yet shows a marked new objectivity in the articulation of the constituent parts of the composition, in the distribution of the functions to the individual figures, and in the naturalistic treatment of the surface. The stone Virgin in the Hôtel-Dieu at Troyes[7] is also important, since the identification of the kneeling donor with Abbé Nicolas Forjot of Saint-Loup establishes its date as between 1508 and 1512. This is a relatively conventional Late Gothic draped figure, whose expression is hardened so realistically that the details strike one as being too stark. The moving and impressive monumental St Martha in the Madeleine at Troyes is probably of about the same date. In this impressive work of masterly sculptural autonomy, body and drapery combine to convey a new idealized harmony. As a document of the Early Renaissance it may be compared with the Mourning Virgin from the group of the dead Christ with the Virgin and St John by Hans Daucher on the altar of the Fugger Chapel in St Anna at Augsburg, though in making this comparison I merely wish to draw readers' attention to the common character of sculpture in France and Germany at this time. Further works attributed to the master of this St Martha[8] cannot be listed here, as they lie outside the scope of our survey. But mention must be made of the stone Pietà in the church at Bayel (Aube) and the stone Entombments in the churches at Villeneuve-l'Archevêque (Yonne; Plate 192B) and at Chaource (Aube),[9] the latter bearing the date 1515. The degree of formal perfection in such works demonstrates how fifteenth-century Franco-Burgundian sculpture had paved the way for such a harmony.

An enigmatic document of Eastern French sculpture before 1500 is the beautiful pearwood figure of a female saint (later given the accessories of St Mary Magdalen) in the Bayerisches Nationalmuseum in Munich (Plate 189B).[10] The sculptural autonomy of this figure and its severe linear structure are astonishing, but at the same time it is suffused with a new idealization of form and self-consciousness of expression. It is but a short step from this type of Late Gothic to the new style associated with the Troyes School, which is seen in the stone Virgin from Rouvroy (Haute-Marne), now in the Louvre, dating from the early sixteenth century.[11]

The large walnut figures of mourners from either an Entombment or a Lamentation, now in the Städtische Skulpturengalerie at Frankfurt (Plate 188, A and B),[12] were acquired at Nevers. The incredible expressive power of these fragments gives one some idea of the treasures that have been lost. We sense here the monumental context, the violence of the inner urges and the fetters of a severe form. They remind us most forcibly of Spanish works of sculpture whose Netherlandish provenance we have already stressed, e.g. the altarpiece from the Oppenheim Collection in the Metropolitan Museum in New York (Plate 186A), the wooden Mater Dolorosa in the Museo del Greco at Toledo, and the kneeling figures of mourners in a Crucifixion in Cordova

Cathedral.[13] However great its resemblance to the Mater Dolorosa at Toledo, we cannot exclude the possibility that Nevers was the real home of the Frankfurt group. What do we know of the Franco-Burgundian stopping-places of South Netherlandish peripatetic sculptors, who then ultimately found in Spain an almost unlimited field of activity and became Spaniards just as they previously had been Frenchmen?

In the Île-de-France, outstanding works of this period are rare. The stone seated Virgin, holding in her lap the Child pointing out words in a book, in the church at Le Luat, Fresnoy-le-Luat (Oise),[14] still follows completely the traditional type of Late Gothic draped figure. The Virgin wears an elegant, richly embroidered dress; the throne has become a faldstool; the Virgin's face has sharp features – these are all ingredients of a novelistic superficiality, which around 1500 is countered by sculptural works bent on reducing the number of symbolic attributes in order to achieve a new harmonious beauty and calm. This tendency is seen in the wooden Mater Dolorosa in the church of Bulles (Oise), and more especially in the wooden St Anne with the Virgin as a child in the church of Poissy (Seine-et-Oise).[15] From instances such as these – only in Troyes and Champagne does the number of surviving examples merit the name of a school – we see that in the sculptural activities of the various French regions about 1500 a new idea of the autonomy of the sculptural figure was emerging, and in the realization of this only the traditional representational types were being taken over from Late Gothic. The Netherlandish sources of these prototypes recede into the far background, and a sculpture of a pronouncedly French character arises. The formal language loses its conventional features.

The earliest evidence of this new tendency is the monumental composition of the Entombment in the abbey of Solesmes (Sarthe) which dates from 1496 (Plates 190 and 191, A and B);[16] the portrait medallions made in Lyon in 1499 by Nicolas Leclerc, Jean de Saint-Priest, and Jean Lepère for King Louis XII and his wife, Anne of Brittany;[17] and the early works of Michel Colombe at Tours, in particular the gold medallion for King Louis XII, 'Semper Augustus Victor Triumphator', for which Colombe made the model.[18] Of vital significance is the fact that in the important centres of France in the late fifteenth century – here again it was the court and not the middle-class, as in Netherlandish and German Late Gothic, which exercised the decisive influence – itinerant Italian sculptors were entrusted with outstanding commissions. Between 1461 and 1466 Francesco Laurana, a native of Dalmatia,[19] was active in Southern France, clearly owing to the initiative of King René of Anjou. In 1477 he returned from Naples to Marseille. His large stone relief of Christ bearing the Cross on the altar of the Célestin church at St Didier originated in Avignon and dates from 1478. In 1494 King Charles VIII went to Italy to raise the claim of the House of Anjou to the throne of Naples, and he returned to Tours in 1495, bringing with him a number of Italian artists. Among these was Guido Mazzoni from Modena, who was responsible for the large monument erected to the king in the abbey of St-Denis after his death in 1498 (unfortunately this was destroyed in 1793). Girolamo Viscardi of Genoa was responsible for the monument to the dukes of Orléans (now in St Denis) and, in 1507, for the altarpiece in the Ste Trinité at Fécamp (Seine-Inférieure). In 1507 the Lombards Antonio della

Porta, called Il Tamagnino, and Pace Gagini erected a marble fountain with a statue of John the Baptist in the château of Gaillon, at the instance of Cardinal Georges d'Amboise. This list shows how complex were the manifestations of Italian Renaissance sculpture in France in the second half of the fifteenth century and at the turn of the century. We cannot emphasize enough that these contacts between France and Italy reflect an inner affinity which distinguishes them sharply for instance from the isolated character of the work of Adriano Fiorentino at the court of Dresden, or the purchase of Michelangelo's marble Madonna by the Mouscron family at Bruges in 1506.

Vitry and Pradel have shown clearly in their monographs on the subject how this Italian-inspired rejuvenation of French sculpture in the last decade of the fifteenth century flourished with greatest vigour in the districts which had remained untouched by the tide of Late Gothic in the preceding epoch: Berry, Bourbonnais, Touraine, and Burgundy. This being so, it is understandable that in surveying these traditions retrospectively from the point of view of French Renaissance sculpture which culminates in the work of Germain Pilon, Pradel should see in Michel Colombe 'le dernier Imagier gothique'; whereas for us in our survey of Late Gothic sculpture of the fifteenth century in Europe, which found its highest fulfilment in the work of the Netherlandish carvers, this same Michel Colombe represents one of the great pioneers of that 'style nouveau' which, through contact with the intellectual forces of Humanism in the sense of the Italian Early Renaissance of the fifteenth century, led in the North also to a radical change in the potentialities and functions of art.

Michel Colombe was active at Tours from 1473 onwards, but his surviving works date only from the beginning of the sixteenth century. They are the monument to François II of Brittany and Marguerite de Foix in Nantes Cathedral, which dates from 1502–7 and was originally in the Carmelite church there; and the relief of St George and the Dragon, dating from 1508–9 and made for the château of Gaillon (now in the Louvre). These are both striking evidence of the masterly translation of Italian prototypes into the French style of the Renaissance. What process of development lies behind these works? Their maturity is proof that they were not the result of an isolated assimilation, but the outcome of organic growth. And there are other works which, though they cannot have come from Michel Colombe's hand, nevertheless reveal a similar artistic situation. The specifically French quality in which the 'clandestine' Renaissance character of the late works of Burgundian traditions manifests itself is seen, I think, most clearly in the stone Entombment at Solesmes (Plates 190 and 191, A and B). This work, as we have seen, carries the date 1496, and, according to the arms it bears, the donor was Prior Guillaume Cheminart. His period of office terminated in 1495. Thus design and commission must have been made before 1496. Even if a painter was responsible for the design – in the case of Colombe's tomb at Nantes we know it to have been Jean Perréal of Lyon – it is the Renaissance character of the sculptural work, even to the perfection of the surface details, that is decisive here, not the Italian language of the architectural surround of the recess and its ornamental features – this language might well have been learnt – and there were enough ornamental engravings to be followed. But the logical consistency in the articulation of the background of the scene cannot have come from itinerant Italian artists. Most impressive of all is the crouching figure of the mourning Magdalen in the foreground (Plate 191B), a figure whose expressive force springs from a Late Gothic way of feeling. Here, then, something remarkable has happened: in a composition stressing in a Renaissance way the importance of the independent figure, Late Gothic evocative sentiment has become the secret power which holds the 'picture' together, though the thematic centre, the figure of the dead Christ, has already lost its binding magic, as understood by the Late Middle Ages.

There is another work which should be related directly to the Solesmes Entombment. This is the small statue of St Cyr as a child in the church at Jarzé (Maine-et-Loire), which we can probably associate with the name of the sculptor Louis Mourier[20] of Anjou.

In order to show the complex significance of this new sculptural style in France even before Michel Colombe's works at Nantes and Château Gaillon, two further examples can be quoted: first, the truly astonishing marble Magdalen at St Pierre de Montluçon (Allier), which no doubt dates from the last decade of the fifteenth century. It is easy to see how this figure follows a traditional Bourbonnais style, developed in the late fifteenth century (cf. the marble female saint in the museum at Moulins). But now suddenly a completely new independence has appeared in the figure, which lends to the content a hitherto unknown self-awareness and bestows on all the details of the surface a new optical significance.[21] This is one of the most magnificent achievements of French sculpture at the turn of the century. It seems as though the legacy of the Late Gothic were no longer any more than a pretext for the expression of a totally new artistic and human experience.

The second example is the three stone figures from the chapel of Anne de Beaujeu's château at Chantelle (Allier), now in the Louvre (Plate 189A).[22] These were the work of Master Guillaumet, known as Jean de Chartres, a pupil and friend of Michel Colombe, between 1500 and 1503. In these figures what strikes us most forcibly is the harmonious union of traditional French types – seen most clearly in the figure of St Peter – with features derived from Italian Early Renaissance sculpture.[23]

From Southern France two works are in a corresponding stylistic position. Their dates of origin are characteristic too. The first is the small silver statuette of St Foy in the treasury of the abbey of Conques (Aveyron), made in 1497 by the goldsmith Pierre Frechrieu at Villefranche-de-Rouergue, a work harmoniously self-contained within its supple, generous lines. The second, of 1504, is the large wooden valves of the door of Aix Cathedral, carved with relief figures, which are still graphically conceived in the Late Gothic way, but which are smothered by the wealth of accompanying Renaissance ornament and are therefore merely decorative in their effect.

In Spanish sculpture the marble monument to Cardinal Pedro González de Mendoza in Toledo Cathedral (arranged for before his death in 1495) represents a similar watershed. The infiltration of Italian sculpture and sculptors into Spain during the second half of the fifteenth century was even more extensive than into France, and proves an inner affinity between Spain and Italy which became even clearer with the advent of the Renaissance. The bronze monument to Lorenzo Suárez de Figuerosa, who died in

1505 while Spanish ambassador in Venice, in the cloister of Badajoz Cathedral[24] has been attributed to the Venetian founder Pier Zuanne delle Campane. But of what nationality may the sculptor have been who was responsible for the model of the portrait?

French and Spanish sculpture was spared the stylistic crisis round 1500 which was experienced everywhere in the Netherlands and Germany. But nevertheless the turn of the century marks a decisive break for French and Spanish sculpture too. It was a question of the birth of a completely new world of sculptural creation such as had taken place in Florence in the early Quattrocento, as the result of a new understanding of the beauty of classical Antiquity.

LIST OF THE PRINCIPAL ABBREVIATIONS

A.	Annales
Arch.	Archéologie, -ique
Bull.	Bulletin
Cat.	Catalogue
d.	der, etc.
Exhib.	Exhibition
f.	für
J.	Jaarboek, Jahrbuch, Journal
Kunstd.	Kunstdenkmäler
Kunstg.	Kunstgeschichte, etc.
Kunsth.	Kunsthistorische, etc.
Kunsts.	Kunstsammlung, etc.
Kunstw.	Kunstwissenschaft
R.	Royal, etc.
Rev.	Revue
Z.	Zeitschrift
A.S.R. Arch. de Bruxelles	*Annales de la Société Royale d'Archéologie de Bruxelles*
G.B.	*Gentsche Bijdragen tot de Kunstgeschiedenis*
J.d.P. Kunsts.	*Jahrbuch der preussischen Kunstsammlungen*
Münch. J.d.b.K.	*Münchner Jahrbuch der bildenden Kunst*
Rev. belge	*Revue belge d'archéologie et d'histoire de l'art*

Catalogues of exhibitions and museums quoted in abbreviated form in the Notes will be found cited in full under the appropriate city in the Bibliography, pp. 232–4.

NOTES

CHAPTER 1

p. 2   1. F. Zschokke, *Z. f. schweizerische Arch. und Kunstg.*, XVIII (1958), 181.

p. 3   2. Especially illuminating for the confluence of workmen are the sources for the history of Milan Cathedral, begun in 1386. Cf. U. Nebbia, *La scultura del Duomo di Milano* (Milan, 1908); C. Baroni, *Scultura gotica lombarda* (Milan, 1944), 123–52; H. Siebenhüner, *Deutsche Künstler am Mailänder Dom* (Munich, 1944).

3. O. Kletzl, 'Zur Parler-Plastik', *Wallraf-Richartz-J.*, N.F. II/III (1933/4), 126.

4. A. Six, 'Die monumentale Plastik der Prager Dombauhütte', *Kunstg. J. der Zentralkommission Wien*, II (1908), 69; K. M. Swoboda, *Peter Parler* (Vienna, 1940), 31; A. Matějček, 'Gotická Plastika v chrámu Sv. Víta v Praze', *Umění*, II (1954), 1; A. Kutal, *České gotické sochařství 1350–1450* (Prague, 1962).

5. B. Lázár, *Studien zur Kunstgeschichte* (Vienna, 1917), 1; J. Balogh, *Márton és György Kolozsvári szobrászok* (Cluj, 1934); J. Pečírka, 'Socha sv. Jíří na hradě Pražkém', *Umění*, VII (1934), 365.

6. J. Ernyey, '"Csák Máté" Hermája', *Magyar Régészeti Társulat Evkönyve*, II (1923–6), 196.

7. T. Müller, *Mittelalterliche Plastik Tirols* (Berlin, 1935), 52; Cat. Vienna Exhib. 1962, no. 425.

p. 4   8. E. Wiegand, 'Beiträge zur südostdeutschen Kunst um 1400', *J. d. P. Kunsts.*, LIX (1938), 67.

9. L. H. Labande, *Le Palais des Papes et les monuments d'Avignon au XIVe s.* (Marseilles, 1925), 30.

10. G. Troescher, *Claus Sluter* (Freiburg im Breisgau, 1932), 43.

11. Cat. Aubert, Paris, nos. 228–30, 223–4.

p. 5   12. J. Braun, *Der christliche Altar* (Munich, 1924), II, 302 ff.

13. J. Sarrète, *Vierges ouvertes, vierges ouvrantes* (Lézignan, 1913); W. Fries, 'Die Schreinmadonna', *Anzeiger des Germanischen Nationalmuseums Nürnberg* (1928/9), 5; A. Schmid, 'Die Schreinmadonna von Cheyres', *Lebendiges Mittelalter, Festgabe für Wolfgang Stammler* (Freiburg, Switzerland, 1958), 130.

14. J. von Schlosser, 'Die flämischen Kaiser-   p. 6 medaillen des Herzogs von Berry', *J.d. Kunsth. Sammlungen des a.h. Kaiserhauses*, XVIII (1897), 75; J. Babelon, *La médaille en France* (Paris, 1948), 13; Cat. Vienna Exhib. 1962, nos. 565–6.

CHAPTER 2

1. D. Roggen, 'Hennequin de Marville en zijn   p. 7 Atelier te Dijon', *G.B.*, I (1934), 173; P. Quarré, 'Les statues de l'Oratoire Ducal à la Chartreuse de Champmol', *Recueil public à l'occasion du cent-cinquantenaire de la Soc. Nat. des Antiquaires de France* (1955), 245.

2. J. Duverger, 'De Brusselsche Steenbickeleren   p. 8 uit de XIV en de XV eeuw', *Bouwstoffen to de Nederlandsche Kunstgeschiedenis* (Ghent, 1933); W. Medding, 'Herkunft und Jugendwerke des Claus Sluter', *Z.f. Kunstg.*, III (1934), 341; D. Roggen, 'Les origines de Klaas Sluter', *A. de Bourgogne*, IV (1932), 293; V (1933), 263, 385; D. Roggen, *G.B.*, II (1935), 103 ('Is Klaas Sluter van duitsch Afkomst?'); XI (1945/8), 7 ('Klaas Sluter voor zijn vertreck naar Dijon in 1385'); XVI (1955/6), 130 ('Klaas Sluter').

3. D. Roggen and L. Verleyen, 'De Portaalsculpturen van het Brusselsche Stadhuis', *G.B.*, I (1934), 123.

4. J. Squilbeck, *Rev. belge*, V (1935), 329; A. Louis, *Rev. belge*, VII (1937), 199; A. Janssens de Bisthoven, *G.B.*, X (1944), 7; Cat. Bruges-Detroit Exhib. 1960, no. 68.

5. R. Hamann, 'Spätgotische Skulpturen der Wallfahrtskirche in Hal', in P. Clemen, *Belgische Kunstd.*, I (1923), 203; D. Roggen and M. de Vleeschouwer, 'De Apostolen en de Aanbidding der Driekoningen in de St Maartens Kerk te Halle', *G.B.*, I (1934), 149.

6. J. Baum, 'Die Lütticher Bildniskunst im   p. 9 14. Jh.', *Belgische Kunstd.*, I (1923), 168.

7. M. Devigne, 'Les rapports de Claus Sluter avec le milieu franco-flamand de Paris', *Oud Holland*, LIV (1937), 115.

8. A. Liebreich and H. David, 'Le portail de l'église de Champmol', *Bull. Monumental* (1935),

349; D. Roggen, 'De Portalsculpturen van Champmol', *G.B.*, IV (1937), 107.

p. 10   9. H. David and A. Liebreich, 'Le Calvaire de Champmol', *Bull. Monumental* (1933), 419; D. Roggen, 'De Kalvarienberg van Champmol', *G.B.*, III (1936), 31; P. Quarré, 'La polychromie du Puits de Moïse', *Mémoires de la Commission des Antiquités de la Côte-d'Or*, XXIII (1947); Cat. Vienna Exhib. 1962, no. 419. A reconstruction of the Crucifixion is in the museum of Dijon.

p. 11   10. We have a further reference to such a contact of Claus Sluter with a painter when Duke Philip sent him in 1393 together with Jean de Beaumez to the château of Mehun-sur-Yèvre 'pour visiter' the works of art being completed there at the instance of the Duke of Berry. Cf. D. Roggen, 'André Beauneveu en de visite van Klaas Sluter te Mehun', *G.B.*, II (1935), 114.

p. 12   11. A. Kleinclausz, 'L'art funéraire de la Bourgogne au moyen-âge', *Gazette des Beaux-Arts* (1901), II, 441; (1902), I, 299.

12. E. Andrieu, 'Les pleurants aux tombeaux des Ducs de Bourgogne', *Rev. de Bourgogne* (1914), 95; *idem*, 'Les tombeaux des Ducs de Bourgogne', *Bull. Monumental* (1933), 171; D. Roggen, 'De "plorants" van Klaas Sluter te Dijon', *G.B.*, II (1935), 127; P. Quarré, 'Les pleurants des tombeaux des ducs de Bourgogne à Dijon', *Bull. de la Société Nationale des Antiquaires de France* (1948/9), 124; Cat. Vienna Exhib. 1962, no. 420.

13. D. Roggen, 'Klaas van de Werve', *G.B.*, VII (1941), 211; Cat. Vienna Exhib. 1962, no. 341.

14. Cat. Cluny, pierre, no. 652. Cf. the weepers in the Musée des Beaux-Arts, Dijon; Cat. Vienna Exhib. 1962, no. 420.

p. 13   15. A. Soliet, 'Les retables de Jacques de Baerze', *Bull. de l'Académie de Dijon* (1922), 144; D. Roggen, 'De twee Retabels van de Baerze te Dijon', *G.B.*, I (1934), 91. Altar carvings by the same master in the church of Dendermonde (Termonde) and in the abbey of Bijloke are supposed to have served as models. Cat. Vienna Exhib. 1962, no. 375.

16. Cf. Cat. Exhib. 'La Chartreuse de Champmol' (Musée de Dijon, 1960).

17. E.g. Cat. Aubert, Paris, nos. 189–92; figure of a weeping Madonna from a Calvary group, Notre-Dame de Louviers, Eure (Cat. Rouen Exhib. 1931, plate XXX; Cat. Paris Exhib. 1950, no. 172); oak relief of the Kiss of Judas, Cluny, Musée Ochier; alabaster groups at the foot of a Crucifixion from the end of the fourteenth century, New York, Metropolitan Museum (*Bull.*, XXI (1926), 144–5); carved, coloured relief fragments from a retable of the Passion in the Musée des Arts Décoratifs, Paris.

18. Cat. Cluny, pierre, no. 646; G. Troescher, *Die burgundische Plastik des ausgehenden Mittelalters* (Frankfurt, 1940), 33; Cat. Vienna Exhib. 1962, no. 338. The South Netherlandish character is in my opinion underlined by the affinity in kind of the marble Maria lactans in the Mayer van den Bergh Museum at Antwerp (*Cat. Musée Mayer van den Bergh, Anvers* (Brussels, 1933), no. 185; J. Geisler, *Oberrheinische Plastik um 1400* (Berlin, 1957), II, figure 13).

19. O. Goetz, 'Der Gekreuzigte des Jacques de Baerze', *Festschrift Carl Georg Heise* (Berlin, 1950), 158.

20. D. Roggen, 'Beauneveu en het Katharinebeeld van Kortrijk', *G.B.*, XV (1954), 223.

21. Cat. Vienna Exhib. 1962, no. 102.

22. L. Raynal, *Histoire du Berry*, II (Bourges, p. 14 1844), 442 ff.; P. Gauchery, 'Le Palais du Duc Jean et la Sainte Chapelle', *Mémoires des Antiquaires du Centre*, XXXIX (1920), 46; XL (1921), 197.

23. Apostles: G. Troescher, 'Drei Apostelköpfe', *J. d. P. Kunsts.*, LXIII (1942), 79; Prophets: Cat. Vienna Exhib. 1962, no. 337.

24. P. Pradel, 'Nouveaux documents sur le p. 15 tombeau de Jean de Berry', *Fondation Eugène Piot, Monuments et Mémoires*, IL (1957), 151.

25. Drawings in the Kunstmuseum, Basel. Cf. F. Zschokke, 'Die Zeichnungen Hans Holbeins nach den Statuen in Bourges', *Z. f. schweizerische Arch. und Kunstg.*, XVIII (1958), 181; Cat. Exhib. 'Die Malerfamilie Holbein in Basel' (Basel, 1960), nos. 277–8. The two badly treated kneeling figures now in the apsidal chapel of Bourges Cathedral (with restored heads) hardly show anything of the original atmosphere.

26. Cat. Paris Exhib. 1950, no. 177. Marble.

27. D. Roggen, 'Postsluteriaanse Sculptuur', *G.B.*, XVI (1955/6), 146; Cat. Vienna Exhib. 1962, no. 377.

28. S. Pajot, 'La sculture en Berry à la fin du moyen-âge et au début de la Renaissance', *Mémoires de la Société des Antiquaires du Centre*, XLVIII (1938–41) (Issoudun, 1941), 74; Cat. Aubert, Paris, no. 315; H. Bober, 'André Beauneveu and Mehunsur-Yèvre', *Speculum*, XXVIII (1953), 741.

29. Cat. Aubert, Paris, no. 321.   p. 1

30. R. Berliner, 'Raphaels Sixtinische Madonna', *Das Münster*, XI (1958), 91.

31. Cf. the relief on the base of the seated Madonna of 1334 in Sens Cathedral; M. Aubert, *La Bourgogne, La Sculpture* (Les richesses d'art de la France) (Paris, 1927), 17; memorial tablet to the Boudoche de Heu family in the church of St Martin at Metz (J. Ernst-Weis, 'Ein Meisterwerk gotischer Plastik in Lothringen', *Elsass-Lothringisches J.*, XIV (1935), 87).

32. J. Evans, *Life in Mediaeval France* (London, 1925), figure 183B; *idem, Art in Mediaeval France 987–1498* (London, 1948), figure 29. The place name is erroneously given as Marognes.

33. H. Naef, 'La Chapelle de Notre-Dame à Genève', *Genava*, XV (1937), 102. Also a crowned head of Christ, stone fragment with remains of paint, from the Dominican friary at Avignon (Musée Calvet).

p. 17 34. Cf. E. Müntz, *Le mausolée du Cardinal de Lagrange à Avignon* (Paris, 1890). Also the 'Transi' on the tombstone of Guillaume de Harcigny (d. 1393), physician of King Charles VI, originally in the Franciscan friary at Laon, now in the museum there, and the 'Transi' of Cardinal Pierre d'Ailly (d. 1412) in Cambrai Cathedral. The effigy of Jacques Germain (d. 1424) completely enveloped in his shroud from the Église des Carmes, now in the Dijon museum, dates from the post-Sluter generation. More extreme realism is the representation simply as skeletons of the two stone effigies of Richard de Chancey (d. 1434) and his wife (d. 1422) in the Oratorian church of Dijon (J. Guibert, *Les dessins d'archéologie de Roger de Gaignières* (Paris, n.d.), plate I, 576).

35. Metropolitan Museum, New York: J. Breck, *Bull. of the Metropolitan Museum of Art*, XXIV (1929), 213; Musée du Louvre, Paris: Cat. Aubert, Paris, no. 266; Cat. Vienna Exhib. 1962, no. 405; Cat. Baltimore Exhib. 1962, no. 95.

36. L. Bégule, *L'église Saint-Maurice de Vienne* (Lyon, 1914).

37. *Fondation Eugène Piot, Monuments et Mémoires*, X (1903), 178; Fr. Abbad Rios, *Catálogo monumental de España: Zaragoza* (Madrid, 1957), 64, figures 143–4. Cf. the silver reliquary bust of St Gauderic, partly enamelled, of c. 1400 by Pierre Boucaut, Toulouse, church of Fanjeaux, Aude: Cat. Exhib. 'Trésors d'orfevrerie' (Montpellier, Musée Fabre, 1954), no. 20.

38. Cat. Aubert, Paris, nos. 223–4. Cf. P. Pradel, p. 18 'Les tombeaux de Charles V', *Bull. Monumental*, CIX (1951), 273, and *Actes du XVIIme Congrès International d'Histoire de l'Art* (La Haye, 1955), 257.

39. Cat. Aubert, Paris, nos. 220–1; L. Stone, *Sculpture in Britain: The Middle Ages* (Pelican History of Art) (Harmondsworth, 1955), 192.

40. F. de Fossa, *Le château de Vincennes* (Paris, p. 19 1929).

41. Cat. Aubert, Paris, nos. 281–2; Cat. Vienna Exhib. 1962, nos. 365–6.

42. L. Régnier, *L'église Notre-Dame d'Écouis* (Paris, 1913), 163; Cat. Paris Exhib. 1950, no. 171.

43. Cat. Paris Exhib. 1937, no. 1007. p. 20

44. Chanoine Poirée, *Réunions de la Société des Beaux-Arts des Départ.*, XX (1896), 316. There is a similarity to the granite figures in the Portico of the Apostles of the church of Le Folgoët, Finistère (Brittany), after 1422; M. Pobé and J. Roubier, *Das gotische Frankreich* (Vienna and Munich, 1960), plate 94.

45. T. Müller and E. Steingräber, 'Die französische Goldemailplastik um 1400', *Münch. J. d. b. K.*, III F., V. (1954), 29; U. Middeldorf, *Gazette des Beaux-Arts*, LV–LVI (1960), 233.

46. J. Guiffrey, *Inventaires de Jean, Duc de Berry* p. 21 (Paris, 1894/6), I, 17.

47. Ivory: Seated Virgin with Child, Koechlin, no. 706, Paris, Louvre (Cat. Vienna Exhib. 1962, no. 361); Koechlin, no. 982, Baltimore, Walters Art Gallery. Silver: Seated Virgin with Child, Paris, Musée de Cluny (no. 5014, ex Soltikoff Collection).

48. M. E. J. Soil de Moriamé, *Les industries d'art* p. 22 *tournaisiennes* (Tournai, 1912), plates XXXIII–XLIII; G. Ring, 'Beiträge zur Plastik von Tournai im 15. Jahrhundert', *Belgische Kunstd.*, I (1923), 275.

49. G. Troescher, *Claus Sluter* (Freiburg im Breisgau, 1932), 43.

50. J. Destrée, 'Étude sur la sculpture brabançonne au moyen-âge', *A. S. R. Arch. de Bruxelles*, VIII (1894), 76; R. Maere, 'Le retable d'Hakendover', *Annales de l'Académie R. d'Arch. de Belgique*, LXVIII (1920), 70; D. Roggen, 'Het Retabel van Hakendover', *G.B.*, I (1934), 108. The stylistic similarity between the carving on the Hakendover altar and the figures in the monstrance (1409) in the church of St Martin at Halle is so great that I cannot subscribe to Roggen's theory that the Hakendover altar dates from as late as 1432 (cf. R. Hamann,

'Spätgotische Skulpturen der Wallfahrtskirche in Hal', *Belgische Kunstdenkmäler* (1923), 217). One should also compare the carved reliefs of the Life of the Virgin in the lower section of a retable of the late fifteenth century in St Léonard at Zoutleeuw (Léau) (cf. J. de Borchgrave d'Altena, 'Notes pour servir à l'inventaire des œuvres d'art du Brabant', *A. S. R. Arch. de Bruxelles*, XLIII/XLIV (1939/40), 249) and fragments of a Coronation of the Virgin in the Musée Curtius at Liège and of seated Prophets in the Musée du Cinquantenaire at Brussels and the Städtische Skulpturengalerie at Frankfurt. Cf. G. Troescher, *op. cit.* (Note 18), plate II; J. de Borchgrave d'Altena, 'Sculptures de vers 1400', *Bull. des Musées R. d'Art et d'Histoire Bruxelles*, 4e série, 25e année (1953), 2; J. Geisler, 'Studien zu niederländischen Bildhauern', *Wallraf-Richartz-J.*, XVIII (1956), 143; Cat. Bruges-Detroit Exhib. 1960, nos. 69–70; Cat. Louvain Exhib. 1962, no. B/113; Cat. Baltimore Exhib. 1962, no. 87.

p. 23   51. Cat. Cluny, bois, nos. 125–6.

52. Brussels: J. Geisler, in *Wallraf-Richartz-J.*, XVIII (1956), 152; Paris: Cat. Aubert, Paris, no. 368. The reliefs on the choir stalls of St Martin at Zaltbommel are characteristic of the linear clarity of Netherlandish sculpture in the early fifteenth century.

53. M. Devigne, *La sculpture mosane* (Paris-Brussels, 1932), 202; Cat. Exhib. 'Art mosan' (Liège, 1951), no. 442; Cat. Vienna Exhib. 1962, no. 479.

54. Cat. Bange, Berlin, 1, no. 3106.

55. Carrand Collection no. 1351; Gerspach, 'La Coll. Carrand', *Les Arts* (1904), figure 68; Cat. Vienna Exhib. 1962, no. 342. Recently proof has turned up of the existence as early as the fourteenth century of small Franco–South-Netherlandish boxwood sculpture related to goldsmiths' work and of a quality higher than that current among the ivory carvers. This proof is the statuette of a Virgin acquired by the Bayerisches Nationalmuseum in Munich; *Münch. J. d. b. K.*, III F., XIV (1963), 245.

p. 24   56. J. Baum, 'Eine gotische Marmormadonna', *Pantheon*, x (1932), 295; Cat. Vienna Exhib. 1962, no. 364.

57. London, Victoria and Albert Museum, no. A.17 – 1941; Cat. Vienna Exhib. 1962, no. 395. I would also mention in this connexion the boxwood Virgin with Child, no. 4440 – 1857, Victoria and Albert Museum.

58. Utrecht, Centraalmuseum, Inv. no. 6363, found during excavations in the Cathedral Square, on the site of the former church of Holy Saviour. It is the fragment of a Virgin or a female saint.

CHAPTER 3

1. For the problems connected with distinguish- p. 25 ing between earlier and later parts of the sculpture of the Portal of St Peter see W. Quincke, *Das Petersportal am Dom zu Köln* (Bonn, 1938). Cf. also O. Kletzl, 'Zur Parler-Plastik', *Wallraf-Richartz-J.*, N.F. II/III (1933/4), 109; A. Huppertz, 'Die Künstlersippe der Parler und der Kölner Dom', *Festschrift der Kölner Dom* (Cologne, 1948), 152; Cat. Exhib. 'Der Kölner Dom' (Cologne, 1956), 38–9.

2. Cat. Schnitzler, Cologne (1961), no. 99; Cat. Vienna Exhib. 1962, no. 379.

3. E. Trier, 'Die Propheten-Figuren des Kölner Rathauses', *Wallraf-Richartz-J.*, XV (1953), 79; XIX (1957), 193; Cat. Schnitzler, Cologne (1961), no. 104.

4. D. Roggen and L. Verleyen, 'De Portaalsculpturen van het Brussel'sche Stadhuis', *G.B.*, 1 (1934), 123.

5. Records prove here that carved 'forms' were used as models for the stone sculpture (E. Waldmann, *Die gotischen Skulpturen am Rathaus zu Bremen* (Strassburg, 1908), 3).

6. G. Migeon, Cat. des Bronzes et Cuivres, Mus. Nat. du Louvre (1904), no. 666; I. Geisler, *Oberrheinische Plastik um 1400* (Berlin, 1957), plate 12; Cat. Vienna Exhib. 1962, no. 362; Cat. Exhib. Coll. E. and M. Kofler-Truniger (Zürich, 1964), no. 938.

7. Cf. the boxwood statuette of a Virgin and p. 26 Child, originally from Marienbaum Abbey near Xanten, now Berlin, Deutsches Museum (Cat. Bange, Berlin, 2, no. 8016).

8. In addition there is the tympanum from the Ratskapelle (1426) in Cologne. K. Schaefer, 'Der Meister des Saarwerdengrabmals', *Wallraf-Richartz-J.*, V (1928), 1; Cat. Schnitzler, Cologne (1961), no. 101. More recently H. P. Hilger, *Der Skulpturenzyklus im Chor des Aachener Domes* (Essen, 1961).

9. Now deposited at the Focke Museum, Bremen. K. Schaefer, 'Ein Hauptwerk der böhmischen Bildhauerschule', *Cicerone*, XIV (1922), 849. A. Kutal, *České gotické sochařství 1350–1450* (Prague, 1962), 108.

p. 26   10. Paris, Bib. Nat., MS. fr. 14420, fol. 92 v. In opposition to the usual contrast of West and East, W. Paatz in his *Prolegomena zu einer Geschichte der deutschen spätgotischen Skulptur* (Heidelberg, 1956) has shown the great tangential movements and opened our eyes to more promising aspects of differentiation for a reassessment.

p. 27   11. Strasbourg: 1404 'ein künstlich Marienbild von Prag, das sollen die Junkern von Prag gemacht haben' (O. Kletzl, *Die Junker von Prag* (Frankfurt, 1936), 12).

12. R. Wallrath, 'Zwei Rheinische "Schöne Madonnen"', *J. d. kölnischen Geschichtsvereins*, XXI (1939), 256; cf. H. P. Hilger, *op. cit.*, 112; P. Bloch, *Kölner Madonnen* (Mönchen Gladbach, 1961), 25, etc.

13. An example of this is the carved, over-life-size virgin in the Hospital at Hollogne-sur-Geer; M. Laurent, 'Claes Sluter et la sculpture brabançonne', *XXXe Congrès de la Fédération arch. et historique de Belgique, J.* (Brussels, 1936), 263.

14. In this church there is also a stone Pietà of the Bohemian type (*De Monumenten van Geschiedenis en Kunst in de Provincie Limburg*, I, 4 (1938), 534, 532 resp., I, 3 (1935), 436).

15. V. Thorlacius-Ussing, '"Bertram"-Kunst in Schweden und Dänemark um 1400', *Resumés des communications présentées au XIIIe congrès international d'histoire de l'art* (Stockholm, 1933), 79; J. C. Jensen, 'Über die Bildschnitzkunst von Meister Bertram', *Der Wagen, Lübeckisches J.* (1957), 45.

28   16. B. Martens, *Meister Francke* (Hamburg, 1929) (rev. G. Graf Vitzthum, in *Repertorium f. Kunstw.*, LI (1930), 247). Altar reliefs such as those at Schledehausen near Osnabrück prove how the new painting in the style of Master Francke influenced Westphalian and Lower Saxon sculpture (V. C. Habicht, in *Z. f. bildende Kunst*, N.F. XXVI (1914/15), 231).

17. Cat. Demmler, Berlin, 56, nos. 7632–45, 8408.

18. W. Paatz, *Die lübeckische Steinskulptur der ersten Hälfte des 15. Jahrhunderts* (Lübeck, 1929), 67; *idem, Prolegomena zu einer Geschichte der deutschen spätgotischen Plastik* (Heidelberg, 1956), 42.

19. D. P. R. A. Bouvy, *Middeleeuwensche Beeldhouwkunst in de Noordelijke Nederlanden* (Amsterdam, 1957), plate 52.

20. W. Paatz, *op. cit.* (1929), no. 29; Cat. Vienna Exhib. 1962, no. 381. No doubt on account of a crack in the material, the bust of Queen Margaret

was separated from the figure while it was being made and replaced by a piece joined on. The original piece is still extant at Lübeck in the St Annenmuseum (Lübeck, St Annen-Museum, M. Hasse, *Die sakralen Werke* (1964), no. 21).

21. W. Paatz, 'Münster, Bremen und Lübeck', *Festschrift Martin Wackernagel* (Cologne, 1958), 80.

p. 29   22. A. Lindblom, *Den heliga Birgitta* (Stockholm, 1918), 19; *Vägledning, Vadstena Klosterkyrka* (Stockholm, 1949), 25.

23. It seems to me to be impossible that these two works could, as Sten Karling suggests (*Medeltida träskulptur i Estland* (Stockholm, 1946), 109), date from as late as 1460. As regards the style, I would remind readers of the head of the Man of Sorrows (1429) by Multscher in Ulm Cathedral. For the same reason they cannot in my opinion be ascribed to Clawes Sittow (a native of Mecklenburg), active at Tallinn from 1454, especially not if the latter was responsible for the Annenaltar (1460–70) originally in the Pühalepa church, Hiiumaa (Dagö), now in the Tallinn Museum of Art.

24. W. Paatz, 'Eine nordwestdeutsche Gruppe von frühen flandrischen Schnitzaltären', *Westfalen*, XXI (1936), 49; I. Achter, *J. d. Rheinisches Denkmalpflege*, XXIII (1960), 212.

p. 30   25. Cat. von der Osten, Hanover, 74, no. 62.

26. Cat. Demmler, Berlin, 54, no. 5863B; Cat. Maedebach, Berlin, 33, no. 18.

27. Cat. Demmler, Berlin, 61, no. 7946; K. Gerstenberg, 'Zur niederländischen Skulptur des 15. Jahrhunderts', *Oudheidkundig J.*, III (1934), 12. H. P. Hilger, *op. cit.* (Note 8), 106, refers to the important date 1415 on a bell in the Überwasser church at Münster on which a Virgin is represented anticipating the type which a little later is supposed to have been characteristic of Utrecht.

28. K. Wilhelm-Kästner, 'Gnadenstuhl und Madonna als Doppelfigur', *Festschrift M. Wackernagel* (Cologne, 1958), 82.

29. A. Feulner, 'Der Bildhauer Madern Gerthner', *Z. d. deutschen Vereins f. Kunstw.*, VII (1940), 1. Cf. the plans for a Holy Sepulchre and tabernacle ascribed to Madern Gerthner in the Kupferstichkabinett, Berlin (R. Wallrath, in *J. d. P. Kunsts.*, LXIV (1943), 73; Cat. Vienna Exhib. 1962, no. 268); F. W. Fischer, *Die spätgotische Kirchenbaukunst am Mittelrhein* (Heidelberg, 1962), 23, 26, 27.

p. 31   30. The tomb of Werner Weiss (d. 1395) provides an incunabulum of a Fair Virgin. Cf. the

'Madonna della Pace' of 1394 by Hans von Fernach in S. Petronio, Bologna (H. Siebenhüner, *Deutsche Künstler am Mailänder Dom* (Munich, 1944), 48).

p. 31   31. Most similar is the Veronese-looking fresco of 1417 in the fourth arcade of the cathedral cloisters at Brixen (Bressanone). This type is rooted in the supranational style of illuminated manuscripts of *c.* 1400.

32. W. Paatz, *op. cit.* (Note 10), 57: Zuschreibung an Niklas Eseler. Cf. F. W. Fischer, *op. cit.* (Note 29), 89.

33. F. Back, *Ein Jahrtausend künstlerischer Kultur am Mittelrhein* (Darmstadt, 1932), 83.

34. E. Zimmermann-Deissler, 'Vier Meister mittelrheinischer Plastik um 1400', *Städel-J.*, III/IV (1924), 9. A limewood Death of the Virgin formerly in the collection of Ottmar Strauss, Cologne (sale Hugo Helbing, Frankfurt, 1934, cat. no. 31), is also believed to come from Oberwesel (I. Futterer, *Oberrheinische Kunst*, IV (1928), 51).

p. 32   35. Schnütgen Museum, Cologne: Cat. Exhib. 'Grosse Kunst des Mittelalters aus Privatbesitz' (Cologne, 1960), no. 45; Cat. Schnitzler, Cologne, 1961, no. 88; Cat. Vienna Exhib. 1962, no. 378.

36. L. Kalinowski, 'Geneza piety średniowieczny', *Polska Ak., Prace Kom. Inst. sztuki*, X (Cracow, 1952), 152; H. Eickel, 'Zur Marienklage aus Unna', *Westfalen*, XXXII (1954), 66; M. Meiss, 'The Madonna of Humility', *Art Bull.*, XVIII (1936), 435; Cat. Vienna Exhib. 1962, no. 390.

37. A. Schädler ('Zum Werk des Meisters der Lorcher Kreuztragung', *Münch. J. d. b. K.*, III F. V. (1954), 80) has convincingly disproved the date 1404 for the Lorch group which was supposed to be founded on documents. Cat. Vienna Exhib. 1962, no. 391.

38. Cat. Vienna Exhib. 1962, no. 382.

p. 33   39. J. Hattemer, 'Zur gotischen Tonplastik am Mittelrhein', *Festgabe G. Lenhart* (Mainz, 1939), 101.

40. E.g. in the parish church of Steinheim, Prov. Starkenburg (Cat. Darmstadt Exhib. 1927, no.111); and in the parish church of Marienthal near Haguenau in Alsace (I. Geisler, *op. cit.* (Note 6), Cat. II, no. 31).

41. W. Pinder, *Mittelalterliche Plastik Würzburgs* (Leipzig, 1924), 129–41.

42. *Kunstd. Bayerns, Unterfranken*, XIX, *Aschaffenburg* (Munich, 1918), 107; Cat. Vienna Exhib. 1962, no. 344.

43. Cat. Josephi, Nuremberg, no. 93; Cat. Vienna Exhib. 1962, no. 398.

44. T. Müller, in *Repertorium f. Kunstw.*, LI (1930), p. 3 196.

45. G. André, 'Der Meister der "Schönen Maria" in der Sebalduskirche zu Nürnberg', *Z. f. bildende Kunst*, LXIV (1930/1), 167.

46. *Kunstd. in Württemberg, Oberamt Künzelsau* (1962), 335. Cf. in St Sebald, Nuremberg, the bronze font with figures of apostles (F. Kriegbaum, *Nürnberg* (Munich, 1961), plate 33). Earlier examples of this sculpture in bronze dating from about 1400 are the figure from the fountain from the Hospital of the Holy Ghost and an effigy of a woman from the Unschlitthaus in the Germanisches Museum, Nuremberg (Cat. Vienna Exhib. 1962, nos 396–7).

47. Cat. Exhib. 'Nürnberger Malerei, 1350–1450' (Nuremberg, Germanisches Museum, 1931), no. 51.

48. Cf. on the following the plates in H. Kunze, *Die gotische Skulptur in Mitteldeutschland* (Bonn, 1925), and Overmann, *Die Kunstdenkmäler der Stadt Erfurt* (Erfurt, 1911).

49. K. Gerstenberg, *Conrad von Einbeck* (Halle, p. 3 n.d.).

50. Drawings, originally belonging together, in the University Library at Erlangen and in the Anhalt Library at Dessau. The inscription dates probably from the sixteenth century, but is none the less significant for that. The title 'Junker von Prag' is probably the title of honour given to the Parlers in Prague. O. Kletzl, *Titel und Namen von Baumeistern deutscher Gotik* (Munich, 1935), 44; O. Kletzl, *op. cit.* (Note 11), 26; Cat. Exhib. German Drawings, U.S.A., 1955–6, no. 1; Cat. Vienna Exhib. 1962, no. 244; R. W. Scheller, *A Survey of Medieval Model Books* (Haarlem, 1963), 120.

51. A. Herrmann, *Das Ulmer Münster* (Stuttgart, 1950), 11.

52. Related also is the beautiful monument of p. Count Konrad von Kirchberg (d. 1417) in the abbey church of Wiblingen near Ulm (J. Baum, *Gotische Bildwerke Schwabens* (Augsburg, 1921), plate 122).

53. Württembergisches Landesmuseum, Stuttgart, Cat. Baum, no. 40; Cat. Vienna Exhib. 1962, no. 430. T. Musper, *Gotische Malerei nördlich der Alpen* (Cologne, 1961), 79, dates this 'about 1400'. Related to the carvings of the Dornstadt altar are

e.g. the Virgins of the Misericord from Herlaz-hofen near Leutkirch, now in the Suermondt-museum, Aachen, and from Gösslingen, now in the Lorenz-Kapelle at Rottweil; cf. G. Otto, *Die Ulmer Plastik des frühen 15. Jahrhunderts* (Tübingen, 1924).

54. A. Legner, *Bildwerke aus dem Liebighaus, Frankfurt* (1962), plate 26. Cf. Pietà, clay, Schloss Öttingen (*Kunstd. Bayerns, Schwaben*, I, *Landkreis Nördlingen* (Munich, 1958), plate 506).

55. V. Beyer, *Rev. des Arts*, IX (1959), 27; Cat. Vienna Exhib. 1962, no. 423.

56. H. Christ, 'Ein Statuetten-Zyklus auf dem Turme des Strassburger Münsters', *Monatshefte f. Kunstw.*, VII (1914), 283.

p. 37   57. I. Futterer, *Gotische Bildwerke der deutschen Schweiz 1220–1440* (Augsburg, 1930), nos 213–19.

58. References in I. Geisler, *op. cit.* (Note 6); Cat. Vienna Exhib. 1962, no. 400.

59. I. Futterer, *op. cit.*, 184, no. 167; H. Reiners, *Burgundisch-Alemannische Plastik* (Strasbourg, 1943), plate 110.

p. 38   60. References in J. Baum, *op. cit.*; Cat. Demmler, Berlin, 84, no. 5556.

61. L. Schürenberg, 'Der kreuztragende Christus im Freiburger Münster', *Oberrheinische Kunst*, VII (1936), 104.

62. Cat. Demmler, Berlin, 69, no. 2185; G. Lill, in *Pantheon*, XVI (1935), 404.

63. Alte Pinakothek, Munich, Cat. II (Munich, 1963), 126 (no. 12426); K. Martin, *Neue Beiträge zur Archäologie und Kunstgeschichte Schwabens, J. Baum gewidmet* (Stuttgart, 1952), 74.

64. *Kunstd. Bayerns, Mittelfranken*, I, *Stadt Eich-stätt* (Munich, 1924), 49, 85, 266.

65. *Geschichte der bildenden Kunst in Wien*, II (1955), 68; K. Ginhart, 'Die gotische Plastik in Wien'.

66. V. Kotrba, 'Kaple svatováclavská v pražske katedrále', *Umĕni*, VIII (1960), 329.

67. A. Kutal, *op. cit.* (Note 9); J. Pešina and J. Homolka, 'K problematice európskeho umĕni kolem roku 1400', *Umĕni*, XI (1963), 161; J. Ho-molka, 'K problematice čcské plastiky 1350–1450', *Umĕni*, XI (1963), 414.

68. W. Pinder, 'Zum Problem der "Schönen Madonnen" um 1400', *J. d. P. Kunsts.*, XLIV (1923), 148; F. Kieslinger, 'Österreichs frühgotische Madonnenstatuen', *J. d. österreichischen Leo-Gesell-schaft* (1932), 180; A. Feulner, 'Der Meister der Schönen Madonnen', *Z. d. Deutschen Vereins f. Kunstw.*, X (1943), 19; K. H. Clasen, *Die Schönen Madonnen* (Königstein i.T., 1951); M. S. Frinta, 'A Master Bust by the Master of Beautiful Madonnas', *The Art Quarterly* (1960), 36.

69. A. Six, 'Die monumentale Plastik der Prager   p. 39
Dombauhütte', *Kunstg. J. d. Zentralkommission Wien*, II (1908), 69; J. Opitz, *Plastik Böhmens zur Zeit der Luxemburger* (Prague, 1936); A. Matĕjček, 'Gotická Plastika v chrámu Sv. Víta v Praze', *Umĕni*, II (1954), 1.

70. R. Ernst and E. Garger, *Die früh- und hoch-gotische Plastik des Stefansdoms* (Munich, 1927).

71. T. Müller, 'Die Madonna vom Sonntags-berg', *Pantheon* (1940), 1; Cat. Vienna Exhib. 1962, no. 433.

72. O. Demus, 'Der Meister der Michaeler Plastiken', *Österreichische Z. f. K. und Denkmal-pflege*, VII (1953), 1; A. Kosegarten, 'Die Chor-statuen der Kirche Maria am Gestade in Wien', *Österreichische Z. f. K. und Denkmalpflege*, XVII (1963), 1.

73. A. Kosegarten, *Plastik am Wiener Stephans-dom unter Rudolf dem Stifter*, Diss. (Freiburg i. Br., 1960).

74. Cat. Vienna Exhib. 1962, no. 436.

75. A. Kutal, 'K problému horinzontálnich Piet', *Umĕni*, XI (1963), 321.

76. W. Körte, 'Deutsche Vesperbilder in Italien', *Kunstg. J. d. Bibliotheca Hertziana*, I (1937), 1; A. Kutal, 'Le "Belle" pietà italiane', *Boll. dell'Istituto storico čescoslovacco*, II (Prague, 1946), 5; W. Krönig, in *Wallraf-Richartz-J.*, XXIV (1962), 106, note 39.

77. The Vierge au Croissant from the Livre de Prières of Philip the Bold in the Bibliothèque Royal, Brussels (F. Lyna, *Mélanges Hulin de Loo* (Brussels, 1931), plate XXXII) is the most beautiful example of the idealization of the Virgin in contemporary Netherlandish art.

78. V. Denkstein and F. Matouš, *Südböhmische Gotik* (Prague, 1955), plates 56, 58, 72; A. Kutal, *op. cit.*, plates 127, 128, 130, 131.

79. R. Ernst, 'Die Krumauer Madonna', *J. d.*   p. 40
Kunsth. Institutes der Zentralkommission f. Denkmal-pflege Wien, XI (1917), 109; A. Kutal, 'O Mistru Krumlovské Madony', *Umĕni*, V (1957), 29; D. Grossmann, 'Die Schöne Madonna von Krumau und Österreich', *Österreichische Z. f. K. und Denk-malpflege*, XIV (1960), 103; Cat. Vienna Exhib. 1962, no. 424; Kunsthistorisches Museum Wien, *Kat.*

d. Sammlung f. Plastik und Kunstgewerbe, I (1964), 155.

p. 40   80. T. Müller, *Mittelalterliche Plastik Tirols* (Berlin, 1935), 77. Cf. R. W. Scheller, *op. cit.* (Note 50), 104. The beautiful Virgin at Marienberg preserves its original colouring, in a harmonious chord of white, gold, red, and blue, and is perhaps just a little precious. The figure allows one to experience the sublimated concordance of colour with forms which the Krumau Virgin must also originally have possessed.

81. L. A. Springer, *Die bayrisch-österreichische Steingussplastik der Wende vom 14. zum 15. Jahrhundert* (Würzburg, 1936); K. Rossacher, 'Technik und Materialien der Steingussplastik um 1400', *Z. Alte und moderne Kunst* (1964), 2.

82. E. Wiese, *Schlesische Plastik* (Leipzig, 1923), 39.

83. K. Garzarolli von Thurnlackh, *Mittelalterliche Plastik in Steiermark* (Graz, 1941), 31; D. Grossmann, *loc. cit.* (Note 79), 110.

84. I am indebted to Dr Hönigschmid for drawing my attention to these important references: V. Schmidt and A. Picha, *Urkundenbuch der Stadt Krummau,* I (Prague, 1908), nos 478/9.

85. T. Müller, *Pantheon,* XXXI (1943), 113; H. Wentzel, in *J. d. Berliner Museen,* II (1960), 71. The alabaster statuette is in elevation, as it were, much like the silver statuette of a Fair Virgin from Salzburg, now in the Carrand Collection, Florence; Cat. Vienna Exhib. 1962, no. 343.

p. 41   86. Cat. Demmler, Berlin, 79, no. 2743; Cat. Vienna Exhib. 1962, nos. 403, 422; Cat. Halm-Lill, Munich, no. 156; Cat. Vienna Exhib. 1962, no. 412; K. Garzarolli von Thurnlackh, *op. cit.,* plates 29, 43, 30. The exhibition of 1962 in Vienna proved that, in spite of careful investigations, a really comprehensive catalogue of Austrian and Bohemian sculpture in stone and cast stone, including all indications of what must be original and what may be replicas, is still badly needed.

87. Orszagos Szépmüvészéti Muzeum: J. Balogh, *A Régi Szoborosztály, Kiállitása* (Budapest, 1956), 23, plate 26. Surely not from Amiens! A. Kutal, 'La "Belle Madone" de Budapest', *Bull. du Musée Hongrois des Beaux-Arts,* XXIII (1963), 21.

88. Cat. Vienna Exhib. 1962, no. 343. The portrait of Archduke Ernst der Eiserne, kneeling in front of a Fair Virgin, as it appears in an illuminated manuscript of *c.* 1415 (by Heinrich Aurhaym, from

Rein in Styria, now Vienna, Österreichische Nationalbibliothek: K. Oettinger, in *Festschrift für A. Goldschmidt* (1935), 57; Cat. Vienna Exhib. 1962, no. 190), proves that these Fair Virgins, also in the way they were worshipped, were individual pieces, not just a universally accepted type.

89. E. Kris, 'Über eine gotische Georgs-Statue und ihre nächsten Verwandten', *J. d. Kunsth. Sammlungen in Wien,* N.F. IV (1930), 121; K. Garzarolli von Thurnlackh, *op. cit.,* plates 30, 31, 36, 40; Cat. Vienna Exhib. 1962, nos 383–6, 407.

90. E. Cevc, *L'art du moyen-âge en Slovenie* (Ljubljana, 1956); *idem, Srednjeveška Plastika na Slovenskem* (Ljubljana, 1963).

91. V. Roth, *Die deutsche Kunst in Siebenbürgen* (Berlin, 1934), plates 123–5: Sibiu (Hermannstadt), Brukenthal Museum, Pietà from the parish church; plates 127–8: Sibiu, Chapel of the Holy Cross, stone Crucifixion of Master 'Petrus Lantregen von oestreich' of 1417.

92. See note 76. The finest of these replicas in Italy seem to be the stucco Pietàs in the Museo Nazionale in Florence (from Friuli) and formerly in the Deutsches Museum in Berlin (Cat. Demmler, Berlin, 81). On the export of Pietàs to Spain, see G. Weise, *Spanische Plastik aus sieben Jahrhunderten,* I (Reutlingen, 1925), 42 (examples at Toledo and Valladolid).

93. Cat. Exhib. Gotische Plastik (Düsseldorf, 1929), no. 52.

94. Cat. Paris Exhib. 1957, nos. 177–81, 185, 187, 188.

95. A. Kutal, 'Madona ve Sternberku a jeji mistr', *Uměni,* V (1957), 111.

96. A. Liška, 'Gotická Parallela', *Uměni,* V (1957), 151.

97. Musée National de Varsovie (1963), figure 75.

98. *Sprawozdania Komisyi Historji Sztuki* (Cra-   p. 4 cow, 1906), 152; E. Behrens, in *Z. d. Deutschen Vereins f. Kunstw.,* X (1943), 49.

99. The losses of works of art at the end of the Second World War are here particularly sad and painful. See D. Kaczmarzyk, *Straty wojenne polski w dziedzinie Rzeżby* (Warsaw, 1958).

100. K. H. Clasen, *Die mittelalterliche Bildhauerkunst im Deutschordensland Preussen* (Berlin, 1939), 350.

101. F. Rademacher, 'Die "Schöne Madonna" im Bonner Landesmuseum', *Pantheon,* XVII (1936),

14; Cat. Rheinisches Landesmuseum Bonn, 1963, no. 113.

102. G. von der Osten, in *Z. d. Deutschen Vereins f. Kunstw.*, II (1935), 525.

p. 43 103. T. Müller, *Alte Bairische Bildhauer* (Munich, 1950), plates 36–42, 44–5.

104. T. Müller, *op. cit.* (1937), plate 49; *Verhandlungen des Historischen Vereins für Niederbayern*, LXXXI (Landshut, 1955), 7; A. Ress, *Studien zur Plastik der Martinskirche in Landshut*, LXXXIV (1958), 5; T. Herzog, 'Meister Hanns von Burghausen', *ebenda*, LXXXIV (1958).

105. This is true also of wooden figures such as the fine St George in the Bayerisches Nationalmuseum, Munich (Cat. Halm-Lill, no. 228; Cat. Vienna Exhib. 1962, no. 334).

106. P. M. Halm, *Studien zur süddeutschen Plastik* (Augsburg, 1926–7), I, 1–65; Cat. Halm-Lill, Munich, no. 210.

p. 44 107. T. Müller, *op. cit.* (1950), plate 48.

108. Cat. Halm-Lill, Munich, no. 158; T. Müller, *op. cit.* (1950), plates 58–61; H. K. Ramisch, in *Mitteilungen der Gesellschaft für Salzburger Landeskunde*, CIV (1964), 23.

109. Cat. Vienna Exhib. 1962, no. 411. The seated Bishop of wood in the Germanisches Museum, Nuremberg (cf. T. Müller, in *Anzeiger des Germanischen Museums Nürnberg* (1928/9), 71), is in my opinion an earlier work by the Master of the Irrsdorf Doors.

110. T. Müller, *op. cit.* (1935), 61.

111. The altarpiece was brought from the Neukloster in Wiener-Neustadt to St Stephen. Cf. K. Ginhart, *Die gotische Plastik in Wien* (Vienna, 1955), 105.

112. Cat. Exhib. Arte Medioevale nell'Alto Adige (Bolzano, 1949), 23, nos 44–6; Cat. Exhib. Innsbruck 1950, nos. 35–6; T. Müller, 'Die Marienkrönung aus Tschengels im Germanischen Nationalmuseum', *Anzeiger d. German. Nationalmuseums* (1963), 45. The relationship of the reliefs from the high altar at Bozen (at Deutschnofen, in the Bayerisches Nationalmuseum, Munich, and in the Museum of Decorative Art, Zagreb) to the Marian reliefs in the Ursulinenkirche at Bruneck (cf. T. Müller, *op. cit.* (1935), 79) is still not clear.

113. T. Müller, *Frühe Beispiele der Retrospektive in der deutschen Plastik* (Munich, 1961), 10.

114. N. Rasmo, 'Il crocifisso ligneo di S. Giorgio Maggiore a Venezia', *Festschrift K. M. Swoboda* (Vienna, 1959), 237.

115. W. Lotz, in *Kunsth. Institut Florenz, Jahresbericht 1939/40, Deutsche Kunstwerke in Italien*, III. p. 45 A similar mixture of styles appears in the Mourning of Christ in the cathedral of Trieste (D. Westphal, in *A. Goldschmidt zu seinem 70. Geburtstag* (Berlin, 1935), 64).

116. A. Kampis, *A Közepkori magyar faszobrászat történetének vázlata 1450–ig* (Budapest, 1932); K. Šourek, *Umění na Slovensku* (Prague, 1938), plates 373–9, 391–5.

117. Kopéra-Kwiatkowski, *Rzeźby z epoki średniowiecza i odrodzenia w Muzeum Narodowem w Krakowie* (1931), nos 9–10, 11–12.

118. See E. Wiese, *Schlesische Plastik vom Beginn des 14. bis zur Mitte des 15. Jahrhunderts* (Leipzig, 1923), and H. Braune and E. Wiese, *Schlesische Malerei und Plastik des Mittelalters* (Leipzig, 1929).

119. J. Dutkiewicz, *Małopolska rzeźba średniowieczna 1300–1450* (Cracow, 1949). For the traditional representation of the Calvary in the fourteenth century in Bohemia cf. A. Kutal, 'Krucifix z Klaštera Barnabitek na Hradčanech', *Umění*, I (1953), 115.

120. H. Braune and E. Wiese, *op. cit.*, nos. 55 ff.; Cat. Demmler, Berlin, 78, no. 8032; Cat. Maedebach, Berlin, no. 19.

121. E. Hintze and K. Masner, *Goldschmiedearbeiten Schlesiens* (Breslau, 1911), plate IV; H. Kohlhaussen, *Geschichte des deutschen Kunsthandwerks* (Munich, 1955), figure 181; Musée Nationale de Varsovie (1963), figure 151.

122. J. Sarrèk, *Iconographie Mariale* (Lezignan, p. 46 1913); W. Fries, *Anzeiger des Germanischen Museums Nürnberg* (1928/9), 11.

123. K. H. Clasen, *op. cit.*, 216, 224.

124. S. Karling, *op. cit.* (Note 23).

125. W. Paatz, *op. cit.* (1929; Note 18), no. 32. The family of donors called Junge is not related to the Lübeck sculptor Johannes Junge. I also do not believe that the retable at Stralsund by Junge originated in the Lübeck workshop of Johannes Junge, as Paatz, *op. cit.* (1956; Note 18), 34, suggests

126. I. Rácz and R. Pylkkânen, *Art Treasuries of Medieval Finland* (Helsinki, 1960), figure 235.

CHAPTER 4

p. 47   1. Cat. Aubert, Paris, nos. 281, 282; Cat. Vienna Exhib. 1962, nos. 365–6.

2. Cat. Aubert, Paris, nos. 283, 284.

3. M. Vloberg, *La vierge et l'enfant dans l'art français* (Paris-Grenoble, 1954), illustrations on pp. 90, 78, 138, 256, 221, 160.

p. 48   4. R. Krautheimer, *Lorenzo Ghiberti* (Princeton, 1956), 79, note 33; W. Paatz, 'Zur Herkunft des Typus der "Schönen Madonnen"', *Festschrift Kurt Bauch* (Munich, 1957), 130.

5. The somewhat lustreless stone figure of a Fair Virgin in the Louvre (Cat. Aubert, Paris, no. 331) is called Burgundian and was called this still at the Vienna Exhibition of 1962 (Cat. no. 339). I think there can be no doubt that it is of Salzburg origin.

6. Cat. Paris Exhib. 1950, no. 180.

7. Cat. Aubert, Paris, nos. 274, 359 (from Ermingen, Mosel).

8. Cat. Aubert, Paris, no. 362. Cf. H. D. Hofmann, in *A. Universitatis Saraviensis, Philos. Fakultät*, VIII, fasc. 4 (1959), 299, and in *idem, Die Lothringische Skulptur der Spätgotik* (Saarwerden, 1962), 69–89.

9. J. Geisler, *Oberrheinische Plastik um 1400* (Berlin, 1957), 29; Cat. Beyer, Strasbourg, no. 258.

10. Cat. Aubert, Paris, no. 394; H. D. Hofmann, *op. cit.* (1962), 412, no. 487; before the middle of the fifteenth century and not the beginning of the sixteenth. S. Hausmann, *Monuments d'art de la Lorraine* (Strasbourg, n.d.), no. 25; H. D. Hofmann, *op. cit.*, 397, no. 321.

p. 49   11. E.g. the Virgin in the Metropolitan Museum, New York, and that at Bussy-la-Pesle are replicas of the Virgin on the portal of Champmol; G. Troescher, *Claus Sluter* (Freiburg, 1932), plate XXI, and *idem, Die burgundische Plastik des ausgehenden Mittelalters* (Frankfurt, 1940), figure 272.

12. G. Troescher, *op. cit.* (1932), 62; K. Gerstenberg, 'Zur niederländischen Skulptur des 15. Jh.', *Oudheikundig J.*, III (1934), 12; cf. plate 6 in H. Wentzel, *J. d. Berliner Museen*, II (1960), 65.

13. Cat. Dijon Exhib. 1949, nos. 13–15; *Claus Sluter en de Kunst te Dijon* (Rotterdam, 1950), no. 16.

14. G. Troescher, *op. cit.* (1932), plates VI, XX, and in *idem, op. cit.* (1940), 104.

15. J. A. Schmoll, 'Die Burgundische Madonna des Hamburger Museums und ihre Stellung in der Sluter-Nachfolge', *J. d. Hamburger Kunsts.*, VI (1961), 7.

16. G. Troescher, *op. cit.* (1932; Note 11), plate V.

17. Cat. Aubert, Paris, no. 332 (in the list of p. 50 plates in the catalogue, the captions of nos. 332 and 333 are transposed).

18. Cat. Aubert, Paris, no. 333.

19. Cat. Cluny, pierre, no. 301.

20. G. Troescher, *op. cit.* (1940; Note 11), figures 334–5.

21. J. Rorimer, *Bull. of the Metropolitan Museum of Art*, XXIX (1934), 192.

22. Cat. Aubert, Paris, no. 356. I think the figure is older than the work by Le Moiturier, to whom it is ascribed.

23. G. Troescher, *op. cit.* (1940; Note 11), 103, 104, 111, 119, 120, 139.

24. G. Troescher, *op. cit.*, 103.   p. 51

25. Cat. Aubert, Paris, no. 368; height, 32 ins. (82 cm.). See Chapter 2, Note 52.

26. Dijon, Musée: Abbot (Cat. Grangier Collection, Dijon, no. 92; companion piece to the St Stephen in the Louvre, Cat. Exhib. 'Claus Sluter' (Rotterdam, 1950), no. 19); Dijon, Quioc Collection: St Peter (belonging with the statuettes from Theuley near Langres, in the Louvre); Munich, J. Böhler Collection: Apostle with Book (Cat. Vienna Exhib. 1962, no. 340) (Plate 17c); Munich, private collection: St Judas Thaddeus; Paris, Louvre: Prophet, Deacon, and St Stephen, originally from the Cistercian abbey of Theuley near Langres (Cat. Aubert, Paris, nos. 341–3); Paris, Musée de Cluny: St Geneviève (Cat. Cluny, bois, no. 20, from Notre-Dame at Poissy, Seine-et-Oise); Paris, private collection: Apostle with Book, originally from a château near Épernay; Zürich, Bührle Collection: Annunciation (*Festschrift des Kunsthauses Zürich* (1958), 48, no. 27) (Plate 17B). Average height: 15–20 ins.

27. Cf. on the following especially M. de Bevotte, *La sculpture dans la région de Toulouse, d'Albi et de Rodez* (Paris, 1936).

28. Cf. the stone figure of an enthroned Maria Lactans in Notre-Dame-du-Port, Clermont-Ferrand (M. Vloberg, *op. cit.* (Note 3), 75).

29. K. Gerstenberg, 'Die niederländische Plastik p. 52 des 15. Jahrhunderts in ihrer europäischen Auswirkung', *XIIIe Congrès International d'Histoire de*

l'Art, Actes (Stockholm, 1933), 164; D. Roggen, *G.B.*, XIII (1951), 199; XVI (1955/6), 149. Cf. otherwise on what follows J. Ainaud de Lasarte and A. Duran Sanpere, *Escultura gótica (Ars Hispaniae*, VIII) (Madrid, 1956).

30. Cf. R. dos Santos, *A escultura em Portugal*, 2 vols (Lisbon, 1948, 1950).

31. Cf. stone figures on the Puerta del Marte at Palma de Mallorca (1422); D. Roggen, *G.B.*, XVI (1955–6), 153, figure 24.

p. 53   32. Cat. Vienna Exhib. 1962, no. 421.

p. 54   33. Abbad Rios, *Catálogo monumental de España: Zaragoza* (Madrid, 1957), 61, 109–14.

34. A. Schmarsow, 'Juliano Florentino', *Abhandlungen d. philolog.-histor. Klasse d. Sächsischen Gesellschaft d. Wissenschaften*, XXIX, no. III (1911). Of course, there is in my opinion no question of a connexion between Giuliano Fiorentino and Ghiberti's work. Cf. J. Ainaud de Lasarte and A. Duran Sanpere, *op. cit.*, 297.

35. H. David, 'Quelques artistes méridionaux en Bourgogne', *A. du Midi*, XLVII (1935), 329; D. Roggen, 'Postsluteriaanse Sculptuur', *G.B.*, XVI (1955/6), 151; P. Quarré, *La chartreuse de Champmol* (Dijon, 1960), 16.

p. 55   36. L. Courajod, in *Gazette Archéologique*, 10e année (1885), 236; H. Drouot, 'Jacques Morel et l'école de Dijon', *A. de Bourgogne*, II (1930); H. David, *loc. cit.*, 355, and *A. de Bourgogne*, II (1930), 254; F. Deshouilières, *Souvigny et Bourbon-l'Archambault* (Paris, 1935), 52; J. Thuile, 'Une œuvre de Jacques Maurel', *Bull. Monumental*, CXIV (1956), 181. Thuile explains the initials I.M. on the base of a stone figure of St Anthony in the church of Charny (Côte d'Or) as being Morel's signature.

37. Kleinclausz, 'L'art bourguignon dans la vallée du Rhône', *A. de Bourgogne*, I (1929), 23.

38. Bosseboeuf, 'Le tombeau d'Agnès Sorel à Loches', *Mémoires de la Société Arch. de Tours* (1900).

p. 56   39. Cat. Aubert, Paris, no. 351.

40. Cat. Dijon Exhib. 1949, nos. 31, 21.

41. C. Oursel, *L'art de Bourgogne* (Paris-Grenoble, 1953), 145.

42. *Op. cit.*, 142.

43. Cat. Aubert, Paris, no. 336.

p. 57   44. G. Troescher, *op. cit.* (1940; Note 11), 120.

45. *Bull. of the Metropolitan Museum of Art*, XXVII (1933), 74; XII (1957), 134.

46. 'Jean à la longue barbe'; H. David, *Bull. Monumental* (1928), 223; idem, *De Sluter à Sambin*, I (Paris, 1933), 18.

47. Cat. Aubert, Paris, no. 322; Exhib. Limoges p. 58 1956, no. 57.

48. H. de Man, *Jacques Cœur* (Bern, 1950).

49. In the same church is a Virgin and Child in the 'painterly' Burgundian style.

50. M. E. J. Soil de Moriamé, *Les anciennes* p. 59 *industries d'art tournaisiennes* (Tournai, 1912); G. Ring, 'Beiträge zur Plastik von Tournai im 15. Jahrhundert', in P. Clemen, *Belgische Kunstd.* (Munich, 1923), I, 275; P. Rolland, *Les primitifs tournaisiens* (Brussels-Paris, 1932); J. Warichez, *La cathédrale de Tournai*, II (Ars Belgica, II) (Brussels, 1935), nos. 24–37; P. Rolland, 'Stèles funéraires tournaisiennes gothiques', *Rev. belge*, XX (1951), 189; D. Roggen, 'Postsluteriaanse Sculptuur', *G.B.*, XVI (1955/6), 165 ff. The monumentally stylized reliefs in the typical black Tournai marble on the tomb of Pierre de Bouffremont (d. 1452) from St Bénigne at Dijon prove that the export of these tomb-lids extended from Tournai as far as Burgundy. Cf. P. Quarré, *Bull. Monumental* (1955), 103.

51. J. Borchgrave d'Altena, *Notes pour servir à l'inventaire des œuvres d'art du Brabant. Arr. de Bruxelles* (1947), 6.

52. D. Roggen, 'Gentsche Grofplastiek uit den p. 60 tijd der van Eyck', *G.B.*, IX (1943), 99.

53. At the same time King René had a painting of himself as a skeleton affixed to his tomb in Angers Cathedral. The tomb, now unfortunately destroyed, was partly by Jacques Morel.

54. J. de Borchgrave d'Altena, in *A. S. R. Arch. de Bruxelles*, XLVII (1947), plate IX.

55. P. Rolland, 'La double école de Tournai, peinture et sculpture', *Mélanges Hulin de Loo* (Brussels, 1931), 296; idem, 'Une sculpture polychrome par Campin', *Rev. belge*, II (1932). The following notes throw light upon the mutual relationship of sculpture and painting at this decisive moment. Jacques Daret lived, according to P. Rolland (*loc. cit.* (1932), 87 ff.), 'au sein d'une véritable dynastie de sculpteurs'. In 1434 he designed a retable for the Chapel of St Nicholas in a church of the same name which was to be executed by the sculptor Jean de Sandres (*loc. cit.*, 57). Jan van Eyck in 1434/5 coloured eight statues in Bruges Town Hall. Had he also designed them? Cf. A. Janssens de Bisthoven, 'Het Beeldhouwerk van het

Brugsche Stadthuis', *G.B.*, x (1944), 28. Regarding the question whether Roger van der Weyden's father Henri was a 'sculpteur' or a 'coutelier' at Tournai, see Wauters, in *Burlington Magazine*, xx/xxi (1912), and A. Hocquet, in *Rev. tournaisienne* (1913), 153. In 1458 Roger coloured the bronze figures of Jacques de Gérines, discussed later, and in 1461 the stone figures of St Philip and St Elizabeth. Cf. L. Maeterlinck, 'Roger van der Weyden, sculpteur', *Gazette des Beaux-Arts*, ii (1901), 265, 399; *idem*, in *Mémoires publiés par l'Academie de Belgique*, lx (1901); M. J. Friedländer, *Rogier van der Weyden und der Meister von Flémalle* (Leiden, 1934), 48.

p. 61   56. G. Ring, in *Z. f. bildende Kunst*, N.F. xxxiii (1922), 36. P. Rolland, 'La chapelle de Michel de Gand dans l'église Saint-Piat à Tournai', *Rev. belge*, iii (1933), 357; J. Borchgrave d'Altena, 'Des caractères de la sculpture brabançonne vers 1500', *A. S. R. Arch. de Bruxelles*, xxxviii (1934), figure 20.

57. J. Destrée, 'Étude sur la sculpture brabançonne', *A. S. R. Arch. de Bruxelles*, xiii (1899), 310; M. Devigne, in *Onze Kunst*, xxxix (1922), 49; J. Six, in *Onze Kunst*, xl (1922), 65; L. Serbal, in *Bull. Monumental*, lxxxviii (1929), 382; M. Weinberger, in *Art Bull.*, xxii (1940), 185.

p. 62   58. J. Leeuwenberg, 'De tien bronzen "Plorannen" in het Rijksmuseum te Amsterdam, hun herkomst en de Vorbeelden waaran zij zijn outleend', *G.B.*, xiii (1951), 13; R. van Luttervelt, in *Oud Holland*, lxxii (1957), 73, 139; J. Leeuwenberg, in *Oud Holland*, lxxiii (1958), 156; Cat. Bruges-Detroit Exhib. 1960, nos. 101–2 (with a survey of the whole literature).

59. J. Lestocquoy, in *Rev. belge*, vii (1937), 220.

60. *De Nederlandsche Monumenten van Geschiedenis en Kunst*, i, 1, *Noordbrabant* (Breda-Utrecht, 1912), 102.

p. 63   61. R. Hamann, 'Spätgotische Skulpturen der Wallfahrtskirche in Hal', *Belgische Kunstd.*, i (1923), 241. Cf. the rood of Willem van Goelen, Antwerp, in the church of Zoutleeuw (Léau), 1453.

62. J. de Borchgrave d'Altena, in *A. S. R. Arch. de Bruxelles*, xlvii (1947), plate xxxi.

63. J. de Borchgrave d'Altena, 'Notes pour servir à l'étude des stalles en Belgique', *A. S. R. Arch. de Bruxelles*, xli (1937), 238.

64. J. Geisler, *op. cit.* (Note 9), figure 87; D. Bouvy, *Beeldhouwkunst, Aartsbisschopelijk Museum Utrecht* (1962), no. 24.

65. J. Roosval, *Schnitzaltäre in schwedischen Kirchen und Museen aus der Werkstatt des Jan Bormann* (Strasbourg, 1903); M. Voegelen, 'Die Gruppenaltäre in Schwäbisch-Hall', *Münch. J. d. b. K.*, xiii (1923), 121; W. Paatz, 'Eine nordwestdeutsche Gruppe von frühen niederländischen Schnitzaltären', *Westfalen*, xxxi (1936), 49; *idem*, *Süddeutsche Schnitzaltäre der Spätgotik* (Heidelberg, 1963), 16.

66. G. Swarzenski, 'Deutsche Alabasterplastik des 15. Jahrhunderts', *Städel-J.*, i (1921), 379.

67. L. Stone, *Sculpture in Britain: The Middle Ages* (Pelican History of Art) (Harmondsworth, 1955), 217.

68. E. Scheyer, 'Eine Pariser Alabastergruppe um 1430', *Schlesiens Vorzeit*, N.F. x (1933), 35.

69. H. Loriquet, *Mémoires de la Commission Dép. des Monuments Historiques du Pas-de-Calais*, i (1889), 69; Hulin de Loo, 'An Authentic Work by Jacques Daret', *Burlington Magazine*, xv (1909), 202; L. Lestocquoy, 'Le rôle des artistes tournaisiens à Arras au XVe s.', *Rev. belge*, vii (1937), 211; W. Paatz, *Scritti di storia dell' arte in onore di Mario Salmi* (Rome, 1961). Cf. the alabaster statuettes in the Musée at St Omer.

70. G. Swarzenski, *Bibliothek Warburg, Vorträge 1926/7* (Leipzig, 1929), 22; R. Krautheimer, *Art Bull.*, xxix (1947), 25; Cat. Vienna Exhib. 1962, nos. 387–9.   p. 64

71. W. Körte, 'Deutsche Vesperbilder in Italien', *Kunstg. J. d. Bibliotheca Hertziana*, i (1937), 41 ff. Cf. the alabaster Pietàs in the Louvre, the Landesmuseum at Wiesbaden, the Victoria and Albert Museum (Cat. Vienna Exhib. 1962, no. 388), and the church of Oud-Zevenaar.

72. M. J. Friedländer, *Die altniederländische Malerei*, ii, *Rogier van der Weyden und der Meister von Flémalle* (Leyden, 1934), 23: 'In those days it was usual for the painter to have a knowledge of sculpture, since he would have to colour works of sculpture; it was usually incumbent upon the painter to evoke the sculpture in paintings on altar wings. That Rogier stood, as it were, on the watershed between painting and sculpture when creating his masterpiece proves much about his talent, whether or not he ever worked as a sculptor.'

73. W. Paatz, 'Stammbaum der gotischen Alabasterskulptur', *Kunstgeschichtliche Studien für Hans Kauffmann* (Berlin, 1956), 127; W. Paatz, 'Mit dem gemalten Band', *Festschrift Kurt Bauch* (Munich,

1957), 126. Cf. also H. Wentzel, in *J. d. P. Kunsts.*, N.F. II (1960), 55.

74. Cat. Vienna Exhib. 1962, no. 393.

p. 65   75. J. Mihalik, 'Die Esztergomer Kalvarie', in E. von Szalay, *Die historischen Denkmäler Ungarns* (Budapest, 1896), II, 209; S. Mihalik, *Emailkunst im alten Ungarn* (Budapest, 1961), plate 17. In my study written in conjunction with E. Steingräber for the *Münch. J. d. b. K.*, III. F.V. (1954), on French gold enamel sculpture round 1400, I referred on p. 74 to the Calvary at Esztergom as being a gift from Queen Isabel to King Sigismund in 1424. I am indebted to T. Straub for pointing out that records prove that the Esztergom Calvary cannot be identified with her gift. I should like to change my dating now to *c.* 1430.

CHAPTER 5

p. 66   1. H. P. Hilger has examined the cycle in a monograph called *Der Skulpturenzyklus im Chor des Aachener Domes* (Essen, 1961); he has distinguished the traditional and progressive elements and has shown the close connexion between the latter features and André Beauneveu's successors.

2. E. Kühnemann, *Kölner Domblatt*, VI/VII (1952), 39.

p. 67   3. The style of physiognomical characterization appears to have an echo in the reliquary bust of St Peter (dated 1473) from the hand of the Frankfurt goldsmith Hans Dirmstein in the treasury of the Stiftskirche at Aschaffenburg; *Kunstdenkmäler Bayerns, Unterfranken*, XIX: *Aschaffenburg* (Munich, 1918), 107; W. K. Zülch, *Frankfurter Künstler* (Frankfurt, 1935), 172.

4. Cf. for example the Virgin on the monument of Canon Peter Schenk von Weibstadt (d. 1437) in the Stiftskirche at Aschaffenburg; *Kunstdenkmäler Bayerns, Unterfranken*, XIX: *Aschaffenburg* (Munich, 1918), 139.

5. Exhaustively presented in the excellent study by G. André, 'Konrad Kuene und der Meister des Frankfurter Mariaschlafaltars', *Marburger J. f. Kunstw.*, XI (1938–9) [1941], 159. Cf. H. Appel, *Wallraf-Richartz-J.*, X (1938), 91. The Annunciation at St Kunibert in Cologne does not seem to me to be a work of Kuene's.

p. 68   6. A. Legner, *Kleinplastik aus dem Liebighaus* (Frankfurt, 1960), no. 25. Formerly in the Fürstlich Hohenzollernsche Collection, Sigmaringen; Cat. Sprinz, Sigmaringen, no. 64. Cf. A. Schädler,

Z. f. württembergische Landesgeschichte, XIV (1955), 418.

7. W. Passarge, *Cicerone*, 16. Jahrg. (1924), 972.

8. C. G. Heise, *Lübecker Plastik* (Bonn, 1926), plate 30.

9. W. Paatz, 'Hans Hesse, Johannes Stenrat und p. 69 ihr Kreis', *Nordelbingen*, VII (1928), 56.

10. W. Paatz, 'Der Meister der Lübeckischen Steinmadonnen', *J. d. P. Kunsts.*, XLVII (1926), 168; M. Hasse, 'Bildwerke des mittleren 15. Jahrhunderts in Lübeck und Vadstena', *Niederdeutsche Beiträge zur Kunstg.*, I (1961), 187.

11. *Bau- und Kunstdenkmäler in Sachsen*, XL (1919), 282.

12. H. Höhn, *Nürnberger gotische Plastik* (Nurem- p. 70 berg, 1922), plates 55–6; G. André, 'Der Meister der schönen Madonna in der Sebalduskirche', *Z. f. bildende Kunst*, LXIV (1930/1), 167.

13. Traces of a Netherlandish style of presentation are also visible in the groups of figures of the Altar of St Catherine (1462–4) in St Sebald at Nuremberg.

14. *Kunstdenkmäler Bayerns, Unterfranken*, XIX: *Aschaffenburg* (Munich, 1918), 137, 147; XII: *Würzburg*, 269, 69; *Pfalz*, III: *Speyer*, 280.

15. R. F. Burckhardt, *Der Basler Münsterschatz* p. 71 (Basel, 1933), no. 27.

16. J. Geisler, *Oberrheinische Plastik um 1400* (Berlin, 1957), 12.

17. Cf. H. Reiners, *Burgundisch-Alemannische Plastik* (Strasbourg, 1943).

18. H. Reiners, *Das Münster unserer Lieben Frau* p. 72 *zu Konstanz* (*Die Kunstdenkmäler Südbadens*, I) (Constance, 1955), 158, 250, 447; Cat. Exhib. 'Gotische Baurisse der Wiener Bauhütte' (Akad. d. Bild. Künste, Vienna, 1962), nos. 18–19.

19. H. Reiners and W. Ewald, *Kunstdenkmäler zwischen Maas und Mosel* (Munich, 1921), 200; M. Dumoulin, Avioth: *Congrès Archéologique de France: Nancy et Verdun, 1933* (Paris, 1934), 467.

20. C. Sommer, 'Eine oberrheinische Plastik der p. 73 "dunklen Zeit"', *Anzeiger f. schweizerische Altertumskunde*, XXXVI (1934), 55.

21. A. Schädler, 'Die Frühwerke Hans Multschers', *Z. f. Württembergische Landesgeschichte*, XIV (1955), 385.

22. The most important of these Apostles in the choir of Aachen Cathedral (dating from *c.* 1425–30), for whose style the St Matthew (Plate 76B) is

especially significant, bear on their base a stone-mason's mark (cf. K. Faymonville, *Der Dom zu Aachen* (Munich, 1909), 192; H. P. Hilger, *op. cit.* (Note 1), 124), which – surprisingly – Schädler has identified twice in the painted presentations of Multscher's Wurzach Altar. Can these (signed) statues in Aachen be early works by Multscher? I see no similarity between them and Multscher's early works in Ulm.

p. 73 23. The real portrait of the 'Bearded' Duke is to be seen in the stone relief of a tympanum in the interior of his Marienkirche at Ingolstadt. Cf. T. Müller, *Festschrift für Wilhelm Pinder* (Leipzig, 1938), 312.

p. 74 24. Cat. Müller, Munich, no. 79.

25. O. Schmitt, 'Die Grabfigur der Gräfin Mechthild von Württemberg', *Z. d. deutschen Vereins f. Kunstw.*, VIII (1941), 179.

26. Cat. Exhib. Innsbruck 1950, 65; T. Müller, 'Ein Beitrag zum Sterzinger Altar', *Festschrift für Hans Jantzen* (Berlin, 1951), 128.

p. 75 27. M. Weinberger, 'A Bronze Bust by Hans Multscher', *Art Bull.*, XXII (1940), 185.

28. *Kunstdenkmäler in Württemberg: Oberamt Künzelsau* (1962), 335.

29. M. Voegelen, in *Münch. J. d. b. K.*, XIII (1923), 156.

30. K. Oettinger, in *J. d. Kunsth. Sammlungen Wien*, N.F. VIII (1934), 56.

31. T. Müller, 'Zur monumentalen Salzburger Plastik des frühen 15. Jahrhunderts', *Z. d. deutschen Vereins f. Kunstw.*, VI (1939), 244.

32. E. Grill, *Monatshefte f. Kunstw.*, V (1912), 475; H. K. Ramisch, 'Zur Salzburger Holzplastik', *Mitteilungen d. Gesellschaft f. Salzburger Landeskunde*, CIV (1964), 21.

33. F. Lübbecke, *Die Plastik des deutschen Mittelalters* (Munich, 1922), II, plate 105.

p. 76 34. *Österreichische Kunsttopographie*, VII (Vienna, 1911), xxvi, 51, and xxii, 243.

35. T. Müller, *Alte bairische Bildhauer* (Munich, 1950), plate 71.

36. K. Ginhart, 'Die gotische Plastik in Wien', *Geschichte d. bildenden Kunst in Wien*, II (1955), 105.

37. Cat. Halm-Lill, Munich, nos. 188–91.

38. Stylistically similar are *inter alia* a Virgin in a private collection, the small figure of a Bishop formerly in the Bloch Collection in Vienna, and two somewhat cruder demi-figures of Holy Virgins in the Szepmüvészeti Muzeum in Budapest.

39. L. Baldass, 'Der Wiener Schnitzaltar', *J. d.* p. 77 *Kunsth. Sammlungen in Wien*, N.F. IX (1935), 29.

40. A. Stange, *Deutsche Malerei der Gotik*, X (Munich, 1960), 63.

41. The best analysis of the situation of sculpture in Vienna in the middle of the century is to be found in B. Fürst, *Beiträge zu einer Geschichte der Österreichischen Plastik in der ersten Hälfte des 15. Jahrhunderts* (Leipzig, 1931). Also L. Baldass, 'Malerei und Plastik um 1400 in Wien', *Wiener J. f. Kunstg.*, XV (1953), 7.

42. K. Garzarolli von Thurnlackh, in *Belvedere*, XIII (1938/9), 148; A. Lhotsky, in *J. d. Kunsth. Sammlungen in Wien*, N.F. XIII (1944), 72.

43. It conforms exactly to the style of presentation of the stone figure of a standing Virgin and Child in the church of Telgte in Westphalia (*Bau- und Kunstdenkmäler Westfalens: Kreis Münster*, plate 111).

44. A. Liška, 'České sochařství v době slohové preměny kolem roku 1450', *Uměni*, IX (1961), 372; X (1962), 334.

45. D. Frey, *Pantheon*, XXXI (1943), 35; K. p. 78 Estreicher, 'Grobowiec Władysława Jagiełły', *Rocznic Krakowski*, XXXIII (1953).

CHAPTER 6

1. W. Paatz, 'Nikolaus Gerhaerts', *Heidelberger* p. 8 *J.*, III (1959), 68 ff.; C. Sommer, 'Bemerkungen zu Nikolaus von Leyden', *Kunstchronik*, XIII (1960), 284.

2. O. Wertheimer, *Nicolaus Gerhaert* (Berlin, 1929); Cat. Beyer, Strasbourg, nos. 274–7.

3. E. Graf zu Solms-Laubach, *Bärbel von Ottenheim* (Frankfurt, 1936); R. Will, 'Le portail de l'ancienne Chancellerie de Strasbourg', *Cahiers Alsaciens d'Archéologie, d'Art et d'Histoire* (Strasbourg, 1959), 63.

4. H. Eichler, *Münch. J. d. b. K.*, III.F. III/IV (1952– p. 8 3), 184.

5. F. Wimmer and E. Klebel, *Das Grabmal* p. 8 *Friedrichs III im Wiener Stephansdom* (Vienna, 1924); K. Ginhart, 'Die gotische Plastik in Wien', *Geschichte der bildenden Kunst in Wien* (1955), 144.

6. H. K. Frenz, *Der Schulkreis Nikolaus Gerhaerts an Mittelrhein und Oberrhein* (unpublished Diss. Univ. Freiburg, philos. Fakultät, 1943); W. Deutsch, *Die Konstanzer Bildschnitzer der Spätgotik*

und ihr Verhältnis zu Niklaus Gerhaert (unpublished Diss. Univ. Heidelberg, philos. Fakultät, 1957).

7. I cannot agree with Ginhart's view (*loc. cit.*, Note 5, 145) that the marble monument of Empress Eleonora of Portugal (d. 1467) in the Neuklosterkirche at Wiener Neustadt is also to be ascribed to Nicolaus. Perhaps the design alone may be his work. Cf. W. M. Schmid, *Münch. J. f. b. K.*, N.F. XIII (1938), 18.

8. Not only the restorer is to blame for the lack of impact made on us by this work. Nevertheless, J. A. Schmoll, in his essay 'Madonnen Nikolaus Gerhaerts, seines Kreises und seiner Nachfolge' (*J. d. Hamburger Kunsts.*, III (1958), 70), stressed the significance of this work for our understanding of Nicolaus. The figure, according to its previous owner, was discovered in Vienna, but it was perhaps not executed by Nicolaus himself. The fragment of a male head in the Bayerisches Nationalmuseum, Munich, also came originally from Vienna (Cat. Müller, Munich, no. 112). The stone St Christopher in St Stephen shows how strong was Nicolaus's influence on Viennese sculpture. Cf. P. Baldass, *Österreichische Z. f. Kunst und Denkmalpflege*, IV (1950), 6.

9. Cat. Amsterdam Exhib. 1958, no. 293.

10. W. Vöge, 'Nicolaus von Leydens Strassburger Epitaph und die holländische Steinplastik', *Oberrheinische Kunst*, IV (1930), 35. Cf. too the fragments of the sculptural decoration of the funerary chapel (dating from 1464) of Bishop Rudolf van Diepholt (d. 1455) in Utrecht Cathedral.

11. D. P. R. A. Bouvy, *Middeleeuwensche Beeldhouwkunst in de Noordelijke Nederlanden* (Amsterdam, 1957), 85.

p. 83   12. New York, Metropolitan Museum, no. 22.60.4.

13. D. P. R. A. Bouvy, *op. cit.*, figure 104.

14. Cat. Rouen Exhib. 1931, plate LI.

15. O. Wertheimer, *op. cit.* (Note 2), figure 8.

16. P. Bloch, *Kölner Madonnen* (Mönchen Gladbach, 1961), plate 33.

17. O. Wertheimer, *op. cit.*, plate 1. However, Wertheimer did not know the original when he made the attribution.

18. The broad basis of this style in South Netherlandish sculpture is shown by the clearly 'painterly' (and more precisely Roger van der Weyden) inspiration of the scenes in the niches of the tabernacle of Mathieu de Layen (dating from 1450)

in St Pierre at Louvain (Leuven; Plate 72B); the stone relief (dating from 1458) in the refectory of St Bavo, near Ghent; the funerary tablet of Jean Keynoghe in the choir of St Pierre at Louvain (cf. J. Destrée, in *A. S. R. Arch. de Bruxelles*, VIII (1894), IX (1895), and XIII (1899)); and the contemporary (unfortunately badly damaged) *stèles funeraires* of Tournai (cf. P. Rolland, *Rev. belge*, XX (1951), 189).

19. P. Pradel, *La sculpture belge au musée du Louvre* (Brussels, 1947), no. 11.

20. Cat. Bruges-Detroit Exhib. 1960, no. 133.

21. J. Baum, 'Vesperbild aus dem Kreise Rogiers van der Weyden', *Pantheon*, IV (1929), 563.

22. S. Fliedner, in *Musées Royaux des Beaux-Arts, Brussels*, VII (1958), 186. The Virgin at Tongerlo cited in that paper, among others, as by Nicolaus Gerhaerts I regard as a replica of *c.* 1470–80, perhaps based on a print.   p. 84

23. Built between 1459 and 1481, at the instance of the Provincial Guistelli. The Sibyls' Corbel in the choir of the church of Lhuitre (Aube) is similar. Cf. P. Vitry, *Michel Colombe* (Paris, 1901), 54.

24. *Bull. of the Metropolitan Museum of Art*, IX (1951), 185.

25. Cf. the wooden St Margaret from the collection of J. Frésart at Liège in the Gruuthuse Museum at Bruges (Cat. Bruges-Detroit Exhib. 1960, no. 72).

26. Cat. Aubert, Paris, no. 347.   p. 85

27. Cat. Aubert, Paris, no. 349.

28. Cat. Demmler, Berlin, 135, no. 2095.

29. H. David, 'Les Bourbons et l'art slutérien', *A. du Midi*, XXXXVIII (1936), 337.

30. Cat. Aubert, Paris, no. 298.

31. New York, Metropolitan Museum, no. 47.42. Limestone, less than life-size. Similar realism is to be seen in the corbel figure of St Jerome, wearing spectacles, from the central west portal of St Étienne at Meaux.

32. C. Sterling, *La peinture française: Les primitifs* (Paris, 1938), 87.   p. 86

33. New York, Metropolitan Museum, no. 06.1215 (Rogers Fund); Cat. Sculpture (1913), no. 148. The back is uncarved. It was originally placed in a recess.

34. M. Aubert, *La sculpture française au moyen-âge* (Paris, 1946), 410.

35. Cat. Aubert, Paris, no. 308; Metropolitan Museum, no. 16.32.184 (ex Hoentschel Collection).

NOTES

Cf. P. Vitry, in *Gazette des Beaux Arts*, XXXI/XXXII (1904), 46, 116; P. Pradel, *Michel Colombe* (Paris, 1953), 39, 123; Cat. Exhib. 'L'art du Val de Loire' (Musée de Tours, 1952), no. 92.

p. 87   36. P. Vitry, *op. cit.* (Note 23), 77; J. Evans, *Life in Mediaeval France* (London, 1925), figure 256b.

37. P. Vitry, *op. cit.*, 82; M. Aubert, *op. cit.*, 410.

38. P. Vitry, *op. cit.*, 97; J. Evans, *Dress in Mediaeval France* (Oxford, 1952), figure 54.

39. M. Aubert, *op. cit.*, 408.

40. Cat. Paris Exhib. 1937, no. 1220.

41. Acquired in 1931; cf. *Theodor Demmler zum 60. Geburtstag: Erwerbungen für das Deutsche Museum 1919–1939* (Berlin, 1939), 24; G. Troescher, *Claus Sluter* (Freiburg im Breisgau, 1932), plate 24.

CHAPTER 7

p. 88   1. J. J. M. Timmers, *Houten Beelden* (Antwerp, 1949), figures 34–5; D. P. R. A. Bouvy, *Middeleeuwensche Beeldhouwkunst in de Noordelijke Nederlanden* (Amsterdam, 1957), 141.

2. Cat. Amsterdam Exhib. 1958, no. 267.

3. O. Wertheimer, 'Der Meister der Molsheimer Reliefs', *Pantheon*, III (1929), 115; Cat. Beyer, Strasbourg, no. 288.

4. Cat. Amsterdam Exhib. 1958, nos. 268–9; Cat. Demmler, Berlin, 132, no. 8333.

5. Cat. Amsterdam Exhib. 1958, no. 293. P. T. A. Swillens (*Oud Holland*, LXVI (1951), 231) has proved that this group of figures did not belong to the sculptural decoration of the burial chapel of Bishop Rudolph van Diepholt in Utrecht Cathedral, constructed under the direction of Jacob van der Borch (E. H. ter Kuile, *De Dom van Utrecht* (Maastricht, n.d.), 62).

p. 89   6. Wood figures of St Martin in the Centraal Museum, Utrecht, *c.* 1490, and in the J. P. Morgan Collection in the Wadsworth Atheneum at Hartford, Conn., *c.* 1510 (Cat. Amsterdam Exhib. 1958, nos. 300, 302). Bronze group of St Martin, dating from 1494, at Valencia (A. L. Mayer, *Z. f. bildende Kunst*, LIX (1925/6), 307).

7. I have never been able to agree with Wertheimer (*loc. cit.*, 122) that the equestrian figure of St Martin (Deutsches Museum, Berlin; Cat. Demmler, Berlin, 140, no. 7655) came from the Upper Rhine.

8. B. Meier, in *Westfalen*, VII (1915), 105; J. Leeuwenberg, 'Een nieuw facet aan de Utrechts

beeldhouwkunst V', *Oud Holland*, XXVII (1962), 79; Cat. Amsterdam Exhib. 1958, 198, nos. 291–2.

9. J. de Borchgrave d'Altena, in *A. S. R. Arch. de Bruxelles*, XLI (1937), 243 (especially figure 59); J. S. Witsen Elias, *Koorbanken, Koorhekken en Kansels* (Amsterdam, 1946), plates 29–42; M. Coppens, *Gothic Choir-stalls in the Netherlands* (Amsterdam-Brussels, n.d.), I, no. 43.

10. Cat. Amsterdam Exhib. 1958, nos. 273–4. I am more inclined to regard the Virgin of the Misericord from Erle in Westphalia (Münster, Diocesan Museum) as a work from the Lower Rhine.

11. Cat. Amsterdam Exhib. 1958, nos. 330, 294. The oak Virgin in the Begijnhof in Amsterdam (*loc. cit.*, no. 333) is similar.

12. Cat. Amsterdam Exhib. 1958, no. 331.

13. M. J. Friedländer, *Altniederländische Malerei*, V (Leiden, 1934), plate XIII.

14. P. T. A. Swillens, 'De Utrechtsche beeldhouwer Adriaen van Wesel', *Oud Holland*, LXIII (1948), 149; LXVI (1951), 228; J. Leeuwenberg, 'Het werk van den Meester der Musiceerende Engelen', *Oud Holland*, LVIII (1948), 164; Cat. Amsterdam Exhib. 1958, nos. 295–7; J. Leeuwenberg, in *Oud Holland*, LXIX (1959), 109.

15. Cat. Demmler, Berlin, 350, no. 2396; Cat. p. 90 Amsterdam Exhib. 1958, no. 299.

16. Cat. Amsterdam Exhib. 1958, no. 305.

17. J. Leeuwenberg, *Beeldhouwkunst*, I (1957), plate 4.

18. D. P. R. A. Bouvy, *op. cit.* (Note 1), 131.   p. 91

19. Cat. Amsterdam Exhib. 1958, no. 337.

20. I refer throughout the following to J. Destrée, 'Étude sur la sculpture brabançonne au moyen-âge', *A. de la Société d'Archéologie de Bruxelles*, VIII (1894), 7; IX (1895), 363; XIII (1899), 273.

21. E. H. Langlois, *Stalles de la cathédrale de Rouen* (Rouen, 1838). A. de Champeaux and P. Gauchery, in *Les travaux d'art exécutés pour Jean de France, Duc de Berry* (Paris, 1894), J. Destrée (*loc. cit.* (1899), 300), and Jouen, in *La cathédrale de Rouen* (Rouen-Paris, 1932), 52, have made extensive and illuminating contributions towards an understanding of the organization of the work on these stalls.

22. *Les chefs-d'œuvre d'art ancien à l'exposition de la Toison d'or* (Brussels, 1908), plate 1; Tentoonstelling

212

'Margareta van Oostenrijk en har Hof' (Malines, 1958), Cat. no. 112.

23. J. Casier and P. Bergmans, *L'art ancien dans les Flandres (Région de l'Escaut)* (Brussels-Paris, 1914), plate LVI, no. 88.

24. M. Devigne, *La sculpture mosane* (Paris-Brussels, 1932), plate LV, 276.

p. 92 25. O. Wertheimer, *Nicolaus Gerhaert* (Berlin, 1929), plate I.

26. D. P. R. A. Bouvy, *op. cit.* (Note I), 91, figure 104; Cat. Louvain Exhib. 1962, 179, no. Engeland/9, St Mary's College, Oscott.

27. Cat. Bruges-Detroit Exhib. 1960, nos. 101–2.

28. *Old Masters Drawings*, VIII (1934), 10, plate 12. Of similar character is a design for an angel for a tomb; *Old Masters Drawings*, VI, no. 48 (The Cleveland Museum of Art, *Bull.*, November 1962).

p. 93 29. D. Roggen, *G.B.*, XVI (1955–6), 172; Cat. Bruges-Detroit Exhib. 1960, 267, nos. 103–4.

30. E. Marchal, *Mémoire sur la sculpture aux Pays-Bas* (Brussels, 1895); J. de Bosschère, *La sculpture anversoise* (Brussels, 1909); H. Huth, *Künstler und Werkstatt der Spätgotik* (Augsburg, 1923), 65; M. Fransolet, 'La signature et le blason de l'imagier bruxellois Jan Bormann', *Rev. de l'Art* (1929); G. van Doorslaar, 'Marques de sculpteurs et de polychromeurs malinois', *Rev. belge*, III (1933), 159.

31. Cat. Exhib. 'Bewahrte Schönheit', Mittelalterliche Kunst der Sammlung Hermann Schwartz, Aachen, 1961; *Aachener Kunstblätter*, XXI, Cat. no. 35.

p. 94 32. C. Oursel, *L'art de Bourgogne* (Paris-Grenoble, 1953), 132; R. Journet, *Deux retables du quinzième siècle à Ternant* (Paris, 1963.)

33. I. Achter, in *J. d. Rheinischen Denkmalpflege*, XXIII (1960), 207.

34. R. Maere, *De Kunst der Nederlanden*, I (1930), 201; M. Hasse, *Der Flügelaltar* (Dresden, 1941), 40, note 52; I. Achter, *loc. cit.*, 219.

35. M. Voegelen, 'Die Gruppenaltäre in Schwäbisch Hall', *J. d. b. K.*, XIII (1923), 121; W. Paatz, *Süddeutsche Schnitzaltäre der Spätgotik* (Heidelberg, 1963), 16.

36. J. Roosval, 'Retables d'origine néerlandaise dans les pays nordiques', *Rev. belge*, III (1923), 136.

p. 95 37. C. Oursel, *op. cit.*, 152. Cf. Scourging of Christ, *c.* 1470–80; carving from an Altar of the Passion at St Trond, Couvent des Frères Mineurs; Christ bearing the Cross, fragment of an altar,

c. 1480, London, Victoria and Albert Museum (J. de Borchgrave d'Altena, *La Passion du Christ dans la sculpture en Belgique* (Brussels, 1946), figures 13, 14); Descent from the Cross, Schnütgen Museum, Cologne (Cat. Schnitzler, Cologne (1961), no. 124; Cat. Bruges-Detroit Exhib. 1960, nos. 86–9.

38. Aert de Maelder, mentioned in records, was probably the painter and not the carver. Cf. Cat. Bruges-Detroit Exhib. 1960, no. 73; Cat. Louvain Exhib. 1962, no. B/114.

39. P. Pradel, *La sculpture belge au musée du Louvre* (Brussels, 1947), no. VIII. Cf. fragment of an Altar of the Annunciation in the Musées Royaux d'Art et d'Histoire de Bruxelles, picture book (1958), no. 47; Cat. Bruges-Detroit Exhib. 1960, no. 99.

40. Cat. Demmler, Berlin, 344, no. 8077.

41. van Herck, *Het passie-retabel van Geel* (Antwerp, 1951); Cat. Bruges-Detroit Exhib. 1960, nos. 74–7.

42. Cf. Roosval, *loc. cit.* (Note 35). The Altar of p. 96 the Passion in the church of Vehmaa (Finland) also has the Brussels town mark and a carver's stamp. Cf. K. K. Meinander, *Œuvres d'art flamand du moyen-âge en Finlande* (Helsinki, 1930), 21.

43. J. Destrée, 'À propos de l'influence de Rogier van der Weyden sur la sculpture brabançonne', *A. S. R. Arch. de Bruxelles*, XXVIII (1919), I.

44. J. de Borchgrave d'Altena, in *A. S. R. Arch. de Bruxelles*, XXXVIII (1934), figure 33; Cat. Brussels Exhib. 1953, 110–11; D. Roggen, in *G.B.*, XVI (1955–6), 173, plate 38; N. Verhaegen, in *Bull. of the Detroit Institute of Arts*, XLI (1962), 64.

45. Cf. J. de Bosschère, *op. cit.* (Note 30).

46. *Kunstdenkmäler der Rheinprovinz*, XII, 4; *Kreis Wittlich* (1934), 65.

47. Cat. Demmler, Berlin, 336, no. 7700. p. 97

48. J. de Borchgrave d'Altena, *loc. cit.*, 188.

49. J. de Borchgrave d'Altena, *loc. cit.*, figure 32.

50. Cat. Bruges-Detroit Exhib. 1960, no. 72.

51. J. de Borchgrave d'Altena, in *A. S. R. Arch. de Bruxelles*, XLVII (1947), plate XLI.

52. J. de Borchgrave d'Altena, 'Notes pour servir à l'étude des stalles en Belgique', *A. S. R. Arch. de Bruxelles*, XLI (1937), 240.

CHAPTER 8

p. 98 1. G. André, in *Marburger J. f. Kunstw.*, XI (1938/9) [1941], 159; H. P. Hilger, *Der Skulpturenzyklus im Chor des Aachener Domes* (Essen, 1961).

2. F. Witte, *Tausend Jahre deutscher Kunst am Rhein* (Berlin, 1932), Tafelband III, 264.

3. *Op. cit.*, Tafelband II, 185.

4. *Kunstdenkmäler der Rheinprovinz*, I, 3, *Dom zu Köln* (1937), 247.

5. Cat. Schnitzler, Cologne (1961), no. 125; E. Lüthgen, *Gotische Plastik in den Rheinlanden* (Bonn, 1921), plate 80.

6. H. Appel, 'Studien zur niederrheinisch-kölnischen Plastik', *Wallraf-Richartz-J.*, XXIV (1962), 230.

p. 99 7. The Crucifix was replaced about 1600. R. Klapheck, 'Kalkar', *Rheinischer Verein f. Denkmalpflege und Heimatschutz*, XXIII, 2 (1930), 43; J. H. Schmidt, *Kalkar* (Ratingen, 1950), 35.

8. F. Witte, *op. cit.*, Tafelband II, 192–4.

9. Cat. Amsterdam Exhib. 1958, nos. 305, 304.

10. Cat. Amsterdam Exhib. 1958, no. 371; U. Hüneke, 'Drei spätgotische Figuren aus Kalkar', *J. d. rheinischen Denkmalpflege*, XXIII (1960), 296.

p. 100 11. R. Klapheck, *Der Dom zu Xanten* (Berlin, 1930); W. Bader, *Sechzehnhundert Jahre Xantener Dom* (Cologne, 1964), 298.

12. J. Leeuwenberg and F. Gorissen, in *Oud Holland*, LXXIII (1958), 18; Cat. Amsterdam Exhib. 1958, no. 353.

13. *Kunstdenkmäler der Rheinprovinz*, VI, 4; *Kirchen Kölns*, I (1916), 216; F. Witte, *op. cit.*, IV, plate 266.

p. 101 14. Cat. Josephi, Nuremberg, nos. 457–8; Cat. Schweitzer, Aachen, plate XXIV; Cat. Demmler, Berlin, 310, no. 8089; Országos Szépmüvészeti Muzeum, Budapest; J. Balogh, *A Régi Szoborosztály Kiallitása* (Budapest, 1956), 23.

15. Cat. Schnitzler, Cologne (1961), no. 116; Cat. Bange, Berlin, 5, no. 420.

16. Cat. Schnitzler, Cologne (1961), no. 114; J. Leeuwenberg, in *Oud Holland*, LXIX (1959), 109.

17. H. Hofmann, *Die lothringische Skulptur der Spätgotik* (Saarbrücken, 1962), 69, 86.

18. H. Hofmann, *op. cit.*, 219.

19. Clemen, *Grabmäler der Grafen von Nassau-Saarbrücken* (Düsseldorf, 1899); *Kunstdenkmäler*

Saarbrücken (1933), 161; F. Witte, *op. cit.*, Tafelband II, 180.

20. The Erzbischöfliche Diözesanmuseum, p. 102 Cologne, Cat. (1936), nos. 244–5. Cf. the Dolorosa in the Pfarrkirche at Vic; H. Hofmann, *op. cit.*, 219.

21. H. Lückger, 'Zur gotischen Plastik in Trier', *Wallraf-Richartz-J.*, V (1928), 27; W. Zimmermann, 'Zur Trierer Bildnerei der Gotik', *Trierer Z.*, XIII (1938), 128; W. Paatz, *Süddeutsche Schnitzaltäre der Spätgotik* (Heidelberg, 1963), 94.

22. H. Eichler, 'Ein Wappenrelief aus dem Kreis des Nikolaus Gerhaert', *Münch. J. d. b. K.*, III. F., III/IV (1952/3), 181.

23. J. A. Schmoll gen. Eisenwerth, 'Madonnen Niklaus Gerhaerts', *J. d. Hamburger Kunsts.*, III (1958), 59.

24. Cat. Demmler, Berlin, 138, no. 5898.

25. *Kunstdenkmäler der Rheinprovinz*, XIII, 3: p. 102 *Kirchen Trier* (1938), 250; XV, 2: *Landkreis Trier* (1936), 298.

26. O. Schmitt, 'Strassburg und die deutsche Bildhauerkunst am Ausgang des Mittelalters', *Elsass-Lothringisches J.*, XX (1942), 124; Cat. Beyer, Strasbourg, no. 257.

27. A. Schwarzweber, *Das Heilige Grab* (Freiburg, 1940), 21.

28. *29. Jahresbericht der öffentlichen Basler Denkmalpflege und des Stadt- und Münstermuseums in kleinen Klingenthal* (1947), 5; A. Kaufmann-Hagenbach, *Die Basler Plastik* (Basel, 1952), 25.

29. H. Reinhardt and A. Rais, 'Neue Beiträge zu einigen Stücken des Basler Münsterschatzes', *Historisches Museum Basel, Jahresbericht 1946*, 27; Cat. Exhib. 'Der Basler Münsterschatz' (Historisches Museum Basel, 1956), nos. 37–8.

30. Cat. Beyer, Strasbourg, no. 288; J. Futterer, in *Oberrheinische Kunst*, III (1928), 51; O. Wertheimer, 'Der Meister der Molsheimer Reliefs', *Pantheon*, III (1929), 115.

31. Cat. Demmler, Berlin, 131, no. 8108; E. p. 10 Hessig, *Die Kunst des Meisters E.S. und die Plastik der Spätgotik* (Berlin, 1935), plate 7, figure 5.

32. H. Schwartz Collection, Mönchen-Gladbach. Cf. Cat. Cologne Exhib. 1960, no. 59; Exhib. 'Bewahrte Schönheit' (Aachen, 1961), Cat.: *Aachener Kunstblätter*, XXI (1961), no. 40. For the South Netherlandish origin cf. the more naïve walnut group of the Adoration in the Netherlandish

triptych from Rieden in the Württembergisches Landesmuseum in Stuttgart (M. Voegelen, in *Münch. J. d. b. K.*, XIII (1923), 140).

33. Cat. Beyer, Strasbourg, no. 287.

34. Cat. Beyer, Strasbourg, no. 294.

35. B. Meier, in *Westfalen*, VII (1915), 129; J. Leeuwenberg, in *Oud Nederland* (1950), 73; Cat. Amsterdam Exhib. 1958, 198.

36. Cat. Sprinz, Sigmaringen, no. 26.

p. 105   37. Cat. Demmler, Berlin, 143, no. 7016.

38. E.g. Cat. Demmler, Berlin, 105–10, nos. 7660, 7041, 3031, 7661.

39. T. Müller, *Mittelalterliche Plastik Tirols* (Berlin, 1935), 153, note 3; G. Otto, 'Die Reliefs am Chorgestühl der Frarikirche', *Mitteilungen d. Kunsth. Instituts in Florenz*, V (1940), 173; O. Schmitt, in *Elsass-Lothringisches J.*, XX (1942), 131; F. Kieslinger, 'Die Schnitzreliefs am Chorgestühl der Frarikirche in Venedig', *Mitteilungen d. Gesellschaft f. vergleichende Kunstforschung in Wien*, I–III (1948–51), 72; T. Müller, 'A Venetian Altarpiece in Hartford', *Art Bull.*, XVII (1954), 365; J. A. Schmoll gen. Eisenwerth, 'Zum Werk des Strassburger Frari-Meisters von 1468', *A. Universitatis Saraviensis, Reihe Philosophie*, V (1956), 276.

40. J. Braun, *Der christliche Altar* (Munich, 1924), 470, plate 209.

41. On Conrad Sifer and his work see Chapter 12 (p. 167).

42. H. Rott, 'Oberrheinische Meister des 15./16. Jahrhunderts', *Oberrheinische Kunst*, III (1928), 55.

43. L. Fischel, *Nicolaus Gerhaert und die Bildhauer der deutschen Spätgotik* (Munich, 1944), 72; M. L. Hauck, 'Der Bildhauer Conrad Sifer von Sinsheim und sein Kreis', *A. Universitatis Saraviensis, Philosophie*, IX (1960), 213.

p. 106   44. The type of presentation is still in the succession of the 'Burgundian' St John the Baptist at Ludgo (Sweden).

45. *Kunstdenkmäler Bayerns: Pfalz*, III: *Speyer* (1934), 284, 251; for the dating c. 1483 see M. L. Hauck, *loc. cit.*, 197.

46. 'Fialenbüchlein des Hans Schuttermayer', *Anzeiger f. Kunde d. deutschen Vorzeit*, N.F. XXVIII (1881), 65; L. Fischel, *op. cit.*, note 70.

47. W. Paatz, *op. cit.* (Note 21), 19; W. Deutsch, 'Die Konstanzer Bildschnitzer der Spätgotik und ihr Verhältnis zu Niklaus Gerhaert', *Schriften d. Vereins f. Geschichte d. Bodensees*, LXXXI (1963), 11.

48. J. Eschweiler, *Das Konstanzer Chorgestühl* (Friedrichshafen, 1949).

49. G. Habich, in *Münch. J. d. b. K.* (1907/I), 76;   p. 107 L. Fischel, *op. cit.*, 114.

50. N. Pevsner, 'An unknown Statue by Nicolaus Gerhaert', *Burlington Magazine*, XCIX (1957), 40; D. Grossmann, in *Z. f. Kunstg.*, XX (1957), 190; Cat. Exhib. German Art (Manchester, 1961), no. 49.

51. Cat. Beyer, Strasbourg, 57, nos. 295–7.

52. M. R. Rogers and O. Goetz, *Handbook to the Lucy Maud Buckingham Medieval Collection* (Chicago, 1945), no. 12.

53. O. Schmitt, *Oberrheinische Plastik im ausgehenden Mittelalter* (Freiburg, 1924), plate 22.

54. Cat. Demmler, Berlin, 144, no. 2240; Cat.   p. 108 Maedebach, Berlin, 38, no. 23.

55. Cat. Demmler, Berlin, 143, no. 7055.

56. The question as to how far in this phase of development engravings were reproductions or prototypes of sculptural works is investigated in L. Fischel's excellent study (*op. cit.*).

57. O. Schmitt, *op. cit.*, plates 42–7.

58. L. Fischel, 'Nouvelles attributions au maître de la Vierge de Dangolsheim', *Archives Alsaciennes*, XVI (1936), 53.

59. Cat. Demmler, Berlin, 146, no. 8387.

60. *Kunstdenkmäler Bayerns, Schwaben*, II: *Stadt*   p. 109 *Nördlingen* (Munich, 1940), 87.

61. *Kunstdenkmäler Bayerns, Mittelfranken*, VIII: *Rothenburg, Kirchliche Bauten* (Munich, 1959), 158.

62. *Münch. J. d. b. K.*, III. F., XIII (1962); J. Schroth, 'Zum Werk des Schnitzers Hans Wydyz', *Z. f. schweizerische Arch. und Kunstg.*, XXII (1962), 87.

63. O. Schmitt, *op. cit.*, plate 49. Was Nicolaus   p. 110 Gerhaerts' high altar in Constance Minster the prototype for this kind of chapel-like altarpiece? W. Paatz, *op. cit.* (Note 21), 97. Cf. the altarpiece with St Anne and the Virgin and Child in the parish church of Lautenbach in Alsace (O. Wertheimer, *Nicolaus Gerhaert* (Berlin, 1929), plate 23).

64. J. Rorimer, *Bull. of the Metropolitan Museum of Art*, XII (1953), 81.

65. J. A. Schmoll, *op. cit.* (Note 23); H. Hofmann, *op. cit.* (Note 17), 247.

66. R. Schnellbach, 'Zwei unbekannte Strass-   p. 111 burger Skulpturen der Spätgotik', *Form und Inhalt*,

Kunstgeschichtliche Studien für Otto Schmitt (Stuttgart, 1950), 211; O. Schmitt, *Gotische Skulpturen des Freiburger Münsters* (Frankfurt, 1926), plate 257B.

p. 111   67. *Kunstdenkmäler in Württemberg: Kreis Waldsee* (1943), 40.

68. J. Baum, *Die Ulmer Plastik um 1500* (Stuttgart, 1911), 21; W. Vöge, *Jörg Syrlin der Ältere und sein Bildwerke* (Berlin, 1950); A. Hermann, *Ulmer Münster* (Stuttgart, 1950), 21.

p. 112   69. L. Fischel, *Bilderfolgen im frühen Buchdruck* (Constance, 1963), 50.

p. 113   70. G. Troescher, *Die Burgundische Plastik des ausgehenden Mittelalters* (Frankfurt, 1940), 161, pointed out a convincing formal affinity between the sedilia at Ulm and those from the Sainte-Chapelle in Bourges, now at Morogues.

71. W. Pinder, *Die deutsche Kunst der Dürerzeit* (Leipzig, 1940), 92.

p. 114   72. J. Eschweiler, *Das Konstanzer Chorgestühl* (Friedrichshafen, 1949); W. Deutsch, *Die Konstanzer Bildschnitzer der Spätgotik* (Diss. Heidelberg, 1957).

73. M. Schuette, *Der schwäbische Schnitzaltar* (Strasbourg, 1907), plate 65; H. Huth, *Künstler und Werkstatt der Spätgotik* (Augsburg, 1923), 42.

74. J. Baum, *op. cit.*, 33.

75. Cat. Müller, Munich, no. 83; Cat. Legner, Frankfurt (1961), nos. 4–5; Pée, *Führer durch das Ulmer Museum* (1958), 45.

p. 115   76. H. Rott, *Quellen und Forschungen* (Stuttgart, 1933 ff.), II, lx.

77. G. Otto, *Die Ulmer Plastik der Spätgotik* (Reutlingen, 1927), 112.

78. G. Otto, 'Der Bildhauer Michel Erhart', *J. d. P. Kunsts.*, LXIV (1943), 17; K. Feuchtmayr, 'Über Gregor Erhart', *Z. f. bildende Kunst*, LX (1926/7), 25; H. Müller, 'Michel und Gregor Erhart', *Lebensbilder aus dem Bayerischen Schwaben*, V (Munich, 1956), 16; G. Otto, *Gregor Erhart* (Berlin, 1943); W. Boeck, 'Neues zu Michel Erhart-Frage', *Z. d. deutschen Vereins f. Kunstw.*, XVII (1963), 77.

p. 116   79. Cat. Demmler, Berlin, 206 ff., nos. 421–3.

80. Museen zu Berlin, IV, W. Vöge, *Die deutschen Bildwerke* (Berlin, 1910), no. 111. F. Kieslinger (*Pantheon*, VI (1930), 389) has published an illustration of a little painted wooden Virgin and Child in a private collection in Vienna, as the model for this silver statuette. I do not believe that such an *opus perfectum* can have been a Late Gothic goldsmith's model. I have no doubt that this little wooden figure is only a replica of the 'model' of the Hufnagel figure.

81. G. Otto, *op. cit.* (Note 77), 108; Cat. p. 117 Demmler, Berlin, 142, no. 408; O. Wertheimer, *op. cit.* (Note 63), 97, note 14; Cat. Maedebach, Berlin, 39, no. 24.

82. Cat. Exhib. 'Bayerische Frömmigkeit' (Munich, 1960), no. 351.

83. P. M. Halm, *Erasmus Grasser* (Augsburg, 1928), 149.

84. Cat. Demmler, Berlin, 242, nos. 5875–7; Cat. Maedebach, Berlin, no. 26.

85. Cat. Müller, Munich, nos. 34–7; T. Müller, *Alte Bairische Bildhauer* (Munich, 1950), plates 88–9.

86. The wooden altarpiece in the pilgrimage p. 118 church of St Salvator at Heiligenstadt (Landkreis Eggenfelden, Lower Bavaria) is dated 1480. Cat. Müller, Munich, nos. 25–6.

87. T. Müller, *op. cit.*, plate 72.

88. T. Müller, *op. cit.*, plate 73.

89. F. Wimmer and E. Klebel, *Das Grabmal Friedrichs III. im Wiener Stephansdom* (Vienna, 1924); E. Klebel, *Die Skulpturen des alten Chorgestühls zu St Stephan in Wien* (Vienna, 1925); B. Fürst, *Beiträge zu einer Geschichte der österreichischen Plastik in der 1. Hälfte des 15. Jahrhunderts* (Leipzig, 1931); K. Oettinger, *Lorenz Luchsperger* (Berlin, 1935); B. Fürst, rev. Oettinger, in *Kritische Berichte*, VII (1938), 84; K. Oettinger, *Das Taufwerk von St Stephan in Wien* (Vienna, 1949); K. Ginhart, 'Die gotische Plastik in Wien', *Geschichte der bildenden Kunst in Wien*, II (Vienna, 1955), 68.

90. D. Radocsay, 'Der Hochaltar von Kaschau p. 119 und Gregor Erhart', *Acta Historiae Artium*, VII (1960), 19. Cf. J. Balogh, 'L'origine du style des sculptures en bois de la Hongrie médiévale, II', *Acta Historiae Artium*, VI (1959), 21.

91. Košice was the outpost of the mountain towns of the Zips, whose churches contain many Late Gothic altars. I cite, as examples from the two following decades, the Nativity and the Altar of the Crucifixion in the parish church of Bardejov (Bartfeld); cf. K. Šourek, *Umění na Slovensku* (Prague, 1938). An important example of Lower Austrian sculpture of *c.* 1490 is a wooden Virgin from Olomouc in the Zemské Museum at Brno (Brünn); J. Krčálová, in *Umění*, IV (1956), 43.

р. 120   92. K. Garzarolli von Thurnlackh, *Mittelalterliche Plastik in Steiermark* (Graz, 1941), plate 91.

93. Cat. Legner, Frankfurt (1961), no. 24.

р. 121   94. T. Müller, 'Zur Erforschung der spät-gotischen Plastik Tirols', *Veröffentlichungen des Museums Ferdinandeium*, XX–XXV (1940–5) (Innsbruck, 1948), 79.

95. A. Schwabik, *Michael Pachers Grieser Altar* (Munich, 1933).

р. 122   96. 'Bayer. Nationalmuseum, München, Erwerbungsbericht 1961', *Münch. J. d. b. K.*, III. F. XIII (1962), 266.

р. 124   97. *Kunstdenkmäler von Bayern, Mittelfranken*, VIII, 1: *Rothenburg, Kirchen* (Munich, 1959), 168. Cf. the tombstones of Friedrich V Schenken von Limpurg (d. 1474) and his wife Susanna von Tierstein at Grosskomburg (J. Baum, *Niederschwäbische Plastik des ausgehenden Mittelalters* (Tübingen, 1925), plates 4–5).

98. The figure was re-erected about 1522 in the centre of the new high altar of the Frauenkirche at Nuremberg, donated by Jakob Welser (cf. *Katalog der Veit Stoss-Ausstellung* (Nuremberg, 1933), no. 57).

99. At the outset we have the St Nicholas from the Nicholas Altar in St Lorenz, donated in 1452, and the high altar of the Katharinenkirche, now in the Germanisches Museum, donated by Marx Landauer and his daughter *c.* 1468.

100. Cat. Müller, Munich, no. 164.

125   101. W. Pinder, *Die deutsche Plastik des 15. Jahrhunderts* (Munich, 1924), plate 39; J. Baum, *op. cit.* (Note 97), plate 11.

102. The latest contribution to this subject is H. Wentzel, 'Die Marienklage aus Alabaster in Mergentheim', *J. d. Berliner Museen*, II (1960), 55.

103. Cat. Müller, Munich, no. 129. Alabaster was quarried in the neighbourhood of Erfurt. Does the Annunciation hail from Erfurt?

104. O. Wertheimer, *op. cit.* (Note 63), plate 8.

105. Bol. Przybyszewski, in *Biuletyn Historii Sztuki*, XIV (1952), 62. On the genealogy of Veit Stoss, see A. Jäger, *Veit Stoss und sein Geschlecht* (Neustadt, 1958); T. Müller, *Veit Stoss* (*Die grossen Deutschen*, v) (Berlin, 1957), 73.

127   106. Archbishop Zbigniew Oleśnicki commissioned the Danzig carver Hans Brand to complete the marble tomb destined for the bones of St Adalbert in Gniezno Cathedral, which had been initiated by his predecessor James III of Siena (d. 1480). The splendid tomb lid with a pontifical effigy of the saint is related to the heritage of Nicolaus Gerhaerts in Vienna. Cf. too the monument of Bishop Georg Schomberg in red marble (1470) in Bratislava (Pozsony, Pressburg) Cathedral; L. Eber, 'Schomberg György siremléke', *Magyarország müemleki*, III (Budapest, 1913).

107. H. Kohlhaussen, in *Münch. J. d. b. K.*, III. F. I (1950), 170.

108. Was Jörg Huber of Passau the master of the stone statues in the style of Nicolaus Gerhaerts on the portal of Passau Town Hall? (T. Müller, *op. cit.* (Note 85), plate 72.)

109. Cat. Nuremberg Exhib. 1933, no. 5.   p. 128

110. Cat. Josephi, Nuremberg, no. 50; H. Höhn, *Nürnberger gotische Plastik* (Nuremberg, 1922), plate 61.

111. Study drawing in the Staatl. Graphische Sammlung, Munich; see E. Buchner, in *Beiträge zur Geschichte d. deutschen Kunst*, II (1928), 472.

112. M. Hasse, 'Bildwerke des mittleren 15. Jahrhunderts in Lübeck und Vadstena', *Niederdeutsche Beiträge zur Kunstg.*, I (1961), 187.

113. A. L. Mayer, *Gotik in Spanien* (Leipzig, 1928), 129.

114. W. Paatz, *Bernt Notke und sein Kreis* (Berlin,   p. 129 1939), plate 1b.

115. A. Lindblom, *Den heliga Birgitta* (Stockholm, 1918).

116. J. Roosval, in *Nordelbingen*, XII (1936), 109.

117. B. Thordeman, *Norddeutsche Kunst in schwedischen Kirchen* (Stockholm, 1930), plates 16, 19.

118. S. Karling, *Medeltida träskulptur i Estland* (Stockholm, 1946).

119. Notke's frieze of a *danse macabre* in the mortuary chapel of the Marienkirche in Lübeck was dated 1463.

120. M. Hasse, *Das Triumphkreuz des Bernt Notke im Lübecker Dom* (Hamburg, 1952).

121. J. Roosval, *Riddar St Görani Stockholms*   p. 130 *stora eller Nikolaikyrka* (Stockholm, 1919); *ibid.*, *Nya St Görans Studier* (Stockholm, 1924); S. Anjou, in *Fornvännen*, Årg. 33 (1938), 349.

122. H. Keller, 'Ursprunge des Gedächtnismales in der Renaissance', *Kunstchronik*, VII (1954), 135; H. Keutner, 'Über die Entstehung und die Formen

Q   217

des Standbildes im Cinquecento', *Münch. J. d. b. K.*, III. F. VII (1956), 138.

p. 130   123. At the same time Notke carved the kneeling figure of King Charles VIII of Sweden (now preserved in Gripsholm Castle). It probably belonged originally to a memorial tablet, perhaps at Vadstena.

p. 131   124. Cat. Beyer, Strasbourg, nos. 294, 295.

125. P. Pieper, 'Die silbernen St Georgsfiguren aus Elbing', *Festschrift für Erich Meyer* (Hamburg, 1957), 93; R. Rückert, 'Museum für Kunst und Gewerbe Hamburg, Erwerbungen 1950–9', *J. d. Hamburger Kunsts.*, V (1960), 154.

p. 132   126. J. Roosval, 'Hinrich Wylsynk', *Nordisk Tidsskrift för Bok- och Biblioteksväsan*, XXIII (1936), 181.

127. S. Karling, *op. cit.*, 182.

CHAPTER 9

p. 134   1. M. Weinberger, in *J. of the Walters Art Gallery, Baltimore*, IX (1946), 9; P. Pradel, *Michel Colombe* (Paris, 1953), 25.

2. P. Pradel, *op. cit.*, 29; Cat. Aubert, Paris, no. 325.

3. P. Pradel, *op. cit.*, plate VI.

4. Cat. Paris Exhib. 1937, no. 1010; P. Pradel, *op. cit.*, 92, plate XVIII, 2.

5. C. Oursel, *L'art de Bourgogne* (Paris-Grenoble, 1953), 142, 144.

6. *Op. cit.*, 143.

p. 135   7. P. L. Duchartre, *Mittelalterliche Plastik in Frankreich* (Munich, 1925).

8. *Inv. général des richesses d'art de la France, Province, Monuments religieux*, III (Paris, 1901), 185, 187.

9. Cat. Cluny, pierre, 1922, no. 663.

p. 136   10. C. Oursel, *op. cit.*, 136.

11. *Festschrift T. Demmler* (Berlin, 1939), 24.

12. C. Oursel, *op. cit.*, 138.

13. Cat. Aubert, Paris, no. 349.

14. Cat. Dijon Exhib. 1949, nos. 35, 37. Cf. also *loc. cit.*, no. 36, Angel of the Annunciation in the church of Flavigny-sur-Ozerain.

15. P. Pradel, *op. cit.*, 32 ff.

16. Cat. Aubert, Paris, no. 355.

p. 137   17. H. Drouot, in *Rev. belge*, VI (1936), 117.

18. Cat. Aubert, Paris, no. 335.

19. L. H. Labande, *Les Primitifs français* (Marseilles, 1932), I, 35.

20. The name of Jehan Morant vouches for the existence of a tradition of bronze monuments in Paris, but his works in the abbey of St-Denis (1468) and in the collegiate church of Cléry have been destroyed.

21. W. Bode, *Collection of J. P. Morgan, Bronzes of the Renaissance* (Paris, 1910), I, no. 2; M. Aubert, *La sculpture française au moyen-âge* (Paris, 1946), 410; P. Pradel, *op. cit.*, 40.

22. D. Roggen, 'Prae-Sluteriaanse, Sluteriaanse, Post-Sluteriaanse Nederlandse Sculptuur', *G.B.*, XVI (1955–6), 163; M. de Bevotte, *La sculpture dans la région de Toulouse, d'Albi et de Rodez* (Paris, 1936), 47 ff.

23. M. Aubert, *op. cit.*, 404.

24. Cat. Limoges Exhib. 1956, no. 12.   p. 13

25. P. Pradel, *op. cit.*, plate XVIII, 1, 2.

26. P. L. Duchartre, *op. cit.*, plate 39; P. Pradel, *op. cit.*, note 377.

27. P. Vitry, *Michel Colombe* (Paris, 1901), 250 ff. and 253; choir stalls by Pierre Pintard and Raoullet Micheau in St Pierre at Saumur, completed in 1475 by Philippe Amy.

28. P. Pradel, *op. cit.*, 20.   p. 13

29. *Op. cit.*, 36.

30. P. Vitry, *op. cit.*, 324.

31. H. Zanettacci, *Les ateliers picards de sculptures*   p. 14 *à la fin du moyen âge* (Paris, 1954), 103, 138.

32. P. Vitry, *op. cit.*, 260–1.

33. Cat. Paris Exhib. 1950, no. 196.

34. Cat. Paris Exhib. 1950, no. 195; M. Vloberg, *La vierge et l'enfant dans l'art français* (Paris-Grenoble, 1954), plate 183.

35. H. Zanettacci, *op. cit.*, 88.

36. Cat. Paris Exhib. 1950, no. 184.

37. Cat. of the sale of the Figdor Collection (Vienna, IV, Berlin, 1930, nos. 166–7). The work is now in private ownership in Vienna. The companion piece from the same altarpiece is in the Bayerisches Nationalmuseum.

38. J. Lestocquoy, 'Sculptures d'origine ou d'influence brabançonne en Artois ("jardin-clos")', *A. S. R. Arch. de Bruxelles*, XXXXI (1937), 76.

39. M. Aubert, *op. cit.*, 392–3.   p. 1

CHAPTER 10

p. 142   1. C. Justi, *Miscellaneen aus drei Jahrhunderten spanischen Kunstlebens* (Berlin, 1908), I, 294; B. G. Proske, *Castilian Sculpture* (New York, 1951), 470, no. 3.

p. 143   2. G. Weise, *Spanische Plastik aus sieben Jahrhunderten* (Reutlingen, 1925), I, plate 112; II (1927), plates 94–5; III, 1, plates 8–9.

3. D. Roggen, in *G.B.*, XVI (1955–6), 172 (3).

4. R. dos Santos, *A escultura em Portugal*, II (Lisbon, 1950), plates XIX, XX.

5. R. dos Santos, *op. cit.*, II, plates XXIII, XXIV.

6. South Netherlandish altarpieces from the second half of the fifteenth century are to be found, e.g. at Santibañez-Zarzaguda (Burgos); Sotopalacios (Burgos); Laredo (Santander), S. María; Medina del Campo (Valladolid), S. Martín; and from Fuentes (Valladolid) dated 1492, in the U.S.A. art market.

7. Especially Joseph Braun, S.J.

8. M. Hasse, *Der Flügelaltar* (Dresden, 1941).

p. 144   9. B. Proske, *op. cit.*, 108 ff.; J. Ainaud de Lasarte and A. Duran Sanpere, *Escultura gótica* (*Ars Hispaniae*, VIII) (Madrid, 1956), 303 ff.

p. 145   10. J. Ainaud de Lasarte and A. Duran Sanpere, *op. cit.*, figure 307.

11. B. Proske, *op. cit.*, figure 118.

12. *Op. cit.*, figure 92.

p. 146   13. H. E. Wethey, *Gil de Silhoe and his School* (Cambridge, Mass., 1936).

p. 147   14. J. Ainaud de Lasarte and A. Duran Sanpere, *op. cit.*, 366 ff.

p. 148   15. V. von Loga, *Spanische Plastik* (Munich, 1923), figure 7; A. L. Mayer, *Mittelalterliche Plastik in Spanien* (Munich, 1922), figure 35.

16. A fine wooden Virgin of 1470, signed by the sculptor Juan de Córdoba, is in the Boston Museum (J. Ainaud de Lasarte and A. Duran Sanpere, *op. cit.*, 373).

17. If the two corbels of the Virgin and St John from the Capilla de S. Jorge in the abbey of Poblet (J. Ainaud de Lasarte and A. Duran Sanpere, *op. cit.*, 244) really date from 1452, this shows the persistence of types of presentation from the early years of the fifteenth century in the style of the monumental sculpture of Toulouse.

18. J. Ainaud de Lasarte and A. Duran Sanpere, *op. cit.*, 243, 287; F. Abbad Rios, *Catalogo monumental de España: Zaragoza* (Madrid, 1957), 61.

19. J. Ainaud de Lasarte and A. Duran Sanpere, p. 149 *op. cit.*, 288; F. Abbad Rios, *op. cit.*, 55. The style of the Virgén Blanca points to the same period as the retablo mayor and suggests that the provenance of the sculptor was Flanders or the Southern Netherlands.

20. The closest parallel is the wooden Pietà by Bernt Notke from the Heiliggeistspital in the St Annenmuseum in Lübeck. Similarly the wooden figure of San Blas in the church of Mainar (J. Ainaud de Lasarte and A. Duran Sanpere, *op. cit.*, figure 277) most resembles the St Ansgar of Bernt Notke in the Petrikirche in Hamburg.

21. A. L. Mayer, in *Z. f. bildende Kunst*, LIX, N.F. XXXV (1925/6), 307; J. Ainaud de Lasarte and A. Duran Sanpere, *op. cit.*, 298.

22. Cf. the wooden St Martin, Musée de Tirlemont (J. Casier and P. Bergmans, *L'art ancien dans les Flandres* (*Région de l'Escaut*) (Brussels–Paris, 1914), I, no. 71, plate XLI). The Netherlandish type of composition goes back to the St Martin, dating from *c.* 1450, in the Utrecht Museum.

23. J. Ainaud de Lasarte and A. Duran Sanpere, p. 150 *op. cit.*, figure 370.

24. *Op. cit.*, 374.

25. Cat. Schnitzler, Cologne (1958), plate 117.

26. E.g. the wooden Altar of the Virgin in the east wall of the Capilla de la Buena Mañano in S. Gil in Burgos.

27. R. H. Randall, 'Flemish Influences on Sculp- p. 151 ture in Spain', *Bull. of the Metropolitan Museum of Art*, XIV (1956), 257.

28. Cat. Demmler, Berlin, 355, no. 7023.

29. B. Proske, *op. cit.*, 9, note 8; J. Ainaud de Lasarte and A. Duran Sanpere, *op. cit.*, 355.

30. A. L. Mayer, 'Simon de Colonia', *Wallraf-Richartz-J.*, III/IV (1926/7), 74; B. Proske, *op. cit.*, 22; J. Ainaud de Lasarte and A. Duran Sanpere, *op. cit.*, 356 ff.

31. J. Ainaud de Lasarte and A. Duran Sanpere, *op. cit.*, 360.

32. These problems are discussed most thoroughly p. 152 in the monograph by Wethey, *op. cit.*, 56 and 113. Cf. B. Proske, *op. cit.*, 11, and J. Ainaud de Lasarte and A. Duran Sanpere, *op. cit.*, 342.

33. H. E. Wethey, *op. cit.*

p. 153   34. Were there traditions of funerary sculpture in Burgos which might have influenced the monument to Alonso de Cartagena? I should like, for instance, to date the effigy of St Lesmes in the church of S. Lesmes in Burgos (J. Ainaud de Lasarte and A. Duran Sanpere, *op. cit.*, 365, figure 344), *c.* 1470.

35. In any case not from the hand of Diego de Siloe, who, as far as we can see, was not active in Burgos before 1516.

p. 154   36. *Kunstchronik*, VII (1954), 39. Cf. the mid-century wooden figure of a seated Virgin in the parish church of Laredo near Santander (G. Weise, *op. cit.*, III, 1, plate 18). The silver Virgin on the high altar of Burgos Cathedral (G. Weise, *op. cit.*, plate 30) dates from the end of the fifteenth century.

CHAPTER II

p. 156   1. J. Casier and P. Bergmans, *L'art ancien dans les Flandres (Région de l'Escaut)* (Brussels-Paris, 1914), no. 33, plate XV (very similar are two statuettes of prophets in the Musée de Cluny, Paris, Cat. nos. 134, 135), nos. 43, 44, 45, plate XXIV. For the whole following section, see J. Destrée, 'Étude sur la sculpture brabançonne au moyen-âge', *A. S. R. Arch. de Bruxelles*, IX (1895), 363; XIII (1899), 273.

2. Cat. Louvain Exhib. 1962, no. B/72.

3. J. de Borchgrave d'Altena, in *Bull. de la Société d'Arch. de Bruxelles* (1938), 31; Cat. Bruges-Detroit Exhib. 1960, nos. 81–4.

4. J. de Borchgrave d'Altena, *Het St Joris-Retabel van Jan Borman* (Amsterdam–Antwerp, 1947).

p. 157   5. An example of a Brussels hallmark on a completely preserved altarpiece from the period 1490–1500 is the Altar of the Family of Christ from the Dominican house at Tallinn (Reval) in the Estonian Museum (S. Karling, *Medeltida träskulptur i Estland* (Stockholm, 1946), 238).

6. J. Roosval, 'Retables d'origine néerlandaise dans les pays nordiques', *Rev. belge*, III (1933), 136; E. Fründt, *Spätgotische Plastik in Mecklenburg* (Dresden, 1963), 20.

7. J. de Bosschère, *La sculpture anversoise* (Brussels, 1909), 95. Cf. Cat. Demmler, Berlin, 332, no. M 82; 339, nos. 496, 497.

8. Cat. Demmler, Berlin, 330, no. 7072.

9. M. Konrad, *Meisterwerke der Skulptur in Flandern und Brabant* (Leipzig, 1929–35), figure 42.

10. Cat. Amsterdam Exhib. 1951, nos. 208–9; p. 15 Cat. Brussels Exhib. 1951, no. 195; Cat. Tournai Exhib. 1958, no. 147; S. Fliedner, in *Musées R. des Beaux-Arts, Bull.*, VII (Brussels, 1958), 197; Cat. Bruges-Detroit Exhib. 1960, nos. 78–9; Cat. Louvain Exhib. 1962, no. B/3.

11. J. de Borchgrave d'Altena, in *A. S. R. Arch. de Bruxelles*, XXXVIII (1934), 204, figures 26–7. Cf. also the Crucifixion group at Wisbecq: *idem, La Passion du Christ dans la sculpture en Belgique* (Brussels, 1946), figures 11, 21.

12. The master of the highly effective Crucifixion in the parish church of Beek, who was active in Oppergelder, was also certainly of Brabant origin: J. J. M. Timmers, *Houten Beelden* (Antwerp, 1949), plates 69, 71–3. M. Devigne ('La sculpture flamande', *Trésor de l'art flamande*, II (Paris, 1932), 151) was reminded of Franconian sculpture by the Crucifixion in Liège Cathedral. In this connexion a particularly impressive Crucifixion from a church in the Scheldt area must be mentioned: J. Casier, in *Onze Kunst*, XL (1922), 175. This is now in a private collection in Ghent. Cf. also the attendant figures of a Crucifixion, not belonging to this latter group, formerly in the Demotte Collection, Paris: J. Casier and P. Bergmans, *op. cit.*, plate XXIV. It is necessary to trace such works as these in order to gain an idea of the possibilities of this new monumental type of statue, since important works, documentarily recorded, have been destroyed, and those still in use in the churches have for the most part lost their original appearance through renovation.

13. P. Pradel, *La sculpture belge au musée du Louvre* (Brussels, 1947), nos. III–VII.

14. S. Fliedner, 'Die Brabender', *Musées R. des* p. 15 *Beaux-Arts, Bull.*, VII (Brussels, 1958), 141, shows that the Brabender family of carvers, active at Münster in Westphalia, came from Brabant, and attributes three of the Apostles at Nivelles as well as the Crucifixion from Nivelles, now in the Louvre, to the elder Brabender, and the Evangelists at Nivelles to the younger Brabender. I have the impression that all the figures at Nivelles are by one hand, but that the Crucifixion in the Louvre is definitely superior to them in its grace of movement and power of feeling.

15. T. Müller, 'Zur südniederländischen Kleinplastik der Spätrenaissance', *Festschrift für Erich Meyer* (Hamburg, 1957), 196. Cf. E. F. Bange, *Die Kleinplastik der deutschen Renaissance* (Florence-Munich, 1928).

16. P. Vitry and M. Aubert, *Musée National du Louvre, Catalogue des sculptures du moyen-âge, de la Renaissance, etc.* (Paris, 1922), no. 518; P. Pradel, *op. cit.*, no. VIII. Relief of the Annunciation in the Musées Royaux d'Art et d'Histoire, Brussels, no. 1006: Cat. Bruges-Detroit Exhib. 1960, no. 99. A little later is the charming relief of the Birth of Christ from Antwerp in the M. Baus Collection, Ypres: J. Casier and P. Bergmans, *op. cit.*, no. 85, plate LIV.

17. *Musées R. d'Art et d'Histoire Bruxelles, Archéologie National, Industrie de l'Art* (1958), 45, attributed to Jan Borman; Cat. Bruges-Detroit Exhib. 1960, no. 80.

18. J. de Borchgrave d'Altena, *loc. cit.* (1934; Note 11), plate 1, and Musées Royaux d'Art et d'Histoire de Bruxelles, picture-book (1958), no. 46. Cat. Louvain Exhib. 1962, no. B/50; P. Vitry and M. Aubert, *op. cit.*, no. 517; P. Pradel, *op. cit.*, no. IX; Cat. Demmler, Berlin, 347, no. 8104. The example in the Orphanage at Antwerp seems weaker (J. de Bosschère, *op. cit.*, figure 4).

19. Cat. Bruges-Detroit Exhib. 1960, no. 85.

20. Should one not include here the astonishingly static St Melchior from an Adoration of the Magi in the Schnütgen-Museum in Cologne (Plate 113B; Cat. Schnitzler, Cologne (1961), no. 117)? This figure is closely allied to the sculpture of the altarpiece at Covarrubias (Chapter 10, p. 150; Plate 152B).

21. Cat. Demmler, Berlin, 346, no. 8076.

22. J. Leeuwenberg, 'Zeven Zuidnederlandse Reisaltaarjes', *Belgisch Tijdschrift voor Oudheidkunde en Kunstgeschiedenis*, XXVII (1958), 95.

23. C. Poupeye, 'Les jardins clos et leurs rapports avec la sculpture malinoise', *Bull. du Cercle Arch. de Malines*, XXII (1912), 50; G. van Doorslaer, 'Marques des sculptures et de polychromeurs malinois', *Rev. belge*, III (1933), 159; J. Lestocquoy, 'Sculptures d'origine ou d'influence brabançonne en Artois', *A. S. R. Arch. de Bruxelles*, XLI (1937), 76; W. Godenne, 'Préliminaires à l'inventaire général des statuettes d'origine malinoise I/II', *Bull. du Cercle Arch. de Malines* (1958/9); J. de Borchgrave d'Altena, 'Statuettes malinoises', *Bull. des Musées Royaux*, IV, 31 (1959), 2.

24. J. Duverger, 'De Meesters van het Grafmonument van Maria van Boergondie te Brugge', *J. der Kon. Vl. Acad. van Belgie*, VIII (1946), 131. There is a particularly interesting record that Jan

Borman was commissioned by the Brussels Municipality to carve models for bronze figures for the façade of a building, after which the models were to be cleaned and coloured for use elsewhere.

25. Cat. Bruges-Detroit Exhib. 1960, nos. 103–4.

26. S. Collon-Gevaert, *Histoire des arts du métal en Belgique* (Brussels, 1951), 259.

27. J. von Schlosser, *Präludien* (Berlin, 1927), 304: ' "Armeleutekunst" alter Zeit'. This study demonstrates that this was a European phenomenon.

28. R. Klapheck, *Der Dom zu Xanten* (Berlin, 1930), 127; E. Meyer, 'Der gotische Kronleuchter in Stans', *Festschrift Hans R. Hahnloser* (Basel-Stuttgart, 1961), 177.

29. Cat. Amsterdam Exhib. 1958, no. 302.

30. J. J. M. Timmers, *op. cit.* (Note 12), plates 78–9.

CHAPTER 12

1. F. Witte, *Tausend Jahre deutscher Kunst am Rhein* (Berlin, 1932), II. Tafelband, 208–14.

2. F. Witte, *op. cit.*, II. Tafelband, 203; A. Kamphausen, *Die niederrheinische Plastik im 16. Jahrhundert* (Düsseldorf, 1931); R. Klapheck, 'Kalkar am Niederrhein', *Rheinischer Verein f. Denkmalpflege und Heimatschutz, Z.*, XXIII, Heft 2 (1931), 85.

3. F. Witte, *op. cit.*, II. Tafelband, 215–18.

4. U. Hüneke, in *J. d. Rheinischen Denkmalpflege*, XXIII (1960), 293. F. Witte (*Rheinischer Verein f. Denkmalpflege und Heimatschutz* (1931), Heft 2, 85), instead of ascribing the usual importance to Master Arnt of Zwolle, postulates a career extending over several decades for Dries Holthuys. I am unable to subscribe to this theory. The sole accredited work by Dries Holthuys is the Virgin of 1496 at Xanten: a typical, relatively conventional piece of stone sculpture, which in my opinion has none of the passionate quality we see in the carving of the Cleves choir stalls or in the Kalkar Altar of St Anne, both of which Witte attributes to Dries Holthuys. Cf. also Cat. Exhib. Kleve 1963.

5. O. H. Förster, *Die Sammlung Dr R. von Schnitzler* (Munich, 1931), no. 95.

6. *Kunstdenkmäler der Rheinprovinz*, VII, 1: *Köln.* The translation of this style into the spirit of the early years of the sixteenth century finds its most beautiful expression in the St John in St Johannes (F. Witte, *op. cit.*, III, 267; H. Appel, 'Studien zur

p. 161

p. 162

p. 163

p. 164

. 160

niederrheinisch-Kölnischen Plastik der Spätgotik I', *Wallraf-Richartz-J.*, XXIV (1962), 251).

p. 164   7. S. Fliedner, 'Die Brabender', *Musées R. des Beaux-Arts, Bull.*, VII (Brussels, 1958), 141.

p. 165   8. H. Kohlhaussen, 'Mittelalterliche Bildwerke im Hamburgischen Museum für Kunst und Gewerbe', in A. Donath, *J. f. Kunsts.*, III (1923), 57.

9. F. Stuttmann and G. von der Osten, *Niedersächsische Bildschnitzerei des späten Mittelalters* (Berlin, 1940), 112.

10. See on the following W. Paatz, *Bernt Notke und sein Kreis* (Berlin, 1939).

11. C. G. Heise, *Lübecker Plastik* (Bonn, 1926), plate 47.

p. 166   12. See also S. Karling, *Medeltida träskulptur i Estland* (Stockholm, 1946), 193; M. Hasse, 'Lübecker Maler und Bildschnitzer um 1500', *Niederdeutsche Beiträge zur Kunstg.*, III (1964), 296.

13. Cat. Demmler, Berlin, 328, no. 8059.

14. Though it has been assumed by scholars, I do not in fact see South German influences in Lübeck sculpture until the first decade of the sixteenth century.

15. J. Roosval, 'Retables d'origine néerlandaise dans les pays nordiques', *Rev. belge*, III (1933), 136; J. Johansson, 'Altarskåpet vid Strängnäs Domkyrkas Lögaltare', *Kyrkohistorisk Arsskrift*, IV (1943), 157; J. de Borchgrave d'Altena, *Retables brabançons conservés en Suède* (Brussels, 1948), with a map of the places.

p. 167   16. According to Karling (*op. cit.*), individual figures were added in 1652.

17. W. R. Deutsch, 'Gotische Bildwerke des Deutschordenslandes', *Pantheon*, XII (1933), 344. In the altarpiece dating from 1504–9 in Frombork (Frauenburg) Cathedral (Ermland), the antiquated East German style has still been retained, with the main figure in the shrine flanked by small figures or groups of figures arranged in layers, while the charming, life-like, painterly quality of the central figure of the Virgin presupposes Saxon or Franconian sources.

18. H. Neuber, *Ludwig Juppe von Marburg* (Marburg, 1915). Especially similar is the style of the figures and altar shrines of the school of Kalkar and the style of the Altarpiece of St Anthony in Xanten Cathedral (F. Witte, *op. cit.* (Note 1), III, plate 233).

19. O. Schmitt (*Schriften des Historischen Museums, Frankfurt*, I (1925), 13) makes a distinction between the striking individual style of the 'Adalbert Master' and the soft, sensuous quality of the two upper side figures of the tomb. Both of these he attributes convincingly to a collaborator who may be identified as the Frankfurt sculptor Hans von Düren. Cf. E. Graf zu Solms-Laubach, in *Städel-J.*, IX (1935–6), 54.

20. H. Reinhardt, 'Der Bildhauer Conrad Sifer',   p. 168 *Münch. J. d. b. K.*, N.F. XI (1934), 233; O. Schmitt, 'Strassburg und die deutsche Bildhauerkunst am Ausgang des Mittelalters', *Elsass-Lothringisches J.*, XX (1942), 136; J. A. Schmoll, gen. Eisenwerth, in *A. Universitatis Saraviensis, Philosophie*, II (1953), 299; Cat. Beyer, Strasbourg, nos. 310–12; M. L. Hauck, in *A. Universitatis Saraviensis, Philosophie*, IX (1960), 113.

21. F. Back, *Ein Jahrtausend künstlerischer Kultur am Mittelrhein* (Darmstadt, 1932), 110, 216; M. L. Hauck, *loc. cit.*, thinks it probable that Conrad Sifer designed the series of reliefs, begun in 1484, at Worms.

22. Cat. Demmler, Berlin, 138, nos. 5597–8; R. Schnellbach, 'Werke aus der Jugend- und Reifezeit des Hans Syfer', *J. d. P. Kunsts.*, L (1929), 105; W. Fleischhauer, 'Zu Hans Syfer', *Form und Inhalt, Festschrift Otto Schmitt* (Stuttgart, 1950), 203; M. L. Hauck, *loc. cit.*, 197.

23. This Netherlandish–Lower Rhenish feature is seen most clearly in the figures of a Crucifixion from an altarpiece in the Dominican church at Wimpfen-am-Berg.

24. K. Oettinger, *Anton Pilgram und die Bildhauer*   p. 169 *von St Stephan* (Vienna, 1951); H. Koepf, 'Neu entdeckte Bauwerke des Anton Pilgram', *Wiener J. f. Kunstg.*, XV (1953), 119; F. W. Fischer, *Die spätgotische Kirchenbaukunst am Mittelrhein* (Heidelberg, 1962), 208.

25. R. Schnellbach, 'Ein unbekanntes Frühwerk des Anton Pilgram', *Wallraf-Richartz-J.*, N.F. I (1930), 202.

26. T. Demmler, 'Der Kanzelträger des Deutschen Museums', *J. d. P. Kunsts.*, LIX (1938), 161; G. Troescher, 'Der Kanzelfuss der Tübinger Stiftskirche', *Z. f. Kunstw.*, IV (1950), 131; Cat. Maedebach, Berlin, no. 27. – There is a magnificent altarpiece in this same abbey of Öhringen (near Heilbronn) which dates from c. 1500; with its impressive shrine figures and the precise sharpness of the carving it is undoubtedly a masterpiece of Franconian Late Gothic sculpture.

27. K. Gerstenberg, in *Die Kunst*, LV (1957), 84.

28. O. Schmitt, *Gotische Skulpturen des Strassburger Münsters* (Frankfurt, 1924), II, figure 238; ibid., *Strassburg und die Bildhauerkunst am Ausgang des Mittelalters* (Freiburg im Breisgau, 1924), 136.

p. 170 29. H. Rott, 'Oberrheinische Meister des 15./16. Jahrhunderts', *Oberrheinische Kunst*, III (1928), 74.

30. Cat. Beyer, Strasbourg, nos. 338–47; M. L. Hauck, *loc. cit.* (Note 20), 159.

31. W. Vöge, *Niclas Hagnower* (Freiburg im Breisgau, 1931).

p. 171 32. Cat. Beyer, Strasbourg, nos. 351–2.

33. M. L. Hauck, *loc. cit.*, 233: the 'Hagenauer Problem'!

34. Presumably Hans Weiditz was the father of Christoph Weiditz the painter, draughtsman, and engraver of medals.

35. J. Schroth, 'Zum Werk des Schnitzers Hans Wydyz', *Z. f. schweizerische Arch. und Kunstg.*, XXII (1962), 87.

p. 172 36. E. F. Bange, *Die Kleinplastik der deutschen Renaissance* (Florence-Munich, 1928), 54; T. Müller, *Deutsche Plastik der Renaissance* (1963), 4.

37. A. Kaufmann-Hagenbach, *Die Basler Plastik des 15. und frühen 16. Jahrhunderts* (Basel, 1952).

38. O. Schmitt, *Oberrheinische Plastik im ausgehenden Mittelalter* (Freiburg, 1924), figure 89.

39. G. von der Osten, in *Z. d. deutschen Vereins f. Kunstw.*, II (1935), 430.

40. J. Baum, *Meister und Werke spätmittelalterlicher Kunst in Oberdeutschland und in der Schweiz* (Lindau-Constance, 1957), 66.

41. L. Volkmann, *Der Überlinger Rathaussaal des Jakob Russ* (Berlin, 1934).

42. Is the fine Altar of the Annunciation in the Unterstadt-Kapelle at Meersburg on Lake Constance an early work by Ivo Strigel? Cf. G. Otto, in *Z. f. schweizerische Arch. und Kunstg.*, X (1948/9), 57.

43. Niclaus Türing of Memmingen was for example the master of the so-called 'Goldenes Dachl', erected by the Emperor Maximilian in 1500 as a spectators' gallery in the old castle at Innsbruck. The highly dramatic stone statues are now in the Landesmuseum Ferdinandeum at Innsbruck; Cat. Exhib. Innsbruck 1950, no. 182.

44. K. Feuchtmayr, 'Über Gregor Erhart', *Z. f. bildende Kunst*, LX (1926–7), 25; G. Otto, 'Der Bildhauer Michel Erhart', *J. d. P. Kunsts.*, LXIV (1943), 17; H. Müller, 'Michel und Gregor Erhart',

Lebensbilder aus dem Bayerischen Schwaben, V (Munich, 1956), 16; Cat. Müller, Munich, 108, no. 94; W. Boeck, 'Neues zur Michel Erhart-Frage', *Z. d. deutschen Vereins f. Kunstw.*, XVII (1963), 77.

p. 173 45. In 1493 Hans Holbein, citizen of Ulm, together with Michel Erhart, was responsible for an altarpiece for Weingarten Abbey. In 1494 Hans Holbein was a taxpayer in his native town of Augsburg.

46. Cat. Demmler, Berlin, 212, no. 452.

47. I think the problem of distinguishing between the hands of father and son is at its most difficult in the Virgin in the Bayerisches Nationalmuseum, Munich, and the attendant figures of St Cosmas and St Damian in the parish church of Kaufbeuren, which perhaps form part of the same group. (Cf. Cat. Müller, Munich, 111, no. 59.)

p. 174 48. From the Schatz- und Kunstkammer in the Burg at Graz. Cf. J. von Schlosser, *Vanitas* (Vienna, 1922); *idem*, *Präludien* (Berlin, 1927), 376.

49. Exhib. 'Early German Art' (Burlington Fine Arts Club, London, 1906), 118, case A, nos. 14, 16. Apparently carved in limewood, which is unusual. Perhaps this use of softwood helps to confirm the early dating; T. Müller, *op. cit.* (Note 36), 11.

50. E. F. Bange, in *J. d. P. Kunsts.*, XLV (1924), 212; *idem*, *Die deutschen Bronzestatuetten des 16. Jahrhunderts* (Berlin, 1949), no. 132.

51. Monument to Diepold and Anna von Stain in the parish church of Jettingen (d. before 1501), memorial tablets of Canon Ulrich von Rechberg (d. 1501) and Dr Adolf Occo (d. 1503) in the cloisters of Augsburg Cathedral, of Dean Ulrich von Wolfersdorf (d. 1504) in the mortuary chapel of the same, and tombstone of Philipp von Stain (d. 1509) in the parish church of Jettingen.

52. E.g., tombs of Bishop Friedrich II of Hohenzollern in Augsburg Cathedral, of Bishop Wilhelm von Reichenau in Eichstätt Cathedral, of Bishop Georg Altdorfer in St Martin, Landshut, and of Provost Maier in the collegiate church at Moosburg. P. M. Halm, *Studien zur süddeutschen Plastik* (Augsburg, 1926–7), I, 102 ff.

53. K. Feuchtmayr, 'Der Augsburger Bildhauer Jörg Muscat', *Münch. J. d. b. K.*, XII (1921), 99; Kunsthistorisches Museum, Vienna: L. Planiscig, *Die Bronzeplastiken* (Vienna, 1924), nos. 305, 306. But there is no connexion with the busts planned for the Emperor Maximilian's tomb.

54. C. von Fabriczy, 'Adriano Fiorentino', *J. d. P. Kunsts.*, XXIV (1903), 83.

p. 175   55. Cat. Exhib. 'La toison d'or' (Bruges, 1962), no. 348.

56. H. Reinhardt and André Rais, in *Historisches Museum Basel, Jahresbericht* (1946), 33.

57. Museen Berlin: IV: W. Vöge, *Die deutschen Bildwerke* (Berlin, 1910), 57, no. III; A. Rosenberg, *Der Goldschmiede Werkzeichen*, 3rd ed. (Frankfurt, 1922), I, no. 113.

58. I thought there was a link between this silver figure and the goldsmith Jörg Seld, of whom we have records in Augsburg from 1484 (N. Lieb, 'Die Augsburger Familie Seld', *Lebensbilder aus dem Bayerischen Schwaben*, VI (Munich, 1958), 38). Apparently I was wrong; for accredited works by Jörg Seld – beginning with the small silver altarpiece of 1492 from St Walburg at Eichstätt (Munich, Wittelsbacher Ausgleichsfond) – already show that remarkable uncertainty of style which appeared occasionally during the attempt of the German Late Gothic to come to terms with the new idealized notions of form and which generally resulted in an exaggeration of the decorative elements.

59. Exhib. 'Early German Art' (Burlington Fine Arts Club, London, 1906), 115, case A, no. 8; Cat. Exhib. 'German Art' (Manchester Art Gallery, 1961), nos. 59, 68 (sketch in the manner of Holbein the Elder). The sketch and model of a silver statuette of St Christopher, also originally from Kaisheim, dating from 1493 and in the same collection, are by another hand (Exhib. London, 1906, 117, case A, no. 12; Cat. Exhib. Manchester, no. 56).

60. T. Müller, *Alte Bairische Bildhauer* (Munich, 1950), plates 91, 88–9.

p. 176   61. F. Burger, *Der Meister der Skulpturen von Blutenburg* (Munich, 1914). The character of a wooden figure of St James in the Academy in Vienna is softer (A. Feulner, *Die deutsche Plastik des 16. Jahrhunderts* (Leipzig, 1926), plate 3).

62. P. M. Halm, *op. cit.* (Note 52), I, 139; T. Müller, *op. cit.*, plate 90.

63. It is uncertain whether among the many masters who are known to have collaborated in this work the chief master is the one responsible for the monogram A T on the biretta of one of the figures; also whether, as suggested by G. Lill (*Hans Leinberger* (Munich, 1942), 26), these initials refer to Andre Taubenpeck, who became a citizen of Landshut in 1494.

64. O. Demus, in *Österreichische Z. f. Kunst und Denkmalpflege*, XI (1957), 1.

65. M. Hasse, in *Z. f. Kunstw.*, I (1947), 89; F. Dworschak, *Krems, Stein und Göttweig in der Kunst des ausgehenden Mittelalters* (Krems, 1948), 177; W. Paatz, *Süddeutsche Schnitzaltäre der Spätgotik* (Heidelberg, 1963), 56.

66. Cat. Müller, Munich, no. 25.

67. We have to consider how much Swabian influence we may presume in the art of the Master of Kefermarkt (and also in his figure of the Virgin at Kájov (Gojau) in the Bohemian Forest).

68. O. Benesch, 'Der Zwettler Altar', in E. Buchner and K. Feuchtmayr, *Beiträge zur Geschichte der deutschen Kunst*, II (1928), 230.

69. K. Oettinger, *Lorenz Luchsperger* (Berlin, p. 177 1935), figures 36 ff.

70. K. Oettinger, *op. cit.* (Note 24); W. Fleischhauer, *op. cit.* (Note 22).

71. I cannot subscribe to the theory of M. Capra (in *Mitteilungen d. Gesellschaft f. vergleichende Kunstforschung in Wien*, IV (1952), 21) that Pilgram's pulpit statues in Vienna date from between 1495 and 1502. On the contrary, the date 1513 on the organ bracket proves unequivocally that at this time Pilgram was still producing traditional types. Moreover work on the tomb of the Emperor Frederick III in St Stephen was not completed until about 1510. The dating 1510 of the relief of St Barbara in the Diocesan Museum in Vienna (M. Capra in *Alte und Neue Kunst*, IV (1955), 34) proves that various styles existed simultaneously, i.e. the Swabian–Upper Rhenish style was being superseded by elements of the Danubian style.

72. Marble busts of King Matthias and Queen Beatrix in the Szepmüvészeti Muzeum, Budapest. E. Hoffmann, 'Der künstlerische Schmuck der Corvinus-Codices', *Belvedere*, VIII (1925), 130; J. Balogh, *Müvészet Mátyás Király Udvaraban* (Budapest, 1964).

73. K. Gerstenberg, 'Riemenschneider und der p. 17 niederländische Realismus', *Z. d. deutschen Vereins f. Kunstw.*, I (1934), 37; J. Bier, 'Die Anfänge Tilman Riemenschneiders', *Kunstg. Gesellschaft zu Berlin, Sitzungsberichte* (1956/7), 9; J. A. Schmoll, gen. Eisenwerth, in *J. d. Hamburger Kunsts.*, III (1958), 94; J. Bier, Introduction Cat. Exhib. Raleigh 1962.

74. Cat. Müller, Munich, no. 129.

75. Early works in alabaster by Riemenschneider include: Annunciation supposed to be from a

monastery at Bamberg, now Amsterdam, Rijks-museum (Cat. Schmitt-Swarzenski, Frankfurt, no. 144); St Barbara, at Bremen, Roselius-Haus (Plate 173B); Virgin of the Annunciation supposed to be from St Peter at Erfurt, now Paris, Louvre (Cat. (1922), no. 555); St Jerome, in the Cleveland Museum of Art (Cat. Schmitt-Swarzenski, Frankfurt, no. 143). Cf. E. Redslob, 'Erfurt als künstlerische Heimat Tilman Riemenschneiders', *Festschrift Friedrich Winkler* (Berlin, 1959), 171.

76. K. Gerstenberg, 'Der Magister mit dem Buch, ein unbekanntes Jugendwerk Tilman Riemenschneiders', *Die Kunst*, LV (1957), 84.

. 179   77. Cat. Demmler, Berlin, 167, nos. 2628, 402-5; Cat. Müller, Munich, no. 131.

78. Riemenschneider's wooden St Sebastian (c. 1490) is preserved with its old, partly original colouring in the Bayerisches Nationalmuseum in Munich (Cat. Müller, Munich, no. 130); it is allegedly from Zell Abbey near Würzburg.

79. The decision of the city council of Würzburg at this time to move the old figures of Adam and Eve into the inside of the chapel is also expressive of a new, optical evaluation.

80. T. Müller, in *Die Kunst*, LIV (1956), 128. Cf. Riemenschneider's Virgin and Child, sandstone, Frankfurt, Städtische Skulpturengalerie, originally in the Stiftskurie in the Martinsgasse at Würzburg.

180   81. G. Poensgen, *Der Windsheimer Zwölfbotenaltar von Tilman Riemenschneider* (Munich, 1955).

82. F. Winzinger, 'Ein zerstörtes Hauptwerk Tilman Riemenschneiders', *Das Münster*, IV (1951), 129.

83. Cat. Exhib. 'Der Bildschnitzer Peter Breuer' (Zwickau, 1935).

182   84. Sandrart expressly states that Stoss was 'not only a sculptor but was also acquainted with etching, engraving, and painting'. Cf. A. Stange, *Deutsche Malerei der Gotik*, IX (Munich, 1958), 79. Drawings by Veit Stoss, preserved at Budapest, Göttingen, and Cracow, are sketches for sculptural work. To Riemenschneider too we may attribute certain drawings (cf. K. Gerstenberg, in *Münch. J. d. b. K.*, III, F.1 (1950), 187; J. Bier, in *Niederdeutsche Beiträge zur Kunstg.*, I (1961), 219).

183   85. G. Barthel, *Die Ausstrahlungen der Kunst des Veit Stoss im Osten* (Munich, 1944).

86. V. A. F. Kotrba, *Levočský oltár Majstra Paula* (Bratislava, 1955); J. Homolka and others, *Majster Pavol z Levoče* (Bratislava, 1961).

87. Cat. Weihrauch, Munich, no. 21; G. von der   p. 185
Osten, 'Über Peter Vischers törichten Bauern', *Anzeiger d. Germanischen Nationalmuseums Nürnberg* (1963), 71.

88. The bronze tablets, dating from c. 1489, in Ellwangen Abbey and in Merseburg Cathedral show how Peter Vischer emancipated himself from the traditions of his father's foundry. Cf. E. F. Bange, 'Die künstlerische Bedeutung Peter Vischers des Älteren', *J. d. P. Kunsts.*, L (1929), 167; T. Müller, in *Wissenschaftliche Z. d. Karl Marx-Universität Leipzig*, V (1955/6), 223; H. Stafski, 'Die Vischerwerkstatt und ihre Probleme', *Z. f. Kunstg.*, XXI (1958), 1; D. Wuttke, 'Die Handschriftenzeugnisse über das Wirken der Vischer', *Z. f. Kunstg.*, XXII (1959), 324; H. Stafski, *Der jüngere Peter Vischer* (Nuremberg, 1962).

89. The existence of business relations between   p. 186
Veit Stoss and the Vischer foundry is all the more interesting. As a sculptor and carver Veit Stoss was not himself permitted to undertake any casting. After the death in 1496 of Filippo Buonaccorsi, known as Callimachus, private secretary to the Polish king, Veit Stoss, who had now returned to Nuremberg, owing to his connexions with the Polish court was commissioned to carve the monument of Callimachus for the Dominican church at Cracow. Veit Stoss prepared the sketch and model for the work, but the surround appears to emanate from the Vischer workshop of about 1505. This same workshop also carried out other important commissions for Poland, e.g. the monumental slabs of the Voivod Peter Kmita (d. 1505) in the Cathedral on the Wawel at Cracow and of Peter Salomon (before 1510) in St Mary at Cracow.

90. Full justice has not been done to this tomb because in the windowless tower-porch of Magdeburg Cathedral it could only be seen and photographed by artificial light. After the damage suffered by the cathedral during the Second World War, however, it was possible to see it in daylight. I therefore refer readers to the new photographs by Günther and Klaus Beyer, reproduced in F. Kämpfer's *Peter Vischer* (Dresden, 1960).

91. I now incline more to the opinion of E. F. Bange that Peter Vischer the Younger was chiefly responsible for the figures on the shrine. Presumably, then, Peter Vischer the Younger was also responsible for the statuette of Hercules and Antaeus in the Bayerisches Nationalmuseum in Munich (Cat. Weihrauch, Munich, no. 22) after a model by one of the Pollaiuolo circle.

p. 187 92. V. Oberhammer, *Die Bronzestandbilder des Maximiliansgrabmals in der Hofkirche zu Innsbruck* (Innsbruck, 1935), 406; F. Winkler, *Die Zeichnungen Albrecht Dürers*, III (Berlin, 1938), nos. 676, 677.

93. Cat. Müller, Munich, no. 124. The attribution to Anton Pilgram comes from Wilhelm Vöge (in *J. f. Kunstw.* (1927), 33).

94. G. Troescher, *Conrat Meit von Worms* (Freiburg i. Br., 1927), J. Duverger, *Conrat Meijt* (Ghent, 1934).

CHAPTER 13

p. 189 1. Cat. Cluny, bois, nos. 344–429.

2. Cf. choir stalls in St Seurin, Bordeaux. The carvings on the choir stalls in St Martin-aux-Bois (Oise) followed slightly later.

3. M. Aubert, *La sculpture française au moyen-âge* (Paris, 1946), 392–3.

4. Late Gothic panel paintings and documentary records prove the great artistic traditions of Amiens. Cf. C. Dehaisnes, 'L'art à Amiens vers la fin du moyen âge dans ses rapports avec l'école flamande primitive', *Rev. de l'Art Chrétien* (1889), 467; *ibid.* (1890), 25, 183, 269; G. Durand, 'Les tailleurs d'images d'Amiens', *Bull. Monumental*, XC (1931), 333; XCI (1932), 5.

5. Antoine Ancquier was also commissioned for the monument of Bishop Adrien de Hénencourt (d. 1530), who had provided so generously for the decoration of the choir of Amiens Cathedral. A drawing made by Guillaume Laignier(?) of the bishop on his deathbed was the basis of the sculptor's work.

p. 190 6. R. Koechlin and J. J. Marquet de Vasselot, *La sculpture à Troyes et dans la Champagne* (Paris, 1900).

7. C. Oman, in *Pantheon*, XVIII (1960), 10.

8. E. Gayelle and P. Piétresson de St Aubin (Lille, 1924) attributed a Visitation in St Jean-au-Marché in Troyes, which is approximately a decade later and by another hand, to Nicolas Halins, called 'le Flamand', known to have been active in Troyes.

9. M. Aubert, *op. cit.*, 309, 418, 419.

10. Cat. Müller, Munich, no. 123.

11. Cat. Aubert, Paris, no. 383.

12. Cat. Legner, Frankfurt (1961), nos. 40–2.

13. R. H. Randall, in *Bull. of the Metropolitan* p. 191 *Museum of Art* (1956), 257; B. G. Proske, *Castilian Sculpture* (New York, 1951), figure 118; G. Weise, *Spanische Plastik aus sieben Jahrhunderten*, I (Reutlingen, 1925), plates 150–1.

14. Cat. Paris Exhib. 1950, no. 184; M. Vloberg, *La vierge et l'enfant dans l'art français* (Paris-Grenoble, 1954), 201.

15. Cat. Paris Exhib. 1950, nos. 182, 181.

16. P. Pradel, *Michel Colombe* (Paris, 1953), 32.

17. J. Babelon, *La médaille en France* (Paris, 1948), 19.

18. P. Pradel, *op. cit.*, 41.

19. F. Burger, *Francesco Laurana* (Strasbourg, 1907). See also Anthony Blunt, *Art and Architecture in France: 1500–1700* (Pelican History of Art) (Harmondsworth, 1953), and Charles Seymour Jr, *Sculpture in Italy: 1400–1500* (Pelican History of Art) (Harmondsworth, 1965).

20. Louis Mourier delivered a multi-figured Entombment to Jarzé in 1504. Cf. S. Pajot, in p. 19: *Mémoires de la Société des Antiquaires du Centre*, XLVI (1934/5), 61.

21. For Michel Colombe, see also A. Blunt, *op. cit.*

22. The statue of St Mary Magdalen at Limeray (Indre-et-Loire) is more conventional and less delicately organized.

23. Cat. Aubert, Paris, nos. 405–7.

24. Among the works attributed by Pradel to p. 19 Jean de Chartres, the Pietà of 1499/1506 in the church of Varennes-sur-Tèche (Allier), donated by Hugues de Montjournal, seems to me to be especially remarkable on account of the strength of its religious expression, the clear anatomy of Christ's body, and the intensity of expression on the face of the votive offerer.

25. M. Gómez-Moreno, *La escultura del rinascimento en España* (Florence-Barcelona, 1932), plate 8; J. M. Azcárate, *Escultura del siglo XVI* (Ars Hispaniae, XIII) (Madrid, 1958), 18.

BIBLIOGRAPHY

I. GENERAL

BAZIN, G. *Peinture française des origines au XVIe s.* Paris, n.d.

BRAUN, J. *Der christliche Altar.* Munich, 1924.

DVOŘAK, M. *Kunstgeschichte als Geistesgeschichte.* Munich, 1924.

FOCILLON, H. *Art d'Occident.* Paris, 1938.

GUDIOL, J. M. *Pintura gótica (Ars Hispaniae,* IX). Madrid, 1955.

HASSE, M. *Der Flügelaltar.* Dresden, 1941.

HUIZINGA, J. *The Waning of the Middle Ages.* London, 1924; Harmondsworth, 1955.

HUIZINGA, J. *Im Bann der Geschichte.* Amsterdam-Zürich-Brussels, 1942.

HUTH, H. *Künstler und Werkstatt der Spätgotik.* Augsburg, 1923.

MARTIN, H. *La miniature française du XIIIe au XVIe s.* Paris, 1923.

MICHEL, A. *Histoire de l'Art,* vol. III, 1, 2, Paris, 1907-8; vol. IV, 2, Paris, 1911.

OSTEN, G. VON DER. *Der Schmerzensmann.* Berlin, 1935.

PANOFSKY, E. *Early Netherlandish Painting.* Cambridge, 1953.

PORCHER, J. *L'enluminaire française.* Paris, 1959.

RING, G. *A Century of French Painting, 1400–1500.* London, 1949.

SCHELLER, R. W. *A Survey of Medieval Model Books.* Haarlem, 1963.

SCHLOSSER, J. VON. *Die Kunst des Mittelalters.* Berlin, n.d.

SCHMITT, O. (ed.). *Reallexikon zur deutschen Kunstgeschichte,* II. Stuttgart, 1948.

    col. 582: Bildhauer, Bildschnitzer (T. Müller)

    col. 625: Bildhauerzeichnung (H. Keller)

    col. 1081: Bozzetto (H. Keller)

STANGE, A. *Deutsche Malerei der Gotik.* Berlin-Munich, 1934-61.

STERLING, C. *La peinture française: Les primitifs.* Paris, 1938.

STONE, L. *Sculpture in Britain: The Middle Ages (Pelican History of Art).* Harmondsworth, 1955.

THOBY, P. *Le crucifix.* Nantes, 1959; Supplément, Nantes, 1963.

TROESCHER, G. *Kunst- und Künstlerwanderungen in Mitteleuropa.* Baden-Baden, 1953-4.

WESCHER, P. *Jean Fouquet.* Basel, 1948.

II. REGIONS

A. AUSTRIA

ERNST, R., and GARGER, E. *Die früh- und hochgotische Plastik des Stefansdoms.* Munich, 1927.

GARZAROLLI VON THURNLACKH, K. *Mittelalterliche Plastik in Steiermark.* Graz, 1941.

KIESLINGER, F. *Die mittelalterliche Plastik in Österreich.* Vienna, 1926.

KOHLBACH, R. *Steirische Bildhauer.* Graz, 1956.

KUTAL, A. *České gotické sochařství 1350–1450.* Prague, 1962.

MÜLLER, T. *Mittelalterliche Plastik Tirols.* Berlin, 1935.

OETTINGER, K. *Altdeutsche Bildschnitzer der Ostmark.* Vienna, 1939.

OETTINGER, K. *Anton Pilgram und die Bildhauer von St Stephan.* Vienna, 1951.

B. CZECHOSLOVAKIA, HUNGARY, YUGOSLAVIA, POLAND, AND THE EASTERN BALTIC STATES

AGGHÁZY, M. *Alte Holzfiguren in Ungarn.* Budapest, 1958.

BROSIG, A. *Rzeźba gotycka.* Poznań, 1928.

BUČINA, F., and STEHLIK, L. *Gotische Madonnen.* Prague, 1958.

CEVC, E. *Srednjeveška Plastika na Slovenskem.* Ljubljana, 1963.

CLASEN, K. H. *Die mittelalterliche Bildhauerkunst im Deutschordensland Preussen.* Berlin, 1939.

DENKSTEIN, V., and MATOUŠ, F. *Südböhmische Gotik.* Prague, 1955.

DUTKIEWICZ, J. E. *Małopolska rzeźba średniowieczna 1300-1450.* Cracow, 1949.

HEKLER, A. *Ungarische Kunstgeschichte.* Berlin, 1937.

KACZMARCZYK, D. *Straty wojenne Polski w Dziedzinie Rzeźby.* Warsaw, 1958.

KARLING, S. *Medeltida träskulptur i Estland.* Stockholm, 1946.

KLETZL, O. *Die Junker von Prag in Strassburg.* Frankfurt, 1936.

KUTAL, A. *České gotické sochařství 1350-1450.* Prague, 1962.

OPITZ, J. *Plastik Böhmens zur Zeit der Luxemburger,* I. Prague, 1936.

SCHÜRER, O., and WIESE, E. *Deutsche Kunst in der Zips.* Brno, 1938.

ŠOUREK, K. *Umění na Slovensku.* Prague, 1938.

C. FRANCE

AUBERT, M. *Les richesses d'art de la France, La Bourgogne, La Sculpture.* Paris, 1927-30.

AUBERT, M. *La sculpture française au moyen-âge.* Paris, 1946.

AUBERT, M. *Sculptures du moyen âge (Encyclopédie photographique de l'art).* Paris, 1948.

BABELON, J. *La médaille en France.* Paris, 1948.

BEAULIEU, M., and BAYLE, J. *Le costume en Bourgogne de Philippe le Hardi à la mort de Charles le Téméraire.* Paris, 1956.

BERGIUS, R. *Französische und belgische Konsol- und Zwickelplastik im 14. und 15. Jahrhundert.* Diss., Munich, 1936.

BEVOTTE, M. DE. *La sculpture dans la région de Toulouse, d'Albi et de Rodez.* Paris, 1936.

CALMETTE, J. *Les Grands Ducs de Bourgogne.* Paris, 1949.

CARTELLIERI, O. *Am Hofe der Herzöge von Burgund.* Basel, 1926; English ed., trans. M. Letts, *The Court of Burgundy.* London, 1929.

CHAMPEAUX, A. DE, and GAUCHERY, P. *Les travaux d'art exécutés pour Jean de France, Duc de Berry.* Paris, 1894.

COLOMBIER, P. DU. *Les chantiers des cathédrales.* Paris, 1953.

CROSBY, S. McK. *L'abbaye royale de Saint-Denis.* Paris, 1953.

DAVID, H. *De Sluter à Sambin,* I. Paris, 1933.

DAVID, H. *Philippe le Hardi.* Dijon, 1937.

DUCHARTRE, P. L. *Mittelalterliche Plastik in Frankreich.* Munich, 1925.

EVANS, J. *Life in Mediaeval France.* London, 1925.

EVANS, J. *Art in Mediaeval France 987-1498.* London, 1948.

GERMAIN, A. *Les Néerlandais en Bourgogne.* Brussels, 1909.

GRODECKI, L. *Ivoires français.* Paris, 1947.

HOFMANN, H. D. *Die lothringische Skulptur der Spätgotik.* Saarbrücken, 1962.

HUMBERT, A. *La sculpture sous les Ducs de Bourgogne.* Paris, 1913.

JOUEN. *La cathédrale de Rouen.* Rouen-Paris, 1932.

JOURNET, R. *Deux retables du 15ème s. à Ternant.* Paris, 1963.

KIEINCLAUSZ, A. *Claus Sluter et la sculpture bourguignonne au XVe s.* Paris, 1905.

KOECHLIN, R., and MARQUET DE VASSELOT, J. J. *La sculpture à Troyes et dans la Champagne.* Paris, 1900.

KOECHLIN, R. *Les ivoires français.* Paris, 1924.

LABORDE, DE. *Les ducs de Bourgogne,* II. Paris, 1849-52.

LUC-BENOIST. *La sculpture française.* Paris, 1945.

MÂLE, E. *L'art religieux de la fin du moyen-âge en France.* Paris, 1922.

MASSEY TOVELL, R. *Flemish Artists of the Valois Courts.* Toronto, 1950.

OURSEL, C. *L'art de Bourgogne.* Paris-Grenoble, 1953.

RÉAU, L. *L'art religieux du moyen-âge (La sculpture).* 1946.

REINERS, H. *Burgundisch-Alemannische Plastik.* Strasbourg, 1943.

ROUSSEL, J. *La sculpture française, Époque gothique.* Paris, 1930.

TROESCHER, G. *Die burgundische Plastik des ausgehenden Mittelalters.* Frankfurt, 1940.

VITRY, P., and BRIÈRE, G. *Documents de sculpture française du moyen-âge.* Paris, 1904.

VITRY, P. *La sculpture française du XIIe au XVI s.* Paris, n.d.

VLOBERG, M. *La vierge et l'enfant dans l'art français.* Paris-Grenoble, 1954.

ZANETTACCI, H. *Les ateliers picards de sculpture à la fin du moyen âge.* Paris, 1954.

D. GERMANY

BACK, F. *Mittelrheinische Kunst.* Frankfurt, 1910.

BACK, F. *Ein Jahrtausend künstlerischer Kultur am Mittelrhein.* Darmstadt, 1932.

BANGE, E. F. *Die Kleinplastik der deutschen Renaissance.* Florence–Munich, 1928.

BANGE, E. F. *Die deutschen Bronzestatuetten des 16. Jahrhunderts.* Berlin, 1949.

BAUM, J. *Die Ulmer Plastik um 1500.* Stuttgart, 1911.

BAUM, J. *Gotische Bildwerke Schwabens.* Augsburg, 1921.

BAUM, J. *Niederschwäbische Plastik des ausgehenden Mittelalters.* Tübingen, 1925.

BEENKEN, H. *Bildwerke Westfalens.* Bonn, 1923.

BRAUNE, H., and WIESE, E. *Schlesische Malerei und Plastik des Mittelalters.* Leipzig, 1929.

CLASEN, K. H. *Die mittelalterliche Bildhauerkunst im Deutschordensland Preussen.* Berlin, 1939.

CLASEN, K. H. *Die schönen Madonnen.* Königstein, 1951.

DECKERT, H., FREYHAN, R., and STEINBART, K. *Religiöse Kunst aus Hessen und Nassau.* Marburg, 1932.

FEULNER, A., and MÜLLER, T. *Geschichte der deutschen Plastik.* Munich, 1953.

FISCHEL, L. *Nicolaus Gerhaert und die Bildhauer der deutschen Spätgotik.* Munich, 1944.

FRENZ, H. K. *Die Schulkreise Nicolaus Gerhaerts am Mittel- und Oberrhein.* Diss., Freiburg i. Br., 1943.

FRÜNDT, E. *Spätgotische Plastik in Mecklenburg.* Dresden, 1963.

GEISLER, J. *Oberrheinische Plastik um 1400.* Berlin, 1957.

GRIMME, E. G. 'Die grossen Jahrhunderte der Aachener Goldschmiedekunst', *Aachener Kunstblätter*, XXVI (1962).

HABICH, G. *Die deutschen Schaumünzen des XVI. Jahrhunderts.* Munich, 1929–34.

HABICHT, C. *Hanseatische Malerei und Plastik in Skandinavien.* Berlin, 1926.

HALM, P. M. *Studien zur süddeutschen Plastik.* Augsburg, 1926–7.

HEISE, C. G. *Lübecker Plastik.* Bonn, 1926.

HENTSCHEL, W. *Sächsische Plastik um 1500.* Dresden, 1926.

HESSIG, E. *Die Kunst des Meisters E.S. und die Plastik der Spätgotik.* Berlin, 1935.

HILGER, H. P. *Der Skulpturenzyklus im Chor des Aachener Domes.* Essen, 1961.

HOFMANN, H. D. *Die lothringische Skulptur der Spätgotik.* Saarbrücken, 1962.

HÖHN, H. *Nürnberger gotische Plastik.* Nuremberg, 1922.

KAUTZSCH, R. *Der Mainzer Dom und seine Denkmäler.* Frankfurt, 1925.

KAUTZSCH, R. *Der Dom zu Worms.* Berlin, 1938.

KLETZL, O. *Die Junker von Prag in Strassburg.* Frankfurt, 1936.

KUNZE, H. *Die gotische Skulptur in Mitteldeutschland.* Bonn, 1925.

LEONHARDT, K. F. *Spätgotische Grabdenkmäler des Salzachgebietes.* Leipzig, 1913.

LÜTHGEN, E. *Die niederrheinische Plastik von der Gotik bis zur Renaissance.* Strasbourg, 1917.

LÜTHGEN, E. *Gotische Plastik in den Rheinlanden.* Bonn, 1921.

MÜLLER, T. *Alte Bairische Bildhauer.* Munich, 1950.

MÜLLER, T. *Frühe Beispiele der Retrospektive in der deutschen Plastik (Sitzungsberichte der Bayer. Akademie der Wissenschaften, Phil.-Hist. Klasse).* Munich, 1961.

OTTO, G. *Die Ulmer Plastik der Spätgotik.* Reutlingen, 1927.

PAATZ, W. *Die Lübeckische Steinskulptur der ersten Hälfte des 15. Jahrhunderts.* Lübeck, 1929.

PAATZ, W. *Bernt Notke und sein Kreis.* Berlin, 1939.

PAATZ, W. *Prolegomena zu einer Geschichte der deutschen spätgotischen Plastik (Abhandlungen der Heidelberger Akademie der Wissenschaften, phil.-hist. Klasse).* Heidelberg, 1956.

PAATZ, W. *Süddeutsche Schnitzaltäre der Spätgotik.* Heidelberg, 1963.

PASSARGE, W. *Das deutsche Vesperbild im Mittelalter.* Cologne, 1924.

PETERS, H. *Der Dom zu Köln.* Düsseldorf, 1948.

PINDER, W. *Die deutsche Plastik vom ausgehenden Mittelalter bis zum Ende der Renaissance.* Berlin, 1914 ff.

PINDER, W. *Mittelalterliche Plastik Würzburgs.* Leipzig, 1924.

PINDER, W. *Die deutsche Plastik des 15. Jahrhunderts.* Munich, 1924.

PINDER, W. *Die deutsche Plastik des 14. Jahrhunderts.* Munich, 1925.

ROTT, H. *Quellen und Forschungen zur südwest-deutschen und schweizerischen Kunstgeschichte im XV. und XVI. Jahrhunderts.* Stuttgart, 1933 ff.

SCHÄDLER, A. *Deutsche Plastik der Spätgotik.* Königstein, 1962.

SCHMITT, O. *Oberrheinische Plastik im ausgehenden Mittelalter.* Freiburg, 1924.

SCHMITT, O. *Gotische Skulpturen des Strassburger Münsters.* Frankfurt, 1924.

SCHMITT, O. *Gotische Skulpturen des Freiburger Münsters.* Frankfurt, 1926.

SCHNELLBACH, R. *Spätgotische Plastik im unteren Neckargebiet.* Heidelberg, 1931.

SCHROTH, I. *Mittelalterliche Goldschmiedekunst am Oberrhein.* Freiburg, 1948.

SCHÜRER, O., and WIESE, E. *Deutsche Kunst in der Zips.* Brno, 1938.

SCHWARZWEBER, A. *Das Heilige Grab in der deutschen Bildnerei des Mittelalters.* Freiburg, 1940.

SIEBENHÜNER, H. *Deutsche Künstler am Mailänder Dom.* Munich, 1944.

STUTTMANN, F., and OSTEN, G. VON DER. *Niedersächsische Bildschnitzerei des späten Mittelalters.* Berlin, 1940.

THORDEMAN, B. *Norddeutsche Kunst in schwedischen Kirchen.* Stockholm, 1930.

WENTZEL, H. *Niederdeutsche Madonnen.* Hamburg, 1941.

WIESE, E. *Schlesische Plastik vom Beginn des 14. bis zur Mitte des 15. Jahrhunderts.* Leipzig, 1923.

WILM, H. *Gotische Tonplastik in Deutschland.* Augsburg, 1929.

WILM, H. *Die gotische Holzfigur.* 3rd ed. Stuttgart, 1962.

WITTE, F. *Tausend Jahre deutscher Kunst am Rhein.* Berlin, 1932.

E. NETHERLANDS

BERGIUS, R. *Französische und belgische Konsol- und Zwickelplastik im 14. und 15. Jahrhundert.* Diss., Munich, 1936.

BORCHGRAVE D' ALTENA, J. DE. *Sculptures conservées au pays mosan.* Verviers, 1926.

BORCHGRAVE D'ALTENA, J. DE. 'Des caractères de la sculpture brabançonne vers 1500', *A.S.R. Arch. de Bruxelles,* XXXVIII (1934), 188.

BORCHGRAVE D'ALTENA, J. DE. 'À propos de l'exposition "Les Madones du Limbourg"', *Bull. S.R. Arch. de Bruxelles,* nos 2/3 (1936), 5.

BORCHGRAVE D'ALTENA, J. DE. 'Notes pour servir à l'inventaire des œuvres d'art du Brabant, Arrondissement de Louvain', *A.S.R. Arch. de Bruxelles,* XLIII/XLIV (1939/40).

BORCHGRAVE D'ALTENA, J. DE. *Les retables brabançons.* Brussels, 1942.

BORCHGRAVE D'ALTENA, J. DE. 'Notes pour servir à l'inventaire des œuvres d'art du Brabant, Arrondissement du Bruxelles', *A.S.R. Arch. de Bruxelles,* XLVII (1944/6) [1947].

BORCHGRAVE D'ALTENA, J. DE. *La passion du Christ dans la sculpture en Belgique.* Brussels, 1946.

BORCHGRAVE D'ALTENA, J. DE. *Les retables brabançons conservés en Suède.* Brussels, 1948.

BORCHGRAVE D'ALTENA, J. DE. 'De Beeldhouwkunst in de zuidelijke Nederlanden', in Gelder, van, and Duverger, J., *Kunstgeschiedenis der Nederlanden,* I. Utrecht, 1954.

BORCHGRAVE D'ALTENA, J. DE. *Notes pour servir à l'inventaire des oeuvres d'art du Brabant. Arrondissement de Nivelles.* Brussels, 1961.

BOSSCHÈRE, J. DE. *La sculpture anversoise.* Brussels, 1909.

BOUVY, D. P. R. A. *Middeleeuwensche Beeldhouwkunst in de Noordelijke Nederlanden.* Amsterdam, 1957.

CASIER, J., and BERGMANS, P. *L'art ancien dans les Flandres (Région de l'Escaut).* Brussels-Paris, 1914.

COLLON-GEVAERT, S. *Histoire des arts du métal en Belgique.* Brussels, 1951.

COPPENS, M. *Gothic Choir-stalls in the Netherlands.* 2 vols. Amsterdam–Brussels, n.d.

DESTRÉE, J. 'Étude sur la sculpture brabançonne au moyen-âge', *A.S.R. Arch. de Bruxelles,* VIII (1894), 7; IX (1895), 363; XIII (1899), 273.

DEVIGNE, M. *La sculpture mosane.* Paris–Brussels, 1932.

DEVIGNE, M. 'La sculpture flamande', in *Trésor de l'art flamande,* II, 69. Paris, 1932.

DUVERGER, J. *De Brusselsche Steenbickeleren der XIVe en XVe eeuw – Klaas Sluter en zijn Brusselsche Medewerkers te Dijon.* Ghent, 1933.

GABRIELS, J. *De vlaamsche Beeldhouwkunst.* Antwerp, 1942.

GERMAIN, A. *Les Néerlandais en Bourgogne.* Brussels, 1909.

HERCK, J. VAN. *Het Passie-Retabel van Geel.* Antwerp, 1951.

KONRAD, M. *Meisterwerke der Skulptur in Flandern und Brabant.* Leipzig, 1929–35.

LOUIS, A. *L'église de N.-D. de Hal (Saint Martin) (Ars Belgica,* VI). Brussels, 1936.

MAETERLINCK, L. *Le genre satirique dans la sculpture flamande et wallone.* Paris, 1910.

MARCHAL, E. *La sculpture et les chefs-d'œuvre de l'orfèvrerie belges*. Brussels, 1895.

MASSEY TOVELL, R. *Flemish Artists of the Valois Courts*. Toronto, 1950.

MEINANDER, K. K. *Œuvres de l'art flamande du moyen âge en Finlande*. Helsinki, 1930.

POUMON, E. *Le Hainaut, Les retables*. Vilvorde, 1948.

PRADEL, P. *La sculpture belge au musée du Louvre*. Brussels, 1947.

ROGGEN, D. 'Beeldhouwkunst, Einde der XIVde en XVde eeuw', *Geschiedenis van de vlaamsche Kunst*, I, 236 ff. Antwerp–The Hague, 1937.

ROLLAND, P. *Les primitifs tournaisiens, peintres et sculpteurs*. Brussels–Paris, 1932.

ROLLAND, P. *La sculpture tournaisienne*. Brussels, 1944.

ROOSVAL, J. *Schnitzaltäre in schwedischen Kirchen und Museen aus der Werkstatt des Jan Bormann*. Strasbourg, 1903.

ROOSVAL, J. 'Retables d'origine néerlandaise dans les pays nordiques', *Rev. belge*, III (1933), 136.

SOIL DE MORIAMÉ, M.-E.-J. *Les anciennes industries d'art tournaisiennes*. Tournai, 1912.

TIMMERS, J. J. M. *Houten Beelden*. Antwerp, 1949.

VOGELSANG, W. 'De Noordnederlandse Beeldhouwkunst', in Gelder, van, and Duverger, J., *Kunstgeschiedenis der Nederlanden*, I. Utrecht, 1954.

WITSEN-ELIAS, J. S. *Koorbanken, Koorhekken en Kansels*. Amsterdam, 1946.

F. PORTUGAL AND SPAIN

AINAUD DE LASARTE, J., and DURAN SANPERE, A. *Escultura gótica (Ars Hispaniae, VIII)*. Madrid, 1956.

DIEULAFOY, M. *La statuaire polychrome en Espagne*. Paris, 1908.

GUDIOL RICART, J. *Arte de España: Cataluña*. Barcelona, 1955.

MAYER, A. L. *Gotik in Spanien*. Leipzig, 1928.

PROSKE, B. G. *Castilian Sculpture*. New York, 1951.

SANTOS, R. DOS. *A escultura em Portugal*, I, Lisbon, 1948; II, Lisbon, 1950.

WEISE, G. *Spanische Plastik aus sieben Jahrhunderten*, I–III. Reutlingen, 1925–30.

WETHEY, H. E. *Gil de Silhoe and his School*. Cambridge (Mass.), 1936.

ZERVOS, C. *L'art de la Catalogne*. Paris, [1937].

G. SCANDINAVIA AND FINLAND

BORCHGRAVE D'ALTENA, J. *Les retables brabançons conservés en Suède*. Brussels, 1948.

CORNELL, H. *Norlands kyrkliga Konst*. Uppsala-Stockholm, 1918.

ENGELSTADT, E. S. *Senmiddelalderens Kunst i Norge*. Oslo, 1936.

HABICHT, C. *Hanseatische Malerei und Plastik in Skandinavien*. Berlin, 1926.

HEISE, C. G. *Lübecker Plastik*. Bonn, 1926.

KARLING, S. *Medeltida träskulptur i Estland*. Stockholm, 1946.

LINDBLOM, A. *Den heliga Birgitta, bildverk i skulptur och maleri fran Sveriges medeltid*. Stockholm, 1918.

LINDBLOM, A. *Sveriges Konsthistoria*. Stockholm, 1944.

MEINANDER, K. K. *Medeltida Altarskap och Träsniderier i Finlands Kyrkor*. Helsingfors, 1908.

MEINANDER, K. K. *Œuvres de l'art flamande du moyen âge en Finlande*. Helsinki, 1930.

RÁCZ, I. *Suomen keskiajan taideaarteita* ('Art Treasures of Medieval Finland'). Helsinki, 1960.

ROOSVAL, J. *Schnitzaltäre in schwedischen Kirchen und Museen aus der Werkstatt des Jan Bormann*. Strasbourg, 1903.

ROOSVAL, J. 'Retables d'origine néerlandaise dans les pays nordiques', *Rev. belge*, III (1933), 136.

THORDEMAN, B. *Norddeutsche Kunst in schwedischen Kirchen*. Stockholm, 1930.

THORDEMAN, B. *Medieval Wooden Sculpture in Sweden*. Stockholm, 1964.

THORLACIUS-USSING, V. *Danmarks Billedhuggerkunst*. Copenhagen, 1950.

H. SWITZERLAND

BURCKHARDT, R. F. *Der Basler Münsterschatz (Die Kunstdenkmäler der Schweiz, IV)*. Basel, 1933.

FUTTERER, J. *Gotische Bildwerke der deutschen Schweiz 1200–1440*. Augsburg, 1930.

GANTNER, J. *Kunstgeschichte der Schweiz*, II. Frauenfeld, 1947.

KAUFMANN-HAGENBACH, A. *Die Basler Plastik des 15. und frühen 16. Jahrhunderts*. Basel, 1952.

KOVÁCS, F. *Stalles de Hauterive*. Posieux-Fribourg, n.d.

REINERS, H. *Burgundisch-Alemannische Plastik*. Strasbourg, 1943.

ROTT, H. *Quellen und Forschungen zur südwestdeutschen und schweizerischen Kunstgeschichte im XV. und XVI. Jahrhundert*. Stuttgart, 1933 ff.

III. SCULPTORS

BORMAN, Jan
Borchgrave d'Altena, J. de. *Le retable de Saint Georges de Jan Borman.* Brussels, 1947.
Roosval, J. *Schnitzaltäre in schwedischen Kirchen und Museen aus der Werkstatt des Jan Bormann.* Strasbourg, 1903.
COLOMBE, Michel
Pradel, P. *Michel Colombe.* Paris, 1953.
Vitry, P. *Michel Colombe.* Paris, 1901.
DOUVERMANN, Heinrich
Nüss, J. F. *Heinrich Douvermann.* Duisburg, 1963.
ERHART, Gregor
Otto, G. *Gregor Erhart.* Berlin, 1943.
GERHAERTS, Nicolaus
Fischel, L. *Nicolaus Gerhaert und die Bildhauer der deutschen Spätgotik.* Munich, 1944.
Frenz, H. K. *Die Schulkreise Nicolaus Gerhaerts am Mittel- und Oberrhein.* Diss., Freiburg i. Br., 1943.
Wertheimer, O. *Nicolaus Gerhaert.* Berlin, 1929.
GRASSER, Erasmus
Halm, P. M. *Erasmus Grasser.* Augsburg, 1928.
HAGNOWER, Niclas
Vöge, W. *Niclas Hagnower.* Freiburg i. Br., 1931.
JUPPE, Ludwig
Neuber, H. *Ludwig Juppe von Marburg.* Marburg, 1915.
KRAFT, Adam
Schwemmer, W. *Adam Kraft.* Nuremberg, 1958.
KUENE, Konrad
André, G. 'Konrad Kuene', in *Marburger J. f. Kunstw.*, XI, XII (1938/9), 159.
MULTSCHER, Hans
Gerstenberg, K. *Hans Multscher.* Leipzig, 1928.
Rasmo, N. *Der Multscher-Altar in Sterzing.* Bolzano, 1963.
NOTKE, Bernt
Paatz, W. *Bernt Notke und sein Kreis.* Berlin, 1939.
PACHER, Michael
Hempel, E. *Michael Pacher.* Vienna, 1931.
Stiassny, R. *Michael Pachers St Wolfganger Altar.* Vienna, 1919.
PARLER, Peter
Kletzl, O. *Peter Parler.* Leipzig, 1940.
Swoboda, K. M. *Peter Parler.* Vienna, 1940.
PILGRAM, Anton
Oettinger, K. *Anton Pilgram und die Bildhauer von St Stephan.* Vienna, 1951.
RIEMENSCHNEIDER, Tilman
Bier, J. *Tilmann Riemenschneider*, I, Würzburg, 1925; II, Augsburg, 1930.

Freeden, M. H. von. *Tilmann Riemenschneider.* Munich–Berlin, 1954.
Gerstenberg, K. *Tilman Riemenschneider.* Munich, 1962.
RUSS, Jacob
Volkmann, L. *Der Überlinger Rathaussaal des Jacob Russ.* Berlin, 1934.
SIFER, Conrad
Hauck, M.-L. 'Der Bildhauer Conrad Sifer von Sinsheim und sein Kreis', *A. Universitatis Saraviensis, Philosophie*, IX (1960).
SILOE, Gil de
Wethey, H. E. *Gil de Silhoe and his School.* Cambridge (Mass.), 1936.
SLUTER, Claus
David, H. *Claus Sluter.* Paris, 1951.
Kleinclausz, A. *Claus Sluter et la sculpture bourguignonne au XVe s.* Paris, 1905.
Liebreich, A. *Claus Sluter.* Brussels, 1936.
Troescher, G. *Claus Sluter.* Freiburg i. Br., 1932.
STOSS, Veit
Barthel, G. *Die Ausstrahlungen der Kunst des Veit Stoss im Osten.* Munich, 1944.
Dettloff, S. *Wit Stosz.* Wrocław (Polska Akademia Nauk, Komitet Nauk o Sztuce), 1961.
Dobrowolski, T., and Dutkiewicz, J. E. *Wit Stwosz, Oltarz Krakowski.* Warsaw, 1953.
Kopéra, F. *Wita Stwosza Wielki Oltarz.* Cracow, 1912.
Lossnitzer, M. *Veit Stoss.* Leipzig, 1912.
Lutze, E. *Veit Stoss.* Berlin, 1938.
Skubiszewski, P. *Rzeźba Nagrobna Wita Stwosza.* Warsaw, 1957.
SYRLIN, Jörg the Elder
Vöge, W. *Jörg Syrlin der Ältere und seine Bildwerke*, II. Berlin, 1950.
VISCHER, Peter
Kämpfer, F. Dresden, 1960.
Meller, S. *Peter Vischer der Ältere und seine Werkstatt.* Leipzig, 1925.

IV. SPECIAL CATALOGUES OF MUSEUMS AND EXHIBITIONS

AACHEN, Suermondt-Museum
Schweitzer, H. D. *Die Skulpturensammlung.* Aachen, 1910.
AMSTERDAM, Das Niederländische Museum
Vogelsang, W. *Die Holzskulptur in den Niederlanden*, II. Utrecht, 1912.

AMSTERDAM, Rijksmuseum
Pit, A. *La sculpture hollandaise*. Amsterdam, 1903.
Exhib. 'Bourgondische Pracht'. 1951.
Leeuwenberg, J. *Beeldhouwkunst*, I. Amsterdam, 1957.
Exhib. 'Middeleeuwse Kunst der Noordelijke Nederlanden'. 1958.

BALTIMORE, Walters Art Gallery
Exhib. 'The International Style'. 1962.

BERLIN, Deutsches Museum
Demmler, T. *Die Bildwerke*, III: *Grossplastik*. Berlin, 1930.
Bange, E. F. *Die Bildwerke*, IV: *Kleinplastik*. Berlin, 1930.

BERLIN–DAHLEM, Staatliche Museen
Metz, P. *Europäische Bildwerke von der Spätantike bis zum Rokoko*. Munich, 1957.

BERLIN-OST, Staatliche Museen
Maedebach, H. *Deutsche Bildwerke aus sieben Jahrhunderten*. Berlin, 1958.

BRUGES
Exhib. 1907 'Les chefs-d'œuvre de l'art ancien à l'exposition de la Toison d'or'. Brussels, 1908.

BRUGES, Musées Communaux
Exhib. 'Le siècle des primitifs flamands'. 1960.

BRUSSELS
Exhib. 'Cinq siècles d'art'. 1935.
Exhib. 'Le Siècle de Bourgogne'. 1951.
Exhib. 'Bruxelles au XVme siècle'. 1953.
Exhib. 'Trésors d'art du Brabant'. 1954.

BRUSSELS, Les Musées du Parc du Cinquantenaire et de la Porte de Hal
Destrée, J., Kymeulen, A. J., and Hannotiau, A. Brussels, n.d.

BRUSSELS, Musées Royaux d'Art et d'Histoire
Archéologie Nationale, Industries d'Art, Folklore. Brussels, 1958.

BUDAPEST, Országos Szépmüvészeti Múzeum
Balogh, J. *A régi szoborosztály, Kiállítása*. Budapest, 1956.

COLOGNE, Schnütgen-Museum
Witte, F. *Die Skulpturen*. Berlin, 1912.
Exhib. 'Grosse Kunst des Mittelalters aus Privatbesitz'. 1960.
Schnitzler, H. *Eine Auswahl*. 1961.

DARMSTADT, Hessisches Landesmuseum
Exhib. 'Alte Kunst am Mittelrhein'. 1927.

DETROIT, Institute of Arts
Exhib. 'Flanders in the Fifteenth Century, Art and Civilization'. 1960.

DIJON, Musée des Beaux-Arts
Exhib. 'Chefs-d'œuvre de la sculpture bourguignonne'. 1949.

Exhib. 'Le grand siècle des ducs de Bourgogne'. 1951.
Quarré, P. *Catalogue des sculptures*. Dijon, 1960.
Quarré, P. *La Chartreuse de Champmol*. Dijon, 1960.

FRANKFURT
Schmitt, O., and Swarzenski, G. *Meisterwerke der Bildhauerkunst in Frankfurter Privatbesitz*, I. Frankfurt, 1921.

FRANKFURT, Städtische Skulpturengalerie (Liebieghaus)
Legner, A. *Kleinplastik*. Frankfurt, 1960.
Legner, A. *Spätgotische Bildwerke*. Frankfurt, 1961.

GHENT
Exposition rétrospective, 'L'art ancien dans les Flandres (Région de l'Escaut)'. 1913.
Casier, J., and Bergmans, P. *Mémorial*. Brussels, 1914.

HANNOVER, Niedersächsische Landesgalerie
Osten, G. von der. *Katalog der Bildwerke*. Munich, 1957.

INNSBRUCK, Tiroler Landesmuseum Ferdinandeum
Exhib. 'Gotik in Tirol'. 1950.

KARLSRUHE, Badisches Landesmuseum
Schneider, A. von. *Die plastischen Bildwerke*. Karlsruhe, 1938.
Schnellbach, R. *Spätgotische Bildwerke*. Karlsruhe, 1962.

KLEVE, Städtisches Museum
Die Klevischen Beeldensnyder. 1963.

LIMOGES, Musée
Exhib. 'Sculptures gothiques du Haut-Limousin et de la Marche'. 1956.

LOUVAIN, Stedelijk Museum
Exhib. 'Ars antiqua sacra'. 1962.

LÜBECK, St Annen-Museum
Die sakralen Werke des Mittelalters. 1964.

LYON, Musée de
Jullian, R. *La sculpture du moyen-âge et de la Renaissance*. Lyon, 1945.

MILAN, Fabbrica del Duomo
Bicchi, U. *Il Museo del Duomo*. Milan, 1956.

MUNICH, Bayerisches Nationalmuseum
Halm, P. M., and Lill, G. Cat. XIII, 1: *Die Bildwerke vom 12. Jahrhundert bis 1450*. Augsburg, 1924.
Müller, T. Cat. XIII, 2: *Die Bildwerke von der Mitte des 15. bis gegen Mitte des 16. Jahrhunderts*. Munich, 1959.
Weihrauch, H. R. Cat. XIII, 5: *Die Bildwerke in Bronze*. Munich, 1956.

MÜNSTER, Landesmuseum der Provinz Westfalen
Meier, B. *Die Skulpturen*. Berlin, 1914.

NUREMBERG, Germanisches National-Museum
Josephi, W. *Die Werke plastischer Kunst*. Nuremberg, 1910.
Lutze, E. *Katalog der Veit Stoss-Ausstellung*. 1933.

PARIS, Musée de Cluny
Haraucourt, E., and Montremy, F. de. *Cat: La pierre, le marbre et l'albâtre*. Paris, 1922.
Haraucourt, E., Montremy, F. de, and Maillard, E. *Cat. des bois sculptés et meubles*. Paris, 1925.

PARIS, Musée National du Louvre
Vitry, P., and Aubert, M. *Catalogue des sculptures du moyen-âge, de la Renaissance et des temps modernes*. Paris, 1922.
Aubert, M. *Descr. rais. des sculptures*, 1: *Moyen âge*. Paris, 1950.
Exhib. 'Cathédrales'. 1962.

PARIS, Palais du Trocadero
Courajod, L., and Marou, P. F. *Musée de sculpture comparée, XIVᵉ et XVᵉ s*. Paris, 1892.

PARIS
Exhib. 'Chefs d'œuvre de l'art français'. 1937.
Exhib. 'La vierge dans l'art français'. 1950.

PARIS, Musée des Arts Décoratifs
Exhib. 'L'art ancien en Tschécoslovaquie'. 1957.
Exhib. 'L'art en Champagne'. 1959.

RALEIGH
Exhib. 'Sculptures of Tilmann Riemenschneider'. 1962.

ROUEN
Exhib. 'Art religieux ancien', 1931. Rouen, 1932.

SIGMARINGEN, Fürstlich Hohenzollernsche Sammlung
Sprinz, H. *Die Bildwerke*. Stuttgart–Zürich, 1925.

STRÄNGNÄS
Utställningen af äldre kyrklig Konst. 1910.
Curman, S., and Roosval, J. *C.R. af Ugglas, Studier*. Stockholm, 1913.

STRASBOURG
Beyer, V. *La sculpture médiévale du Musée de l'Œuvre Notre-Dame*. Strasbourg, 1956.

STUTTGART, Württembergische Altertümersammlung
Baum, J. *Deutsche Bildwerke des 10. bis 18. Jh.* Stuttgart, 1917.
Walzer, A. *Schwäbische Plastik*. Stuttgart, n.d.

TOURNAI, Cathédrale
Exhib. 'Arts Reliquieux'. 1958.

UTRECHT, Aartsbisschoppelijk Museum
Vogelsang, W. *Die Holzskulptur in den Niederlanden*, 1. Utrecht, 1911.
Bouvy, D. *Beeldhouwkunst Aartsbisschoppelijk Museum Utrecht*. Utrecht, 1962.

VIENNA, Kunsthistorisches Museum
Exhib. 'Europäische Kunst um 1400'. 1962.
Katalog der Sammlung für Plastik und Kunstgewerbe, 1. 1964.

ZÜRICH, Schweizerisches Landesmuseum
Baier-Futterer, J. *Die Bildwerke der Romanik und Gotik*. Zürich, 1936.

THE PLATES

Claus Sluter: Zacharias from the Moses Fountain, 1395–1403. *Dijon, Chartreuse de Champmol*

(B) Claus Sluter: Virgin and Child from the portal, 1391–7. *Dijon, Chartreuse de Champmol*

(A) Claus Sluter: St John the Baptist and Philip the Bold from the portal, 1391–7. *Dijon, Chartreuse de Champmol*

(B) Claus Sluter: Jeremiah from the Moses Fountain, 1395–1403.
Dijon, Chartreuse de Champmol

(A) Claus Sluter: Prophet, corbel from the portal (cast), 1391–7.
Dijon, Chartreuse de Champmol

3

Claus Sluter: Moses, David, and Jeremiah from the Moses Fountain, 1395–1403.
Dijon, Chartreuse de Champmol

Claus Sluter: Isaiah from the Moses Fountain, 1395–1403. *Dijon, Chartreuse de Champmol*

Claus Sluter: Head of Christ from the Moses Fountain, 1395–1403. *Dijon, Musée Archéologique*

6

Juan de la Huerta (?): Virgin from the reredos, 1448. *Rouvres-en-Plaine, church*

7

(B) Claus Sluter: Monk, 'pleureur' from the monument to Philip the Bold, 1404/5. *Dijon, Musée de la Ville*

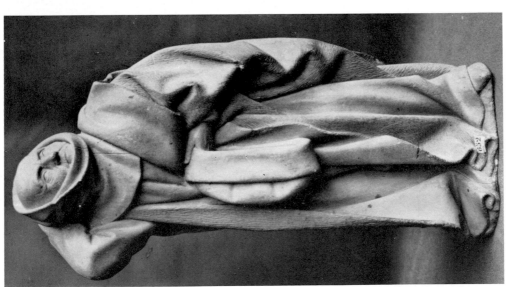

(A) Claus Sluter: Monk, 'pleureur' from the monument to Philip the Bold, 1404/5. *Paris, Musée de Cluny*

8

(B) Virgin and Child, *c.* 1390–1400. *Halle (Hal), pilgrimage church, south-west portal*

(A) Virgin and Child from Dijon, *c.* 1410–20. *Paris, Louvre*

9

Virgin from the Coronation of the Virgin, *c.* 1400–10. *Liège, St Jacques, portal*

10

(A) Annunciation, early fifteenth century. *Écouis, church*

(B) Votive relief, early fifteenth century. *Écos, church*

(A) Coronation of the Virgin (cast), 1392/1407. *La Ferté–Milon, château, archway*

(B) Relief of the legend of St Servatius from Maestricht, 1403.
Hamburg, Museum für Kunst und Gewerbe

12

Reliquary bust of St Valerius, given in 1397. *Zaragoza Cathedral*

Goldenes Rössel, 1403. *Altötting, collegiate church*

(A) Christ carrying the Cross, *c.* 1410–20. *Paris, Musée de Cluny*

(B) Jacques de Baerze: Altarpiece from the Chartreuse de Champmol, 1390–9. *Dijon, Musée*

Jacques de Baerze: Altarpiece from the Chartreuse de Champmol, 1390–9. Detail. *Dijon, Musée*

16

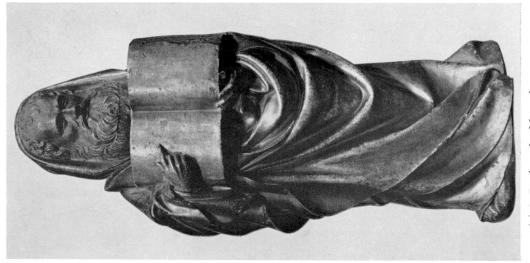

(A) St John the Baptist, early fifteenth century.
Paris, Louvre

(B) Virgin from an Annunciation, early
fifteenth century. *Zürich, Bührle Collection*

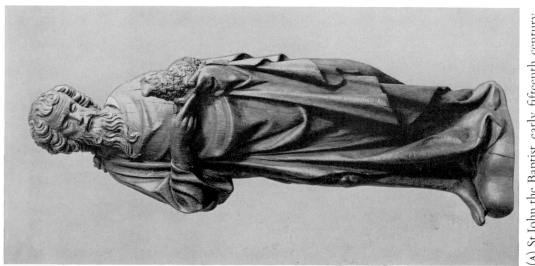

(C) St Paul, early fifteenth century.
Private collection

Group from the retable of the high altar, *c.* 1410–20. *Hakendover, St Sauveur*

High altar, *c.* 1420–5. *Dortmund, Reinoldikirche*

(B) St Elzéar from Apt, c. 1373. *New York, Metropolitan Museum of Art*

(A) Jean de Cambrai: Virgin and Child,
c. 1408. *Marcoussis, church of the Célestins*

(B) André Beauneveu (?): Presentation in the Temple, c. 1390–1400.
Paris, Musée de Cluny

(A) South Netherlandish (?): Virgin
and Child, early fifteenth century.
Amsterdam, Rijksmuseum

Jean de Cambrai: Tomb of Jean, duc de Berry, from the Sainte 'Chapelle, begun 1405. *Bourges Cathedral, crypt*

(B) Jean de Cambrai (?): Head of an Apostle from Mehun-sur-Yèvre, 1408/16. *Paris, Louvre*

(A) André Beauneveu: Head of an Apostle from the Sainte Chapelle, after 1392. *Bourges, Musée*

23

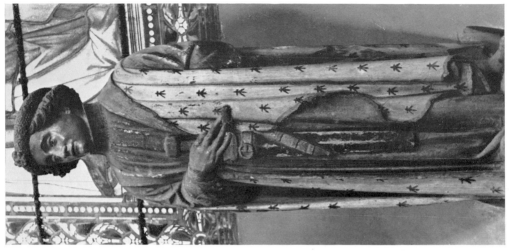

(B) Louis de Châtillon (?) from the Sainte Chapelle, Bourges (?), early fifteenth century. *Morogues, church*

(A) Virgin and Child from the trumeau, late fourteenth century. *Riom, Notre-Dame-du-Marthuret*

(B) Man of Sorrows, early fifteenth century. *Bourges, Musée*

(A) God the Father from Bourges, early fifteenth century.
Paris, Louvre

25

(A) Pope Urban V, d. 1370. *Avignon, Musée Calvet*

(B) Monument to Cardinal Jean de la Grange, d. 1402, from St Martial. Detail.
Avignon, Musée Calvet

(B) God the Father in Benediction from the church of the Célestins,
c. 1400. *Avignon, Musée Calvet*

(A) Fragment from the monument of Cardinal Jean de la Grange,
d. 1402, from St Martial. *Avignon, Musée Calvet*

Monument to Pierre d'Évreux-Navarre, Count of Mortain, from the Chartreuse, Paris, 1412/13 (?). *Paris, Louvre*

28

Monument to Catherine d'Alençon from the Chartreuse, Paris, 1412/13 (?).
Paris, Louvre

(B) Westphalian Master: Figures from the Burgkirche, 1399–1401.
Lübeck, St Annenmuseum

(A) Annunciation from tomb-chest of Archbishop Friedrich of
Saarwerden, before 1414. *Cologne Cathedral*

30

Eligius of Liège: Effigy from the tomb-chest of Archbishop Friedrich of Saarwerden, before 1414. *Cologne Cathedral*

(B) Pietà from Unna, early fifteenth century.
Münster, Westphalian Landesmuseum

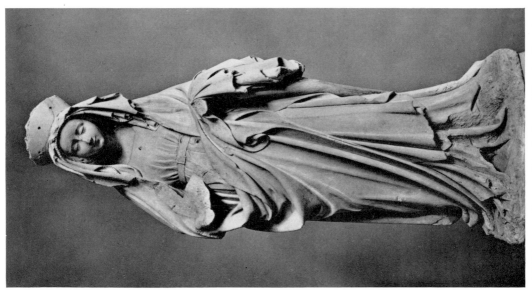

(A) Johannes Junge: Virgin from Niendorf, early
fifteenth century, Lübeck, *St Annenmuseum*

32

(B) Virgin and Child, c. 1420–5.
Würzburg, Marienkirche

(A) Christ on the way to Calvary from Lorch, early fifteenth
century. *Berlin-Dahlem, Staatliche Museen*

(B) Master Hartmann: St Martin, after 1417.
Ulm Cathedral, west portal

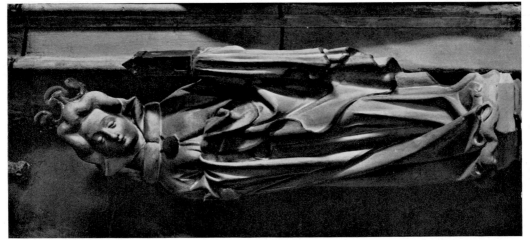

(A) St Barbara, c. 1424–5.
Mainz Cathedral, Memorienpforte

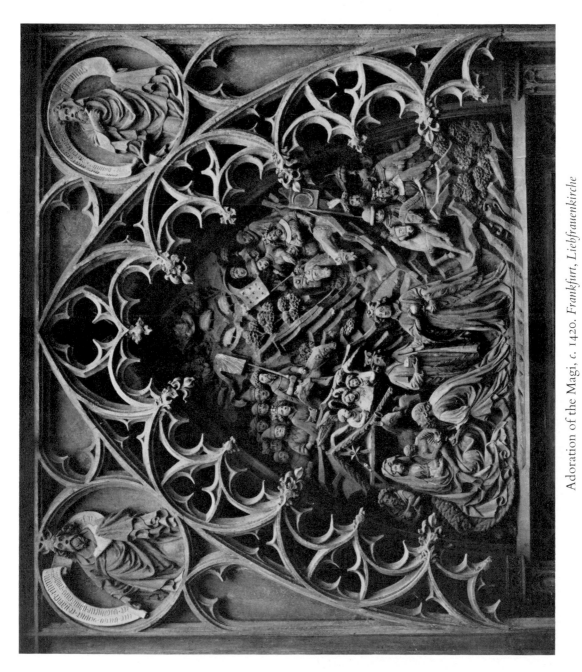

Adoration of the Magi, *c. 1420. Frankfurt, Liebfrauenkirche*

Ulrich von Ensingen (?): St Catherine, *c.* 1390. *Strasbourg Minster, steeple, north-west pier*

36

Apostle, early fifteenth century. *Nuremberg, Germanisches National-Museum*

37

Fair Virgin, *c.* 1425–30. *Nuremberg, St Sebald*

Krumau Virgin, *c.* 1390. *Vienna, Kunsthistorisches Museum*

(B) Fair Virgin, c. 1390–1400. *Marienberg Abbey, main portal*

(A) Fair Virgin from St Elizabeth, Wrocław (Breslau), c. 1400. *Warsaw, Muzeum Narodowe*

Pietà from Seeon, c. 1400. *Munich, Bayerisches Nationalmuseum*

(B) Crucifixion, c. 1430. Wrocław (Breslau), St Elizabeth

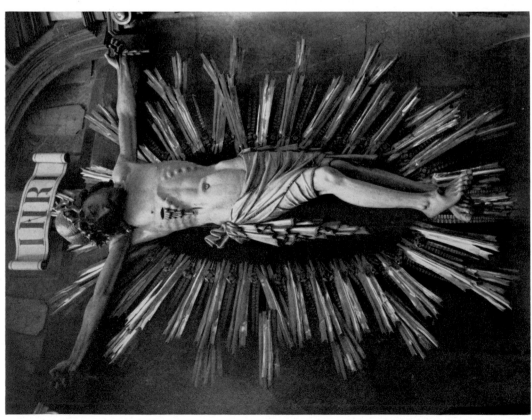

(A) Crucifixus, c. 1420. Prague, Týn Church

(B) Fair Virgin, *c.* 1410. *Gdańsk (Danzig), St Mary, Reinhold Chapel*

(A) Reliquary bust of St Dorothea from the Chapel of the City Council, Wrocław (Breslau), *c.* 1410. *Warsaw, Muzeum Narodowe*

43

(B) Virgin and Child, early fifteenth century.
Cracow, Museum Narodowe

(A) Pietà, early fifteenth century. *Cracow, St Barbara*

44

(B) Conrad von Einbeck: Self-portrait, after 1382. *Halle, Moritzkirche*

(A) Wenzel von Radecz, 1374/85. *Prague, Sv. Vit (Cathedral)*

(B) Reliquary bust from the South Tyrol, *c.* 1390.
Vienna, Kunsthistorisches Museum

(A) Joseph of Arimathaea from an Entombment, *c.* 1420.
Darmstadt, Hessisches Landesmuseum

(A) Fair Virgin, c. 1420–30.
Budapest, Szépművészéti Museum

(B) Fair Virgin, c. 1390–1400. Formerly
Toruń (Thorn), St John

47

Fair Virgin, *c.* 1390–1400. Detail. *Formerly Toruń (Thorn), St John*

Fair Virgin, *c.* 1390–1400. Detail of Moses. *Formerly Toruń (Thorn), St John*

Self portrait of the architect (?), *c.* 1400–10. *Regensburg Cathedral*

'Master of Seeon': Virgin Enthroned, *c.* 1425. *Munich, Bayerisches Nationalmuseum*

Hans von Judenburg: Coronation of the Virgin, from Bozen (?), 1421. *Nuremberg, Germanisches National-Museum*

(B) Hans von Burghausen, d. 1432, from his monument. *Landshut, St Martin*

(A) Tomb of Ulrich Kastenmayr, before 1431. *Straubing, St Jakob*

Tomb of Philippe de Morvillier from St Martin-des-Champs, Paris, 1427–38. Detail. *Paris, Louvre*

54

Tomb of Gómez Manrique from Fresdeval, *c.* 1430. Detail. *Burgos, Museo Provincial*

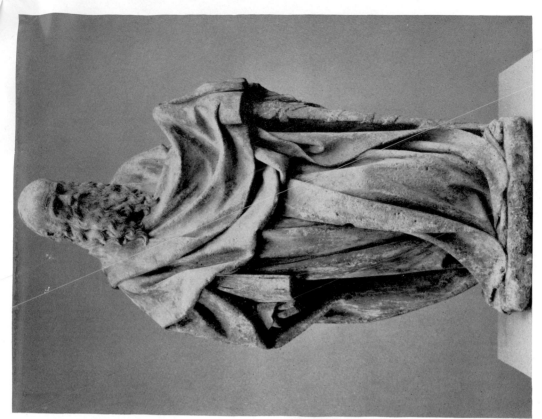

(B) St Paul from Poligny, c. 1420.
New York, Metropolitan Museum of Art

(A) St John the Baptist from Poligny, c. 1420.
New York, Metropolitan Museum of Art

(B) Pietà from Dijon. *Frankfurt, Städtische Skulpturengalerie*

(A) Virgin and Child, *c.* 1430–40.
Auxonne, Notre-Dame

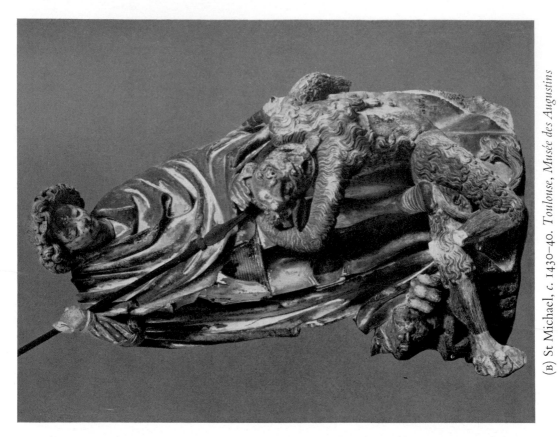

(B) St Michael, c. 1430–40. Toulouse, Musée des Augustins

(A) Nostre-Dame de Grasse, c. 1430–40.
Toulouse, Musée des Augustins

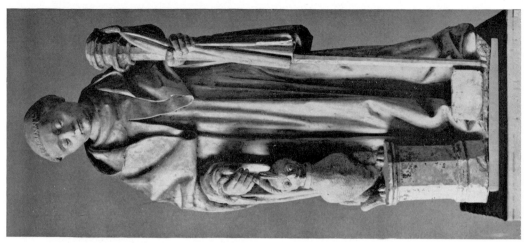

(C) St Jean de Reôme from Rochefort, *c. 1460. Asnières-en-Montagne, church*

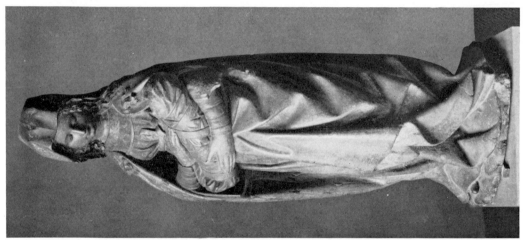

(B) Vierge au Poupon from the chapel of the Hôtel Rolin, *c. 1460. Autun, Musée Rolin*

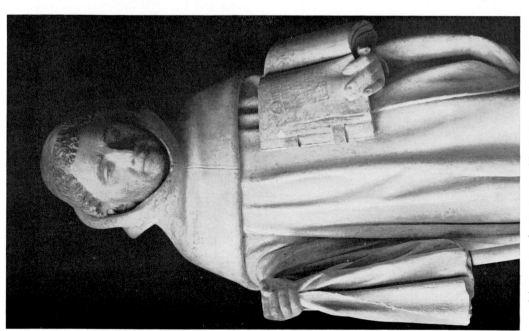

(A) Antoine le Moiturier (?): St Bernard, *c. 1465. Fontaine-lès-Dijon, church*

(A) Virgin and Child, *c.* 1425.
Châteaudun, Sainte-Chapelle

(B) Virgin and Child from the north portal,
c. 1400. *Le Mesnil-Aubry, church*

(A) Fair Virgin, *c.* 1420. *Prado, church*

(B) Virgin and Child, early fifteenth century. *Vassar College, Poughkeepsie*

Pedro Johan: High altar, 1425/36. *Tarragona Cathedral*

Effigy of Doña Aldonza de Mendoza, d. 1435, from Lupiana. *Madrid, Museo Arqueológico*

(A) Monument of Bishop Alonso Carrillo de Albornoz, d. 1439. *Sigüenza Cathedral*

(B) Jacques Morel: Tomb of Charles I of Bourbon and his wife, 1448–53.
Souvigny, St Pierre

Virgin from Poligny, *c.* 1450. *New York, Metropolitan Museum of Art*

Jean Michel and Georges de la Sonnette: Entombment. 1451/4. *Tonnerre, hospital*

(B) Jean Michel and Georges de la Sonnette: St Joseph from Entombment, 1451/4. *Tonnerre, hospital*

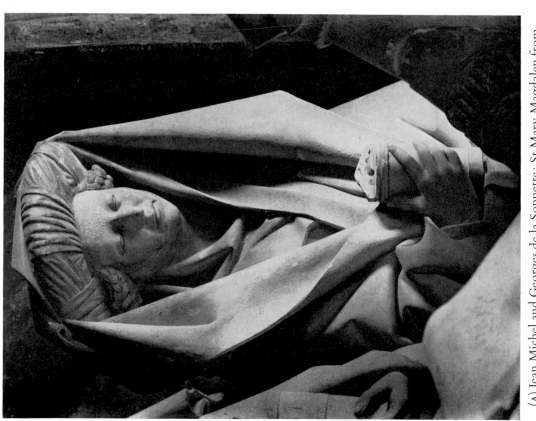

(A) Jean Michel and Georges de la Sonnette: St Mary Magdalen from Entombment, 1451/4. *Tonnerre, hospital*

Monument of Friar Jehan Fiefvés, d. 1425, from Tournai. Brussels, *Musée du Cinquantenaire*

(A) Jehan Delemer and Robert Campin: Angel of the Annunciation, 1428. *Tournai, Ste Marie-Madeleine*

(B) Jehan Delemer and Robert Campin: Virgin of the Annunciation, 1428. *Tournai, Ste Marie-Madeleine*

Votive stone of Ditmar de Brême, d. 1439. *Anderlecht, church*

(B) Monument of Engelbrecht of Nassau, d. 1443, and Johanna of Polanen. *Breda, Groote Kerk*

(A) Nicolas de Bruyn and Gerard Goris: Misericord, 1438/42. *Louvain (Leuven), St Pierre*

71

(B) Mercy-seat from the tabernacle of Mathieu de Layen, 1450.
Louvain (Leuven), St Pierre

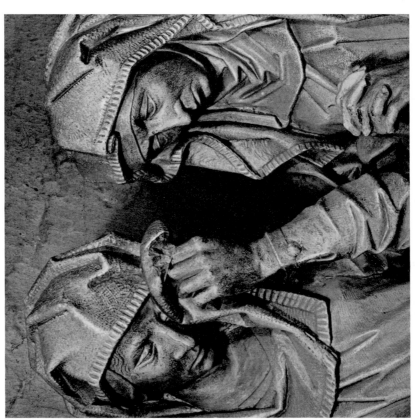

(A) Women at the Sepulchre (detail), c. 1440–50.
Soignies (Zinnik), St Vincent

(B) Crucifixion from Rimini, c. 1430. *Frankfurt, Städtische Skulpturengalerie*

(A) St John the Baptist, c. 1430. *Munich, Bayerisches Nationalmuseum*

Paris: Mourning Women from a Crucifixion, *c.* 1430.
Wrocław (Breslau), Silesian Museum

74

Crucifixion, c. 1430–40. *Esztergom (Gran) Cathedral, treasury*

(A) Virgin and Child, *c.* 1460. *Lübeck Cathedral*   (B) St Matthew, *c.* 1430. *Aachen Cathedral, choir*

(A) Angel of the Annunciation, 1439.
Cologne, St Kunibert

(B) Virgin of the Annunciation, 1439.
Cologne, St Kunibert

Death of the Virgin, *c.* 1440. Detail. *Würzburg Cathedral*

(B) Konrad Kuene: Virgin and Child from the monument of Archbishop Dietrich von Moers, 1460. *Cologne Cathedral*

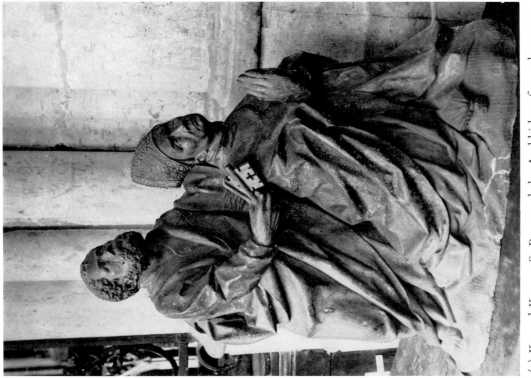

(A) Konrad Kuene: St Peter and the Archbishop from the monument of Archbishop Dietrich von Moers, 1460. *Cologne Cathedral*

Schlüsselfelder St Christopher from St Sebald, 1442.
Nuremberg, Germanisches National-Museum

Seated Man, c. 1430–5. Strasbourg, Musée de l'Œuvre Notre-Dame

(B) Monument of King Vladislav II Jagiello, d. 1434. Detail.
Cracow Cathedral

(A) Monument of Friedrich der Streitbare, Elector of Saxony,
c. 1440–50. Detail. *Meissen Cathedral, Fürstenkapelle*

(B) Hans Multscher: Page from the town hall, Ulm, c. 1427–30.
Ulm, Museum

(A) Head of a bishop from the Minster, c. 1460 (?).
Basel, Klingenthal Museum

Hans Multscher: Model of a tomb lid for Duke Ludwig the Bearded, 1435.
Munich, Bayerisches Nationalmuseum

Hans Multscher: Man of Sorrows, 1429. *Ulm Minster, west portal*

(B) Hans Multscher: Monument to Countess Mechthild, *c.* 1450.
Detail. *Tübingen, Stiftskirche*

(A) Hans Multscher: St Catherine, *c.* 1460.
New York, Frick Collection

86

(c) Hans Multscher: St Apollonia from the altar, 1456–8. *Sterzing (Vipiteno), church*

(B) Hans Multscher: Virgin and Child from the altar, 1456–8. *Sterzing (Vipiteno), church*

(A) Hans Multscher: St Ursula from the altar, 1456–8. *Sterzing (Vipiteno), church*

Jakob Kaschauer: Virgin and Child from the high altar of Freising Cathedral, dedicated 1443.
Munich, Bayerisches Nationalmuseum

(A) Annunciation from the Schnegg, begun 1438. *Constance Cathedral*

(B) Emperor Frederick III, before 1452. *Wiener Neustadt, St Georg*

(B) Nicolaus Gerhaerts: Crucifixus, 1467. *Baden-Baden, Old Cemetery*

(A) Nicolaus Gerhaerts: Monument to Canon Conrad von Busnang, 1464.
Strasbourg Minster

Nicolaus Gerhaerts: Tomb of Archbishop Jacob von Sierck, 1462. *Trier, Bischöfliches Museum*

Nicolaus Gerhaerts: Bärbel von Ottenheim, 1464. *Frankfurt, Städtische Skulpturengalerie*

Nicolaus Gerhaerts: Self portrait (?), c. 1467. *Strasbourg, Musée de l'Œuvre Notre-Dame*

(B) Virgin in the Rose Bower, c. 1460–70.
Berlin–Dahlem, Staatliche Museen

(A) Virgin and Child, c. 1465–70. Private collection

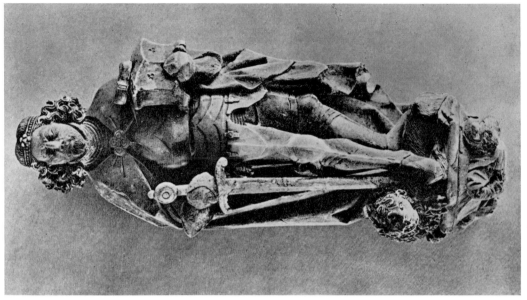

(B) St Adrian, *c. 1460. Brussels, Musées Royaux*

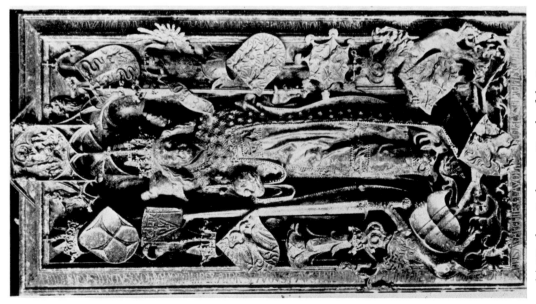

(A) Nicolaus Gerhaerts: Tomb of the Emperor Frederick III, begun 1469. *Vienna, St Stephen*

(B) North Netherlandish: St Bavo, c. 1460.
New York, Metropolitan Museum of Art

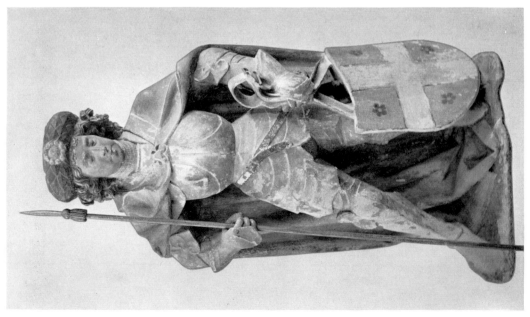

(A) St George, c. 1455–60. *Utrecht, Centraal Museum*

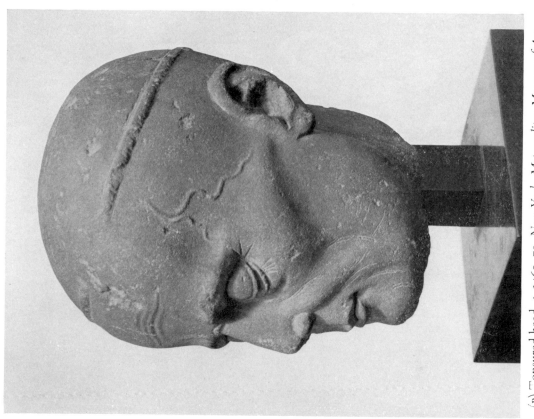

(A) St Christopher from Dijon (?), c. 1480.
St Louis, Missouri, City Art Museum

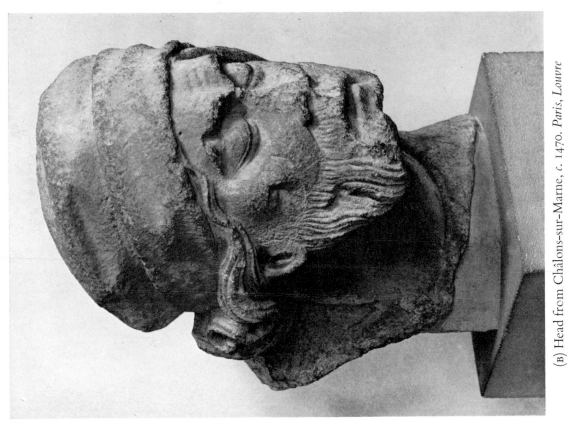

(B) Head from Châlons-sur-Marne, c. 1470. *Paris, Louvre*

(A) Head from Châlons-sur-Marne, c. 1470. *Paris, Louvre*

Prophet, c. 1465–70. Cluny, Chapelle de Bourbon

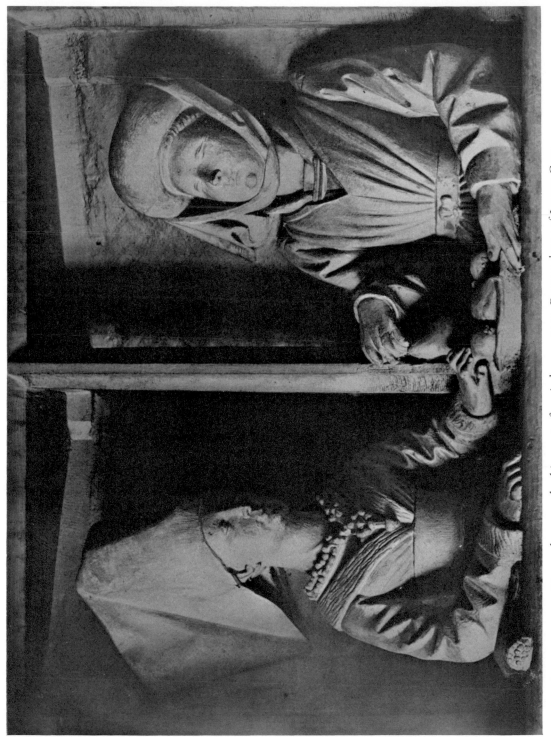

Man and woman looking out of a window, c. 1450. *Bourges, house of Jacques Cœur*

(B) St Mary Magdalen, c. 1464. *Châteaudun, castle, Sainte-Chapelle*

(A) St James from Semur-en-Auxois, c. 1460. *Paris, Louvre*

(A) Nicodemus from an Entombment, *c.* 1470.
New York, Metropolitan Museum of Art

(B) North French (?): St Barbara, *c.* 1460–70.
New York, Metropolitan Museum of Art

(A) St John from Beaugerais, *c.* 1450.
Paris, Louvre

(B) Reliquary head of St Fortunade, *c.* 1450–60.
Sainte-Fortunade, church

(B) St Catherine, c. 1460–70. *Private collection*

(A) Mourning Virgin, c. 1450–60.
Berlin-Dahlem, Staatliche Museen

104

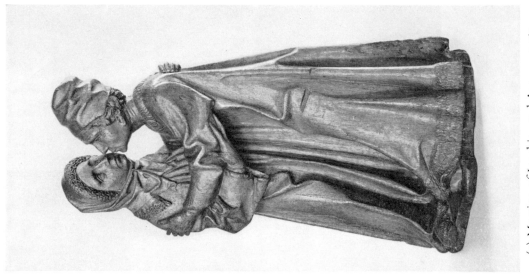

(B) Meeting of Joachim and Anna, *c.* 1460.
Amsterdam, Rijksmuseum

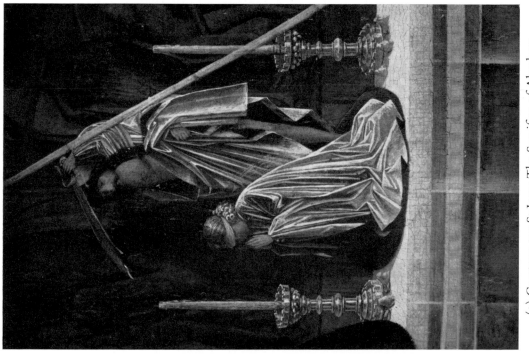

(A) Geertgen tot St Jans: The Sacrifice of Abraham
(detail), *c.* 1480. *Amsterdam, Rijksmuseum*

Jacques de Gérines (?) and Renier van Thienen (?): Tomb of Isabella of Bourbon, 1476. *Antwerp Cathedral*

(A) Jacques de Gérines (?) and Renier van Thienen (?): Philippe de Neveu (?) from the tomb of Isabella of Bourbon, 1476. *Amsterdam, Rijksmuseum*

(B) Jacques de Gérines (?) and Renier van Thienen (?): Anne of Burgundy (?) from the tomb of Isabella of Bourbon, *c.* 1476. *Amsterdam, Rijksmuseum*

(C) Jacques de Gérines (?) and Renier van Thienen (?) Margaret of Burgundy (?) from the tomb of Isabella of Bourbon, *c.* 1476. *Amsterdam, Rijksmuseum*

(D) Renier van Thienen: Figures from a Crucifixion from a candelabrum, 1482–3. *Zoutleeuw (Léau), St Leonard*

Adriaen van Wesel: St Joseph and Angels from an Adoration, *c.* 1475. *Amsterdam, Rijksmuseum*

(A) Altarpiece from Rieden, *c.* 1450. *Stuttgart, Württembergisches Landesmuseum*

(B) St Leonard Altarpiece, 1479 (?). *Zoutleeuw (Léau), St Leonard*

(B) Altar of the Passion, c. 1480–90. Detail. Geel (Gheel), St Dymphna

(A) South Netherlandish: Descent from the Cross, c. 1460–70.
Detroit, Institute of Arts (formerly Arenberg Collection)

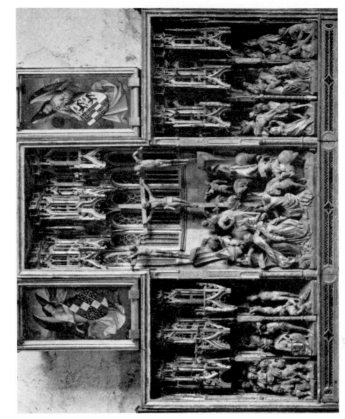

(B) Altar of the Passion, 1466. Ambierle, priory church

(A) Altar dedicated by Claudio de Villa, c. 1470. Brussels, Musées Royaux

(A) Virgin from a Crucifixion, 1469 (?).
Kalkar, St Nikolaus

(B) St John from a Crucifixion, 1469 (?).
Kalkar, St Nikolaus

(A) Virgin, c. 1466.
Cologne, St Maria im Kapitol

(B) Netherlandish: King Melchior from an
Adoration, c. 1490. *Cologne, Schnütgen Museum*

(A) St Anne with the Virgin and Child from Wissembourg, *c.* 1480.
Berlin (East), Staatliche Museen

(B) Annunciation from the Venningen tomb, *c.* 1470. *Speyer Cathedral*

(A) Adoration from Molsheim, *c.* 1465–70. Strasbourg, *Musée de l'Œuvre Notre-Dame*

(B) Adoration from Colmar, *c.* 1470–80. *Amsterdam, Rijksmuseum*

(B) St Michael, 1467. *Erfurt, St Severi*

(A) Monument of Elisabeth of Straubing–Holland, d. 1451.
Trier, Dreifaltigkeitskirche

(B) Friedrich Herlin: High altar, after 1466. *Rothenburg, St Jakob*

(A) High altar, *c.* 1465. Detail. *Nördlingen, St Georg*

(B) Bust from the Hospital of St Marx, c. 1470.
Strasbourg, Musée de l'Œuvre Notre-Dame

(A) Thomas Strayff: Man of Sorrows, 1478.
Wiener Neustadt, parish church

(B) Virgin and Child, c. 1470–80. Downside Abbey

(A) Kneeling Virgin from a Nativity from Wonnenthal, c. 1480.
Berlin-Dahlem, Staatliche Museen

Virgin and Child from Dangolsheim, *c.* 1470. *Berlin-Dahlem, Staatliche Museen*

St George from the high altar, *c. 1465. Nördlingen, St Georg*

(A) and (B) Jörg Syrlin the Elder: Busts from the choir stalls, 1469–74. *Ulm Minster*

(A) and (B) Jörg Syrlin the Elder: Busts from the choir stalls, 1469–74. *Ulm Minster*

(A) and (B) Heinrich Iselin: Stall ends from Weingarten, *c.* 1478. *Berchtesgaden, Schlossmuseum*

Peter Köllin (?): Pietà from Weil, 1471. *Stuttgart, Württembergisches Landesmuseum*

Michel Erhart: Virgin of the Misericord from Ravensburg, *c.* 1480.
Berlin-Dahlem, Staatliche Museen

Erasmus Grasser: Figures from a Crucifixion from Pipping, *c.* 1480–90.
Munich, Bayerisches Nationalmuseum

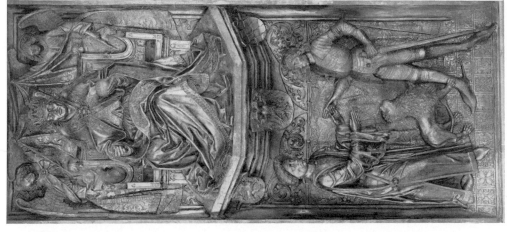

(B) Monument of Emperor Ludwig of
Bavaria, c. 1480 (cast).
Munich, Frauenkirche

(A) Monument of Emperor Ludwig Ludwig of Bavaria, c. 1480.
Detail. *Munich, Frauenkirche*

128

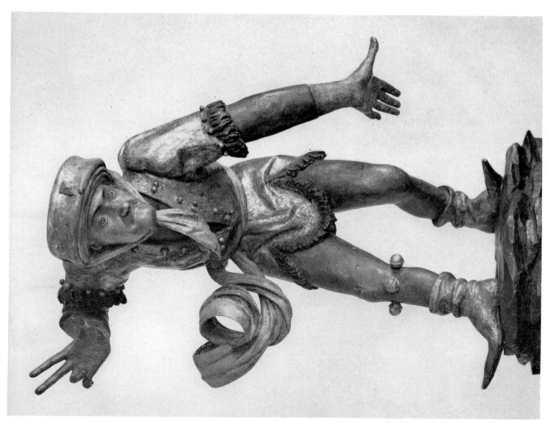

(A) and (B) Erasmus Grasser: Morris Dancers, 1480. *Munich, town hall*

Apostle, *c.* 1490. *Wiener Neustadt, parish church*

High altar, *c.* 1480. *Košice (Kaschau)*, *St Elizabeth*

Michael Pacher: St Wolfgang from the high altar, 1471–81. *St Wolfgang*

Michael Pacher: Coronation of the Virgin from the high altar, 1471–81. *St Wolfgang*

Veit Stoss: Death of the Virgin from the high altar, 1477–89. Detail.
Cracow, St Mary

Veit Stoss: High altar, 1477–89. *Cracow, St Mary*

Veit Stoss: Monument to King Casimir Jagiello, 1492. Detail. *Cracow, Cathedral on the Wawel*

Bernt Notke: St George, 1489. *Stockholm, Storkyrka*

(B) Netherlandish: Virgin and Child, *c.* 1470. *Vadstena*

(A) Bernt Notke: St Mary Magdalen from the Triumphal Cross, 1477. *Lübeck, St Annenmuseum*

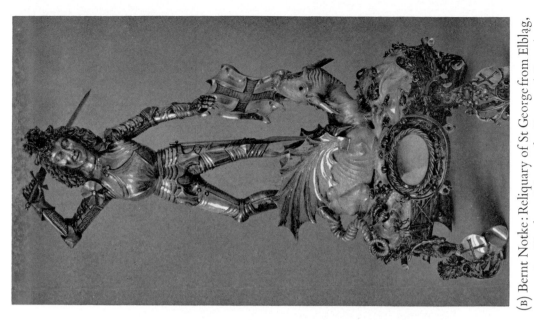

(B) Bernt Notke: Reliquary of St George from Elbląg, c. 1480. *Hamburg, Museum für Kunst und Gewerbe*

(A) Bernt Notke: High altar, 1483. *Tallinn (Reval), Church of the Holy Ghost*

(B) Monument to Charles d'Artois, d. 1471. Detail. *Eu, St Laurent*

(A) Jean II of Bourbon from Bourbon-l'Archambault, *c.* 1470 (?). *Baltimore, Walters Art Gallery*

(B) Votive group from the Carmelite church, given in 1470. *Aix-en-Provence Cathedral*

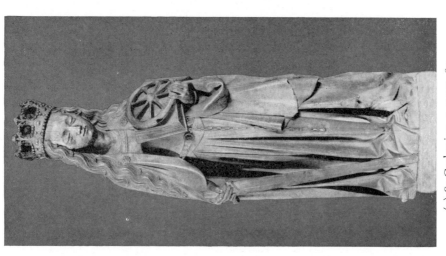

(A) St Catherine, *c.* 1470–80.
Autun, Musée Rolin

Mourner from the tomb of Antoine (?) de Sourches, d. 1485/7.
Malicorne, church

(A) Tomb of Antoine (?) de Sourches, d. 1485/7. *Malicorne, church*

(B) Monument to Philippe Pot from Cîteaux, *c.* 1480. *Paris, Louvre*

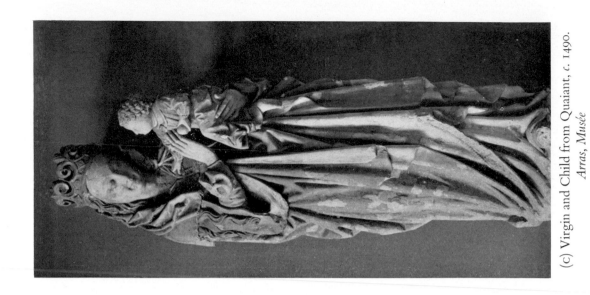

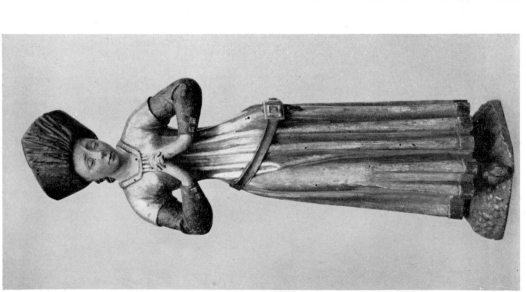

(A) Saint from a Lamentation, c. 1480.
New York, Metropolitan Museum of Art

(B) Virgin and Child, c. 1490. *Amiens Cathedral*

(C) Virgin and Child from Quaiant, c. 1490.
Arras, Musée

144

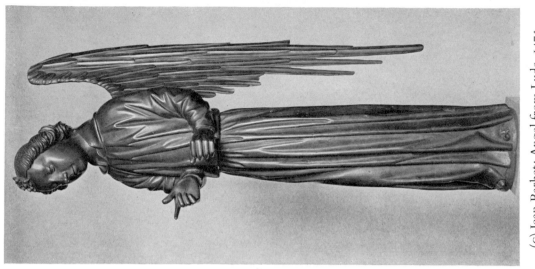

(c) Jean Barbet: Angel from Lude, 1475.
New York, Frick Collection

(B) Prophet from St Sernin, c. 1470–80.
Toulouse, Musée des Augustins

(A) Prophet from the rood screen, c. 1475.
Albi Cathedral

(B) Guillermo Sagrera: Angel, c. 1440-50. *Palma, Lonja*

(A) Juan Alemán: Puerta de los Leones, after 1465. Detail.
Toledo Cathedral

(B) Group of mourners from a Crucifixion, c. 1460–70.
Guadalupe Abbey

(A) St James, after 1477. Toledo, *S. Juan de los Reyes*

147

Martín Vázquez de Arce, from his monument, *c.* 1488. *Sigüenza Cathedral*

Tomb of Juan Fernández de Morales, *c.* 1490. Detail. *Toledo, S. Clara*

(c) Rodrigo Alemán: St Peter from the choir stalls, 1503. *Ciudad Rodrigo Cathedral*

(B) Egas Cueman: Tomb of Alonso de Velasco, 1467–80. *Guadalupe Abbey*

(A) Lorenzo Mercadante: Saint, *c.* 1460. *Gerona Cathedral, treasury*

Sebastián de Almonacid: Monuments of Condestable Álvaro de Luna and his wife, 1489. *Toledo Cathedral, Capilla de Santiago*

(B) Altar, c. 1500. Detail. *Covarrubias, collegiate church*

(A) Hans of Schwäbisch Gmünd: Adoration of the Magi, c. 1500, detail from the high altar. *Zaragoza, La Seo*

(B) Pedro Millán: Christ in Pity, c. 1490. *El Garrobo, church*

(A) Jan van Mecheln (?): Choir stalls, c. 1480. *León Cathedral*

(B) Simon de Colonia: Portal, 1482–98. Detail.
Burgos Cathedral, Capilla del Condestable

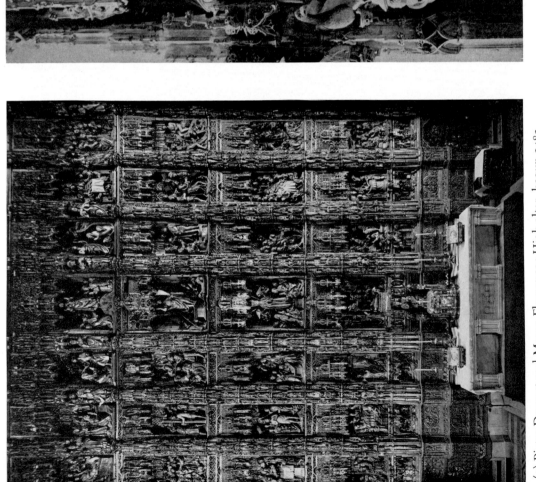

(A) Pieter Dancart and Marco Flamenco: High altar, begun 1482.
Seville Cathedral

Monument of Bishop Alonso de Cartagena, *c.* 1480. *Burgos Cathedral*

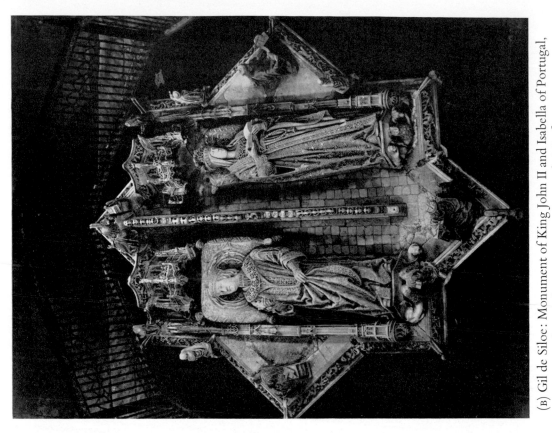

(B) Gil de Siloe: Monument of King John II and Isabella of Portugal, designed 1486. *Burgos, Cartuja de Miraflores*

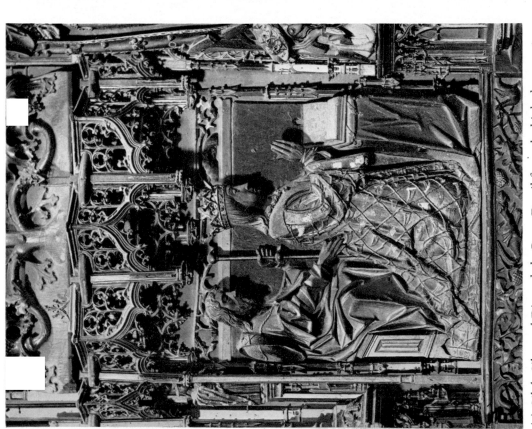

(A) Gil de Siloe and Diego de la Cruz: Detail from the high altar, 1496–9. *Burgos, Cartuja de Miraflores*

(B) Gil de Siloe: Monument of Juan de Padilla from Fresdeval, c. 1500–5.
Burgos, Museo Provincial

(A) Gil de Siloe: Monument of the Infante Alonso, designed 1486.
Burgos, Cartuja de Miraflores

(A), (B), and (C) Crucifixion, *c.* 1490. Details. *Louvain (Leuven), St Pierre*

(A) Crucifixion from Nivelles, late fifteenth century.
Paris, Louvre

(B) Dicing soldiers from a Crucifixion from Antwerp. *c.* 1490–1500.
Munich, private collection

Jan Aert van Maastricht: Font, 1492. 's Hertogenbosch (*Bois-le-Duc*), *St Jan*

(A) Jan Borman (cast by Renier van Thienen): Effigy from the monument of Duchess Mary of Burgundy, 1491–8. *Bruges, Notre-Dame*

(B) Misericord, *c.* 1493. *Diest, St Sulpice*

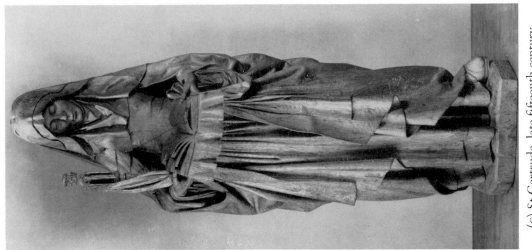

(c) St Gertrude, late fifteenth century.
Etterbeek, St Gertrude

(B) Virgin and Child, *c.* 1490–1500.
Paris, Louvre

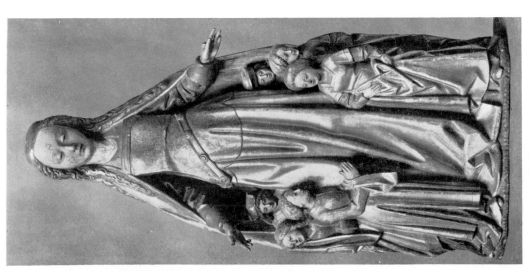

(A) St Ursula from Bruges, *c.* 1490.
Berlin–Dahlem, Staatliche Museen

Jan Borman the Elder: Altar of St George from Louvain, 1493. *Brussels, Musée du Cinquantenaire*

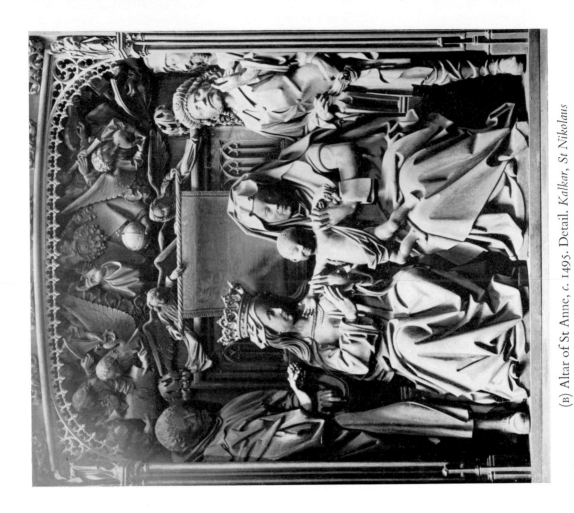

(B) Altar of St Anne, c. 1495. Detail. *Kalkar, St Nikolaus*

(A) Master Loedewich: High altar, 1498–1500. Detail. *Kalkar, St Nikolaus*

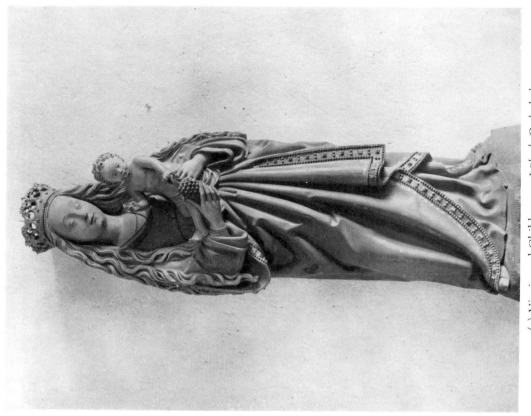

(B) Virgin and Child, 1509, *Lübeck Cathedral*

(A) Henning von der Heyde: St John the Evangelist, *c.* 1505.
Lübeck, Marienkirche

165

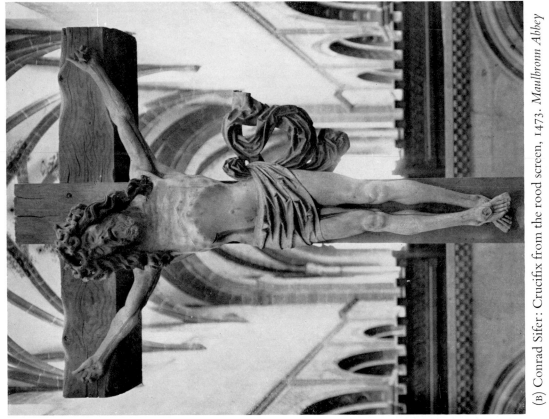

(B) Conrad Sifer: Crucifix from the rood screen, 1473. *Maulbronn Abbey*

(A) Tomb of Dean Bernhard von
Breidenbach, d. 1498. *Mainz Cathedral*

(B) Veit Wagner (?): St Peter from the Mount of Olives, completed 1498.
Strasbourg Minster

(A) Hans Syfer: Bust of a prophet, *c.* 1485.
Berlin (East), Staatliche Museen

167

(A) Niclaus von Hagenau: Self-portrait (?), *c.* 1495.
Strasbourg Minster, St Andrew's Chapel, above the portal

(B) Scholar saint, *c.* 1490. *Würzburg Cathedral, cloisters, tympanum*

168

(B) Hans Syfer: Bust from the high altar, completed 1498.
Heilbronn, St Kilian

(A) Hans Syfer: Detail from the Entombment, 1487–8.
Worms Cathedral, cloisters

169

Niclaus von Hagenau: St Augustine and donor from the Isenheim altar, 1500–10.
Colmar, Musée d'Unterlinden

Michel and Gregor Erhart: High altar, 1493–4. *Blaubeuren, Benedictine monastery*

(B) Hans Weiditz: The Fall of Man, c. 1505.
Basel, Historisches Museum

(A) Gregor Erhart: Vanitas, c. 1500.
Vienna, Kunsthistorisches Museum

(B) Tilman Riemenschneider: St Barbara, c. 1485.
Bremen, Roselius-Haus

(A) Virgin and Child from St Moritz,
c. 1490. Augsburg, Maximiliansmuseum

(B) Erasmus Grasser: St Peter from the high altar, 1492.
Munich, St Peter

(A) Martin Kriechbaum (?): St Christopher from the high altar, c. 1491–8.
Kefermarkt, church

Martin Kriechbaum (?): High altar, c. 1491–8. *Kefermarkt, church*

(A) and (B) Tilman Riemenschneider: Adam and Eve from the Marienkapelle, 1491–3. *Würzburg, Mainfränkisches Museum*

176

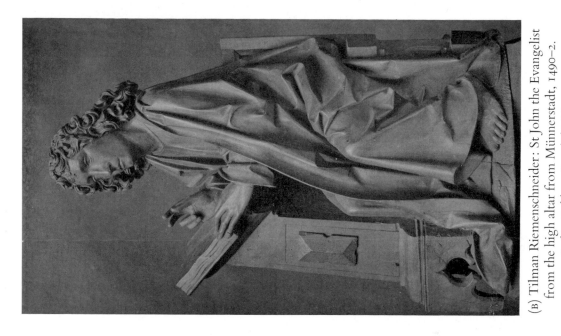

(B) Tilman Riemenschneider: St John the Evangelist from the high altar from Münnerstadt, 1490–2. *Berlin–Dahlem, Staatliche Museen*

(A) Tilman Riemenschneider: Relief from the high altar from Münnerstadt, 1490–2. *Berlin–Dahlem, Staatliche Museen*

Tilman Riemenschneider: Detail from the altar, 1501–5. *Rothenburg, St Jakob*

Veit Stoss: Crucifix from St Sebald, *c. 1500. Nuremberg, St Lorenz*

(B) Veit Stoss: Virgin and Child, c. 1500.
Nuremberg, Germanishes National-Museum

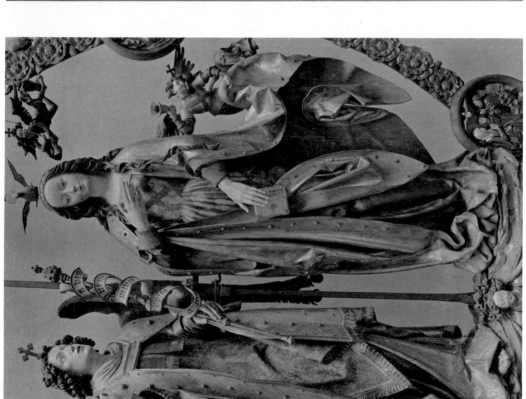

(A) Veit Stoss: Salve Regina, 1517–18. Nuremberg, St Lorenz

(B) Adam Kraft: Christ carrying the Cross, relief from the Schreyer tomb, 1490–2. *Nuremberg, St Sebald*

(A) Veit Stoss: The Kiss of Judas, 1499. *Nuremberg, St Sebald*

Adam Kraft: Self portrait from the tabernacle, 1493–6. *Nuremberg, St Lorenz*

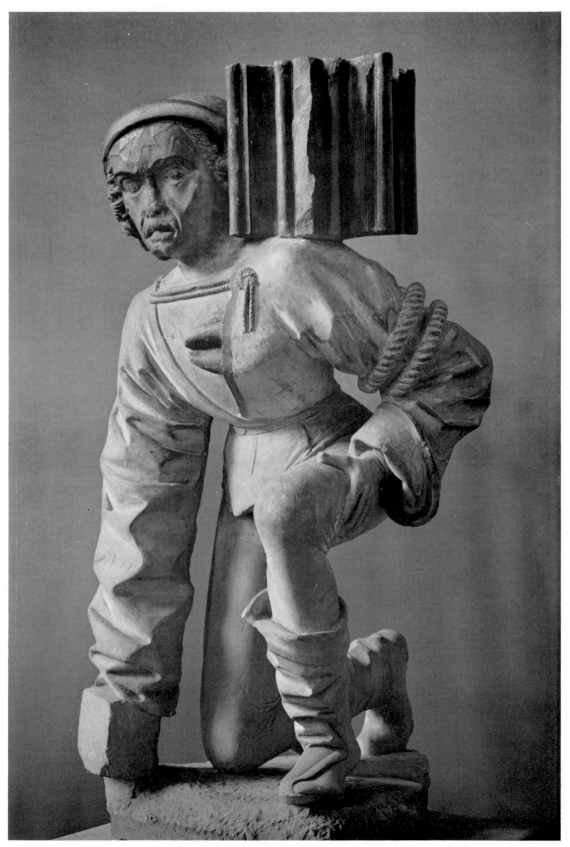

Anton Pilgram: Pulpit-bearer from Öhringen, *c.* 1485–90. *Berlin (East), Staatliche Museen*

Peter Vischer the Elder: Tomb of Archbishop Ernst von Sachsen, 1495.
Magdeburg Cathedral

184

Peter Vischer the Elder: Branch-breaker, 1490. *Munich, Bayerisches Nationalmuseum*

(B) Detail of relief of the Life of St Firmin, begun 1490.
Amiens Cathedral, south choir screen

(A) Altarpiece, from Burgos (?), c. 1490–1500.
New York, The Cloisters Collection

Reliefs of the Life of St Firmin, begun 1490. *Amiens Cathedral, south choir screen*

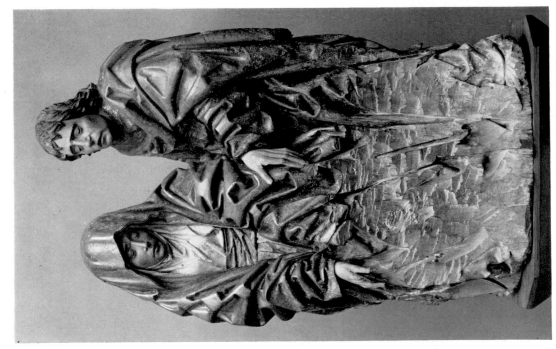

(A) and (B) Mourners from an Entombment from Nevers, c. 1500. Frankfurt, Städtische Skulpturengalerie

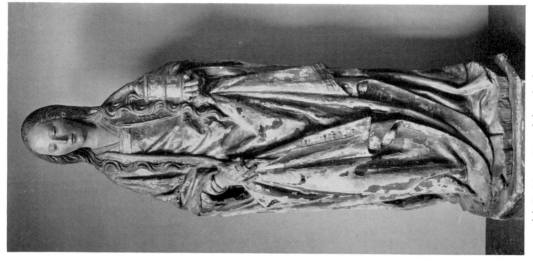

(B) St Mary Magdalen, before 1500.
Munich, Bayerisches Nationalmuseum

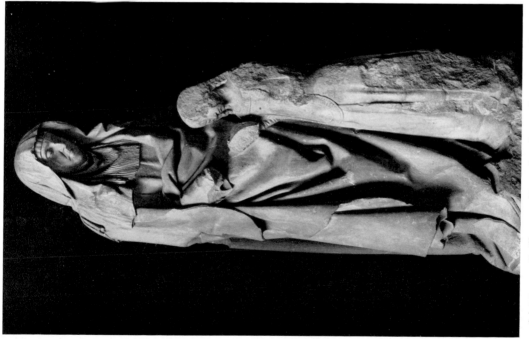

(A) Master Guillaumet (Jean de Chartres): St Anne from
Chantelle, 1500–3. *Paris, Louvre*

Detail from the Entombment, 1496. *Solesmes Abbey*

190

(A) and (B) Details from the Entombment, 1496. *Solesmes Abbey*

(A) Conrat Meit: Entombment, 1496. *Munich, Bayerisches Nationalmuseum*

(B) Entombment, 1528. *Villeneuve l'Archevêque, church*

INDEX

Numbers in *italics* refer to plates. References to the Notes are given to the page on which the Note occurs followed by the number of the Note; thus 197[1] indicates page 197, Note 1. Notes are indexed only when they contain further concrete information and not when the further information is purely bibliographical. Names involving the elements de, von, van, etc., are indexed under the christian name: e.g. Jean de Marville will be found under Jean. Statues of sacred persons are included under the name of the person; exceptions to this rule are statues of Christ and the Virgin, since they are so numerous and it is unlikely that any reader will want to look them up. Themes (e.g. Pietà) and scenes (e.g. Annunciation) are not indexed under subject.

A

INDEX

M

R

Radibor, *Virgin* and *St John Evangelist*, 45
Ramersdorf, Holy Cross Altar, 117
Rampillon, *St Barbara*, 138
Raphael, 126
Ravensburg, 172
  Parish Church, high altar, 116; *Virgin* from, 116; *126*
  St Jodok, corbel figures, 170
Raymond du Temple, 18
Rebeck family, mon., 184
Regensburg, 42
  Cathedral, sculpture, 42–3; *50*
Rein, MS. from, 204[88]
Rembrandt, 62
René of Anjou, king, 135, 137, 191; tomb, 55, 207[53]
Renier van Thienen the Elder, 92, 93, 137, 160, 161; *106, 107, 161*
Renier van Thienen the Younger, 160
Reval, *see* Tallinn
Rheinberg, parish church, altarpiece, 94
Rheine, *St Agnes* from, 99
Richard de Chancey, mon., 199[34]
Rieden, altarpiece from, 94, 215[32]; *109*
Riemenschneider, Tilman, 177–81, 182, 224[75], 225[78,80,84]; *173, 176–8*
Riga
  Great Guild Hall, *Death of the Virgin*, 129; *Virgin*, 132
  Schwarzhäupterhaus, *St George*, 166
Rimini
  Crucifixion from, 63–4; *73*
  S. Francesco, *Pietà*, 64
Rimpar, parish church, mon. of Eberhard von Grumpach, 178
Riom
  Château, 14
  Notre-Dame-du-Marthuret, *Virgin*, 14; *24*
  Sainte Chapelle, 14
Roch, St, Amsterdam, 91; Florence (Stoss), 126; Utrecht, 91
Rochefort (Côte d'Or), palace chapel, *St Jean de Reôme* from, 56, 134; *59*
Rode, Hermen, 129
Rodez, 55
Roger van der Weyden, 32, 60, 61, 62, 63, 64, 74, 79, 81, 84, 86, 87, 93, 94, 96, 107, 109, 117, 123, 126, 140, 142, 143, 150, 151, 156, 158, 161, 163, 164, 208[55,72], 211[18]
Rogge, Conrad, bishop of Strängnäs, 96
Rohr, abbey (Asam), 126
Rois, Robert li, mon., 59
Rolin, Chancellor Nicolas, 79
Rollinger, Wilhelm, 118
Romer, Lienhard, 124
Römhild, Stadtkirche, mon. of Otto IV of Henneberg, 185, 186, 187

Roskilde, cathedral, mon. of Queen Margaret, 28, 29, 201[20]; *St John Evangelist*, 166
Roth IV, Bishop Johannes, mon., 186
Rothenburg
  St Jakob, altar (Riemenschneider), 180; *178*; high altar, 74, 109, 124; *117*
  St Michael, altarpiece from, 180
Rottweil, Lorenzkapelle, pulpit-bearer, 169; *Virgins*, 74, 203[53]; ('Master of Eriskirch'), 38
Rouen, 138, 140, 190
  Cathedral, choir stalls, 91, 138
Roupy, 15
Rouvres-en-Plaine, church, reredos, 49, 56; *7*
Rouvroy, *Virgin* from, 190
Rubens, Sir Peter Paul, 62
Rudolf van Diepholt, bishop, funerary chapel, 211[10], 212[5]
Rudolf von Scherenberg, bishop of Würzburg, mon., 179
Rufach, *Virgin* from, 73
Russ, Jakob, 172
Rytterne, church, altarpiece, *Mass of St Gregory*, 166

S

Sagrera, Guillermo, 142; *146*
St Antoine-en-Viennois, abbey church, west portal, 17
St Apollinaire, château, *Virgin* from, 50
St Arnual, collegiate church, mon. of Johann III, 101
St Bavo, refectory, stone relief, 211[18]
St Benoît-sur-Loire, abbey church, choir stalls, 51
St Denis, mons., 13, 14, 18, 19, 47, 191, 218[20]
St Didier, Célestin church, altar, 191
St Éloi, retable from, 140
Ste Fortunade, church, reliquary, 75, 87, 136; *103*
St Gallen, abbey, statues (M. Erhart), 116
St Jean-de-Losne, hospital, *Virgin*, 49
St Johann in den Tauern, *Virgin* from, 120
St Lambrecht (Hans von Tübingen), 75
St Leonhard im Passeiertal, altar from (Klocker), 123–4
St Lorenzen (S. Lorenzo in Pusteria), altarpiece, 121, 122
St Louis (Miss.), City Art Museum, *St Christopher* from Dijon (?), 85; *97*
St Martin-aux-Bois, choir stalls, 226[2]
St Omer
  Cathedral, Miquel mon., 59, 69
  Musée, alabaster statuettes, 208[69]
  St Bertin, altarpiece (Marmion), 138
St Sigmund (S. Sigismondo), altarpiece, 44
St Trond, Couvent des Frères Mineurs, altar of the Passion, 213[37]
St Wolfgang, church, high altar, 120 ff., 128, 176, 177; *frontispiece, 132, 133*